W9-AVK-661

HORRORS!

HORRORS!

DRAKE DOUGLAS

The Overlook Press
Woodstock, New York

First published in 1989 by
The Overlook Press
Lewis Hollow Road
Woodstock, New York 12498

Book design by Jaye Zimet

Library of Congress Cataloging-in-Publication Data

Douglas, Drake.
Horrors!

1. Horror films—History and criticism. 2. Horror tales—History and
criticism. I. Title.
PN1995.9.H6D6   1988   791.43'09'0916   88-42721
ISBN: 0-87951-325-X

In Memoriam to my parents

Werner Friedrich August Zimmerman
Ann Wilhelmina Skau Zimmerman

With special thanks to

Stephen David Kent

CONTENTS

INTRODUCTION: 1989   1

INTRODUCTION: 1966   13

THE VAMPIRE   31

'For the life of the flesh . . . is in the blood.'

THE WEREWOLF   79

'And there could be seen on his chest the vague markings
of a five-pointed star . . . the sign of the pentagram . . . the
mark of the beast. . . .'

THE MONSTER   113

'I am malicious because I am miserable; if any being felt
emotions of benevolence towards me, I should return them,
an hundred and an hundred fold.'

THE MUMMY   181

'And the body was carefully anointed with the proper
incantations to the gods and a strip of perfumed linen wound
about each joint and the body was placed in the desert
tomb to find eternal rest. . . .'

THE WALKING DEAD   219

'A tall figure appears, walking slowly, looking neither to the
left nor to right, his eyes dull and glazed, filled with visions of
the grave. . . .'

THE SCHIZOPHRENIC 241

'I sought with tears and prayers to smother down the crowd of hideous images and sounds with which my memory swarmed ... and still, bewteen the petitions, the ugly face of my iniquity stared into my soul.'

THE PHANTOM 267

'Imagine ... Red Death's mask suddenly come to life ... to express, with the four black holes of its eyes, its nose, and its mouth, the extreme anger, the mighty fury of a demon; and not a ray of light from the sockets!'

THE HUNCHBACK 299

'Never till now was I aware of how hideous I am. When I compare myself with you, I cannot help pitying myself, poor, unhappy monster that I am. . . . I am something frightful, neither man nor brute, something harder, more shapeless and more trampled upon, than a flint.'

THE CREATORS OF HORROR—I 333

The Alcoholic:
'I became insane ... with intervals of horrible sanity.'

THE CREATORS OF HORROR—II 353

The Rhode Island Recluse:
'The world was at one time inhabited by another race ... who yet live on outside, ever ready to take possession of this earth again.'

THE CREATORS OF HORROR—III 369

The Mystic of Wales:
'Is there no serenity to be had anywhere in this world?'

EPILOGUE: 1966 383

EPILOGUE: 1989 387

FURTHER READING 411

FILM LIST 415

HORRORS!

INTRODUCTION: 1989

There is a dark side to all of us. Perhaps six thousand (or so) years of civilization have still not been able to obliterate those terrible fears of a million (or so) years ago— fears that haunted our hairy progenitors as they huddled in the fire-flickering, shadow-casting, water-dripping cold caves of the first human shelter and trembled before the mysteries of the unknown darkness and the incredible natural violence of that early time that often seemed about to tear their world apart. How and when did the first true thought enter the minuscule mind of the early human? When did those animal eyes first gleam with the initial touch of intelligence? Who was the first humanoid to glance up to the moon and wonder about that silver eye that seemed to watch from the night sky? What beatle-browed hirsute creature first realized the power of the sun and moved to the eerie darkness of the rear of the cave to daub his or her confused thoughts upon the hard walls, thus taking the first step in the creation of religions intended to ease the emerging fear of death? Who was the ape man who first peopled the night with strange and terrible creatures? What grunting caveman clad in animal skins first encountered the fear of the dead, of ghostly apparitions, of humans turned into ravaging animals?

When, how and where did those superstitions arise that still plague the human mind?

For we are still afraid, despite our supposedly ultra-sophisticated society. We choose not to walk under ladders, light three cigarettes on a match, whistle in a dressing room, or feel really comfortable on Friday the 13th. We avoid a black cat that might cross our path; we bless each other when we sneeze; we avoid breaking a mirror. We scoff at such foolishness, of course, but we can't really shake from our minds the guilty sense that all of this may really mean something. Why take chances?

And we are still afraid of the dark. We are uneasy walking down a dark and lonely street in the dead of night, constantly glancing over our shoulders to assure ourselves that we are not being followed. We would not think of entering a cemetery after midnight. We lie uneasy in our beds during a violent electrical storm and immediately turn on the lights when entering a dark house to be certain nothing lurks in the shadows. We are startled by every sudden sound in the darkness, turning sharply: "What's that?!"

Fear, no matter what its source or reason, is an integral part of human nature, perhaps our most ancient heritage from those dark and much older times.

We feel a bit foolish about our fears, and we try to rationalize them with an embarrassed little laugh and an uneasy shrug of our shoulders. After all, we are civilized and intelligent beings, and we must not admit to failings that only remind us of our uncomfortably low beginnings. We know everything has a perfectly logical explanation (Well, doesn't it?) and we are safe and comfortable and not really afraid. No, not really.

Perhaps part of our defense against such foolishness is a somewhat masochistic delight in purposely scaring ourselves, either in the pages of gruesome murder mysteries or in the darkness of a cinema where no one can see our fear. You see, we don't really take such things seriously! We know there are no men who turn into wolves or live on human blood. The monsters that walk our streets now may be just as dangerous, but they were not created in electrically crackling laboratories or by the mysterious spell of the moon. They are an unfortunate product of what we proudly claim to be the most civilized world in the long history of human beings, and which sadly is also one of the most violent. There are no such things as werewolves and vampires. Ghosts? Well, of those tenuous beings we are perhaps not really so sure, but we at least pretend to disbelieve; it's the thing to do. Nevertheless, we will shun old decaying houses that are reputed to be "strange."

While the darkness still frightens, it also fascinates. Fog-swirling swamps with silent bottomless pools . . . the violence of high winds, crackling lightning, and stomach-rumbling thunder . . . dark mansions with sliding panels and secret passages . . . the eerie silence of tumbled, dusty, cobwebbed old castles . . . the mustiness of old tombs . . . the unnatural silence of a graveyard with white tombstones like giant frozen tears, licked by hungry shreds of must. . . .

And tales of Horror.

The book you hold in your hand first appeared in 1966 and was, in fact, originally written nearly twenty years before that, with later revisions. Except for adding a chapter on *The Hunchback of Notre-Dame* and updating the bibliography and filmography, I have left the text of the 1966 edition intact. It remains a somewhat difficult work to define. It is not by any means a history of horror, nor a work of reference; since it encompasses legend, literature, and film, it would take a much larger volume than this to present the entire field, if in fact that can be done.

It is simply a book to be read and enjoyed; nothing more nor less. *Horrors!* was written as a very personal and affectionate remembrance, a tribute, a last, lingering look at part of our past; in fact, it was not originally intended for publication.

During the late 1940s, the great classic monsters had fallen into disrepute, in large part supplanted by the more modern evil creatures of science fiction and radiation. The world had changed radically with the onset of World War II and the Atomic Age, and tastes in horror altered with it. If the old monsters were at all remembered, it was in a quasi-comic sense, and there was little worthy literary output in the field. I felt the final stake had at last been driven into Dracula's heart when he and his old companions the Frankenstein Monster and Lawrence Talbott became foils for the comedy antics of Abbott and Costello. I was outraged; it seemed a form of sacrilege. How could anyone ever again taken these creatures seriously after they had been turned into buffoons? (My sense of humor has improved since then, but it still makes me feel just a bit uncomfortable.)

It was all a great pity, for I had a very real affection for Frankenstein, Dracula, and their ilk, whose more human forms and problems seemed to me more interesting, pathetic, and much more frightening than the weirdly fanciful, nonhuman creatures who took their place. I was too young to see either *Frankenstein* or *Dracula* on their initial releases . . . besides, children in those days were not admitted to see horror films—my, how times have changed! But *Bride of Frankenstein* had a tremendous impact on me. (I saw this film through a deep, bilious-green filter, which incredibly heightened the aspect of horror; it's a pity it is not always shown that way.) I became hooked on horror and had read both *Frankenstein* and *Dracula* more than once before my teen years had ended.

I wanted to remember these creatures in a serious written account penned in a style to approximate the higher literary quality of the original works from which they came, while also paying a belated tribute to their literary, and film, creators. The many blood-filled horror volumes that later filled the bookstores seemed to have no literary quality whatever.

The film section with which each chapter concludes was an after thought. I was more interested in the legends and writings of the genre. But how could I write of the Frankenstein Monster without paying tribute to the most magnificent performance in all horror films, that of Boris Karloff as the Monster? If I mentioned him in this respect, could I ignore him as Imhotep in my section on the Mummy? Or Bela Lugosi as Dracula? The other great film monsters naturally fell into line. Frankly, the film sections are still not my favorite portions of this book, but they seem to have received the greatest attention.

There are two phrases to bear in mind in the reading of this work: "personal reminiscence" and "classic monsters."

I am not an historian, but merely an avid reader and moviegoer particularly drawn to certain genres. This book is my own very personal remembrance of my favorites, and such a book is naturally somewhat restricted by the writer's own preferences. Perhaps you may feel I have neglected favourites of your own. I'm sorry about that but, you know, the reminiscences are my own; if you want to remember other things, you'll have to write a book of your own. The pleasure of the writing, and the reading, would have been lessened by the forced inclusion of matters that were not part of that same fond remembrance. You can find any number of books if you want facts, technical details, gruesome blood-tinted photographs, and that sort of thing. *Horrors!* was written for sheer pleasure and should be read in the same way. I hope I have included enough pleasant memories for anyone interested in this particular field.

Classic monsters. Yes, there is the crux of the matter. My monsters are primarily the creatures of legend and literature, touched by the supernatural or created by the madness of men who "ventured where no man should go," the good old monsters who lurked in gloomy black-and-white settings of Central European villages, ancient castles and tombs, mouldering mansions and stone laboratories filled with mazes of bewildering equipment and the sounds of hummings of electricity, in dark nights and violent storms. Vampires, zombies, werewolves, mummies, schizophrenics. They have haunted the memory of superstitious humans for eons and were created in literature primarily during the nineteenth century and in film

during the great era of the 1930s. Later monsters, save
for those that are worthy extensions of the originals,
have no place here. Do not look for slashers, axe murderers, psychotics. The infamous Jason does not belong
here. Such are not part of my family.

A case in point is the frequent complaint that I have
not included *Psycho* and its weird innkeeper Norman
Bates in these pages. That omission has given rise to
startlingly scathing letters from some of my readers, as
though this single exclusion destroyed any merit the
work might possess.

I have always had the greatest respect for the writings
of Robert Bloch, and for Alfred Hitchcock's superb film.
Psycho is undoubtedly a masterpiece, but in a very different vein. It is a modern masterwork with no connection with the classic era of which I wrote. Bates is a
mental defective, a madman. He is not an undead, an
artificially created being, a supernatural creature, but
an unfortunate product of the pressures of our own mind-
bending times. He is a schizophrenic but can be called a
Jekyll-and-Hyde only in the broadest and most clinical
sense. Stevenson's classic schizo was as much the result
of scientific meddling as was the great Monster of Dr.
Frankenstein; he became two different people in a very
definite and physical sense, not just from the quirks of
his own twisted mind. Norman Bates belongs to another
time and another field, not with Dracula and Talbott;
his is the world of insanity, which is quite another
matter. I will apologize for the omission if you like, but
I must remain true to the spirit of the book. Classic
monsters.

Alien is certainly one of the most frightening of films,
but in spite of the terror it evokes, it is a work of pure
science fiction and that, too, is a world of its own. The
line of division between horror and science fiction can
be irritatingly tenuous. In a sense, the creation of a
monster in a laboratory can be considered a form of
science fiction, but . . . well, you know what I mean. I
have spoken of *The Thing* in these pages, because, al-

though it is also science fiction, there is a strong parallel to the Frankenstein theme.

I considered including a chapter on ghosts but decided against it. This is another form of horror. The chill you feel in the presence of a ghostly wraith is very different from that you experience upon confrontation with Frankenstein's Monster. Each segment of this book is dominated by the outstanding figure of its kind, and there is no such figure in the literature of ghosts, although there has been much fine writing. This unfortunately meant the exclusion of the master ghostwriter M. R. James from the section on creators of horror; but he would not really have belonged—another apology to my readers who resented this omission. There have been some excellent horror-touched ghost films, particularly the frightening *The Uninvited*. Such films as *The Amityville Horror* and *Poltergeist* had much of this, this primarily from the special effects that have become the most important factors of such films. The world of ghosts is far too vast to be compressed into a single chapter.

Witchcraft was another discarded possibility; this, too, is an enormous field. The terrifying film *Black Sunday* was included because while a tale of medieval witchcraft, it was also a superb film about vampirism.

I do not much care for the current field of horror. The films have lost the dark creeping spirit of true horror, dealing as they do with shock and sensationalism rather than with the more cerebral and human aspects of the classics. I think it all began, strangely enough, with the Dracula and Frankenstein films of the Hammer productions from England. These often splendid and visually impressive films (particularly the various Draculas with Christopher Lee) are properly dealt with in this book and rightly praised, but with reservations. They introduced excessively graphic brutality for shock purposes— there was far too much blood covering the screen—and also a totally unnecessary and sometimes uncomfortable sexuality. These elements are all too common in the so-called horror films of today, and as a result, instead of our comfortable old classic monsters, we are inundated with horrendous slashers in goalie masks, axe wielders, and homicidal maniacs. These, too, simply do not belong.

Literature in the field of horror also seems to have deteriorated. There is no Poe or Lovecraft today, with their vivid imaginations and elegant prose, no Machen or Derleth, certainly no Shelley or Stoker. I doubt that *Frankenstein* and *Dracula* are really widely read today, although everyone knows their basic stories. I do feel sorry for those who have never had the great pleasure of reading the two greatest masterpieces of horror! The former is written with too much style and elegance, and the latter is too long. People don't like too many words today; they haven't the time for it. Only the remarkable Stephen King seems able to get away with it. Readers today want the blood to begin running on the first page and go right on to the last. It's a pity. Good writing has always been one of the delights of such novels.

The word "horror" is difficult to define. My trusted dictionary calls it "painful and intense fear, dread or dismay," which is fine; but I prefer the same volume's description of "terror" as "to be afraid . . . scourge . . . frightening aspect . . . an appalling person or thing'. Note the last two phrases. Reminds one of the Frankenstein Monster, doesn't it? Perhaps this is what Karloff had in mind when he expressed his own preference for "terror" to describe his films.

Nothing can be as terrifying as Man himself. All the monsters of the classic works and films bore human forms. Dracula could transform himself into a bat, a wolf, a shred of mist; but in his natural state he was a human like you and me; all we need is a long cape with a high collar and a pair of hypnotic Lugosi eyes. The werewolf is a tormented man who changes form under the influence of the full moon. Once we take the wrappings off a mummy, we see merely a badly desiccated man (or woman) who died long ages ago, and the zombie is in all respects a human being whose mind and will

There was also pathos in Boris Karloff's performance, in his mute
pleading for understanding from a terrified mankind that sought only
to destroy him.
Frankenstein (Universal Pictures, 1931)

have been totally destroyed. Jekyll-Hyde presents a
double-man who is two sides of the same coin; the
Phantom and the Hunchback are creatures whose deformities, human-created, have turned them into monsters.

Having human forms, these monsters also have, to
some extent, human emotions, unfortunately suppressed
by their treatment at human hands. They long for normalcy, for companionship and understanding, even for

love. They are not happy in what they are, and for the most part their depredations are merely the result of their eternal struggle for survival. Dracula does not drink the blood of the living because he likes it; he requires it for survival. Despite the horrid nature of his existence, he battles for survival because life is precious even to one such as he. Yet surely it can become rather tiresome and boring to live forever. Vampires and werewolves are often grateful for the release of death. With his last breath, the Werewolf of London thanks his destroyer. Frankenstein's Monster constantly pleaded for understanding; his acts of violence were the result of his total rejection and the fear and hatred of mankind. The werewolf is the most tragic of them all. It is the animal that kills, not the man; in human form, he can be the gentlest of men.

It is this aspect that provides the sharpest difference between these monsters of old and the so-called monsters of today. We fear them and their horrible appearance, we are terrified by them and appalled by their murderous activities—and yet we can pity them. They are a sorrowful lot, forever battling against the human race, which hates and seeks to destroy them. Yet one of the finer aspects of the human race is its supposed inclination to champion the underdog.

Dr. Frankenstein's creation is both the most terrifying and most pathetic of them all, particularly as portrayed by Boris Karloff, who alone came close to the psychology of Mary Shelley's original creation. (This, of course, is also largely the responsibility of the script.) Once we become accustomed to his hideous exterior, we have a tendency to root for him in his battle against a violently biased humanity. Of course there is a message here, whether Shelley intended it or not. The evils of intolerance. Man too often strikes out with violence at those who are different, those he cannot understand. Boris's creature has become the most beloved of all monsters. Mary Shelley would certainly have approved.

I am very pleased with this new edition of *Horrors!*

Perhaps it means my dear old friends will live a little longer. I do hope members of the younger generations will read this book and discover there are horror monsters greater and more fascinating then the one-dimensional slasher who attacks young lovers busy in their beds or the axe wielder preying on sex-starved teenagers in mountain cabins. For older readers, I hope it will bring back fond memories of their own.

They're still out there in the shadows, these monsters of the past, waiting to frighten and entertain us, ever alert to the danger of the stake in the heart, the silver bullet, the violent hands of fear-stirred men. But they have become old friends by this time, and perhaps we can understand them more easily than we used to.

Here we meet them again. Enjoy yourself.

INTRODUCTION: 1966

Night brings terror. Strange, alien forms move restlessly across the face of the earth. Fear, horror and death follow in their wake. The sky is dark; the moon has not yet risen; the stars seem too frightened to shine. A thick, blue-white fog blankets the denuded forest, gliding like some sluggish, viscous stream through the trees, pausing for a moment now and then to caress as with a sickening affection some gnarled, familiar trunk, then again moving on across the blasted, bloodless land, settling at last in the deep morass of the swamp, a lifeless world of black and grey, cloaked in the very silence of death, where the naked trees stretch their bony limbs in silent, meaningless supplication to the dark sky. No sound of bird or beast disturbs the quiet, for to tread the thick, treacherous mud of the swamp is to vanish forever in the murderous clutch of quicksand; even to rise through the air above is to perish in the noisome vapours that arise from this dead heath. Here only the incorporeal fog can live, twisting in hideous ecstasy, finding its own paradise in a world forever dead, moving through blackened trees that will never again wear the green garb of springtime. This is a world that knows no seasons.

On the very fringes of the silent swamp, the swooping form of a large bat, its leathery wings briefly disturbing the stillness, creates a blacker blot upon the night sky; the long, lean, silvery form of a wolf, its eyes gleaming like twin pinpoints of hell-fire, prowls menacingly through the underbrush. The smaller, gentler animals of the wood shiver in the doubtful security of their burrows, alert eyes darting fearfully about a land that has suddenly become stranger to them. The crickets seem petrified with fear, and a gravelike stillness suffocates the face of earth.

Slowly, a slender silver crescent brightens the ebony of the night sky. Satisfied that her visit is both expected and welcome, the moon raises herself higher, revealing her white, seductive body, and begins her journey across a cloudless sky. It is the night of the full moon, and the Unknown has again descended upon the earth. In the castle of the Carpathians, the mad scientist works feverishly over the massive inert form on the operating table, striving to instil the spark of life. All throughout the world, crumbling castles and mysterious moss-grown mansions conceal their own loathsome horrors. Wolves howl to the new-risen moon and the dark forms of bats throw menacing shadows as they hover before open windows. Innocent men with the taint of the wolf feel an irresistible urge to fall on all fours. Vampires rise from their damned, earth-lined coffins to silently prowl the night in quest of their dreadful sustenance. Strange and unknown terrors rise from the sacred tombs of ancient Egypt, and horrors of which man has never dreamed stalk the lonely night.

Terror walks the face of earth.

2

Horror, says Webster, is a painful and intense fear, dread or dismay. The legendary, literary and, in our time, visual worlds of horror have never lost their hold on the imagination of man. Tales of werewolves and vampires, of undying monsters and mad scientists, still bring their tingle of fear; readers fearfully put aside *Dracula* with nightfall, and the single name Karloff flashed on a screen causes shivers to run down the spines of movie audiences. Belief in witchcraft, satanism and all their attendant evils has by no means vanished from the earth. Peasants in the Carpathians still furtively cross themselves when in the presence of a man reputed to indulge in evil practices, and will tell you quite seriously that certain men, who bear 'the mark of the beast', have the peculiar ability to transform themselves into wolves or other animal forms at the full of the moon. Voodoo remains a powerful, if somewhat concealed, force in the islands of the West Indies, and the mysterious, still comparatively unknown depths of the African jungles abound in frightening superstitions and strange religious practices.

Nor need we go so far afield to find evidence of current belief in various modes of horror and black magic. The Devil's Mass is still celebrated in meetings throughout the world. For the writing of his terrifying *La Bas*, Joris Karl Huysmans immersed himself in the frightening world of satanism at the end of the last century, and in his book on witchcraft[1] of only a quarter of a century ago, William Seabrook relates chilling accounts of vampirism and lycanthropy in modern New York and London. It is not too long ago that witches were still being burned alive at the stake and buried at the crossroads (indeed, it may still be happening) and the barns of the Pennsylvania Dutch are still marked with colourful hex signs. The zombie walks the deserted roads of Haiti and leopard men creep through the jungles of a Congo torn by violence.

Indeed, how many of our most progressive and enlightened citizens wear about their necks a religious medallion to ward off the ever-present and powerful forces of evil?

Skilful writers have long profited from these superstitions, turning them into quite acceptable, sometimes classic, literary fare. Although such tales go back to the earliest times – Petrarch wrote of werewolves, and the first true novel of horror, Horace Walpole's *The Castle of Otranto*, appeared in 1764 – the modern tale of horror, as we know it today, was formed by an American writer, Edgar Allan Poe, whose chilling tales first appeared in 1839. There are few readers who do not know such terrifying stories as *The Fall of the House of Usher*, *The Black Cat* and *The Tell-Tale Heart*.

Poe, who died in 1849, had and has many imitators and successors, the most outstanding being another American, Howard Phillips Lovecraft, the mysterious recluse of our own time who converted a peaceful Rhode Island into the abode of strange and terrifying beings. It is a regrettable example of the peculiar course of literary history that Edgar Allan Poe,

---

[1] *Witchcraft, Its Power in the World Today*.

who died more than a century ago, is so highly regarded today, while Howard Phillips Lovecraft, dead for just over a quarter of a century, is today almost forgotten, although many of his tales, such as *The Outsider*, *The Dunwich Horror* and *The Rats in the Walls* compare quite favourably with the best of master Poe himself, and at least one other tale, *The Colour Out of Space*, is one of the early modern classics of science-fiction horror. Were it not for the anthologic activities of his most ardent disciple, August Derleth, the Lovecraft stories would by now have been lost with the old editions of *Weird Tales* magazines.

Another giant in the field of the uncanny was Arthur Machen, the brooding, brilliant Welshman responsible for the delightful chill of *The Great God Pan* and other stories; William Seabrook once said that Machen, who died in 1947, knew far more of the night world than he would dare or care to admit. We shall meet Poe, Lovecraft and Machen further on in these pages. Nor should we forget such superb craftsmen of horror, both past and present, as Algernon Blackwood, Fritz Leiber, Theodore Sturgeon, J. Sheridan Le Fanu and Lord Dunsany among others.

There are, indeed, few writers who have not tried their hand at tales of the supernatural, although most have turned to the somewhat more literarily acceptable field of the ghost story. *Great Tales of Terror and the Supernatural*, probably the finest anthology of its kind, includes stories by such literary figures as Nathaniel Hawthorne, Honoré de Balzac, Somerset Maugham, William Faulkner and Ernest Hemingway. In the field of the 'pure' ghost story, there are no finer writers than Henry James and Montague Rhodes James, the latter another of our sadly neglected authors.

It is noteworthy, however, that the writings of Poe and Lovecraft, James and Machen, all fall into the category of the short story, for there have been very few really successful tales of horror in the more elongated field of the novel. There may be very cogent reasons for this. Horror is an extremely difficult mood to sustain over a period of several hundred pages, and few authors have dared even to attempt it. Such novels as the previously mentioned *The Castle of Otranto*, Ann Radcliffe's

The Mysteries of Udolpho and Lewis's *The Monk* satisfied horror fans of their day, but are little read in our own time. William Sloane presented an interesting work in *The Edge of Running Water* and in our own time we have seen the classic ghost novel, *The Uninvited*.

When we speak of classics of horror, of course, two magnificent works immediately come to mind. The first of these was written by a young girl just entering her twenties, the wife of one of the greatest poets of the English language. It was in 1818 that Mary Shelley startled the literary world with her frightening tale of the creation of a monster. Few works of fiction have so struck the imagination as has *Frankenstein*. It was neither the first nor the last of Mrs Shelley's writing, but it is the only one of her novels still widely read. In this superb tale of grave robbing and body snatching, of brooding castles and mad scientists, of unearthly creatures, the poet's wife seemed, for a brief time, to have been touched with genius. The very word Frankenstein has now become a part of our English vocabulary, describing man's unleashing of ungovernable forces. We live, indeed, in a Frankensteinian age.

It seems, perhaps, illogical that a young, romantically inclined girl such as Mary Shelley, travelling through Europe in the company of a handsome, brilliant young poet (to whom she was not yet wed) should have produced so morbid a work as *Frankenstein*, yet a somewhat similar situation arose some eighty years later, when the man who, for more than a quarter of a century, served as business manager for the great actor Sir Henry Irving, wrote what is probably the most terrifying novel ever produced. Bram Stoker achieved literary immortality in 1897 with that masterpiece of vampirism, *Dracula*. This bloodcurdling tale, which has none of the psychological undertones of Mrs Shelley's work but is a horror tale pure and simple, has never lost its power.

The motion-picture industry, of course, has, in our time, played a major role in the dissemination of horror. The first true horror film of any artistic value was the brilliant German production of Decla-Bioscop's filming in 1919 of a story by Robert Wiene titled *The Cabinet of Dr Caligari*, presenting

The Monster (Boris Karloff) stares at a little girl floating flowers in the lake. The conclusion of this scene, in which he tosses the girl into the lake thinking she will float like the blossoms, was excised from the final print.
Frankenstein (Universal Pictures, 1931)

the great Conrad Veidt as the somnambulist. Soon after, Lon Chaney began to chill audiences as 'the man of a thousand faces', a title which his son, to a somewhat lesser degree, was to assume in later years. Movie horror as we know it today, however – the horror of the undead, the vampires, the were-wolves – had its beginning in the early 1930s, when some imaginative moviemaker conceived the clever notion of utilizing the works of Mrs Shelley and Mr Stoker. In 1931,

Boris Karloff, as the Monster in *Frankenstein*, brought a new kind of terror to the screen; Bela Lugosi, repeating the role he had first brought to the Broadway stage, appeared as the infamous vampire count of the Carpathians in *Dracula*, and soon after Lon Chaney, Jr, began his series of performances as Lawrence Talbot, the Wolfman. These were milestones in filmmaking, setting a standard of sheer horror which has seldom been equalled.[2]

These early films filled the coffers of Universal Studios, and plans were promptly made to squeeze every bloody penny from this new trend. The monsters were not permitted to die; all became immortal. The terrible creation of the well-intentioned Victor von Frankenstein was destroyed by fire, sulphur, explosion, flood and quicksand, but always he rose again, to spread horror and death throughout the village of Frankenstein (or Vasaria, or Oberndorf) and, to a constantly lessening degree, the movie audience. It was not quite as simple to return Dracula to the world of the nonliving living, for there were tradition-honoured methods of disposing of a vampire, and once slain in this manner, the Transylvanian nobleman could not be resurrected. Of course, Hollywood has never felt itself bound by such tradition. An attempt was made to restore Dracula to life by simply removing the wooden stake embedded in his heart, but this did not go over well with the audiences, who realized full well that the stake in the heart meant permanent death to a vampire. The solution to this particular dilemma turned out to be rather simple. Apparently the infamous count was not so busy searching for blood that he did not have time to attend to the little matter of propagation. The screen became rather quickly and thickly populated with the sons and daughters of Dracula, who also suffered from his taint of vampirism.

Unfortunately, these later films lacked one very essential ingredient which had played a tremendous role in the success

[2] We speak here of the horror films which were outstandingly successful. There were silent Frankensteins and Draculas, long forgotten and a film titled *Vampyr* produced in 1931 by Carl Dreyer.

of the first efforts: the writing genius of the original creators. In an industry whose primary commodity is imagination, no one could be found to match the flights of fancy of Mrs Shelley and Mr Stoker. The films took on a monotonous sameness of writing, direction, production and performance, and finally were suffocated by their own repetitions.

Nor were these constantly resurrected horrors enough. Soon the screen was flooded with a veritable galaxy of monsters: walking Egyptian mummies, indestructible werewolves, bloodthirsty ghouls and a college faculty of mad scientists. Under the weight of all these creations – in a world plunged into the far more realistic horrors of the Second World War – the fad for the superstitious collapsed and the term 'horror' became anathema at the box office.

Another familiar scene in horror films. A horse and carriage, a frightened coachman, in a mist-enshrouded forest.
Brides of Dracula (Hammer Films, 1960)

A decade later, Count Dracula and Frankenstein and their progeny were rudely awakened from what had appeared to be eternal rest at last, and once again set about the business of terrifying a new generation of moviegoers, this time in crimson technicolor. The Egyptian mummy Karis again dragged his linen-wrapped form about a technicolor countryside in search of his lost, violated love, the Princess Ananka. The British created a Frankenstein monster who bore no resemblance to the Karloff horror of a quarter century before, but were markedly more successful in resurrecting the vampire count and the werewolf.

Such traditional, old-time monsters were no longer sufficient for the motion-picture trade, and each so-called screenwriter attempted to surpass the other in dreaming up some new kind of fantastic scourge. There were women who turned into hornets, men a hundred feet tall or two inches small, a man with the head of a fly and a fly with the head of a man, dinosaurs hundreds of feet in height, giant spiders, ants, grasshoppers, praying mantises, and even a man who donned a leather suit and tried to convince the audiences that he had turned into an alligator. We might, with a little stretching of the imagination, believe in a monster such as was portrayed by Boris Karloff, who had the attributes and emotions of a man, but surely it is rather taxing our credulity to ask us to be really frightened by a creature who is half-fish and half-lizard, but with nothing of man in his make-up, who develops a very unfishlike passion for a lovely girl in a flimsy négligé. It is conceivable that an octopus would languish with lust for another octopus, but unlikely that even so charming a temptress as Sophia Loren would create such emotions in an octopoidal heart.

New production companies sprang up whose sole purpose was to cash in on the new horror trend while it lasted. The films were childishly written and in poor taste, cheaply produced, amateurishly directed and embarrassingly performed, appealing only to the emotions of the very young or the extremely naïve. The first of the Karloff Frankenstein films had been artfully tinted a gruesome shade of green to add to the air of horror, but these new productions 'improved' on this interesting technique by presenting their cheaply made films in black and white save for those scenes intended to be particularly horrifying, in which blood suddenly appeared in bursts of bright crimson. Horror seemed to have become the domain of the teenager when a film introduced a descendant of the great Dr Frankenstein who created a new monster with a face so hideous as to be almost comical, set upon the firm, beautifully proportioned figure of a teenage football hero; another presented a high school girl who, in addition to the problems of acne and halitosis, suffered from the rather embarrassing ailment of lycanthropy. The Frankenstein monster, it was reported, died of shame when he became the foil for the comedy antics of Abbott and Costello.

Under these appalling attacks on the integrity of horror, it

David Peel was a blond vampire in the excellent *Brides of Dracula*. His victims were members of a girls' school . . . and his own mother. *Brides of Dracula* (Hammer Films, 1960)

was expected that this new bubble would burst, and films of this type would again be labelled box office poison. But this did not occur. The wildly, childishly fantastic monsters have had their day and have now almost disappeared from the screen. Thanks largely to the intelligent and beautiful productions of classic horror by Hammer Productions of England and the superb presentations by American-International Studios of the tales of Edgar Allan Poe, horror is more alive at the box office today than it has been since the great days of Karloff and Lugosi, and has achieved an aspect of respectability and artistry it has never before possessed. Devotees of horror line up to see Vincent Price, Peter Cushing and Christopher Lee, the current horror kings; the Karloff-Lugosi-Chaney classics can often be seen on the several television programmes which devote themselves to films of this sort. In the literary field as well, horror has suddenly become very much alive. Numerous magazines of short stories are appearing on the news-stands; anthologies of tales of terror are big sellers in paperbacks; *Dracula*, long a popular volume in the Random House Modern Library, has now joined *Frankenstein* as a selection in the beautiful editions of the Heritage Club. The monsters of the past, for a time supplanted by the more fanciful creatures of science fiction, are stirring in their graves, and once again the night is filled with ominous shadow.

3

In a recent anthology of horror tales,[3] Donald Wollheim made much of the fact that the world has changed. Horror – and here we speak of actual belief in the creatures of horror, rather than the mere enjoyment of them through books and films – thrives on the unknown, on darkness, aloneness, fear and ignorance. Our world has made tremendous strides in the past half-century, and most of these ingredients necessary for the belief in horror have been abolished. Science has answered most of our questions concerning the unknown horrors of the

[3] *Terror in the Modern Vein.*

past, has clearly pointed out the impossibility of various superstitions being anything more than just superstitions, and has
made it quite clear that under no circumstances can a man
become a wolf, or a bat, or a creeping shred of smoky mist.
The world today is neither dark (save, perhaps, in a political
sense) nor lonely (at least in the sense of being physically
alone). One cannot imagine a man-made monster or a werewolf creating a panic in the garish world of Times Square;
more than likely he would be looked upon as a further interesting example of the native product. Dracula would simply not
stir up much of a commotion in the bloodsucking centres of
Wall Street or Madison Avenue. These creatures belong to the
dimly lit, foggy back alleys of Victorian London. The invention of the electric and neon light would seem to have been
sufficient to place these monsters permanently in their graves.

Aloneness, too, has changed in recent years. With auto-
mobiles, buses, subways, it is no longer necessary to walk
down dark, unlighted streets. When the son of Dr Frankenstein returned to his ancestral home, he travelled by train in
a coach as gloomy and inhospitable as the terrain through
which he passed; today he might make the same journey in a
comfortable, well-lighted club car. Jonathan Harker on his fatal
real-estate venture to Castle Dracula journeyed through dark
and fearsome forests and mountain passes in an uncomfortable,
horse-drawn carriage; today he might travel quickly by air.
No matter where you might wish to travel today, you can
journey in well-lighted comfort, with sometimes an excess of
companionship. A woman walking down a dark street today
peers anxiously behind her not through fear of vampires, but
of the rapist or mugger. No one walks through a cemetery at
midnight any longer, unless in obedience to some Hallowe'en
daredevilry.

Ruined, deserted castles are not difficult to find in our world,
but the further we move from the trappings of monarchy, the
less interested are we inclined to be in these essentials of
horror. To a modern American, who has never lived under the
tyranny of a robber baron, and has never seen the towers and
battlements of a castle glowering down upon his home, the
past does not have as strong and possessive a hold. A ruined

castle is of interest because of its association with great wealth
and romance, and if the average tourist thinks of such a place
in terms of history, he concentrates on the glamour of kings
and queens, beautiful princesses and handsome princes, rather
than on the oppression and brutality often visited upon the
people in the village below. Even the castle of an actual his-
toric vampire like the infamous Gilles de Rais, or a monster
like the Marquis de Sade, becomes, to the tourist mind, something colourful and exciting.

We must, too, take into consideration the population explosion of the past century or more. Tales of witchcraft and
vampirism were extremely believable in a Europe so much
more sparsely populated than it is today. In, for instance, the
fifteenth century, villages in Central Europe were isolated com-
munities with little contact with an outside world which was
unknown and terrifying. In the comparatively deserted forest-
land surrounding such a village, anything might happen.

Why, then, this fascination for a world that no longer exists,
this desire to be frightened by creatures whom we know lived
only in the imagination of man? Why, in the latter portion of
the ultra-scientific twentieth century, does civilized man still
cling, like the most superstitious peasant and ignorant savage,
to his tales of vampirism, lycanthropy and monster-making?
Why has horror not gone the way of other outmoded fashions?
Perhaps the answer – without involving ourselves in patho-
logical and psychological meandering – lies in the mind of
man itself, springing from mankind's hereditary fear of the dark.

Most of man's religions stress evil as something darkly sinister, festering in and arising from black shadow. From earliest
childhood we have learned of the evil powers of darkness that
forever wait to drag us from the path of moral righteousness;
Satan is referred to as the Black Prince, the Prince of Darkness.
Light is Good, dark is Evil. So has it been since our earliest
ancestors huddled in fear before the fire that held back the
strange, unknown darkness that lay beyond the entrance to
the cave. Such racial memories die hard. Have we, as a people,
ever really forgotten our fear of the dark? Throughout our
long and tortuous history, we have peopled the black shadows
with vague, monstrous forms. Most children are born with

this inherited fear that makes a night light essential in many homes. They know there is nothing standing in the dark corner of the bedroom, they realize there is no reason to hesitate before entering that dark room, but that twinge of fear, the touch of coldness at the base of the spine, remains.

Why, then, do we permit ourselves to revel in literature and films that play on this ancient fear, that help us to people the darkness with the strange and terrifying creatures that, in our early years, caused us to lie trembling in our beds with blankets pulled over our ears? Perhaps we are striking back at our own childhood, subconsciously proving to ourselves that we know those early fears to be groundless and can now turn to them for a source of amusement.

Perhaps Georges Lefebvre had part of the answer when he wrote of another time: 'Melancholy and tears, despair and horror . . . reflection on ancient ruins . . . shook the boredom of ordered life.'[4]

Imagination is one of the most cherished attributes of the human mind, and it is just this attribute which, in our day and age, appears most in danger of extinction. Science has answered just about all our questions concerning life and the world about us. Perhaps it has answered too many questions, left us with too little food for our starving imagination to work upon. An over mechanized world, in which we know the whys and wherefores of all that we do and all that happens to us, can be a rather colourless world in which to live, one in which the fancied worlds of our imagination become doubly valuable to us.

Much tradition and superstition have fallen under the impact of science, but cold, reasonable logic has in no way dimmed the lustrous appeal of horror, perhaps because we never really did believe it, anyway. We do not need to be told that it is impossible for a man to turn into a wolf; we've known that all along. Science smugly informs us that Dracula could not have lived on for hundreds of years, feasting on human blood; well, we never really believed he did, anyway. We are inclined to agree with the scientist that there is no

[4] *The French Revolution, From Its Origins to 1793.*

such thing as a curse issuing from the violated tomb of a long-dead pharaoh, but it makes exciting, imaginative reading.

There may well be, of course, in the still little-understood labyrinths of the human mind, deeper and more ominous reasons for horror's continued fascination. Horror is a world of violence – emotional as well as physical – and even to the most civilized of minds, violence has an inescapable (if somewhat guilty) appeal. This compulsion to violence is part of our emotional composition, and the time in which we live, violent though it may be, gives the individual little opportunity for expression. We all occasionally feel the desire to strike out against supposed personal wrongs, and it is only our civilized nature that prevents us from the violent expression of this psychological urge. In the battle between the Frankenstein monster and a humanity which refused him the understanding he craves, we can find this expression of our own innate hostilities, for there are few of us who do not, at some time or another in our lives, feel we are not properly understood or appreciated. Perhaps, in some small way, the imaginative, often violent, world of horror provides us with a psychological safety valve, a mental expression of the hostilities and the urge to violence which we must subdue within ourselves.

The world of horror is also one of death and the grave, and this, too, may provide a psychological basis for its continued popularity. Sigmund Freud and his followers speak often of the strange death wish which lies concealed in us all. There is a frightening, inescapable fascination about the grave and the insoluble mystery that follows the end of life. From the time of our birth, every moment brings us closer to death. It was Voltaire who possessed a clock which, with the chiming of each hour, intoned the solemn words: 'One hour nearer the grave.' Death is always with us – inescapable, inexplicable. It is the one aspect of life which can not be dismissed, which comes to us all, and there may for all of us be times – times unsuspected – when our minds reach out for the rest, the peace, the mystery of the grave. Perhaps the true fascination of Dracula is not his age-old conquest of death, but the ultimate victory of the spectre which comes for us all.

All this may illustrate the reasons for the existence of this particular form of literature, but is there not something more, some explanation for the sudden, unusual popularity of horror today? To answer this, we need only look at the times in which we live.

Our age has been replete with its own horrors; perhaps we are attempting to forget the terrors of the atomic era by returning to older, somehow more comfortable horrors of the past. It seems peculiar to speak of the literature of horror as 'escapist' fare, but, then, perhaps it depends on what it is we wish to escape from.

There is, too, fear of the future. We are no sooner accustomed to the various threats of the Atomic Age when we have the terrible possibilities of the Space Age thrust upon us. Since the days of H. G. Wells, and before, we have read stories of the monstrous figures and forms of life that may be encountered in other worlds. Wells gave us feeble little Martians with bulbous heads, Wyndham gave us walking plants, Heinlein gave us slugs that attached themselves to the nerve centres of man. For a time the horrors of science fiction quite eclipsed those of vampirism.

But the time when contact may be made with these beings from another world (if they exist, of course) is now coming rather uncomfortably close. We are reaching a point where we would rather not be constantly reminded of the dangers and terrors that may await us once we have been released from the binding gravity of our own world. The monsters of ancient superstition are somewhat easier to understand than the plant people of Venus; at least we know they do not really exist, while Venus has yet to convince us of her harmlessness. Science-fiction monsters will no doubt always retain their own particular appeal, but they have already given way to the tried and true vampire. Our own monsters at least preserve the semblance of human form. Rather the horrors we know, than those we know not of. They come from a world that cannot be touched by progress, science or reasoning – the limitless, frightening but secure world of the imagination.

And now, let us meet them again. Let us go back to the towering, cobweb-enshrouded Carpathian castle of Count Dracula, to the mysterious laboratory of Baron Victor von

Dracula (Bela Lugosi) descends into the crypt of Carfax Abbey.
Upon his death in 1956, Lugosi was buried in the cape that had
become a trademark.
Dracula (Universal Pictures, 1931)

Frankenstein, to the werewolf-infested forests of Central
Europe, to the musty, not quite deserted tombs of ancient
Egypt. Let us examine these strange, persistent ways of life
that science has been unable to demolish. Let us join the vampire in his quest for blood, the mummy in his search for his

stolen beloved, the scientist in his mad quest for the very spark of life. Once again, the light shines in the laboratory tower of the mad scientist, once again the massive oaken door of Castle Dracula opens to admit the unwary guest. They are waiting for us. We need fear nothing, for we know – do we not ? – that these beings do not really exist, that they are figments of the imagination, relics of superstition.

But we will take with us a few wooden stakes and silver bullets – just in case.

THE VAMPIRE

'For the life of the flesh . . . is in the blood.'

We find ourselves in a strange, blasted land, a fearsome country composed of stark blacks, whites and greys. It is almost as though Nature, when painting the world, here found her palette dry of the brighter hues of life, and so daubed this land-scape with the drab and cheerless shadings of death. The trees are denuded wooden spires pointing mutely to a sky never free of glowering clouds. A thick, white mist crawls like some alien invader through the silent forest, wrapping itself about us like some sickeningly affectionate white plasma. The fog works in collusion with the swamp, concealing from us the treacherous bogs which suck hungrily at our feet and try to draw us into their muddy, murderous embrace. We skirt the silent black waters of a bottomless pool and pass along the bank of a small brook, its water unusually dark and impene-trable, cold and forbidding. Our passing disturbs a giant black bird perched in its leafless roost above our heads; it screams at us with the voice of the damned, and flaps its leathery wings as if to frighten us away. It is the only sound we hear in this land which seems suffocated with the silence of the tomb.

We find our way back to the road once again, and continue on our journey, stumbling now and then as our feet slip into age-old wagon ruts in the hard, frozen earth.

We are travelling along the same wild dirt road traversed nearly three-quarters of a century ago, by the most unfor-

tunate real-estate agent in history. His name was Jonathan
Harker, and this roadway was for him the route to a particularly horrifying kind of hell. As the carriage bore him
deeper and deeper into the strange wilderness, Jonathan Harker looked out upon scenes he had never imagined to exist
outside of a bucolic nightmare. The gloom, the depression, the
bleakness weighed heavily upon him. He could not shake from
him the fear instilled in his heart by the people of the village
through which he had passed, who blanched with horror and
crossed themselves fearfully when he mentioned his destination. Such fears were foolish, he told himself. He was merely
on his way to the surely quite respectable castle of a Transylvanian nobleman to discuss the purchase of properties in
England. He would stay a night or two, enjoying medieval
luxury, finish his business and return to England and his
fiancée Mina. Surely no harm could come to him.

We stand now at the crossroads where Jonathan's nightmare of horror began. Here, where the road divides, one
branch descending into the valley and the other winding on
up into the mountain, Jonathan stepped from the public coach
and into the black equippage his host had sent to meet him
and conduct him on the last leg of his strange and terrible
journey.

We follow along Jonathan's route, through country that
becomes wilder and more desolate. This road is little travelled
now, and there is no sign of life. The blood has been drained
from this land, and the closer we come to our objective, the
more strongly are we reminded of a land that has lost its
vitality.

And there, at last, it looms before us, clinging like a monstrous sleeping bat to the side of the precipitous mountain, its
harsh dark towers piercing the heavy black clouds that blanket
the sky. Here is the fount of horror, the original home of
evil, the most terrifying residence in all of Europe.

This is Castle Dracula.

We move, with fear-slowed steps, across the small courtyard to the massive main entrance. The heavy oaken door
opens slowly to our touch, and its rusted hinges seem to cry
in agony after so long a sleep. It was this door that was opened

for Jonathan Harker. When the Englishman stepped inside, he was greeted by the tall, menacing, white-haired (he was grown old from lack of sustenance) figure of the infamous count himself. Covered with dust, its scanty furniture crumbling, the walls themselves beginning to reveal the harsh, unkindly

The impeccable Count (Bela Lugosi) bids welcome at the dust-choked, cobweb-hung entrance of Castle Dracula.
Dracula (Universal Pictures, 1931)

touch of Time, the massive room we enter is still impressive. There, to the right, is the broad stone stairway leading to the upper floors. Here Count Dracula held aside the cobwebs to permit Jonathan Harker to pass through. In the room above, Harker was attacked by the women of the castle, entering his room on a slender moonbeam. From the window, to his un-believing horror, the real-estate man watched the cloaked count crawl down the perpendicular wall into the valley far below, and return with a moving sack of horror on his back.

But we will not pause here, for these are empty rooms with but little interest for us. These are the daylight hours, and what we seek lies below. Little clouds of dust rise up like writhing phantoms from the floor with each step we take, then settle once again, to slow death. There is a haunting silence about the castle which, for centuries, has been the scene of unparalleled horror. It is not strange that we should find ourselves continually looking over our shoulders. Here, some say for five hundred years, the king of vampires has held his unholy and blasphemous feasts. These walls which we pass have looked upon scenes of unequalled bloodthirstiness and horror. The very atmosphere is charged with violence, and we every moment expect it to reach out and take hold of us. Every shadow, every depression in the walls, seems to hold its own particular horror. We should not be too surprised to see Count Dracula himself standing there in that dark corner, his face a deathly white, sparked by two brilliant flames of hell-fire.

Through the long, dust-choked corridors, past empty cham-bers that conceal their own tales of horror, down to the vast cellars we go, picking our way with care along the narrow stone stairway. The cellar is an enormous vaulted chamber, lined with massive stone columns to support the enormous weight of the vast structure above.

And here, in this musty, dust-choked corner of hell, we have at last arrived at our destination.

In this vast catacomb, through centuries of mortal history, the black coffin bearing the infamous coat of arms of the House of Dracula has lain secure from the dangerous eyes of the world. Here, through five centuries of human life, the count has slept during the hours of daylight, replete, his hunger appeased, lying like a monstrous, bloated leech, his face flushed and a thin line of scarlet trickling from the corner of his mouth. With the rising of the moon, he will leave his coffin, crawl through the narrow aperture in the wall, and make his way down into the valley to feast once again.

Van Helsing returned to England secure in the knowledge that Count Dracula would never again repose in this thrice-damned spot, having himself – or so he thought – prevented the count from returning home from his sojourn in England where, having depleted his supply of sustenance in his homeland, he travelled in search of a young and virile country. Harried, pursued, with annihilation facing him, the count sought frantically to return to the safety of these cold stone walls, but his centuries-long career of horror was now in danger of coming to an end. On the hills just north of the castle, in actual sight of his grim fortress that meant salvation, Count Dracula faced extermination. It was here, while his coffin was being borne to the castle by a band of gypsies, that his nemesis caught up with him. Just at the final moment, as the last rays of the sun departed from the sky and freedom of movement was once again to be his, Dracula met his death, and Mina Harker wrote:

. . . in that moment of final dissolution, there was in the face a look of peace. . . .

This, at least, is the story Van Helsing brought back with him but as we stand on the bottom of the stone stairway leading into the crypt, a chill of fear comes over us, and we are suddenly not quite certain what to believe. There have been stories; the people of the valley still glance with fear to the castle on the mountain; they still furtively cross themselves and speak with hushed whispers of the vampire; and we find ourselves wondering if such monumental evil can ever truly die. We find a strange comfort in the fact that we are here during daylight hours. With timid steps, we enter the catacomb and make our way to the small alcove where Jonathan Harker said the coffin was wont to lie all through the blood-dripping centuries.

And we see it there before us, the long, tapering black box

squatting like some giant insect from hell on the stone floor. The dreaded Dracula crest, etched in jewels on the lid, glistens in the light of fading day. We are standing before the unholy bed of the king of vampires.

2

The Bible tells us, in Leviticus, that the life of the flesh is in the blood, and so has it been believed all through history. With all primitive peoples, the gift most pleasing to the gods was the shedding of human blood on the altars of sacrifice. Even the more civilized peoples of ancient Mexico and Central America honoured their gods with veritable torrents of blood; after a war of conquest in 1486, no less than twenty thousand prisoners gave their blood to the Aztec gods on the altars in Tenochtitlan. The Babylonian, the Egyptian, the early Hebrew, even the Greek and the Roman, not to mention the more barbaric tribal peoples of the wild, northern portions of Europe, all appeased their gods through offerings of the life of the flesh. With the further progress of mankind, the more enlightened civilizations substituted an animal or a bird for the human victim, but the great basic offering remained the same – the blood, the very life.

Although the barbarism of such sacrifice has no place in our own modern day, medical practices are clear indication that we have not lost the belief in the source of life. Through transfusion death is often prevented, by the infusion of the blood of the living into the veins of the dying. The Christian religion speaks of the blood of Christ, given for salvation, and this same blood is symbolically drunk in Communion. The life of the flesh is in the blood.

It is not only the gods who hunger for blood. The horror of cannibalism is, in many instances, merely another expression of this old belief. The savage who feasts on the flesh and blood of his enemy is partaking of his strength, his courage, his very life. The death of the body does not always allay this insatiable thirst for blood. In various primitive African tribes of Africa and Asia today it is still custom to offer sacrifices of

blood to the dead who, though in their graves, long still for
the sustenance of life. If such blood is not freely given, the
dead will rise from their graves and attack the living in order
to satisfy their unholy thirst.

From such beliefs, perhaps, came the terrible legend of the
vampire.

The vampire – who is a creature neither truly living nor
really dead – must have blood in order to survive. The food of
mortals is of no value to him. It is blood he requires, the thick,
warm fluid which is the life. He must feed even as mortals do,
and during the hours of darkness – traditionally the time of
evil, which cannot bear the purifying light of day – he roams
the countryside in search of blood. Without it, the spark of
his unholy life grows ever weaker. (It is a belief, however,
in parts of Greece, that the vampire need feed only once each
century.) He is not a gourmet. He will take his sustenance
wherever it is to be found. While he much prefers the rich
blood of a human he will, if necessary, drain the fluid of any
living, warm-blooded creature he is able to ensnare. He feasts
to repletion, and returns to his grave when he has had his fill,
very much, says Montague Summers,[1] like a huge, bloated
leech, filled almost to bursting with his hideous repast.

The vampire is the most loathsome of all creations of God
or man, a being neither living nor dead, but possessed of a
strange, unholy vitality which is a counterfeit of both life and
death; he is not a ghost, but a corporeal, full-blooded being
whose life is wholly dependent on the lives of others. Although
in our time his abode is the wild, rugged Carpathian strong-
holds of Transylvania, his story goes back to far older times
and more ancient lands. He is to be found in all nations and
all civilizations. There are tales of vampirism in the chronicles
of Babylon and Assyria, of Egypt and ancient China. Belief in
his existence is still strong in much of Europe, and particularly
in Greece, where apparently he made his first appearance on
the Continent; he is frequently mentioned by the early writers
of Sparta and Athens. The ravages of this undead creature

---

[1] *The Vampire, His Kith and Kin.*

did not truly spread into other portions of Europe before the latter part of the seventeenth century, at which time there appears to have been a veritable plague of vampirism, particularly in the Slavic nations, centring in Transylvania, where the vampire found a land particularly suited to his mode of existence. He is the most dreaded and most powerful of all the creatures of evil. For as long as he has his bloody sustenance, the vampire lives on, year after year and century after century. There is for him no normal mode of death, no illness, no old age. His ravages can be halted only by his complete annihilation, and such a death is not easily secured. He is cunning, incredibly swift and strong, and, most terrible of all, he is capable of a horrible means of propagation which permits him to increase his numbers with startling speed.

It must again be pointed out that in no sense is the vampire a ghost, a wraith, a walking shade. He is not a walking dead man, although neither can it be said he is a living man.

It is no coincidence that, at least in our civilization, the most famous of the vampires seem all to be counts, barons, or other noblemen, particularly those of Slavic lineage. The vampire belief arose in this part of the world from the seventeenth to nineteenth centuries, the era of the powerful robber barons who ruled their villages with a bloody and brutal hand. The power of life and death over their subjects belonged wholly to them, and they never hesitated to make use of this right. Many were vile, cruel, cold-hearted monsters, using their power for all manner of vice and evil. This was the time of the horrifying Countess Elizabeth Bathory, real-life Transylvanian Queen of the Vampires, who murdered and drank the blood of some 650 young girls. The monster Gilles de Rais – he who had sat in the bowels of a living boy while drinking his blood[2] – was already a terrifying memory. It is not to be wondered that the tyrannized villagers could not conceive of such evil ceasing at the grave. The evil that men do lives after them and so, be he evil enough, does the evildoer himself.

A man – or, of course, a woman – who has led a particularly vile and evil life will almost certainly become a vampire; it is

---

[2] Joris Karl Huysmans, *La Bas.*

his curse for the wicked deeds committed during the natural term of his life, as well as an admission that a powerful evil can not easily be put to rest. Just so, one who dabbles in black magic and the various arts and crafts of Satan and the powers of darkness is a very strong candidate for the life of the undead.

Various parts of the world have their own beliefs concerning the origin of the vampire creature. The result of copulation between the Devil and a witch will be, during his lifetime, a master of the black arts and, at his death, a vampire; most primitive peoples believe that all witches and warlocks become vampires after death. People who are deformed at birth are quite likely to become vampires; this is particularly true of those born with a harelip, which would be a definite asset in the vampire's terrible method of feeding. In Transylvania, those born between Christmas and Epiphany are believed to possess the taint of vampirism, while other peoples believe the same of any child born on a Saturday. Even after death itself, a man is in danger of joining the ranks of the vampire, particularly in the wilder parts of Greece. Here is the belief that any corpse over which an animal leaps or steps will be unable to rest in his grave. For this reason, even today, dogs and cats are securely locked indoors at the time of a funeral. It is even held, particularly in the Orient where such people are a rarity, that redheads, or men with blue eyes, will become vampires.

The lust for revenge also plays a major part in the creation of a vampire. In the Mediterranean lands where the vendetta casts a shadow on the lives of the people, it is strongly believed that a slain man whose murderer is not brought to justice becomes a vampire, thirsting hungrily for blood to replace that of his own which was spilled in violence.

Vampirism is a belief current particularly in many of the Catholic countries of Europe, and the Church plays a large part in both the creation and the extermination of the beast. It is an accepted fact that a man who dies under the ban of excommunication will become a vampire. Montague Summers, the one-time priest who made so intense a study of these creatures of evil (in whose existence he implicitly believed) repeats frequently that there are three necessities for the exis-

tence of the vampire – a dead body, the Devil, and the permission of God – although he is mute as to why God should
permit such an evil. The vampire cannot tolerate holy articles
and can be severely burned by contact with a crucifix or holy
water. The wearing of any holy object is one of the strongest
guards against the attack of such a creature.

The spread of the legend of vampirism was undoubtedly
greatly assisted by the horrors of premature burial, so graphically described in Poe's story of that name. This is a horror
which need not much concern us in these days, but a century
ago – more recently in some backward countries – the burial
of a person in a state of catalepsy or coma was not unusual.
Often people so entombed would revive in the grave and manage to dig their way to freedom. They would then reappear,
wild-eyed, insane with the horror of their experience, dis-
hevelled, bloody, the very spectre of death. To superstitious
minds, they would, indeed, have risen from the grave. Summers
makes much of this, stating that at the turn of the century,
there was at least one premature burial each week in the
United States. There is, he was told by medical experts of the
time (he was writing in 1928), only one certain proof of death,
and that is the actual decomposition of the body. During his
travels in the last century, Mark Twain visited a building in
a Bavarian hamlet where the dead were kept for several days
before burial in order to be certain they were truly dead. The
chamber was equipped with food and drink, and a bell rope by
which those who were not dead could summon aid. Montague
Summers maintains that the great French tragedienne Rachel
died from the shock of a near premature burial. Our present
method of preparation of the body, of course, makes actual
living entombment unlikely today.

Literature has given us a stereotyped portrait of the vampire
which has become quite standard. Count Dracula has been the
model for the past half century (and nowadays generally resembles Bela Lugosi). He is a Transylvanian nobleman, charming, suave and striking, dressed always in evening clothes and
cape. He is extremely wealthy, owns a large, crumbling castle
in the dreary mountains of his homeland, and is possessed of
an indefinable but quite fatal charm which makes him almost

overwhelmingly attractive to women.

The vampire of legend is quite a different figure. He is more apt to be an untitled peasant, a quite average individual possessing nothing but the terrible vampire taint. He is lean and gaunt, extremely pale of face, except for the period just after feeding. His eyes are agleam with an unnatural redness reminiscent of hellfire, and his teeth are extremely white, the canines pointed as fangs. His nails, for some reason, are permitted to grow to an exceptional length and are generally dirty with clots of dried blood and bits of torn flesh. He is remarkable for the terrible, quite unbearable odour of his breath. Indeed, outside of films and novels, the horrible stench of his breath is one of the monster's most outstanding attributes, as it is of any creature whose diet is restricted to blood and carrion. After he has feasted, he lies in his coffin like some monstrous, sated insect, his body heavily bloated, his face flushed, his mouth filthy with the redness of his damned repast. He lies generally with eyes open and is completely aware, even during the hours of daylight, of all that goes on about him. He is, however, unable to act at this time, both because of the barrier of day and the lethargy which follows his feast.

The mentally ill recognized by medicine as vampires are much more conventional in appearance. Certainly there was nothing about John George Haigh, a director of the Onslow Park Hotel in South Kensington, London, to indicate that lust for blood and a twisted, demented religious mania had driven him to the murder of nine people. Haigh, who was also an inventor of some promise, under the direction of religious 'visions', lured his victims into his basement, where he clubbed them from behind, opened their jugular veins and drank down a glassful of hot blood before dissolving the bodies in sulphuric acid. A small and insignificant man with curiously slanted eyes, Haigh went to his well-deserved death on the fifteenth of August in 1949.[3]

Mary Lensfield of Brooklyn, whom William Seabrook encountered on the Riviera in 1932, somewhat resembled an Oriental's idea of a vampire with her pale skin, fiery red hair

[3] Robert Eisler, *Man Into Wolf*.

and bright green eyes. When Seabrook grazed his shoulder on a sharp rock, Mary hungrily fastened her mouth to the wound and 'like a leech' or 'a greedy half-grown kitten with sharp-pointed teeth', sucked at the blood. She revealed her insatiable craving for blood and, on Seabrook's advice, placed herself in the hands of doctors who managed to cure her of her vampiric leanings.[4]

There are various methods of detecting a vampire. Most reliable is the fact that the soulless creature casts no reflection in a glass, mirror or pool of water. It was this trait, above all, that revealed Count Dracula to the alert Professor Van Helsing. The vampire will, generally speaking, be seen only in the hours of darkness. Although it is part of the Grecian legend that there are vampires who can walk in daylight, it is generally held that he is able to leave his grave only two hours before midnight, and must return to it by the first cock-crow of morning or face extermination. The growing of hair on the palms of the hands and an index finger of unusual length, while more generally signs of the werewolf, may also be found in the vampire who, as is the case in many instances, may have been a werewolf during his normal life. The belief that the vampire cannot cross running water is a fallacy, but to many salt water does appear to be an impassable barrier. (The crossing of water did not interfere with the travels of Count Dracula.) The vampire, as previously mentioned, cannot bear to look upon a cross or a crucifix, or any object which might form a cross or cast the shadow of a cross, and he will shun the general area of a church or cathedral.

The world of the vampire is a world of blackest night. As evil cannot survive the light of goodness and reason, so does the vampire perish at the purifying touch of daylight. During the hours when the sun brings its clean brightness to the world, the vampire lies asleep in the hideous privacy of his coffin. This coffin must either lie in its original grave, or its bottom must be strewn with a layer of earth from the vampire's native soil. The coffin is carefully and often ingeniously concealed, for during these daylight hours of his unholy sleep,

[4] *Op. cit.*

the vampire is extremely vulnerable. He is, indeed, completely helpless. Should his life be threatened during this period, he cannot strike back. In spite of the terrifying power of this monster of the undead, the vampire presents absolutely no danger during the daylight hours, and it is then he can most easily be destroyed – providing, of course, his coffin can be found. It is also fatal to the vampire if he is unable to return to his coffin before the rising of the sun.

But when the orb of the sun sinks behind the horizon and the last of its rays slowly fades into death, the terrible world of the vampire comes again into its own and, during this time, he is well-nigh invincible. With the fading of the last glimmer of light in the sky, the bloodthirsty monster rises from his coffin and begins his unholy depredations.

The vampire follows various methods in rising from his little sleep of death, for not all lie above ground in the seclusion and safety of their own castles, as did the coffin of Dracula. To begin his own nightly quest for food, it was necessary only for the diabolical count to raise the lid of his coffin, resting on the floor of the castle dungeons. (Even this simple method has its variations; in a film of some years ago, the son of the infamous count slept in his coffin beneath the brackish waters of a dismal swamp. At moonrise, the coffin slowly rose to the surface of the water, and the vampire then stepped from it.) The majority of vampires were buried underground and returned each night to sleep beneath the earthen mounds of their original graves. Upon close examination, these graves, appearing to the casual glance normal and undisturbed, reveal the presence of several deep tunnels, of the thickness of a human finger, leading down to the coffin itself. It is through these egresses, in the form of a swirling mist, that the vampire makes his exit from the underground lair for, although a vampire is of very corporeal form, he does have the ability, as we shall see, of changing shape at will.

The most likely victims of the vampire are those with whom he was associated in life, and particularly those who were especially close to him during the time of his more normal existence. For this reason, the love of a man fated to become a vampire is a most perilous thing. It is the wife or the

Lon Chaney, Jr., played a suave, debonair Count Alucard (spell it backwards) to the *femme fatale* vampire Evelyn Keyes. *Son of Dracula* (Universal Pictures, 1942)

sweetheart who will feel the first razor-sharp bite of the vampire's teeth.

The physical attack of a vampire follows a very definite pattern. It begins with an ardent embrace, during which the victim, through the strangely hypnotic force of the vampire's eyes, is lulled into a false sense of peace and well-being. A passionate, greedy kiss follows the embrace, after which the vampire lowers his lips and sinks the fanglike, canine incisors into the tender regions of the throat, causing the blood to flow freely into his mouth. The general point of attack is the jugular vein at the side of the throat, an easy mark in a kiss of passion. The teeth, needle-sharp, make a swift and almost completely painless incision here. Apparently the vampire is also possessed of certain curative powers, for before the lips are removed from the bleeding jugular, the wound is closed and the bleeding ceases.

The final fate of the vampire's victim will depend on the quantity of blood drained from the vein. In his attack on Mina Harker, Dracula returned frequently to drain just enough blood to cause considerable lethargy and even illness in his victim, but not enough to bring death. In this way, the count managed to keep alive – and readily available – a constant source of sustenance over whom he had complete dominance. In her more rational moments, Mina had no awareness of what had happened to her. She welcomed, each night, the ardent embrace of the vampire which, each morning, left her near the point of death, but once the count had left her side, she could recall nothing of what had occurred. This is another of the deadly talents of the vampire – his complete mastery, through hypnosis, over the mind of his selected victim.

Often, however, the greedy monster will drain so much of the vital fluid from his victim's veins that death will result after the first such visit. This, unfortunately, does not bring release to the victim, for to die as the result of a vampire's feeding is to join the ranks of the undead. This fact explains the veritable plague of vampirism some centuries ago, for propagation is incredibly swift when death, not birth, brings increase of numbers. This will also provide an answer to the question as to why the vampire invariably attacks those who were dearest to him.

Such a death is quite often the result of the vampire's attack, for the creature is generally almost insatiable in his desire for the blood of his victim, and the slightest taste of the life-giving fluid will send him into an orgy of feasting. One of the most pitiful figures in *Dracula* is the madman Renfield who, having fallen under the baneful influence of the monster count, devours flies, spiders and small birds in his unquench-able thirst for the warmth of blood. There have been instances where vampires, in the agonies of their unholy cravings, have even devoured their own rancid flesh while still in the grave.

The vampire, of course, faces a constant battle for survival.

Feared and dreaded by all living creatures, he is at all times sought out for destruction. In league against him are all the forces of good and decency, including the very real power of the Church. Satan, however, as always, takes care of his own, and he has fortified the vampire with various unusual talents to assist him in this constant battle for survival. Most outstanding and successful of these methods is his remarkable ability to change his shape.

As we have seen, the basic form of the vampire after the death of his human shell remains the same as it was during his normal lifetime. His transition from the world of the living to that shadowed and frightening world of the undead does not in any way alter his physical form. It is only in times of peril, or during the active search for food, that the vampire will transform himself.

He will most often assume the shape of an enormous bat. One of the most terrifying sights in the entire world of horror is that of a large bat, outlined by the silver of the moon, lingering menacingly outside an open window, quietly lulling the sleeper to a sense of security before it swoops silently into the room and, gently flapping its wings, squats on the sleeper's breast and fastens its needlelike teeth in the throat.

Even aside from its connection with the field of horror, the bat is, generally speaking, a feared and despised mammal. With its strange leatherlike wings, its clawlike fingers and its ratlike body and sharp, evil face, the bat is scarcely a creature to become a household pet. They are carnivorous creatures, most of them quite harmless and even beneficial, as they feed on insects and small birds. The vampire bat of South and Central America will feed on the blood of cattle and even, at times, on humans, generally biting through the large toe while soothing the sleeper with his wings. Such attacks, save when they lead to rabies, are seldom fatal to human beings. (It is a remarkable thing that this actual bloodsucking bat should become associated with the vampire legend among people who had no knowledge whatever of the New World vampire bat.) The sight of a crawling bat, hooking itself along with the aid of its thumb, is a particularly unpleasant one, and huge schools of small black bats hanging, sleeping, head down from the limbs of trees or in dark caves present rather a macabre picture.

The bat form, however, is an ideal one for the vampire, and it is not difficult to see why – even apart from the bloodsucking habits – legend has so connected them. The bat is strictly a creature of darkness. Like the vampire, it sleeps during the hours of day and forages for food under the protecting cloak of darkness. In assuming this mammal shape, the vampire achieves the tremendous advantage of considerably more freedom of movement than he can possess in his human form. He need no longer depend on doors and terraces for entry into the sleeping chamber of his victim; an open window will more than suffice. A man trying to force himself through a dark bedroom window may very easily be discovered; a bat can easily do so with but little danger of detection.

Hammer Films provided the most enormous transformation of a vampire into his bat form.
Brides of Dracula (Hammer Films, 1960)

The vampire will often retain this bat form while feeding, gently moving his leathery wings in an effort to lull his sleeping victim. He then can effect his escape in the same manner in which he arrived. This form is also an obvious advantage in fleeing any pursuers.

The vampire may seek safety and advantage in other transformations as well, his life form being plastic and ever changeable. We have seen that, in effecting a departure from his grave, he can also transform himself into a shred of mist. This would seem to be even more of an advantage than the bat shape, and certainly even safer. There can be no bars to mist. As long as there is a keyhole, the slightest crack under a door, the smallest possible opening in a window, the vampire with the ability to became vapour cannot be kept from his quarry. And how to fight a bit of mist? Do you shoot it, stab it or strangle it? How do you take hold of it with your hands? This ability to become mist, however, seems to be a rather rare and unusual trait, and not one of which all vampires are capable; perhaps it is reserved for members of the hierarchy, such as Count Dracula. Some beliefs, in fact, state that the ability to vaporize is restricted to escape from the grave.

The form of a wolf is also assumed by the vampire on occasion. The chief advantage of this form, of course, is that of strength and power.

This unusual and varied ability of transformation is principally what makes the vampire so well-nigh invincible during the feasting hours of the night. He can, chiefly through various religious artifacts, be rendered temporarily harmless, but destruction of the vampire is almost completely a matter of daylight hours. When hard-pressed, he can generally make his escape by changing his form. He need not, however, depend solely on this talent, for in physical combat he is a formidable foe, possessed of the superhuman strength of many men. Nor is he simple to catch. If he finds himself facing overwhelming odds and, for some reason, circumstances do not permit a change of form, he can run with a speed to outstrip any mortal man.

The vampire also has his allies, whom he controls and who will always do his bidding. The wolves obey him, and legend also states that he has complete dominion over flies, mosquitoes, spiders and all blood-drinking creatures, whom he can readily call to his assistance.

But there are disadvantages, too, for along with these peculiar powers which seem to give him so marked an advantage over his mortal foes, the vampire is burdened with certain restrictions which he cannot, even with all his power, overcome. Chief of these, of course, is the fact that, regardless of where he may be or what he may be doing, he must return to his coffin before the first rays of dawn brighten the sky, or he faces immediate and permanent extinction. Here is the vampire's Achilles' heel. Wherever Dracula travelled from his native Transylvania, it was necessary for him to take his coffin along with him, and to place it close enough to the scene of his depredations that he would never run the risk of being unable to return to it before dawn. This seriously restricts the field of operations both in area and time.

Even when he has reached the security of his coffin, the vampire is in great danger, for it is during this period that he is not only harmless but completely vulnerable. With the rising of the sun, all of the vampire's terrible powers leave him and he is at the utter mercy of any who come across him. For this reason, the utmost importance is placed upon the hiding place of his coffin, which must be concealed in such a way that it can not be discovered by his enemies, who can then either slay the vampire while he sleeps, or burn the casket and prevent his returning to it. Count Dracula and his female companions-in-blood returned to sleep in the catacombic cellars of Castle Dracula, which the terrified, superstitious villagers would never have dared to enter. When he arrived in England, the count slept in the cellar of a deserted mansion and, at one time, had several properly prepared coffins secreted in various sections of the city in order to expand the base of his operations without running the danger of being trapped without a resting place at dawn. A vampire may, indeed, have numerous such graves, but each coffin must contain a layer of earth from the original tomb. Wherever it may be placed, the coffin lies always in darkness, away from any possible contact with the disintegrator rays of the sun. Deep cellars of castles or large mansions are highly preferred, or the tumbled rubble of ruins, any place not likely to be frequented by the curious, whose inquisitiveness might endanger the vampire's continued existence. Deep and lonely caverns, desolate moors, treacherous swamps – these are all likely resting places for the sleeping vampire. In *Return of the Vampire*, Bela Lugosi concealed his coffin in the rubble of bombed London, and in the more recent English film, *The Horror of Dracula*, the coffin was kept in a rather obvious but, for that very reason, extremely secure hiding place – the shop of a casketmaker.

While there is no actual cure for those attacked by the vampire, there are protective devices to ward off his murderous kiss. The best preventive, of course, is to stamp out the disease itself, and this is a method followed by many primitive peoples. In certain parts of the African continent, immediate action is taken after the death of a man considered to be in danger of becoming a vampire. It is believed that the most certain way of keeping a man in his grave is to deprive him of both movement and speech. With this in mind, the tongue of the suspect corpse is removed, and the arms and legs are detached from the trunk of the body.

In the Catholic countries, a corpse can be kept in his grave by the placing of a Eucharistic particle in the grave or in the mouth of the corpse itself. The depth of the grave may also have a deterrent effect on the urge to walk. The deeper the grave, the less likely is it that the vampire will be able to rise from it, despite his ability to vaporize. If the thorny stem of a wild rose is placed in the folds of the shroud, the monster will become entangled in the cloth and be unable to leave the grave. By the same token, the vampire's head can be permanently and rather brutally fastened to his coffin by the driving of a long nail through the skull. This again points up the fact that the vampire is not a ghost, but requires the complete freedom of physical movement for his existence.

Despite all these precautions, however, vampires continue to walk, and then other steps must be taken. Most common precaution amongst the peasant people is the scattering of mustard seeds on the roof or threshold of the house where the vampire's visit is expected. Some unwritten law of vampirism

Dracula (Bela Lugosi, right) cringes from Van Helsing's upheld crucifix, in Lugosi's first appearance in the role that would dominate his career.
Dracula (Universal Pictures, 1931)

makes it essential that the monster stop to count each and every one of these seeds; this will generally hold him beyond the rising of the sun, at which time he is, of course, instantly destroyed.

The vampire can not bear the odour of garlic, which reacts upon him much like poison gas. Mina Harker was advised to keep blossoms of garlic in a vase beside her bed, and even to wear a wreath of the plant about her neck while she slept. It was only when this order was not obeyed and the garlic removed that Dracula was able to enter her chamber. If the window and door sills are rubbed with garlic, the vampire is unable to cross the threshold regardless of whatever shape he may care to assume.

Most effective bar to the attack of the vampire, however, is the crucifix, for as the vampire is the very symbol of evil, so is the cross the symbol of good. Devout Catholics throughout the world still wear such an emblem today to ward off evil and, at least in the more backward regions of Central Europe, this evil includes the horrifying attack of the undead. Should the crucifix come into contact with any portion of the vampire's flesh, it will sear and burn him, leaving a permanent scar. Even the shadow of a crucifix, or any shadow falling in the form of a cross, will cause the vampire to flee in panic. Should such a shadow, however, fall directly upon him, he will be unable to move from its imprisonment. Holy water, if thrown upon such a creature, will react upon him like acid, burning him violently and, if thrown in sufficient quantity, destroying him.

For in spite of his impressive supernatural powers, the vampire can be destroyed, and the means of his destruction are very clear, very definite and quite satisfyingly permanent.

Accidental annihilation is a fear of which every vampire is constantly possessed, and this is his inevitable fate should he, for any reason whatsoever, be unable to return to his coffin by the required time. A vampire who is cornered by his enemies becomes filled with panic as the night withdraws and the sun begins to lighten the eastern sky. He knows he must be lying securely in his earth-lined coffin before the first direct rays touch the ground. He becomes a ferocious, dangerous animal as he fights for his very existence. A single beam of the sun falling upon his body will bring instant, complete and absolute disintegration. Much was made of this fact by the pursuers of Count Dracula. It is almost impossible to overcome the vampire during his nightly hours of activity, but one certain way to do so is to prevent his return to his coffin. Physical combat with the creature is always an ill-advised venture because of his great strength and cunning. A far safer method is to find his coffin and destroy it by fire while he is away on his quest for blood. When, sated and lethargic, he returns at the end of the night and finds his coffin in ashes, he is doomed, and not all his trickery can save him.

The Church may also be called upon to put a vampire to

rest, particularly if the creature has become a vampire as the result of death during excommunication. At the reading of absolution over an excommunicated vampire, the body will instantly crumble to dust. Montague Summers reports several accounts of such absolution.

But the time-honoured method of destroying a vampire is through use of the stake to transfix the monster's evil heart. This the vampire cannot survive, and it will put a permanent end to his depredations. It is, however, not quite as simple a deed as it may sound.

First of all, the vampire must be snared while in his coffin, and we have already seen that finding his resting place is no easy task. This, of course, must be done during the hours of daylight or, according to some ancient legends, on a Saturday. (Christmas Eve is also an ideal time for the sport of vampire hunting, for no evil creature has power on this holiest of nights. People born on Christmas Eve are believed to exert considerable influence over vampires and werewolves.) Once the vampire has been found resting in his casket, the danger is still far from over, for a bungled job, even during the hours of daylight, may restore the vampire to his full strength. Here indecision on the part of the attacker may well be fatal. It takes considerable moral courage – and physical strength as well – to drive a wooden stake through a human body, even if it is the body of an undead. The deed must be quickly completed, for great care must be taken that the monster be fully destroyed before the setting of the sun.

The task can also be made ineffectual by the use of improper tools. Not just any wood will serve for the stake. The most acceptable is aspen, which is believed to have been the wood from which the cross of Christ was fashioned. Maple or hawthorn may also be used. The stake must be sharpened to an extremely keen point, but must also be solid enough so that it will not shatter under the force of the blow. In some instances, a dagger consecrated on an altar may be substituted for the wooden stake, but this is not always entirely effective; at any rate, it is always wisest to keep to the tried and true methods.

Other materials are also required for the proper dispatch of a vampire. Of great importance is a sharp-edged sexton's spade for severing the head. A sword, knife or axe simply will not serve. A supply of garlic must also be on hand to complete the ceremony.

The proper ritual for the execution of the great vampire monster is clearly set forth and, for most complete results, must be closely observed. The sharp point of the stake is placed immediately above the slowly beating heart of the creature. An extremely steady hand is required, for the stake must pierce the exact centre of the heart, or the attempt will end in failure and disaster. The strongest nerves are also necessary. The vampire sleeps but in most cases is aware of what is going on about him. His red eyes are open and staring, watching every movement of his would-be assassin. It is only the imprisonment of the daylight hours and the lethargy which invariably follows his night's feeding that prevents the vampire from defending himself.

With the stake now held very firmly in place over the breast, the sexton's spade is raised. Here, now, is the moment of crisis. One moment of weakness or indecision, the slightest wavering of courage and determination, and the vampire will yet be the victor. Using the spade as a hammer, with one powerful stroke, the stake is driven into the black heart of the inert creature. The reaction is immediate, violent and indescribably horrible. The vampire fills the air with his horrid screams as he feels himself being sent into eternal damnation. Just as a mosquito, filled with blood, will seem, when crushed, to burst into an ugly red mass, so will the vampire release in one tremendous red torrent all the mass of stolen blood stored within his unholy body. Bloody foam froths at his lips and trickles down his chin; blood spurts from his nose, his eyes and his ears and even bursts, like some violent cataract that can no longer be held in check, from the very tips of his fingers. He twists and squirms, screaming in almost unbearable agony, swimming in a veritable sea of blood.

It is absolutely imperative that the vampire be transfixed by a single, powerful blow of the sexton's spade. This is, of course, not a simple matter. It requires considerable strength of arm and extreme courage of will and, in light of the above description, a strong stomach as well. A second blow with the spade will have a directly opposite effect from that desired for more than one blow will restore the vampire to the peak of his deadly power, and the would-be destroyer will swiftly become the creature's next victim.

The vampire now lies transfixed in his coffin, an expression of incomparable horror on his twisted features, the coffin glistening with the crimson of blood, the heavy wooden stake extending from the bloodstained chest of the infamous creature. The entire chamber reeks with the odour of blood, which has spattered the destroyer and left its crimson stain on the floor, the ceiling, the furnishings. The chamber resembles a slaughter house.

But all has not yet been done. The vampire has not even now been rendered completely harmless. Now the sexton's spade must once again be raised and, again with one single powerful stroke, the head of the vampire is severed from his body. Those hideous crimson lips must now be forced open, revealing the bloodstained fangs which have been sunk into the throats of so many helpless victims, and the mouth is thickly stuffed with poisonous garlic.

Only now is the vampire completely destroyed, never to rise again. His years, perhaps his centuries, of feeding on the blood of the living have at long last come to an end. While the destroyer watches, the body begins to dissolve, crumbling into dust, and finally disappears from view. The vampire has at last found rest.

Two other methods of extinction might be briefly noted. As we have seen, the most certain way to dispose of the beast, aside from the ritual described above, is through fire. We have previously mentioned that the most complete method of destroying the vampire is to burn his empty coffin, thus preventing the beast from returning to his grave. This, however, has its dangers as well. Those who have perpetrated this deed might well face destruction at the hands of the vampire before death finally claims him. There is also the possibility that, as in the case of Dracula, the vampire may have another coffin to flee to in the event of such a disaster.

More efficacious than this is the burning of the coffin while the monster sleeps within it. Once the vampire has been

burned to ashes, there is nothing that can revive him. Some
legends state that burning must follow the ritual of the stake
in order to make his destruction more certain. This burning
has, however, one further drawback. As has been mentioned,
the vampire has command of many types of insects, and these
may quite possibly come to his assistance. Any insect, worm,
spider, etc., which escapes, unseen, from the funeral pyre may
contain the spirit of the vampire (he has, of course, no soul as
we know it) and carry him on to life again. Even in his last
extremity, the vampire may seek escape through his ability
of transformation.

A silver bullet is sometimes used as a more direct means of
bringing death to a vampire, but this is generally a risky practice, depending on the marksmanship of the gunman. This is

**Irving Pichel stands ready to impale the first great female vampire
(Gloria Holden) in the brooding tale of Dracula's daughter.**
Dracula's Daughter (Universal Pictures, 1936)

the accepted manner of bringing death to a werewolf, and it is possible it affects the vampire only in his wolf form. It is, at best, an impermanent end, for a vampire slain by a silver bullet can be revived by the touch of moonlight.

These, then, are the most accepted methods of bringing final and permanent death to this evil creature. Disposal of the coffin is by far the surest method, followed by the stake and the spade. This latter method, by the way, may sometimes be even more disagreeable than expected, for it must be remembered that there are female vampires as well as those of the male sex. It would take a tremendously strong-willed person, indeed, to hammer the stake into a gently moving female breast, even if her evil nature be quite apparent.

3

Here, then, we have the world of the vampire, a world of blackness lighted by the crimson of blood, of yawning graves and opened coffins, of bats and wolves, of unholy lusts and passions. Of all the creatures of the night, he is the most powerful, the most dreaded, the most invincible.

Although belief in the vampire is today most common in Greece, the writing of Bram Stoker has placed his home in the wilds of Transylvania. It is, indeed, a perfectly logical home. With its dark mountains, its bottomless pools, its swamps and fens, thick, curling fog, the gloomy mountains and forests of this portion of Europe seem indeed a world that has been drained of its vitality. Vampires have been known in all of Eastern Europe, in Paris and in London, in all parts of the world, but Transylvania has become their traditional home.

Here it was that Count Dracula, most famous and terrifying of all the vampires of literature, held the countryside in a centuries-long vice of horror. But there have been other vampires, as well, and these, too, deserve a brief visit from us.

4

There is no scarcity of vampires in literature, although the great age of vampire tales came to an end in the latter part of the last century, culminating in Stoker's *Dracula*. As early examples of vampire tales, Montague Summers cites Goethe's *Die Braut von Korinth* and Bürger's poem *Lenore*, which, chiefly through the interest of Sir Walter Scott, was first translated into the English language in 1796. *Lenore* was to have considerable effect on later writers, and even Coleridge, in *Christabel*, is said to have been strongly influenced by this work.

It was not until 1819, however, that the first great vampire made his appearance. (It is interesting that this is the year following the first appearance of *Frankenstein*.) Just as, in the twentieth century, the name of Dracula became synonymous with vampire, so, in the century preceding ours, Lord Ruthven was the very epitome of vampiric horror.

The writing of *The Vampyre*, which introduced Lord Ruthven to a thrill-hungry reading public, was, for many years, as much of a mystery as the story itself. It was said that the tale had its origin in 1818, in that curious milestone of literary evenings when Percy and Mary Shelley and Lord Byron and other friends gathered on a windy, stormy night to tell ghost stories. During the course of the evening, it was agreed that each member present should concoct a tale based on some supernatural happening. Mary Shelley's contribution, which appeared in print later that same year, was the greatest of all classics of horror, *Frankenstein*. It was announced in 1819, when *The Vampyre* first appeared, that this tale of the undead was the work of Lord Byron, begun in that same story-telling session, and so was it credited through numerous editions; it was even included some years later in the collected works of Byron. The young poet, however, from the first steadfastly insisted that he was not its author, and it was later determined that the infamous Lord Ruthven was actually the creation of still another member of that literary party, Dr John Polidori, physician and companion to Byron.

Like its famous successor *Dracula*, Polidori's tale is a long and involved story of blood-drinking and horror. Since it is long out of print and generally forgotten, a brief synopsis of the tale may not be out of place here.

The story opens in London with the appearance in society of a strange, distant, but charming European nobleman with the disturbing quality of giving a chill to anyone upon whom his dull, grey eyes happen to fall. His name is Lord Ruthven. The strange gentleman becomes friendly with a young man named Aubrey, and the two depart together on a tour of the Continent. In Rome, warned by letters from home which relate strange and terrifying scandals connected with Lord Ruthven, young Aubrey shakes off his companion and travels to Greece, where he meets and loves the beautiful Ianthe, who regales him, and then terrifies him, with tales of vampires, in which she implicitly believes. Aubrey is attacked by one of these undead creatures, and Ianthe loses her life in his defence. As a result of this terrible experience, the young man languishes in Athens with a raging fever. Lord Ruthven makes his appearance at this most opportune time and nurses him back to health, after which the two again become companions. During their journeys in the interior of Greece, they are attacked by robbers, and Lord Ruthven is fatally wounded. Before his death, he forces Aubrey to swear that he will not permit word of his death to reach England. Aubrey, in accordance with another promise, takes the body of his late companion to the pinnacle of a mountain and exposes it to the first rays of the moon. When, shortly after, Aubrey returns to give Ruthven proper burial, the corpse has disappeared.

Aubrey returns to England in time for the society début of his younger sister, at which function, to his horror, he finds Lord Ruthven, who immediately reminds Aubrey of his promise not to reveal the story of his 'death'. To Aubrey's increasing horror, it is announced that his sister is about to become the bride of the Earl of Marsden, who is none other than Lord Ruthven himself.

Aubrey falls ill, but preparations for his sister's wedding

continue. The couple are married and they leave for their honeymoon while Aubrey, now at the point of death, reveals all. But it is too late. Aubrey's sister has met death from the bite of the vampire, and Lord Ruthven has disappeared. Although this ending seems to cry for one or more sequels, it is the rather unsatisfactory conclusion to the tale of this particular vampire nobleman.

The appearance of *The Vampyre* created an immediate sensation. Although largely forgotten today, the tale is well written and reeks of the atmosphere of horror. We might today smile at the young Aubrey persisting in keeping his promise to Ruthven even at the risk of his sister's life and soul, but in the early years of the last century, a man's honour was dependent on keeping his word under any and all circumstances. The revival of Ruthven by the first rays of moonlight is an aspect of vampirism which has largely been forgotten. *The Vampyre* presented the age with an entirely new type of literature – as had *Frankenstein* in the previous year – and the public lapped it up. The original edition ran into numerous reprints and in the same year the tale was translated into both French and German.

Lord Ruthven became the most famous literary villain of his time, and there were soon many imitations of this famous work, all presenting the blood-hungry nobleman as the protagonist. A French writer, one Cyprien Berard, even attempted to write a sequel. On June 13, 1820, *The Vampyre* was presented on the French stage in a dramatization by Charles Nodier, and achieved a considerable success. There followed a veritable flood of stage vampires, both in drama and farce. In England, there was even a one-act comic operetta, and a very popular full-scale opera on the vampire theme was adapted by James Robinson Planche. The Germans created their own vampire opera in Leipzig in 1828, and in 1851 no less a literary figure than Alexandre Dumas presented a drama on the vampire, in which the monster was named, again, Lord Ruthven.

In the following years, the vampire theme was not neglected, although it made its appearance chiefly in such excellent short stories as the *Carmilla* of Sheridan Le Fanu, the terrifying *For the Blood Is the Life* by Marion Crawford and *Four Wooden Stakes* by Victor Roman, one of the finest of all vampire tales.

In the field of the novel, the successor to *The Vampyre* was a book by Thomas Prest, *Varney the Vampire*. Appearing in 1847, this tale of some eight hundred pages is most often compared to Stoker's more famous novel.

In 1897, Lord Ruthven for all time lost his eminence as king of the vampires to Count Dracula, who remains today the very epitome of evil and supernatural cunning.

Stoker was an English professor, and the last person who would be expected to write a classic of horror. Born in 1847 (his name was actually Abraham) he was a sickly child not expected to live, who grew into a hale, hearty, handsome man. He served for twenty-seven years as business manager to the great actor Sir Henry Irving. In the fiftieth year of his life, following a 'too generous helping of dressed crab at supper one night', Stoker had a nightmare of a vampire rising from his tomb, and the story of Dracula was born. (The name of the vampire Stoker took from historical sources dating back to 1455, when Walachia was ruled by a ferocious beast named Voivode Drakula, often referred to in the chronicles as a vampire.) Stoker, whose only other work of importance, seldom read today, was *The Jewel of the Seven Stars*, was a shy, retiring man who preferred to keep out of the limelight and spend his days in solitude at Cuden Bay on the Scottish coast, where much of *Dracula* was written. He died in 1912, at the age of sixty-five.

His novel stands today as undoubtedly one of the most brooding and horrifying works in the English language, and serves well as a study and analysis of vampirism. Here is the dark, mysterious Transylvanian castle, the frightening, mistenshrouded countryside, the blood-lusting lord of the castle and his un-human relatives, the transformation into the form of a bat and a wolf, the attacks on sleeping innocents, all the horrors of a life that reaches beyond the grave.

The story of *Dracula* is too well-known to require retelling

[5] H. Ludlam, *A Biography of Dracula*.

A frequent scene in Dracula films: another victim with bites on her neck. Peter Cushing, Michael Gough.
Horror of Dracula (Hammer Films, 1958)

here. The basic idea is the removal of the vampire curse from its native Transylvania to England. The area about Castle Dracula has been drained of its blood. It is a sterile, hostile land; centuries of feasting by the count and his numerous descendants have taken their toll. Dracula, therefore, seeks greener pastures and plans to migrate to the younger and more virile, untapped land of England. It is as an English real-estate agent that the unfortunate Jonathan Harker visits the count for his terrifying stay at Castle Dracula, and makes it possible for the vampire to visit England. Dracula arrives in the new land on a ship which is found with all its crewmen dead; the count leaves the death vessel in the form of a wolf. He takes up residence in London, where two girls, Lucy Wenstra and Mina Murray, the latter Jonathan Harker's fiancée, become his victims. It is finally through the courage and wisdom of the wily old Professor Van Helsing that Dracula, forced to flee, finally finds his death with the traditional stake in his heart.

Much of the book is a masterpiece of atmosphere, seldom surpassed. The opening portion devoted to the journal of young Harker, recording the agent's visit to the count's Transylvanian stronghold, is as chilling as any writing in the English language. Here is the brooding horror, the brush of the supernatural, the very air of evil, the terror upon terror of the world of the vampire. Stoker has created, in Castle Dracula, perched high on a naked mountain with its bleak towers and battlements reaching upward to a dark sky, a little corner of hell on earth. In later portions of the tale, the constant battles between Dracula and Van Helsing are as enthralling as a detective story, and the vampire's attacks on the innocent Lucy and Mina and the domination of the unfortunate Renfield are graphically drawn.

The story is, however, not without flaws, and the greatest of these, undoubtedly, is its considerable length. As has been previously mentioned, it is extremely difficult to maintain an air of brooding horror over an extended number of pages; for this reason, most of the finest writing in this field is in the form of the short story. *Dracula* has its lagging portions and, in spite of its general excellence, the tale, once Dracula has left Transylvania, never manages fully to recapture the air of horror with which it begins. The battles to save the lives of the two female victims become rather tedious and repetitious. The story would probably have been greatly benefited by considerable cutting.

Be that as it may, *Dracula* remains a brilliant piece of writing, and for more than sixty-five years, has been the last word on vampires. The book achieved immediate and tremendous success, a success which continues to this day.

Dracula was first produced on the stage March 9, 1925, some dozen years after the death of its author. The dramatization was prepared by Hamilton Deane, the son of one of Stoker's childhood friends, and starred Raymond Huntley as the count. At its run in the Little Theatre in London, a hospital nurse was posted in the lobby to assist patrons overcome by fright, a gimmick used today in movie theatres by producers of the cheaper type of horror films. Such antics are now greeted with contemptuous amusement, but in 1925 it helped make Dracula a phenomenal success. Although it was received with less than enthusiasm by the critics, the play ran through a number of productions over a period of years, and was presented in the provinces until 1941.

This dramatization of Dracula was first presented in New York at the Fulton Theatre on October 5, 1927, and was again a considerable success. Starred as Count Dracula was a European actor whose characterization was to bring him fame over the next thirty years – Bela Lugosi.

Dracula brought to an end what might be termed the period of 'creative vampirism' in literature. It is the highest praise of Stoker's work to point out that there have been no outstandingly successful novels on the vampire since Dracula, although there have been many interesting short stories. The finest vampire tale in many years was My Lips Destroy by Cornell Woolrich[6] a chilling story relating the attempts of a bride-vampire to bring her husband into the world of the undead. August Derleth, one of our finest horror writers, told a quietly terrifying vampire tale in The Drifting Snow, in which a trio of vampires stand in the snow outside a lonely mansion and beckon to those within. This same writer's Nellie Foster is a brief, taut story of a housewife who takes matters into her own hands and ends the career of a vampire.[7] Richard Matheson's Gold Medal book I Am Legend, a fascinating combination of horror and science fiction, deals with the last human on

---

[6] Beyond the Night.
[7] These tales, which originally appeared in Weird Tales magazine, are included in Derleth's Not Long For This World.

an earth where all other creatures have become vampires. There is also Theodore Sturgeon's 1961 Ballantine book, *Some of Your Blood*. This is an engrossing vampire tale with a twist, in which the modern vampire – human, undead – feasts on menstrual blood. In the hands of a less capable writer, the theme would have been offensive and shocking, but Sturgeon handles it with a good deal of subtlety and manages considerable horror along the way.

5

Hollywood's first great horror cycle began in the early 1930s. The senior Lon Chaney had brought a touch of the terrifying to the silent screen, but his was a horror produced more by make-up than story element. As Quasimodo in *The Hunchback of Notre Dame* he had, indeed, brought chills to film audiences, and the horrifying skull-face of his *Phantom of the Opera* was certainly enough to satisfy the most avid seeker of the terrifying.

But Chaney's monsters were those created by society – deformed, repulsive misfits – and not those of legend and the undead. There was always an element of pity in these creatures, and the element of horror was generally of secondary importance. (In 1927, Chaney did appear as a vampire in the Metro film *London After Midnight*. His vampire was not the suave and cultured nobleman of later films. His eyes were large and staring, heavily circled by shadow, his teeth double rows of sharply filed points, his hair white and straggly. Dressed in a black cloak, white tie and top hat, he was an extremely unpleasant figure.) It remained for an English actor and a suave Hungarian to bring to the screen the type of horror that comes to mind when we mention the word 'monster'.

In 1930, the great Chaney died, and it was said that Hollywood could never find a replacement for this 'Man of a Thousand Faces'. It was feared that horror had had its day. The following year, however, Universal Studios – Hollywood's traditional 'home of horror' – introduced a film and an actor which marked the beginning of the truly great era of horror. The actor, whose name was to become, through three decades, a very synonym for horror, was an Englishman by the name of Charles Edward Pratt, changed for marquee value to Boris Karloff. The film was *Frankenstein*. We shall be meeting both these gentlemen again.

Frankenstein became a phenomenal success leading to numerous sequels. The audience suddenly became horror-hungry, and Hollywood has always been generous in appeasing such hungers.

A silent *Dracula* had been made in 1921 by the German film director F. W. Murnau, titled *Nosferatu, the Vampire*, since he had neglected to secure permission to use Stoker's title. The producers of the first projected sound version of the vampire tale turned to the greatest master of silent horror – Lon Chaney. Chaney, though impressed by the possibilities of the tale, hesitated at making a talking film and died before a decision was made. The producers then turned to Bela Lugosi. The film, like *Frankenstein*, made screen history, and Lugosi joined Karloff as a true master of horror.

Dracula, although masterfully directed by Tod Browning and boasting the brilliant camera work of the German Karl Freund, seems somewhat dated today and does not stand up as well as does *Frankenstein*, but it is still an effective work. Stoker's original tale is too all-encompassing for a literal translation to the screen, but his basic theme was closely followed. As in the book itself, the opening portions of the film were considerably superior to the closing ones. Castle Dracula was a massive, ancient ruin filled with cobwebs and mystery, sweeping stone staircases and enormous cold fireplaces, a perfect setting for the unnamable horror it concealed. The countryside was blasted and arid, the villagers terrified of the monstrosities dwelling in the fortress on the mountain-top. From the opening scene with agent Renfield and a terrified coach driver riding through the barren countryside, a sense of horror settles upon the screen.

Bela Lugosi was, of course, an ideal choice for the role of the vampire count, and, indeed, throughout his life and career he was never to escape identification with the role. There was a strange and terrible magnetism about his performance as the count. He was suave, he was gallant, he was ever proper and very formal – and he was deadly. Tall, darkly handsome in an almost Oriental fashion with his patent-leather hair and his slow, studied way of speaking, dressed in evening clothes and a long black cape, he was the personification of the Eastern European nobleman. There was a chilling hypnotism in his eyes – intense, burning, soul-searching. Although Mr Lugosi was not far from his fiftieth year when he appeared on the screen, one could not doubt his ability to have women follow him to destruction. The sight of his tall, black-cloaked figure, with the white face and burning eyes, standing motionless in the swirling white mist, is a classic picture of horror.

There are various reasons why the film has lost some of its effectiveness today. Styles in acting and direction have undergone considerable alteration in the past thirty years and more. Much of the performance in *Dracula* today seems considerably overdone, a result, too, of too literal transference from the stage, where broadness of performance is a necessity. The action seems somewhat static, more in keeping with stage production rather than the greater freedom of the film. In many portions the sound was faulty and the photography indistinct. An air of constant silence hovers over the film, for this was before the days of the crashing musical score which is now an integral part of every film. In some scenes – particularly those in which Lugosi, eyes glowing and fangs gleaming, approaches his victim – the complete silence enhanced the air of horror, but today the total lack of musical scoring creates an air of monotony, particularly in the opening scenes at Castle Dracula. The black and white photography, on the other hand, is a decided asset to the film, creating a nightmarish world of black, white, and grey shadows.

Even with these minor faults, however, *Dracula* remains an outstanding film and one of extreme importance in the history of motion-picture horror. Together with *Frankenstein*, it introduced an entirely new concept in the field of the visually terrifying and, certainly not of least importance, launched Bela Lugosi on his long film career as one of the most famous screen monsters.

Hollywood followed the original *Frankenstein* with several successful sequels and, quite naturally, attempted the same money-making device after the success of *Dracula*. The results were somewhat less than fortunate. In 1935, Marguerite Chapman became the victim of *Dracula's Daughter*, in which an extremely evil Gloria Holden lured young girls to their destruction with the aid of a hypnotic ring and a peculiar, stolid, Oriental manservant played by Irving Pichel, later one of Hollywood's major directors. It was a heavy, plodding and dreary film which was not very well received. Apparently the audiences of the day preferred their female vampires to be more on the order of Theda Bara.

The nefarious count himself made some rather unexplained reappearances in subsequent horror films during the cycle of the late thirties. In such films as *House of Frankenstein* and *House of Dracula*, it was apparent that the imaginations of screenwriters were beginning to wear thin, and it was no longer possible to produce an acceptable script constructed on a single idea; these stories presented a hodgepodge of loosely woven incidents, each serving merely to bring a particular monster onto the screen and then dispose of him for the appearance of the next. Thus we were presented with the mad scientist, the hunchback assistant (either male or female), the wolf man, the Frankenstein monster, and Dracula, all in one film. Finally, you could not tell the monsters without a programme, and it was difficult to know if the Frankenstein monster was being played by Lugosi, Karloff, Chaney or Strange. Such films contributed heavily to the collapse of the horror cycle.

Considerably more successful was *Son of Dracula*, one of the last films of this period of horror, released in 1942. With Lon Chaney, Jr., in the title role, assisted ably by Louise Albritton as a female vampire of undeniable charm, the film achieved a high level of horror, was well written, directed and photographed. Although Chaney achieved his greatest success as Lawrence Talbot, the wolf man, he presented a strikingly menacing figure as the charming Count Alucard (spell it backward). After his attempts to bring his lady love into eternal life-death had failed, Alucard met his death by

Count Alucard (Lon Chaney, Jr.) also had his white-haired nemesis—
played by J. Edward Bromberg, cringing here under the attack of the
vampire.
Son of Dracula (Universal Pictures, 1942)

dissolution when he returned to his coffin – removed from the
swamp and placed in a cave – to find it in flames.

Not all vampires were of the Dracula line. In *Return of the
Vampire*, Lugosi appeared as Armand Tesla, a vampire who
sought sustenance in the bombed ruins of wartime London.
The film had several striking sequences: two Cockney grave-
diggers return to the cemetery after an air raid to reinter the
dead. They find one corpse with a spike driven through his
heart. When they remove the spike, the 'corpse' groans; it is
Tesla, who had been staked twenty years before. Tesla's chief
adversary sits playing the family organ, while Lugosi (in evening clothes, of course) threatens her. With a sweeping gesture,
she removes the music book from the rack and reveals a

lighted cross; Lugosi disappears in a clap of thunder. Finally, Tesla – who has slain his werewolf assistant – is dragged into the sunlight and the flesh runs from his skull like melting wax, a delightfully gruesome end.

The failure of later *Dracula* films to achieve great success is not difficult to understand. Mary Shelley's book merely opened the door on man-made monsters, but Stoker's work opened the door on vampires, brought through it just about all possible aspects of this horror and closed the door again. In both literature and films, *Dracula* was complete and definitive. Further tales could be little more than carbon copies.

With the revival of horror in the 1950s, Hammer Studios in England assumed the mantle of the old Universal Studios, remaking many of the old classics of horror in large-scale, expensive technicolor productions. Of these, the Dracula films were by far the most successful.

Horror of Dracula, released in 1958, the year following the death of Bela Lugosi, starred Christopher Lee, with Peter Cushing as Dr Van Helsing. Although certain liberties were taken with Stoker's tale, this film, in many ways, surpassed the original of more than a quarter century before, and ranks with the great horror films of the past. In Cinemascope and technicolor, the film was exquisitely mounted and superbly directed and performed. Colour permitted stress on bloodshot eyes and dripping lips, and the film was replete with startling and horrifying scenes. The one possible complaint – and it is a minor one – might be that the sumptuous and beautiful Castle Dracula lacked the brooding, decadent horror of Lugosi's home. There were here no thick cobwebs, no clouds of dust, no shattered stairways; the castle of the new Dracula was a magnificent palace with broad, well-carpeted stairs, beautifully and tastefully furnished. Perhaps the new count was financially more successful than the old.

Christopher Lee made a thoroughly convincing vampire and his ferociously sudden appearances on the screen, his teeth converted to fangs dripping with blood, his eyes a furious, maniacal red, were terrifying. Cushing, on the other hand, was a calm and quietly effective adversary.

As a fine example of terror, we might cite the scene in

which Harker enters the tomb of the sleeping vampires, during the hours of daylight. Here, resting in their coffins, he finds Dracula and one of his beautiful 'brides'. Harker places the wooden stake above the girl's heart and there is a gushing fountain of crimson blood as he drives it home; the beautiful girl is immediately transformed into a hideous, ancient hag. But while he has been about this task, Harker has neglected to keep an eye on the sun, which has now set. He hears the crashing of the door of the tomb and the victorious laugh of the evil count who, with the death of day, has risen from his coffin and trapped the brave hunter of vampires.

The Hammer Films Dracula series were superbly and lushly mounted, as evidenced in this scene in which the tall, athletic Dracula (Christopher Lee) carries his victim from the castle library.
Horror of Dracula (Hammer Films, 1958)

The film ended brilliantly. Van Helsing is searching for the monster when the door of the study bursts open and Dracula, still dripping with the blood of his recent feeding, leaps into the room. A struggle follows, but the vampire is imprisoned by the power of a crucifix. He falls to the floor, directly into a beam of sunlight. In a sequence of motion-picture magic, he crumbles into dust.

Cushing appeared as the vigorous and brilliant Dr Van Helsing in 1960, in a sequel to this film, *Brides of Dracula*. Although somewhat less successful than its predecessor, it revealed the same careful attention to detail, the same fine craftsmanship and the same feeling for the horrible. There was no attempt to revive the count himself, and no Dracula appeared. This film, however, concentrated on an interesting new theme – the perils of a universal spread of vampirism. The young vampire is imprisoned in chains in the castle of his noble-woman mother until a young girl, as the result of an accident, is forced to spend a night at the castle. The vampire works his charm on her, and she effects his release. The young man then pays court to her at the school, while he spreads his evil amongst the female students, until Van Helsing puts a stop to it.

This film presented several fresh approaches to vampirism and some innovations. Martita Hunt, as the mother who herself becomes a vampire as the result of her own son's attack, is probably the most pathetic of all the undead. With superb artistry, Miss Hunt, while speaking with Van Helsing, manages to keep one hand nervously before her mouth to conceal her fanglike canines. She seeks Van Helsing's help and voluntarily submits to her own extermination, certainly an unusual angle. Use is made of the ability of holy water to cause serious burns on the vampire's flesh. When he himself is bitten by the monster, Van Helsing burns out the taint in his throat by applying fire to the wound. The vampire is ultimately destroyed by being trapped in the shadow of a cross formed by the arms of a windmill.

The film also contains one of those superb little scenes of horror as a madwoman lies on the grave of one of the vampire's lovely young victims and urges her, with promises of rich, warm blood and everlasting life, to rise from the imprisoning earth and follow her new master.

The two Hammer vampire films were beautifully coloured and produced. Even here, however, we are reminded that there was but one supreme vampire – the taint of vampirism is referred to as the curse of Dracula.

Early in 1961, there appeared a minor black and white film made in Europe, titled *Black Sunday*, one of the greatest of all vampire films. Based on a tale by Nikolai Gogol, the story centred upon the Slavic conception that Satan walks the earth but once every hundred years, on Black Sunday.

The horror of this gem of a film begins even before the title is shown upon the screen. In mysterious, misty Moldavia, a vampire trial is being held. A woman is tied to a cross and the golden mask of Satan, its interior lined with sharp iron spikes, is hammered onto her face, the local punishment for witchcraft and vampirism. The scene is startlingly horrifying, with the flickering light of burning fires, naked trees, robed priests, thick fog, and the screaming of the tortured vampires.

The tale itself opens some two centuries later, again on a Black Sunday. A doctor, travelling with his young assistant to a medical convention, comes across a ruined chapel. Their exploration takes them to the vault, where they find a curious, massive stone sarcophagus. Set into the stone, above the head of the corpse, is a glass panel, through which can be seen a horrible golden mask, apparently placed over the face of the corpse. At the breast of the coffin is a stone cross; this would be visible through the faceplate. As they stare with a mixture of curiosity and horror, an enormous bat swoops out upon them. The doctor manages to kill the mammal, in the process breaking the glass of the sarcophagus; the blood of the slain creature drips onto the golden mask.

Meanwhile, in the castle, the ruling prince sits in fear before a massive fireplace flanked by large stone griffins. He knows that this is Black Sunday, and he fears for the safety of his beautiful young daughter, Katya, who strongly resembles the long-slain vampire woman. Uneasy, the prince retires.

In the crypt, the blood has revived the vampire woman who, still in her coffin, silently calls to her follower, who had

The carriage of death moves furiously but silently through the dark misted forest in the superbly atmospheric *Black Sunday.*
Black Sunday **(American-International, 1960)**

perished with her. In the cemetery, the earth moves and the satanist, still wearing his golden mask, rises from the grave. Through a secret passageway, in the griffin fireplace, he enters the castle and presents himself before the terrified prince, who suffers an attack of apoplexy. One of the young doctors is called for, but the male vampire intercepts him and takes him to the crypt, where the woman anxiously awaits his blood. The doctor becomes a vampire and then ministers to the prince.

The following morning, the second young doctor arrives at the castle. He finds the prince dead, with the bite of a vampire on his throat. His medical friend cautions him about 'interference' and disappears.

The young doctor discovers the secret entry to the crypt through the fireplace, where he finds the revived vampire woman. The doctor, rushing to the village, seeks the assistance of the Church. He convinces the village priest of the truth of the vampire tale and they return to the crypt, where they find both Katya and the vampire woman. Katya has been brought to the tomb by the satanist and, through physical contact with her descendant, the vampire has at last gained sufficient strength to rise from her tomb. The young doctor is at first unable to distinguish between the two women, both of whom now claim to be Katya. He finally makes his decision, and moves to destroy the woman whom he believes to be the vampire, when he notices she wears a crucifix about her neck; he realizes the vampire could not wear such an adornment. In a quick gesture, he tears the cloak from the supposed Katya and sees her decayed, worm-covered body. The vampire is overcome and burned at the stake.

Much of the effectiveness of this horrifying film – the most original vampire tale since *Dracula* – is due to its superb photography. There is little sunshine or daylight in *Black Sunday*; it is a film of dreary blackness and a perfect example, so common in horror films, of an instance in which the impression would have been largely destroyed by colour. The atmosphere is brooding and chilling, the characters portraits of the most superb creatures of horror. The slow revival of the vampire woman with the dripping of the blood, the crawling of the spiders and centipedes, the resurrection from the grave of her satanic assistant, the black carriage, in which the satanist takes the young doctor to the castle, moving swiftly but with complete lack of sound, the operation of the secret panel behind the fireplace, the revealing of the vampire's corrupted body – all are superb instances of the tremendous effects visual horror may have on an audience.

6

The shadows begin to lengthen. The brilliant orb of the sun will soon disappear behind the rugged Transylvanian peaks. The sky has lost its colour, and darkness is about to descend upon the world. The full moon awaits in the wings, prepared

at the proper moment to make her next appearance on the
stage of life. Soon the silver rays of the moon will slip their
inquiring fingers through the embrasure in the wall and lightly
kiss the crested box before us. Like lovers, the moonlight and
the king of the vampires will greet each other. Outside the

The dark, hypnotic Lugosi eyes created many a shiver of fear in the
audience, as well as in his victims.
Dracula (Universal Studios, 1931)

castle, the mist will arise from the swamps and lay a blanket upon the earth to serve as a carpet for the feet of Dracula. The wolves will gather and howl their greetings to the moon; bats will raise their rodent bodies on leathery wings and swoop from the pinnacles of the towers in search of that same terrible sustenance which means life to Count Dracula.

We must be long gone from here before that lid begins to open, and the long, white hand of the king of vampires reaches again for the freedom of the night air.

THE WEREWOLF

'And there could be seen on his chest
the vague markings of a five-pointed
star . . . the sign of the pentagram . . .
the mark of the beast. . . .'

The campfires burn low, and another log is thrown upon the flames, sending up a brief shower of sparks that momentarily lights up the dark forest that surrounds us and casts weird and frightening shadows dancing about us. Just a few yards from the circle of the fire, the darkness begins, the darkness of the forest and of a stranger and more terrible world. The tall, gaunt sentinels of the trees conceal their own secrets, and it may be that the movements we see beneath them are phantasms of our own over-activated imagination. The night is silent, and above the dark trees a silver disc appears, now and then hiding her face, as though with fear, behind the dark, fleeting clouds.

It is on such a night that the werewolf walks.

There is comfort for us in the knowledge that we are not alone in this strange world. Encircling the fire with a rim of riotous colour, washed into black where the night has successfully secured its hold, flaming into yellow and crimson where the fire reaches out its strands of light, are the wagons of the gypsies. There is light in some of them, but most are dark. Indistinct forms sit on the wagon steps, wearing voluminous ankle-length skirts, or broad silken pantaloons and tightly pulled kerchiefs. The fire glints on golden earrings.

Wisps of smoke arise from pipes firmly held in narrow lips that have tightened through knowledge of hatred and persecution. From the far outer edge of the circle comes the soft, plaintive sound of a gypsy melody, weeping two thousand years of sorrow to the indifferent night. Someone rises from the steps and enters a wagon, and we can hear, for a moment, the clash of bangles and bracelets. There is, strangely, no sound of merriment or laughter.

Before us by the fire sits the queen of the gypsies herself. She is older, far older, than anyone else we have ever seen, and she squats upon the box which is her seat, much like some small, withered insect. Her clothes are brilliant clashes of silken colour, with a wide sweep of crimson skirt, a yellow satin blouse and a brilliant orange bandanna about her small head. Both arms are covered with cheap bangles of gold and silver, and long loops of beads and amulets dangle about her neck. From each ear hangs an enormous brass half-moon. Whenever she moves her gnarled hands, there is a dazzling sparkle of rings.

She has been silent for some minutes, and we can study that ancient face. The throat is as withered as that of an unwrapped Egyptian mummy, and the face itself a veritable network of fine lines, crisscrossing to form a distinctive pattern of age. Wisps of silver hair escape from the kerchief about her head. The dry mouth is old and sunken; the stem of a battered wooden pipe is held between the white, wrinkled lips. Only the eyes are still supremely alive, gleaming like burning coals in that dead face, red by reflection from the fire, alight with the mysteries of the past and of the future, the eyes of ancient knowledge which have seen more than the rest of us have known in our most terrifying dreams.

With a trembling hand, the gypsy woman tosses another bit of wood upon the dying fire, and the flames leap up momentarily; then, as with a sigh, the bright tongues fall back and let the darkness return.

We have come to this gypsy camp from the castle of Count Dracula to meet the second monster of our study – the werewolf. We have not travelled very far. To our right a blacker, obscene blot against the dark sky, the vampire count's fantastic abode, can still be dimly seen. Even in the early days, the gypsies encamped in this area; indeed, it was with a gypsy band that Dracula made his last frantic flight to the safety of his labyrinthine home.

The gypsy is wise in the ways of the black arts, and as we have seen, knowledge of this kind often brings with it dangers almost too terrible to mention. The very origin of the gypsies is lost in the mists of time. They are believed to be the remnant of some obscure and long-forgotten tribe of India, forced by some ancient catastrophe to leave their native homes and travel throughout the world; their language is a derivative of ancient Sanskrit. In English law they were called Egyptians, and it is by a corruption of this name that they are known today. They carry with them the ancient lore and magic of Egypt during the days of the great Pharaohs, and of India during a time long forgotten by history. For thousands of years they have delved into the secrets of magic, travelling about Europe in their colourful caravans, a race apart from all other races, a people apart from all other peoples, making their living by fortune telling, horse trading, working in metal, music and, now and then, by thieving.

For their audacity of knowledge in forbidden fields, the gypsy has suffered in many ways. They have become a people outcast from the rest of the world, a race despised, doomed to wander from country to country, village to village, feared, hated, persecuted. Clinging through all the centuries to their own peculiar dress and mode of living, they have been looked upon as the spawn of Satan, as witches and magicians, as thieves and murderers, as sex fiends and kidnappers. Nor did they escape the monumental hatred of the Nazis, for they were gathered into the concentration camps of Eastern Europe with other 'undesirable' peoples. In the thousands, the gypsies of Hungary and Rumania were removed from their wagon caravans and herded into the gas chambers of Birkenau. The estimated population of 750,000 gypsies in Europe before the war years was drastically reduced by 1945.

But the gypsies are as accustomed to persecution as are the Jews. During the Middle Ages they were imprisoned, tortured, slain by the hundreds and thousands. All great cities were

The werewolf became the third of the trio of great creatures of horror, providing Lon Chaney, Jr., with his most memorable role. *The Wolf Man* **(Universal Pictures, 1941)**

closed to them and there was no place where they might find rest. (There are many examples of persecution of gypsies in literature. In *The Hunchback of Notre Dame* the barriers were lowered before the entrances to Paris when the gypsy caravan approached; the tragic fate of Esmeralda befell her because of her gypsy blood. The opera *The Bohemian Girl* graphically reveals hatred of the gypsies, who are driven from the lands of Count Arnheim. In true legendary gypsy fashion, they counter by kidnapping his daughter.)

And with all this persecution, the gypsies have suffered still another curse – lycanthropy. The werewolf legend is tightly bound up with the world of the gypsy. This ancient harridan before us, with the two-wise eyes, has seen much. Indeed, it is rumoured that her own son bears the mark of the wolf. It is he who may be out there in the surrounding darkness.

But the old gypsy woman is beginning to stir. She raises her eyes to the black expanse behind us and seems to be examining the trees for some portent of disaster. She removes the pipe from her mouth and begins to speak:

'We call it the curse of the pentagram. . . .'

2

The legend of the werewolf is at least as old as that of the vampire, and as widespread among the superstitious peoples of the world. In Transylvania and other Slavic nations, he is called a *volkodlak*, while in France the common term is *loup-garu*. The Scots call him a *warwulf*, while the German *werwolf* is most similar to our own term. 'Were' means man, which literally translates the term into man-wolf.

Petronius in his *Satyricon* reveals that the werewolf was known to the ancient Roman, and the legend appears in the folklore of most nations. It was in Europe, where the wolf is one of the largest carnivorous animals, that the legend became most popular. We found that the vampire myth had its foundation in the offering of blood to the gods as the supreme sacrifice – the blood is the life. The legend of the werewolf also has its basis in facts somewhat more solid than those of the supernatural. Cannibalism in early man doubtless had considerable importance in the origins of the legend. The more civilized man became, the more horrible became the practice of cannibalism. The eating of human flesh was something unnatural, something beastlike. One who indulged in this particular kind of feasting must be very close to an animal; from here, the next step was belief that such a person actually transformed himself into an animal. In Europe this animal became a wolf, while in other nations, where the wolf was not so common, he became a bear, a tiger, a leopard. Even today, we often use such terms as 'ravening like a wolf', 'fierce as a wolf', etc. Through such terms, we can trace the origins of lycanthropy.

The Romans considered lycanthropy a form of insanity. At certain times of year, particularly in February, said the Romans, certain men were filled with ravening appetites and the strength and cunning of a wolf. Such men would live in the hills, precisely in the manner of wolves, attacking and tearing all who might pass. Later writers indicated that this disease was most prevalent in Bohemia and Hungary, where people afflicted with such madness made their homes in cemeteries, sleeping in despoiled graves, feasting upon corpses and often attacking the living.

Such people were firmly convinced that they had, indeed, taken on the physical form of a wolf, as they had assumed his attributes. In this same sense, lycanthropy is today an accepted form of insanity.

More primitive and superstitious people were easily led to believe that the lycanthrope was actually transformed into a wolf. The belief was very common among various tribes of the American Indian, and the Navajos had a secret society whose emblem was a wolf head, and whose adherents were believed to be possessed of the ability to change their shapes. In the African jungles, the wolf became a leopard, and the terrifying leopard man society brought death and disaster to many a village. While the members of this cruel organization – which is still in existence – merely donned a leopard skin and attacked their victims with sharpened spikes in their hands as a symbol of leopard claws, many believed an actual transformation took place. The same was held to be true of the Africa hyena man and of other instances in which animal characteristics were attributed to men. William Seabrook tells of a visit[1] in North Africa to a panther man named Tei, who was himself firmly convinced that he became a panther when he committed his crimes. He liked it, he stated, for it was far nicer than being a man. Tei achieved his transformation by donning the skin of a panther and executing certain leaps which had the desired effect; this was the same method followed by American Indians. Tei found his end before a firing squad.

One of the strangest of Seabrook's accounts concerns the transformation of a woman into a hyena.[2] An Englishman had shot one of these ugly scavengers and found, to his surprise and horror, that set in the ears of the dead animal was a pair of gold earrings encrusted with semi-precious stones. These stones, it was learned, had belonged to one Sarab'na, daughter of a local chief. She had long lived under the suspicion of lycanthropy, and this was accepted as proof positive. Nor could the people be dissuaded from this belief by the true facts of the case – that the princess, tortured in hopes of extracting a confession of lycanthropy, had been driven to madness and slain. To cover up the murder, her earrings had been placed on a young hyena in hopes of stirring up confusion and leading the people to believe the lycanthropy tale.

Seabrook also tells the story of a Frenchman on the Ivory Coast who kept his wife in a cage because she was a werewolf. The cage was large, roomy, clean and comfortable, and the wife refused to leave it or to prefer charges against her husband, preferring to remain in the safety of her prison, for whenever she was released she returned to her home with her jaws smeared with blood.

As Europe suffered from a plague of vampirism in the seventeenth century, so, less than a hundred years earlier the Continent underwent a blood bath of lycanthropy which, for some unknown reason, seemed to centre itself mostly in France. The tales of suspected or merely disliked persons dragged to their death on a lycanthropic charge is reminiscent of our Salem witchcraft days.

[1] *Witchcraft, Its Power in the World Today.*
[2] *Ibid.*

The legend of the werewolf is closely allied to that of the vampire, and what applies to one very often applies also to the other. The methods of becoming a werewolf are somewhat similar, but his destruction is a different matter.

There is, however, at least one very sharp difference between these two supernatural creatures. The werewolf is not an un-dead like the vampire. The vampire has died and returned to his terrible form of life as punishment for the evil he has committed, or as the result of suffering death at the bite of a vampire. This is not the case with a werewolf, who is a living creature with habits and the practices of the living. Unlike the vampire, he does not spend any part of his day in a deathlike trance, and has no coffin to return to. Save for the hours when the taint is upon him, the werewolf leads a completely nor-mal, human existence.

One who is versed in evil and black magic runs as much danger of becoming a werewolf as he does of joining the ranks of the vampire. According to the ancient Greeks, anyone could transform himself into a wolf; he need only know the proper incantations. Many primitive peoples believed that donning a wolf's skin at certain times of the year enabled the wearer to become one of the pack.

Those who eat the flesh or drink the blood of a sheep that has been killed by a wolf are in danger of becoming either werewolves or vampires, and we have seen werewolves often become vampires after death.

The easiest way of becoming a werewolf is to suffer a bite, or even a scratch, from such a creature; in this respect, were-wolves increase their numbers even more easily than vam-pires. During times of pestilence, war or famine in Central and Eastern Europe, the attack of a wolf was man's most dreaded danger. At such times, the wolves often came down from the hills that were their natural home and prowled about the farms and even the villages of the valley below, often attacking and killing people. The attack of a wolf, while ex-tremely painful and often fatal, was merely one of the dangers of living in such times, but should it be learned or even suspected that a man had been attacked by a werewolf, he was shunned, driven from the village, or put to death by the terrified peasants. The saliva of the werewolf was at all times considered deadlier than the most virulent poison, and one drop of it entering the bloodstream was enough to condemn the victim to a lifetime of hell. Where the victim of a vampire is in such danger only if he dies as the result of the attack, the werewolf's victim faces disaster merely from his touch.

The werewolf is not quite as easily detected as the vampire. He has no fear of mirrors or still water, for, being human, he casts a reflection. He does not sleep during the daylight hours, for he is not strictly a creature of the night. During the periods of normalcy, the artifacts of religion which deter the vampire at all times will have no effect upon him. There are, however, several tried-and-true methods by which such a creature can be discovered.

The hands of a werewolf are the most certain giveaway. There is a certain growth of stiff, coarse and bristly hair in the centre of his palms, also seen, though not as often, in the vampire. Most humans who are werewolves will, of course, keep their palms shaven, but the roughness of the skin caused by such a procedure is almost impossible to disguise. Nothing, however, can disguise the most distinguishing mark of the werewolf – his fingers. In all such creatures, the index finger is the longest digit on the hand, extending considerably beyond the middle finger.

The pentagram is the symbol of lycanthropy, and the werewolf will be branded with it on some part of his body. This, one of the most potent symbols in witchcraft and one of the most dreaded indications of evil, is a five-pointed star. The werewolf generally will find that the pentagram has appeared on some part of his body, usually the chest or hand, soon after his first killing, and that it will remain until his death. It is also believed that the werewolf sees the shadow of the pentagram in the palm of his next victim.

Just as with the vampire, legend and film have made of the werewolf a rather romantic figure; but as with the vampire, the genuine article is quite a different proposition. The true werewolf is a lean, gaunt man with hollowed cheeks and eyes which, like those of a wolf, glow in the dark. His legs are scabrous, covered with sores, and there is in him a constant restlessness which makes repose impossible. He seems always to pace a room like a caged animal. And he is, in truth, even more dangerous than a wild animal escaped from his cage.

In many instances, however, the werewolf is far more to be pitied than the vampire, for his is a world of agony and intense horror. There is here another sharp difference between the two unholy beings. The vampire is completely evil, a satanic monster whose primary concern is the continuance of his own foul existence. Once a creature becomes a vampire, he loses all human feeling and emotion and becomes a thing of damnation.

Not so, however, the werewolf who, during his more nearly normal lifetime, suffers the agonies of damnation. For while the vampire is a true creature of the undead, the werewolf assumes his monstrous appetites only during the period of transformation; at other times, he is a normal being, suffering torture for his hideous crimes. At such times, the werewolf seeks and longs for destruction, but death can only come in certain forms, and suicide is an impossibility.

According to the ancient gypsy legend, first quoted in the film *The Wolf-Man*:

> Even a man who is pure in heart
> And says his prayers by night,
> Can become a wolf when the wolfbane blooms
> And the autumn moon is bright.

Therein lies the tragedy of the werewolf. The taint can come to anyone – to an honest, upright citizen, to a sweet, loving young girl, to a simple housewife. Once the taint is upon someone, his nature does not undergo any visible change. His life will continue as before, but at certain periods of the year he will turn into a ravaging creature of horror. The true agony lies in the fact that this previously honest citizen, once the nightly horror is over and he returns to his normal form, is fully aware of what he has done. The ferocious beast, lying in wait to rip and rend the unwary traveller, may, during the hours of daylight, be a gentle man, a loving husband and father, who would consciously harm no one.

Two forces govern the transformation of man into wolf. Most important of these is the moon. During the cycle of the full moon, the blood of the werewolf undergoes its chemical change, resulting in the transformation of the body and complete subservience of the human nature to that of the beast. From the moment the first rays of the full moon brighten the sky, until it has set behind the hills before the greater radiance of the sun, the werewolf is an animal, walking often on all fours, attacking all who come within his reach, killing, tearing, feeding on the flesh of his victim. Here, again, we see a difference between vampire and werewolf, for the former walks every night, whereas the latter is generally restricted to the nights of the full moon.

That strange plant known as wolfbane is another factor in this terrifying transformation. Wolfbane blooms under the autumn moon, and according to some legends, it is only at this time – with the combination of the blooming wolfbane and the full moon – that the werewolf prowls the countryside.

Much can be learned of the presence of a werewolf by the behaviour of other animals, particularly feline. They are extremely sensitive to the presence of such a creature, and will react immediately and violently to the proximity of a man bearing the mark of the pentagram.

There has been considerable confusion concerning the actual transformation to werewolf, particularly in the matter of clothing. In films, the werewolf has the hairiness and features of a wolf, but is generally fully clothed and walking on two legs. The werewolf of ancient legend, however, is far more a wolf than a man. Once the transformation has taken place, it is impossible to detect any difference between the werewolf and the true wolf, although the werewolf is often somewhat larger, with silvery fur and deep crimson eyes. He will travel on all fours, like the animal he counterfeits, and will not be hindered by clothing. Just how this lack of clothing comes about has not been established. It does not necessarily indicate nudity at the time of transformation. Either the creature tears off the restricting bonds of clothing, or the clothes share in the transformation. At any rate, when a werewolf is slain and returns to human form, he is always found to be naked.

Legend has long placed the gypsy as guardian and protector of the werewolf. Peasants of the Slavic nations where the werewolf legend is today still strong, fear the approach of gypsy bands primarily because of this connection with lycanthropy. Some legends would indicate that lycanthropy is a disease originated with wandering gypsy tribes, but this may be merely another aspect of the belief that the gypsy is an evil being connected with black magic and various forms of satanism.

The world of the werewolf is not the unrelieved black evil of the vampire, but a world of constant dread and agony. Let us examine the life of one such unfortunate creature, whom we shall call, in best Transylvanian tradition, Baron X. He is a wealthy, handsome, personable young nobleman of an ancient and highly distinguished family. He has led a normal life for one of his high station, surrounded by all the well-publicized advantages of wealth, respected by the people of the village. Perhaps he is about to marry, to assure the continuation of the noble line.

One night, while strolling alone through the forest, Baron X is attacked by a wolf. The creature is driven off, and the baron's wounds, though extremely painful, are not serious. There is no reason to believe he has been attacked by other than a bona fide wolf, with which the mountain forests abound.

The change in the baron comes slowly. There is a period of illness, of intense fever, quite natural after the painful wounds he has received. A most peculiar change comes over his aristocratic hands. The index finger seems suddenly elongated, and he rubs constantly at the palms of his hands, which appear suddenly coarsened, as though he had been doing extremely heavy manual labour. A restlessness comes over him and he finds relaxation difficult. Most of the long evenings he paces the floor of his study, like a caged animal longing for freedom. His pet hound, a huge, devoted mastiff and an excellent hunter, becomes violent in the baron's presence and has to be put to death. A peculiar, indistinct figure seems to have been impressed on the baron's chest. It resembles a star.

Then comes the night of the full moon. All throughout that day, Baron X has been more than usually uneasy. Sitting, lying, standing, are all difficult for him. He wanders restlessly about the mansion, unable to remain stationary. He encounters difficulty in breathing, as though there were some obstruction to his respiration, or as though his lungs had undergone some sort of alteration. He can not bear to close the collar of his shirt, which gives him a feeling of strangulation. He is possessed of a fever, and a most peculiar, almost overwhelming desire to drop to all fours.

Night falls. The sky is dark. A slender white mist arises in the quiet forest, moving slowly through the dark recesses of the trees. Baron X now feels seriously ill. He sits slumped in the large chair before the windows which have been opened for a breath of cool night air. His breathing is heavy, strained, rasping. Perspiration gleams brightly on his face.

Slowly the full moon rises above the trees and sheds her silver light into the room. The brilliance of artificial lighting of the lamps suddenly causes unbearable pain to the baron's eyes, and he turns them off. Strangely, he can see as well without their light and credits this to the brightness of moonlight.

And then the transformation begins. Slowly at first a peculiar darkening spreads over the baron's features. His feet become cramped and pained and, in his last conscious act, he reaches down to remove shoes and socks. A haziness enters his mind and his thoughts begin to spin in a dizzy world, until it is impossible for him to pick out clearly any of the objects in the room. His sense of smell becomes more acute, and he scents odours in the room he had never noticed before. His heart begins to beat faster. His head falls back against the chair, and he releases his will to the strange and unknown forces that are now working within him.

The change begins at the feet, which become smaller, the toes shortened like stumps, the arches crumbling, while thick, bristly hair sprouts over them, until they resemble less the human foot and more the blunt paws of an animal. The legs and body become completely covered with hair, and the hands begin to curl in on themselves. The fingers become squat while the nails extend to sharp-pointed claws. Both hands are covered with coarse hair.

The face is the last to change. The throat swells, extends, bursts through the restraint of the collar. The eyes grow longer, tapering, while the normal hairline begins steadily to extend down over the forehead, meeting the level of the eyebrows and merging into one broad covering of hair, joining with the thick, bushy beard that has sprouted from the jaws. The nose becomes fleshy, glistening with moisture, the nostrils broad and quivering. The teeth extend, pushing past the barrier of the lips, extending over the face like long, gleaming white fangs.

There is now nothing human about the baron. The earlier lethargy and illness are gone. He has become a wolf. His small, evil red eyes dart cautiously about the room, ever alert for danger, while the wet nostrils sniff suspiciously at the air. He rises from the chair, and his posture is no longer that of a man. He stands in a slight crouch, his hands extended defensively, his body burly, wiry and strong. He leaps to the sill of the window and out into the night, pausing for one brief moment to raise his hairy head to the moon and bay a greeting. Suddenly he feels wonderfully free and unfettered.

The werewolf stays in the shadows, moving cautiously and swiftly through the trees of the forest or, in the village, keeping to the back alleys. He moves with all the cunning of the animal he has become, his padded feet making no sound on either pavement or forest floor. When someone approaches, he conceals himself until it is safe, then he leaps out upon the victim and, with a swift and savage bite of the jugular vein, tears the life from the body.

In the morning, Baron X awakens in his own bed. Perhaps, for a moment, there is no recollection of the evening before. Remembrance comes finally in a variety of ways. Learning of a brutal death as the result of some wild animal's attack may bring recall. It may even be that it will not be until several killings have taken place, and a chain of recollections form in his mind, that he will realize his own terrible responsibility. On the other hand, as he rises from his bed the morning after his first transformation and his first killing, he may find certain indications – mud tracks on the floor, in the unmistakable shape of an animal's paws, marks and bruises on his own body, the vague remembrance of what he had thought was a nightmare – that will instantly recall to him what had happened during the previous evening.

And now there are even more definite indications, to those who know what to look for. There is no doubt that the index fingers have grown to a quite extraordinary length. There is a peculiar growth of hair in the palms of his hands, and the strange marking on his chest is quite definitely a pentagram, which all efforts to remove prove fruitless. Baron X has had his first blood and is now a true werewolf.

He is doomed to a lifetime of agony. There is no cure for the taint of lycanthropy. At first, he will try numerous preventive measures. During the nights of the full moon, he will lock himself securely in his chamber, leaving strict orders to the servants that under no circumstances, despite any orders or importunings from himself, is the door to be opened before sunrise. This method, however, is not successful, for the werewolf, despite locked doors and windows, can usually find a way to leave the chamber and seek the freedom of the night. The baron may go yet a step further and bind himself to his chair for the hours of night but this, too, is unavailing, for no bonds can secure the powerful werewolf. In desperation, the baron may voluntarily submit himself to the police – who, of course, will not believe his tale – and have himself placed in the supposed security of a prison cell during the hours of peril. This, too, however, proves futile, for the werewolf is possessed of superhuman strength, and not even prison bars will contain him.

Baron X now exists in a particularly horrible kind of personal hell. He is a werewolf and knows it, but there is nothing he can do. He may seek the assistance of others, but this will avail him little. His insistence upon his nature is looked upon as some form of delusion that will pass; his providing of various proofs is called coincidence. The baron begins to long fervently for the release of death, but to the accursed, death is not an easy thing. Having become a creature of the night, the baron can no longer die through normal means, and some

Dr. Edelmann (Onslow Stevens) encounters the Wolf man (Lon Chaney, Jr.) in the last film of the great horror cycle.
House of Dracula **(Universal Pictures, 1945)**

unwritten law makes suicide impossible.

To his family and friends, Baron X remains Baron X, with no outward indication of the horror he has become. As the weeks and months go by, there are, however, alterations in his manner which cause concern in those who are close to him. He becomes nervous and irritable, there is loss of appetite and an inability to sleep. During certain times of the month – is it ever noticed that it is during the time of the full moon? – he behaves as one living under some particular horror. He loses weight, dark circles appear about his eyes, he becomes a shadow of his former self. He talks strangely, wildly, about a curse, about a transformation, about the evil influence of the moon. No one, of course, takes such talk seriously, not even to the extent of remaining with him during one such full moon and seeing for themselves; the baron, knowing the result, will not permit it. It is feared that Baron X is going mad.

For the baron, the horror continues endlessly. With each cycle of the full moon, he kills, not knowing that he is killing, but hearing the next day of some new violence in the village, of yet another attack by some particularly vicious and ferocious wolf who eludes all attempts at capture. The village is, indeed, becoming alarmed. Never before have the wild animals of the hills been so daring, or come so close.

Here and there, among the more ignorant element of the village, there may be whispered talk of a werewolf. The deaths are so obviously due to the attack of a wolf, yet the animal has never been seen and has, with a cunning above that of an ordinary wolf, skilfully avoided all traps set for it. The more responsible elements of the community brush off talk of werewolves as 'medieval superstition'. At any rate, certainly no such talk attaches itself to the baron or his family.

Month after month, the horror continues. The baron-cum-werewolf finds little difficulty in securing victims. A young girl walking through the wood with her lover . . . they hear a sound: the brush before them parts and a dark, hairy form leaps out upon them. The youth tries valiantly to defend her, but both are murdered. An elderly woman, returning late to her home after some errand of mercy in the village, is set upon in some dark alley and the next morning is found dead, her body horribly torn. As the attacks increase a curfew is placed upon the village, and the streets and surrounding areas become dark and silent once night has fallen. But even the homes are not secure, for in several instances this remarkably cunning 'wolf' manages to force entry through doors or open windows.

And each morning, the baron hears of these deaths and realizes that he is responsible for them. Not all the killings are random, and he reacts with horror as he learns that villagers against whom, for some childhood reason, he has harboured a grudge, have been found torn to pieces. Even those he loves are among his victims. He dreads now to take others by the hand, fearing to see in their palms the shadow of the pentagram. Nothing can stop him, nothing can put an end to the hell into which he has plunged. His normal, happy life is over, and a new and unutterably terrible life has begun. He has become one of the creatures of the darkness, an obscenity on the face of the earth, a being with no right to existence. He lives in dread of the transformation and the mornings after, wondering who next will fall to the fury of his claws and fangs. He cries to whatever God he knows, pleads for release, begs for death to save himself and so many others, searching frantically for some manner of forestalling the next change.

Such is the peculiar hell of the werewolf. There is little defence against his attack, which is swift, unpremeditated, brutal and generally fatal. One cannot prepare for his coming, as with the vampire. Mina could be defended against the dangerous visits of Dracula because of his intention of keeping her alive to return again and again to the feast her young blood provided him. The werewolf has neither the need nor the desire to preserve the life of his victim. He does not need them for sustenance, His attack is not one of horrible necessity, as it is with the vampire, but merely a vicious striking out of a wild, ferocious animal. His intention is to kill, not to preserve.

However, if, for some reason, the attack of a werewolf is anticipated, much the same precautionary measures may be taken as will ward off the depredations of a vampire. In a village which has admittedly become the haunt of a werewolf, the use of garlic blossoms or garlic oil on window sills and doorsteps will generally serve as a security measure. Crucifixes and other religious artifacts will avail nothing.

For someone suddenly attacked by a werewolf, there is generally no hope of escape. The creature's attack is too swift and sudden to permit of defensive measures once it has begun. When the werewolf leaps, he reaches for – and generally promptly finds – the jugular vein, and with one tremendously powerful thrust of his clawed paw, or one slashing bite of his fangs, he rips it from the living throat, bringing instant death to his victim. No mortal man can cope successfully with the werewolf's superhuman strength.

The methods of destroying a werewolf are somewhat more limited than those which dispose of a vampire. Since he is not an undead, he is not liable to the supernatural laws which somewhat restrict the movement of the vampire. Sunrise has no disastrous effect upon him, and he does not lie in a coffin during the day. There is, actually, no time when he is immune from death, but this death can be brought to him only in a prescribed manner. These methods are applicable whether the werewolf is in his human or animal form; at no time, however, can he perish by normal means.

A silver bullet entering the werewolf's body at any point will bring instant death. Some legends state that a cross must be cut into the head of the bullet, but this is probably not essential. Any silver object melted down and fired out of a gun will serve the purpose. An ordinary bullet will not harm a werewolf, even though he be in human form.

While the silver bullet appears to be the only infallible way of disposing of a werewolf, he can possibly be beaten to death by some silver object heavy enough to do the job. This would be dangerous, however, to the human because of the close contact that is required.

According to some legends, death does not bring rest to the werewolf. We have previously seen that any creature who leads a particularly evil life runs the risk of vampirism after death. By his very nature, of murder and ferocity, the werewolf is a particularly strong candidate for this life after death, and many do, indeed, become vampires once a silver bullet has put an end to his wolfish existence. It is to be hoped, however, that this refers only to those having become werewolves by choice rather than accident. The involuntary werewolf suffers enough torment during his lifetime and should not be penalized beyond.

3

There is no *Dracula* or *Frankenstein* of the werewolf world,[3] although the screen has created the symbol of lycanthropy in Lawrence Talbot. Most of the popularity of the werewolf is due to his various appearances on the screen. He also appears in many learned dissertations on the supernatural, and is often met with in short stories; no werewolf novels have achieved the durability of the classic works of Stoker and Mrs Shelley.

One of the most striking werewolf tales is *The Kill* by Peter Fleming, written in 1931.[4] The story takes place in a chilly railroad waiting room in the west of England, where two men have been sitting for some time, waiting for a train delayed by fog. One of the two is a young man, the other somewhat older, short, shabbily dressed in black, his skin dark and sallow, with a pointed nose and sharp jaw. The younger strikes up a conversation, during which he learns that the stranger has come to this part of England to enjoy hunting. This leads the young man to relate a peculiar tale of his hunting uncle, Lord Fleer.

During the First World War, Lord Fleer had taken into his home a young displaced Belgian girl, whom he later adopted as his legal heir. This did not sit too well with Fleer's house-keeper, who was in process of bearing him a son, whom she hoped would be the heir; Fleer now refuses to acknowledge him. The housekeeper dies in giving birth to Vom, first cursing Fleer in harsh and bitter terms, stating she had placed a charm on Vom that would make him look after his own interests. It is noted that the newborn babe has a peculiar deformity of the hand – an elongated third finger.

Vom is raised by one of the tenant farmers and the years

---

[3] The closest to a werewolf classic is Guy Endore's *The Were-wolf of Paris*, which is described later.

[4] Reprinted in *Creeps by Night*, selected by Dashiell Hammett.

pass. The Belgian girl, Germaine, grows into a lovely young woman and Lord Fleer tries to forget the curse of a dying woman placed upon anyone who is made his heir above the bastard son. Ten years later, Vom runs away and is not seen again until now, says the young man in the station: Vom, he says, reappeared just a few days ago. Several sheep have been slaughtered by a wild animal, and Lord Fleer has no doubt that this animal was his werewolf son and no doubt of his purpose in returning. He was right. Germaine was attacked and slain by the werewolf.

This finishes the young man's tale in the railway station. Germaine's death has occurred just a few days before, and now he is himself Fleer's heir, on his way to the estate. At this point, the older man rises slowly, his eyes filled with hatred, his mouth dripping with saliva. Just before he leaps upon him, the young heir notices the peculiar deformity of his murderer's hand.

Mr Fleming's tale is brief and effective. The atmosphere of horror is established immediately – two men, strangers to each other, alone in the dead of night, in a cold and barren railway station of an out-of-the-way spot in England, surrounded by fog, and a tale of supernatural murders. The young man's story builds up on this atmosphere of terror, yet the final revelation, that the stranger to whom he tells this tale is Vom, sworn to kill any who stand in the way of his own inheritance, is unexpected and shocking when it finally comes.

One of the very finest werewolf tales of recent years is *There Shall Be No Darkness* by James Blish, better known as one of the finest current writers of science fiction.[5]

This rather lengthy story tells of a werewolf who crashes an elegant houseparty in a Scottish castle. Honoured guest at the gathering is a famous Polish pianist named Jarmoskowski, of remarkable appearance, with eyebrows that meet above his eyes, ears that tilt slightly forward, and index and middle fingers of the same length. His teeth are remarkably long and

[5] In *Thrilling Wonder Stories* (April 1950); reprinted in *Zacherley's Vulture Stew*.

white, and the pianist has the disconcerting habit of constantly scratching his palms.

It is at midnight, with most of the guests asleep or lying in drunkenness, that the horror of the evening begins. One of the guests, Foote, convinced of Jarmoskowski's werewolf nature, faces him in the pianist's bedroom. The musician transforms himself into a wolf before Foote's eyes. The horrified guest manages to slip into the corridor and slam the door behind him. Doris, an ex-love of the Pole, joins him in the corridor, where they are attacked by the werewolf, who has made his exit through the bedroom window. He is driven away with the aid of heavy silver candlesticks.

The entire castle is now alerted to the certainty that there is a werewolf in their midst. Doris is particularly perturbed, fearing that the pianist has seen the pentagram in her palm. Things take quite a different turn, however, when it is discovered that Doris is a witch and, therefore, a great asset to the werewolf.

The guests melt silverplate into bullets, marking them with the sign of the cross, and set out in pursuit of the monster. With the aid of a pack of dogs, Jarmoskowski is trapped, but manages his escape. The party return to the castle where they begin preparations of defence. Orders are placed for the immediate delivery, by plane, of silver bullets, masses of garlic, and silver crucifixes. Thus they are ready for the siege.

New horror strikes when one of the guests is found dead from a werewolf attack, and it is realized that there must be a second creature, in the house itself. When Foote demands an examination of all members of the party to determine which of the guests, apparently injured by the previous night's brush with Jarmoskowski, had become a lycanthrope, one of them instantly becomes a wolf and leaps upon the host, Newcliffe, who batters the animal to death with a silver candlestick. The second werewolf is then revealed to have been their hostess, Caroline Newcliffe.

Later that same night, Doris retires to her room and there is confronted by Jarmoskowski, beckoning to her from the window. Taking in her hand a revolver loaded with silver bullets, Doris opens the window. To her horror, the pianist pleads with her to shoot, thus ending a life which has become a nightmare to him. When Doris finds herself unable to do so, the Pole pleads with her to go away with him, sharing his werewolfism. Just as she is about to surrender to his importunings, Foote enters the room and slays the creature.

The tale is crisply and bluntly told, and the Scottish castle becomes, indeed, a house of horrors. There is revealed a considerable amount of werewolf lore, with particular emphasis on the efficacy of silver in combating the lycanthrope. In some instances, the legends of werewolves become somewhat confused with those of vampirism – such as the statement that, in order to estimate the number of werewolves in the world today, one need only set up an enormous mirror over the crowds in Grand Central Station and see how many of the milling figures on the floor fail to cast a reflection. A frightening idea, this, but werewolves do cast a mirrored reflection. The preparations for the chase in *There Shall Be No Darkness* and the description of the siege of the castle are built up with considerable detail and excitement. The addition of a witch to the cast of characters is an interesting and amusing point, reverting to the sometimes accepted theory that witches have a certain amount of control over werewolves.

Bruce Elliott's 1954 tale *Wolves Don't Cry*[6] offers an amusing switch on the werewolf theme. The story concerns itself rather with a wereman, a wolf cursed with transformation into a man. A nude man is found in the wolf's cage of the zoo, with no knowledge of how he came there. He is taken to a hospital for examination, where his total ignorance of human activities baffles the researchers. The 'man', meanwhile, finds himself in a completely alien life, for he is by nature a wolf. He finds colour extremely painful to his eyes, his sense of smell is deadened, and it is agony for him to sit erect on the base of his spine. In an escape one night, he is picked up as a hitch-hiker by a woman, whom he sexually assaults. From books, he learns the proper incantations to return him to wolf form, and he again makes his way back to the cage at the zoo.

[6] *Magazine of Fantasy and Science Fiction* (1954); reprinted in *Off the Beaten Path*, edited by Judith Merril.

One day the woman who had picked him up in her car passes the cage with her child, a small boy destined to be a werewolf.

The tale is lightly and delightfully written. Elliott reveals the feelings of the wolf in such detail that one might almost suspect him of being the wereman of the story. Of particular interest is the comparison between the unfettered life of a wolf (even in a cage) and the restricted life of man. We have already seen that a werewolf feels a certain exultation from the freedom he achieves after his transformation; the exact opposite, of course, would be true of a wolf-turned-man. The story, although provided with a sufficiency of horror, ends on a delightfully wry note as the wolf sees his male cub wheeled by in a baby carriage.

4

The most famous werewolf is Lawrence Talbot, as played by Lon Chaney, Jr., in the Universal film *The Wolf-Man* of the early 'forties. Talbot is the personable young son of a wealthy landowner, played by Claude Rains. Young Talbot has just undergone a period of schooling abroad, and when he returns to his Transylvanian home, he has neither interest nor belief in the strange peasant legends he has known since childhood. While strolling one night through the dark, mist-covered forest, he rushes to the defence of a woman being attacked by a werewolf, and is bitten, thus becoming a lycanthrope himself. After several murders, the truth of his condition is brought to him by the old gypsy fortune teller (played by Maria Ouspenskaya), whose son (Bela Lugosi) is the werewolf who had attacked Talbot. No one will believe Talbot's wild story, and the murders continue. He finally attacks his own father who, with the aid of a silver cane and the assistance of others (Ralph Bellamy and Warren William), brings about the youth's destruction.

The film is still frequently seen, and remains one of the best of the werewolf series. The excellence of the cast is an indication of the high regard in which horror films were held at that time. The performances were all excellent: the petite, nervous Ouspenskaya was to repeat her role of Maliva, the gypsy woman, in later films. The atmosphere was suitably mysterious and the story had the novelty of freshness.

Lawrence Talbot joined Hollywood's rank of undying monsters and provided Lon Chaney with a role he was to essay for many years, and with which he was identified as closely as Lugosi with Dracula and Karloff with Frankenstein. Little acting was needed for this role, which was chiefly a matter of looking with agonized eyes at the full moon. (This, of course, is no reflection on the younger Chaney, who proved his ability in later films.) Chaney's make-up, with the hair-covered face, the fangs, the crouched posture, became the accepted model for wolf men. The close-ups during transformation were effectively handled.

In *Frankenstein Meets the Wolf-Man*, two great monsters were brought together with mixed results. The story began with a basically interesting plot – Talbot's attempts to free himself from the curse of lycanthropy. The gypsy woman Maliva, played by Ouspenskaya, tells him there is but one person who can help him – Dr Frankenstein. At the village of the good doctor, named Vasaria now, they learn that Frankenstein and his creation have perished in a fire. Talbot, being pursued by the villagers after one of his transformations, stumbles into the ruins of the laboratory, finds the monster immured in a block of ice, and revives him, but the monster cannot assist him. Talbot then turns to the late doctor's daughter, who happens to be in Vasaria. Only after the monster stumbles into a village festival, disrupting the good cheer, does the daughter agree to furnish Dr Frankenstein's diary to Talbot's London friend, Dr Mannering, with the understanding that the doctor will first devote his efforts to destruction of the monster, and then the curing of Lawrence Talbot.

The inevitable happens. Mannering, obsessed with the wonder of Dr Frankenstein's creation, restores the monster to his full strength. This all happens, of course, during the full moon. The monster breaks loose and faces the fury of the wolf man. The two battle in the laboratory, while Mannering and the baroness flee. The villagers, in the meantime, blow up the village dam and drown the laboratory and the battling monsters in its flood waters.

The film has its interesting points, and it set various standard backgrounds and legends for later stories. Chaney did his usual competent job as Talbot, Dr Mannering was played by Patric Knowles and Baroness von Frankenstein by the regally beautiful Ilona Massey. Had the monster been more effectively played, the film would have been far more successful. Unfortunately, Bela Lugosi's performance, which will be discussed later, was the weakest point of the film.

The battle between Talbot and the Frankenstein monster was very highly touted as 'the battle of the century' and 'the battle of the monsters'. It was effectively staged with the proper amount of tossed laboratory equipment, animal growls, monster screams, etc.

Lawrence Talbot did not fare well in later films. It was probably the placing of these two monsters in one film which was responsible for the greatest error of Hollywood horror-makers – the monster rallies. If two monsters are good, why not three, four, half a dozen? Unfortunately, an increase of monsters does not necessarily mean an increase of horror. *House of Dracula* and *House of Frankenstein* followed, neither very successful. The wolf man met his final end from a silver bullet after a rather pathetic love story with a little gypsy girl. A new legend is here introduced, in typical Hollywood fashion: the werewolf can be slain only by a silver bullet 'fired by the hand of someone who loves him enough'. The gypsy girl loved him enough. On the night of the full moon, she waits outside his window, her pistol loaded with silver. Talbot, in wolf form, bursts through the window and leaps upon her. The girl fires the bullet into his body, killing the werewolf, but his attack has also slain her. The werewolf collapses on the young girl's body and returns to the form of Lawrence Talbot.

Although Talbot was the most famous of werewolves, he was by no means the only one. Shortly before the release of the original *Wolf-Man*, Hollywood presented another interesting film on the theme: *The Were-Wolf of London*, directed by Stuart Walker, with another excellent cast which included

Henry Hull, Warner Oland, Spring Byington and Valerie Hobson.

The story had Henry Hull, an outstanding English botanist, travel to Tibet in search of a rare flower called the marifesa, which bloomed only by moonlight. While prowling through the valley in which the plant grows, he is attacked and severely bitten by a werewolf who, for some reason, is also in quest of the plant. Hull brings the rare blossom back to England and attempts to make it bloom with the aid of enormous lamps intended to simulate moonlight. He is visited by a Japanese scientist named Yogami (Oland, of course) who is, in fact, the werewolf who had attacked Hull in Tibet. Oland reveals to Hull that the juice of the marifesa, squeezed onto the skin, is a counter-agent to the spell of lycanthropy. He pleads with Hull to do all in his power to cause the plant to blossom before the next full moon and to give the blossom to him. Hull refuses.

On the night of the full moon, Hull learns that he, too, has become a werewolf. He prowls the streets of London and kills a prostitute. It now becomes of personal importance for him to have the marifesa blossom before the next seizure, but again he fails. He flees to the poorer section of London and rents a room in the home of a constantly tipsy Cockney woman. He locks himself in, hoping to keep himself imprisoned during the period of transformation. This, of course, fails, and he bursts into the street, causing considerable terror and panic for his landlady and her pixilated friend, who had been peering through the keyhole.

The marifesa blooms at last, but the blossom is stolen by Oland. Hull first moves to attack the social party-giver (Byington) but fails. Finally he attacks his young wife (Hobson), but a well-placed shot by a silver bullet fells him as he moves up the stairway at the head of which cower a terrified Miss Hobson and a hysterical Miss Byington. As he lies dead at the foot of the stairs, he resumes his normal shape and, muttering a whispered thanks for his release, he expires.

This film, frequently shown on television, may seem somewhat dated today, but still contains a considerable amount of interest, atmosphere and fine performances. Oland makes his usual satisfying Oriental menace, and Spring Byington is a delightfully scatterbrained social climber. In the scenes involving the tipsy landlady, superbly played by Ethel Griffies, we have probably the finest comedy relief ever provided in a horror film. The Tibetan scenes are eerie and mysterious, and the atmosphere of Hull's London home is greatly increased by the presence of a monstrous flesh-eating plant from Madagascar. Hull's make-up as the wolf man followed the general lines of Lawrence Talbot's, but his facial expression was more elastic and animalistic than Chaney's.

We have seen that the Hammer Studios of London have contributed greatly to the recent resurge of interest in horror by resurrecting the colourful creatures of the past; in 1961, this studio presented its first film on the werewolf, titled *Curse of the Werewolf*, based rather loosely on Guy Endore's *The Werewolf of Paris*. Like all Hammer productions, this was given elaborate production, authentic sets, brilliant colour, fine performances and direction. Nor was it merely the production values which made *Curse of the Werewolf* one of the top-grade horror films. It did not stress cheap horror effects, and even atmosphere was sacrificed for story values. The script concentrated on the legendary traditions of the werewolf, exploring his growth and his habits, the measures to be taken against him and, in particular, the agony of the werewolf's soul and the distress of his family. That the film managed such detail without losing the interest of its audience is a considerable compliment to all concerned.

The film is set in Spain, in the area of Castillo Siniestro at the end of the eighteenth century. Here a beggar approaches the wealthy and brutal marquis on his wedding night. The beggar is humiliated, made sport of and cast into the castle dungeon. The years pass, and the beggar is ignored and forgotten, living chained in filth until he becomes more animal than human. A mute servant girl, having displeased the now aged marquis by resisting his advances, is cast into the dungeon with the animal-like beggar, who rapes her and dies of the certainly unusual exertion. The girl escapes and murders the marquis, then flees. She is found by a Professor Carido, who takes her to his home, where she is cared for by him and

A beggar (Richard Wadsworth) at the wedding feast of the Marquis of Castle Siniestro makes a lewd remark and is cast into a dungeon, where he later rapes a servant girl who gives birth to a werewolf son. *The Curse of the Werewolf* (Hammer Films, 1961)

his housekeeper. A son is born to the girl, and she dies in childbirth. The boy is named Leon and adopted by the professor.

Leon is but six years of age when he is revealed to be a werewolf, responsible for vicious attacks on sheep. The village priest is approached and the professor is told only love can conquer the curse with which Leon is afflicted. Further years pass, and Leon grows to manhood, unaware of his terrible affliction, subdued by the love that surrounds him. He finds romance in the form of a girl named Christine.

But the werewolf merely slumbers. At a cheap dance hall Leon becomes ill in the sordid surroundings. One of the female entertainers takes him to her room, where the transformation seizes him. Leon kills both the woman and a friend who had taken him there. He kills again and again, finally appealing for help to the professor. It is decided to keep him heavily chained. Finding this unbearable, Leon flees. His nature is revealed to Christine, who is certain her love can effect a cure. Before they can flee, Leon is arrested for murder and jailed. That night the moon is full and Leon, again a ravening wolf, shatters the bars of his cell and leaps into the village, snarling with fury, hatred and blood lust. He is swiftly pursued by the villagers. Trapped among the rooftops of the village, he calls to his adopted father in the crowd, pleading for death through the silver bullet he knows his father carries. In the bell tower of the cathedral, Leon and the professor stand face to face. There is the report of a revolver, and the werewolf falls in peaceful death.

The film relies more heavily on characterization and plot for its horror than on such atmospherics as shadows, mists, graveyards and sudden appearances of the werewolf. There are few scenes which can be pinpointed as truly horrifying, yet the overall effect of the film is intensely frightening.

The artistry of performance and make-up are largely responsible for the film's success. The beggar (Richard Wadsworth) is one of the most horrible creatures in horror films. As the years pass in his dungeon, he becomes a mass of long, filth-encrusted hair, his flesh covered with scabrous sores, his teeth sharp as fangs, his eyes wild and bloody. It comes as no surprise that the offspring of so horrible a creature would become a werewolf. In Anthony Dawson, as the marquis, we have a comparably vile and revolting character. When he eyes the mute servant girl, his face is pasty white, syphilitically pitted with scars and scabs. Justin Walter plays the six-year-old werewolf, who has terrible dreams filled with blood, whose palms develop a growth of coarse black hair and who, when the moon is full, leaps screaming at the bars of his window, his teeth fanged and his eyes crimson.

Leon, the werewolf, was played by Oliver Reed, a handsome young actor of powerful and impressive physique. In make-up he was probably the most interesting of the screen's lycanthropes. He was covered, chest and back included, with a mass of gleaming silvery hair, and technicolor made excellent use of blood-dripping fangs and burning red eyes.

All in all, *Curse of the Werewolf* is probably the most satisfying and intelligent of all werewolf films.

We might, in passing, make brief mention of one other interesting film which, though based on the werewolf tradition, offers a slight deviation from the usual lycanthropic tale. This was Val Lewton's *The Cat People*, in which the French actress, Simone Simone, portrayed a woman with the ability to transform herself into a black panther. The film, laid in New York and well directed by Jacques Tourneur, was an interesting atmospheric study in black and white, containing several particularly hair-raising scenes of suspenseful horror: a woman walking alone through the dark, deserted areas of Central Park, while the cat-woman pads silently in pursuit; the same terrified woman floating alone in a darkened indoor swimming-pool, the walls dancing with reflection of the water, while the spitting hiss of the panther reverberates all about her.

The film was extremely successful, and there was an attempt to have the cat-woman, after she had been speared to death by a sword-cane, join the ranks of the various immortal monsters. The sequel, *Curse of the Cat People*, considerably lacked the imagination of the first production, and the poor woman has rested in peace ever since.

5

The campfire of our gypsy caravan has burned low by this time, and the night is far advanced. The ancient gypsy woman – could it be Maliva herself? – still sucking at her unlighted pipe, sits silently, her hands clasped in the voluminous folds of her many-coloured skirt. There is a sadness in her face, and we are again reminded of the rumour that her own son bears the mark of the pentagram.

She has told us all she knows – or all she cares to tell. Generations of gypsy lore have made the werewolf a familiar

Oliver Reed (right) has himself imprisoned on a night of the full
moon in Hammer's intelligent revitalization of the lycanthrope, based
on Guy Endore's *Werewolf of Paris* (changed to Spain).
The Curse of the Werewolf (Hammer Films, 1960)

figure to her. There are those who even claim the gypsies pro-
tect the werewolf and give him care and shelter in their camp,
that they have a pact with these creatures of the supernatural
which protects them from attack. It may be. There is much in
a gypsy encampment which we can never hope to fathom.

We rise and thank our gypsy informant. We hesitate for a
moment before venturing into the dark forest, thinking again
of the old woman's son who may be lurking behind every
tree, but take courage from the spell which she has said over
us and the amulet she has placed around our necks.

After a few steps, we turn and look back. The glow of the
campfire has become small and indistinct, but before it we see

the crouched shadow of the gypsy queen, staring into the dying embers, seeing there things which it is better we do not see.

THE MONSTER

*'I am malicious because I am miserable;
if any being felt emotions of benevolence
towards me, I should return them, an
hundred and an hundred fold.'*

Transylvania, through history and legend, has become the natural habitat of horror. In the dusty, cobweb-covered ruins of a massive stone castle on a bleak, cold mountainside, we have learned of the infamous Count Dracula, king of the vampires, the most evil and powerful of all creatures of Satan. Sitting before a blazing campfire of the gypsy, we have been told the frightening tale of the most unfortunate of the inhabitants of the dark world of superstition, the werewolf.

But we are not yet ready to leave the mysterious, fog-enshrouded blue-black mountains of Transylvania, for there is one more stop to be made, the most frightening of all, for now, for the first time, we will come face to face with a horror of man's own making.

We find ourselves now in one of those quaint, rustic villages so dear to the hearts of poet and travel-poster painters. Here are the narrow cobbled streets, the gingerbread houses with their gables and florid decorations, the village square, the people in leather breeches, Tyrolean hats and gaily flowered skirts. The tall, snow-capped mountains of Transylvania form a colourful background for this fairy-tale world.

But there is something amiss in this pleasant little hamlet, something not quite as it should be. We pause for a moment before realizing what is wrong. According to time-honoured tradition, such a village should be filled with music and gaiety, laughter and song, the sound of violin and accordion. The streets should be festooned with ribbons and flowers, the people gathered in the square about enormous tuns of wine, seated at long wooden tables loaded with the good things of life, laughing, drinking, singing, dancing. This little village is part of Central Europe's unique little fairyland, and here only joy and happiness should prevail.

But we hear no music, no laughter, we see no dancing figures, no smiling faces. We are met with suspicious glances, with dark, glowering expressions; there are no friendly greetings, no smiling hellos. The village seems dark and dreary, as though perpetually hidden from the bright joys of sunlight by some ever-present cloud of blackness. The village square, centre of communal life, is deserted, and isolated scraps of paper dance wildly at the touch of the chilling wind. Now and then a dark, lonely figure rushes across the marketplace, without pausing to speak; trembling fingers move in the sign of the cross as frightened eyes are raised to the desolate jumble of ruins perched high on the mountainside overlooking the village. There is no joy here, no pleasure, no happiness; there is only sorrow, fear, dread and a century of hopelessness.

For this is the ancient little village of Ingolstadt, made so famous – and infamous – by a brilliant and unfortunate scientist by the name of Baron Victor von Frankenstein.

The very stones of this little village seem to exude a peculiar horror of their own, for there was reserved for this charming little hamlet a form of terror unequalled on the face of the earth. Ingolstadt has never recovered from the horror brought to it originally a century and a half ago by a sincere, well-meaning, but tragically foolish young scientist who learned, to his own sorrow and that of the entire village, that there are some things which, perhaps, the inquisitive mind is not intended to approach. The young scientist's tragic error has left an indelible stamp upon the countryside. Reminders are everywhere, and even today, as we travel about the silent village, we can stand on the very spots where the greatest monster of all time struck fear and terror into the hearts of the kindly, simple people of this once happy and prosperous village. Here, in this very marketplace, ringed with music-box houses, during one of the numerous village festivals, when Ingolstadt was filled with good cheer and laughter and song, the monster appeared, bringing death, terror and destruction, the memories of which still cloud the listless eyes of the inhabitants. We can walk along the little stream just outside the village and visit the long-deserted ruins of the small labourer's hut where dwelt the first innocent victim of the monster's long reign of horror. In a wooded region just beyond the outskirts of Ingolstadt we can still see the ashes of the thatched hut where lived the blind fiddler who was the only human being ever to befriend the lonely, frightened monster created by Dr Frankenstein.

But if we wish to know the full harrowing tale of the creation of a living, soulless being, we must leave the village itself and travel up into the hills, to what has become famous as the very birthplace of horror.

Castle Frankenstein has been vacant for many years, and it is unlikely that it will ever again be occupied. It is one of perhaps a handful of former residences around the world which has been marked for all time by the events that once occurred there, and even the bravest of men would hesitate in making it his home.

A high, sturdy wall surrounds the grounds; it is difficult to say whether this is to keep horrors in or the villagers out, for no dweller of Ingolstadt would care to approach the place. Two massive wooden doors set in the walls are the only means of entry. They are kept always closed now, having been shut with a resounding bang on a stormy night when the villagers, horrified by the latest ravages of the monster, had marched upon the castle itself. Beyond this wall, the towers of Castle Frankenstein look dark and ominous against the ever-clouded sky.

A brief cold blast of fear sweeps over us as we push open one of these huge doors and enter the small outer courtyard. It is completely barren now. The earth is dry and caked, here and there are outcroppings of hardy, colourless weeds. As we cross the bare plot of blasted earth and mount the short flight of broad steps leading to the main entrance of the castle, a flock of purple-black ravens, disturbed in their ruminations of horror, rise noisily from the towers and battlements and wheel above our heads. Our hand hesitates a moment as we place it on the massive oaken door that leads into the castle itself. It is a doorway to hell. Perhaps it would be better to permit it to remain closed. We laugh somewhat shamefacedly at our fears and the door groans with many years of disuse as we slowly push it open.

We find ourselves in the vast entrance hall, a cold and utterly cheerless chamber thickly covered with the dust of the years and the cobwebs of many generations of industrious, undisturbed black spiders. To the right is a massive stone fireplace, and beyond this another heavy, closed door; to the left is yet another pair of these gigantic, heavily carved portals, one of which stands partially ajar as though the ghost of some long-dead Frankenstein had just passed through. Directly before us is the enormous stone stairway to the second floor, each step of which seems intended for the tread of a giant. The stairway divides midway at a landing and then branches off to right and left; a gallery encircles the entrance hall. The wall of the landing is covered with an enormous tapestry, too thickly encrusted with dirt and age to permit us to determine its subject. Just above our heads, under the gallery, is a small window through whose begrimed pane comes a limited amount of light. The walls, floor and ceiling are composed of cold, unadorned stone. There is a peculiar, musty smell about the place, such as we generally expect and seldom find in an ancient museum. Cobwebs glisten like fragile diamond strands in the feeble light, and squatting in the centre of some are unpleasantly large spots of blackness. As we walk slowly away from the entrance door, our footsteps kick up small clouds of dust; we run headlong into one of the massive spider projects and feel chilled at the unpleasant, sticky contact.

In the centre of this unfriendly foyer, we pause and let the icy air of the castle of mystery seep into us. Here, indeed, is the original home of horror. In this ancient edifice lived generations of the House of Frankenstein. It is difficult to conceive of a warm family life within these cold, inhospitable

walls, of lovers, of playing children. Yet the Frankensteins
were an honoured and highly respected family until, in the
early part of the nineteenth century, one young member of
the House, too deeply imbued with knowledge and ambition,
unleashed upon the world the most fantastic creature it has
ever known. Here the handsome young baron sat in those last
years, alone, greatly aged by his experiences, facing the incredible and disastrous results of what he had done. Yet it was
to be just the beginning. If ever a family was to be accursed,
it was the family of Frankenstein.

We open the large door to our right and see a massive
dining-room. The table is coated with thick dust, and the
immense high-backed chairs are still in their places. A huge
cobwebbed chandelier glistens in the light. The table seems
still prepared for guests who will never arrive. We might wonder if there is a nightly gathering of shades at this table, with
the great monster seated in that massive chair at the head. We
close the door again – silently, for noise in such a tomb would
be a frightening thing – and enter the room on the left.

This enormous, vaulted chamber, with its high ceiling almost
lost in perpetual darkness, was the library. There are rows of
shelves on all four walls, some of them still holding ancient,
mouldy volumes, and decaying logs still lie untouched in the
giant fireplace. Opposite the door through which we have
entered are two large French doors, opening onto a little
balcony, from which we can look over the entire village of
Ingolstadt.

And there, to the left of us as we stand on the balcony, on
a slight rise of ground, but dimly seen through the eternal
blanket of darkness that seems forever to conceal Frankenstein Castle from the eyes of man, as though it were some
obscene horror, are the ruins of the place we have really come
to see – the laboratory in which Dr Victor von Frankenstein
created his monster.

But within this most famous of all the world's scientific
laboratories, we find only desolation. The roof has long since
fallen in, and most of the equipment has been destroyed or
dismantled and carried away; here and there, leaning unsteadily against the unsturdy walls or lying in a heap of rubble

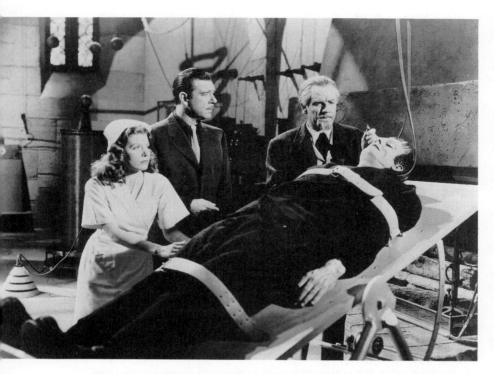

Nina (Jane Adams) wants to lose her hunched back, Talbot (Lon
Chaney, Jr.) wants a cure for lycanthropy and Dr. Edelmann (Onslow
Stevens) wants to restore the Monster (Glenn Strange).
House of Dracula (Universal Pictures, 1945)

on the dirt-and-rock-choked floor are the rusted remains of
unfathomable scientific paraphernalia. All that remains of the
great Dr Frankenstein's famous workshop is a hopeless jumble
of fallen stone, twisted wires, battered panels and shattered
tubings, completely without meaning to us.

But in the very centre of this confused mass, standing alone
and undamaged, as though too fearful an object to be tampered with, even by time itself, there still stands the one thing
about which is clustered this whole incredible tale of horror –
the massive, heavily constructed operating table. Upon this
smooth panel of steel, waiting for the spark of life, lay the
great and fantastic monster of the Frankensteins. While the
violent electrical storm, so essential to the young scientist's

work, screamed its full fury about this damned tower, the enormous, hideous creature waited, tightly bound, its heart, its mind, its organs, ready for that first moment of consciousness, waiting for that first second of supreme horror that the world would never be able to forget.

Yes, indeed, we are in the right place to learn about the creation of monsters. Let us stand here in this infamous ruined laboratory and partake of one of man's greatest dreams. See, the laboratory is no longer in ruins, the wires are properly connected, flashes of electricity spurt from cathode to anode, a tall figure wearing a white laboratory smock stands before the table on which is stretched a heavily bandaged form. There is a light in his eyes – a light of excitement, a light of wonder, a light of insanity. We are about to view the miracle of creation.

2

The beginning of life is the greatest unravelled mystery of mankind, and in all probability will always remain so. From whence came that first spark of consciousness which was to culminate in man himself? It is a question indissolubly bound in controversy between science and religion. What are the truths of evolution? How literally should we take the story of Adam and Eve? Is the Garden of Eden actual fact or just an allegorical fairy tale? Did man and ape descend from a common ancestor, as claimed by science, or was man created as man and placed over all the beasts of earth, as traditionally claimed by some religionists?

The answer undoubtedly lies somewhere between the two. The facts of evolution are certainly too overwhelming to be denied. Neanderthal Man, Java Man, Rhodesian Man, Cro-Magnon Man – these are all obviously steps along the long road leading to homo sapiens. The story of the origin of man is a long, involved and mysterious history told us by bones, artifacts and remains found in various corners of the world. Even during the writing of these lines, a new discovery has been made which extends the story of man beyond the point of two million years. A weathered, beaten skull, so largely animal and yet so obviously human, leading to the great civilizations of Egypt, Greece and our own time – this is the story of life.

Where, then, does this leave the story of Adam and Eve and the Garden of Eden? Probably where it belongs – in the world of religious legend. Legend, it must be remembered, is not necessarily untruth; it is simply a different, often simpler and more interesting method of retelling past events. We have no reason to believe that this tale of the Bible was intended as a completely literal account of the origin of life. If we consider it merely as an allegorical manner of recounting the creation of man, the story becomes perfectly understandable. When the tale told in Genesis was first made known, it was far easier for people to accept, by faith, the story of Adam, Eve, the Tree of Knowledge and the Serpent, than to ask that they accept the story of fossils, evolution and cavemen, even if it had been known at that time.

This need not necessarily affect our belief in the existence of a Supreme Being, a Great Creator, a God. Man may be the result of millions of years of evolution, but can we believe that life itself is a mere accident? The cosmos, the suns and their planets, the evolution of moving, feeling, thinking creatures, the entire process of life had its beginning and, somewhere, had its originator. It does not really matter which came first, the chicken or the egg, the caveman or Cro-Magnon, for, whichever it was, some creative force was responsible for it. The growth of a child in the womb of its mother, the sun that warms the soil and the rain that nourishes it, the diseases and the terrible wars that prevent the overpopulation of our planet, the endless, orderly, never-changing cycle of life and death – these are facts with which we are familiar to the point of accepting without much thought, for they are the regular nature of things, but they are all part of that inexplicable wonder of creation, behind which there must be some cosmic force. The origin of life is too complex, too involved and too wonderful to be sheer accident.

The great dream of the scientist and pseudo-scientist has always been the duplication in the laboratory of this act of creation, for to the man who could actually create life – and, by relation, perhaps defeat the ever-present scourge of death – would belong the riches of the world. There has always been, however, one very serious hindrance to the intensive study of the laws of creation – the violent opposition of the Church.

From the earliest times, the scientist has traditionally been a man apart, a man to be mistrusted, somewhat feared and, as often as not, a being in league with the devil. In early civilizations, science was inseparably bound with religion, astrology, divination, and the supernatural. The astrologer-scientists of Mesopotamia and Babylon, of Egypt and Persia, were looked upon with awe and fear by the people of their time. They were considered not quite of the human species, strange and mystical beings, in league with the gods and possessed of all the strange and terrible powers of darkness. The astrologer served as high priest and diviner of the future of men and empires, and was the repository of all 'scientific' lore. His was the most feared voice in the land, often sounding with greater force and power than that of the king himself. To run counter to the will of such a man was to court instant and terrible disaster, for the astrologer could call on the powers of both man and the supernatural to avenge himself on his enemies. Many of these men were complete charlatans, using the mysterious worlds of science and religion to further their own ends, but the fact that, in spite of the comparative ignorance of these times, there was steady and remarkable advance in the field of science, is clear indication that there were also among them men with sincere inquiring scientific minds. We must not make the error of judging all people by our own time. The astrologer in Chichen-Itza who determined it was time to sacrifice a healthy young man to Huitzilopochtli may have been as sincere in his belief as a Catholic priest calling for a mass to the Virgin.

After the fall of Rome, during that long period when Europe was in the grip of what has been inaccurately called the Dark Ages, the position of scientists underwent an alteration. Still feared for his knowledge of unholy things, still mistrusted for his supposed alliance with the devil, the scientist nevertheless lost his position of pre-eminence. He no longer served as high priest, and his knowledge and power no longer, at least to all appearances, governed the lives of the people. A new force had entered civilization, and the position of the scientist was never again to be quite the same. This new force was the Christian Church, and from this time even to our own day, the forces of religion and science were to be at odds, sometimes agreeing to a form of truce, but more often than not directly opposed to each other, each seeing in the other a dangerous force threatening his own power and authority.

This new position of the scientist during the Dark Ages, and for some time afterward, was not an enviable one. He had completely lost his connection with religion, which had contributed heavily to his great influence in earlier ages. No longer did he occupy the all-powerful post of high priest and arbiter of the gods. The Church had taken this from him. It was the Pope now who served as the emissary of God, the arbitrator between God and his worshippers, and no one was permitted to infringe on the rights of the Holy Father. Thus had the scientist lost his strongest hold on man.

The result was the ostracizing of the scientist and, often, excommunication. The scientist, the alchemist, the astrologer, by whatever name he might be known, was branded an unbeliever, a heretic, a dangerous ally of the devil. His researches were unholy and against the teachings of God. It was the thirst of knowledge that had forever lost man his paradise and only through return to Godliness could that paradise be regained. The scientist was in league with the anti-Christ, and his experimentations would forever bar man from what he had lost. To associate with such evil men was to place your own soul in jeopardy, and to court disaster.

This attitude endured beyond the Dark Ages, even into the period of so-called enlightenment that followed. Sir Francis Bacon was seriously considered to be in league with Satan because of his lifelong search for truth. The Church dominated thought and tried to mould the minds of its followers. In portions of Europe, the terrible Inquisition brought violent and painful death to all nonconformists.

Of these nonconformists, freethinkers and dabblers in the black arts of science were in the forefront. To attempt to delve

Boris Karloff played a descendant of Dr. Frankenstein in this minor effort; its sole interest was that it was Karloff's last appearance in a Frankenstein film.
Frankenstein: 1970 (Allied Artists, 1958)

into the mysteries of life was tampering with the very laws of God and not to be tolerated. Such evil must be stamped out, torn on the rack, burned at the stake. The door of many a scientist's laboratory was suddenly broken in by the dreaded soldiers of the Inquisition and the scientist himself tortured into an admission of consort with the devil and tied to the stake in the market square. It took courage, in those days, to be a scientist. The alchemist of the day was pictured as a wild-eyed, heavily bearded, robed maniac who spent his nights bent over simmering fires, chanting incantations and drawing obscene cabalistic signs to call up the various demons who alone could assist him in his work. He had gone beyond the rim of damnation and was already a hopelessly lost soul. The

scientist – and there was no distinction between scientist,
soothsayer, magician, alchemist and astrologer – was believed
possessed of the power of the evil eye, and was a person
shunned by the community, persecuted, driven from his home
and even put to death for his 'unholy practices', for the har-
bouring of such a creature could bring the wrath of God upon
the entire village, and certainly the wrath of the Church. Even
the most famous astrologer-soothsayer of the Middle Ages,
Nostradamus, despite his devout adherence to the Church and
the firm protection of his sovereign, France's King Henry II,
was feared and shunned by the people.

To a large measure, as the result of increased knowledge
and education, of limitations of the power of the Church, this
constant battle between Church and science has lost its
importance and, while the Church still often disapproves of
many aspects of scientific research, no attempt at serious interference is made.

The scientist today is a well-trained, thoroughly educated,
dedicated man in a white frock coat, working in a clean,
bright laboratory. Here he has, quite recently, finally succeeded, through the bombardment of various substances with
electrical particles, in creating a certain form of artificial life.
True, these are not thinking, moving creatures, but they are
life. Man has already emulated his Creator. Perhaps this is the
first step, the beginning.

The day of the feared, long-robed and bearded, mystical
scientist is at an end, but perhaps there is already at work in
some white, antiseptic laboratory, the future Dr Frankenstein.

3

It was at about the turn of the century, that period when the
new enlightenment of the 1700s was mellowing into the greater
understanding of the 1800s, that the most famous monster-
maker of them all began his fateful research into the forbidden
field concerned with the creation of life. The young Victor
von Frankenstein will be known for all time as the king of
monster-makers. Born of good, noble family which could trace

a highly honoured lineage back for several centuries, he was a young man of considerable intelligence, even of genius as later proved, and of intensely active, inquiring mind. A scientist can not always be held responsible for the results of his experimentations (we can, for instance, not hold the workers on the Manhattan Project responsible for the deaths at Hiroshima), and with this in mind, we cannot consider Frankenstein an evil man. He was a dedicated scientist, devoted to the furtherance of knowledge and the improvement of the lot of man. His researches into the origins of life were not made for personal gain or selfish reasons. Pure science was the greatest hunger of his life. Knowledge for the sake of knowledge might well be pointed out as the dictum by which he lived. Victor von Frankenstein firmly believed that the untapped realms of mental endeavour should be fully explored for the ultimate good of all mankind. His chief motives in attempting to learn the basic reactions and origins of life were praiseworthy. It was his thought that discovery of the key to life might lead to the conquest of death itself.

It was while Frankenstein was a student at the University of Geneva that this hunger to find the origins of life became an obsession, and he determined to devote his life to finding the solution. His unorthodox methods of research, the beliefs and ideas bordering on heresy, caused his expulsion from the university. He returned to the village of Ingolstadt, for centuries the original home of the Frankenstein family. Here, on a small rise of land beside the castle, he erected a tall stone tower to serve as his laboratory, in which he could pursue his studies unhindered.

These studies were to result in the infamous monster of the Frankensteins.

The strange and terrifying tale is told in the book by Mary Shelley which, although written nearly a century and a half ago, remains today the definitive work on monster-making.

Mary Wollstonecraft Shelley was the daughter of William Godwin, an English writer of the late eighteenth century. Godwin, although an ordained minister, was a notorious radical, constantly advocating overthrow of the government, of religion, of every institution of civilization. He believed the institution of marriage to be outmoded, although he was himself twice wed, and considered the sanctity of the family to be nonsense. Mary was born in 1797, when Godwin was past his fortieth year. Her mother died soon after, and her raising was left in the hands of Mary Clairmont, Godwin's second wife, who appears to have been the traditional fairy-tale stepmother.

In 1812, the great poet Percy Shelley entered into correspondence with Godwin, whose writing and ideas he greatly admired. Their association resulted in 1814 in a meeting between Mary and Shelley. They fell in love. Shelley was already married, having eloped in 1811 with Harriet Westbrook, by whom he had twice become a father. Both Mary and Percy, however, shared Godwin's views on marriage, and the existence of a Mrs Shelley meant little to either of them. They left England and toured the Continent. A child was born to them, named William. In 1816, Harriet Westbrook, driven half-insane by her husband's treatment, drowned herself, and Mary and Percy were married. Percy's reputation was further damaged by open scandal when he was declared an unfit father and custody of his two children was given to his deceased wife's family.

The romantic marriage was not to last for long. In 1822, just six years later, Shelley and a friend set out on the Gulf of Spezia in a schooner. A violent storm arose, and Shelley was lost, together with his friend and a young sailor. Mary outlived her husband by nearly thirty years, dying at the age of fifty-four.

Most of Mary Shelley's literary efforts are forgotten today, save for the one story, written when she was twenty-one, which she titled *Frankenstein or the Modern Prometheus*.

The idea of writing *Frankenstein* originated in that remarkable literary evening which we have already mentioned in connection with the vampire legend. Mary, Percy and their constant companion, Lord Byron, were in Switzerland with other friends. During a wild and stormy night, it was suggested that each tell a story of the supernatural. Mary Shelley's contribution was *Frankenstein*.

It is quite possible that, in her travels through Europe, Mary had come across the ruined moats and battlements of a thirteenth-century castle some miles outside of Frankfurt-am-Main, Germany, and heard the Frankensteinian legend connected with the jumbled mass of stone. After the passing of so many centuries, it is impossible to explore the basic truths of such legends or fairy tales, but the tale that is told of the tomb which lies near the castle is a chilling one. The knight who is buried in the tomb, it is said, met his death in a battle with a ferocious 'man-eating monster' which, according to legend, was man-made. Author John Keel, who visited these ruins some years ago and participated in an Army Hallowe'en broadcast from the site, reports that the monster was an animal resembling a boar. It is quite possible that this vague and frightening legend of a man-made creature may have left its mark in Mary's memory and germinated into the tale of Dr Frankenstein.[1]

That so young a girl, accustomed throughout her life to beauty and luxury, should have so intense an understanding of the basic forces and emotions of life as revealed in her novel is not the least remarkable facet of this brilliant work. Under the skilful hand that wielded Mary Shelley's pen, the frightening and tragic story of Dr Frankenstein comes startlingly alive. Here is horror in plenty, as we follow the creation of the monster, trace the course of his violent existence and see the tragic decline of the Frankenstein fortunes. But here, too, is much more than simply a tale of horror, for Mrs Shelley delves deeply into the mind of the young doctor and even, vividly and brilliantly, into the emotions of the monster itself. There are few finer guides to the creation of life and the mind of man than the novel *Frankenstein*.

4

The creation of Dr Frankenstein was no synthetic being, for while the young scientist created life, he did not, in the exact sense, create the vessel into which that life was introduced.

---

[1] *Jadoo*; see also the 1962 summer-fall issue of *Famous Monsters* magazine.

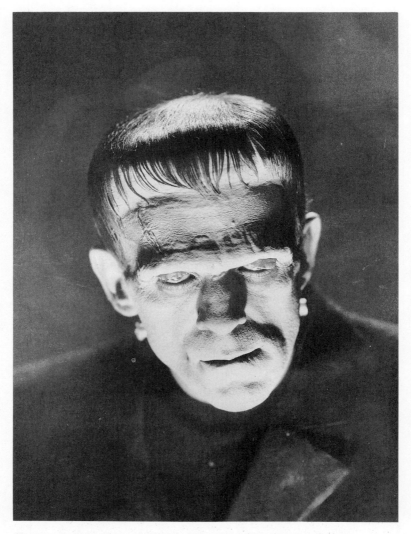

The greatest Monster of all time: Boris Karloff in *Frankenstein*. The power and impact of the Monster was largely lost when he abandoned the role.
Frankenstein (Universal Pictures, 1931)

The actual physical form of the monster was assembled from the limbs and organs of cadavers, bodies stolen from their graves or executed criminals cut down from the gallows.

To secure these necessary body parts for his great work, the young Frankenstein was obliged to resort to various questionable means. The world was not yet as open to the research scientist as it is today. The process of dissection was considered an abomination, an unforgivable transgression of the laws of decency, morality, religion and society. More than this, it was illegal, and the doctor apprehended in such a practice faced the loss of his licence, heavy fine and a long term of imprisonment. Such restrictions were typical of the difficulties under which doctors of the day were forced to do their work. In order to understand the body, to study and examine the origins and results of disease, a doctor must be in a position to secure first-hand knowledge. He must be able to dissect, to examine the various organs, to become completely familiar with the composition and performance of the body. If he cannot do this, he is groping in the dark. If a woman required an operation in those days, her form was covered with a sheet and the doctor performed with his hands beneath the sheet, unable to see what he was doing. The direct result of such bans on study of the human organism was the rush of grave robbing so common in Europe during this time. Research scientists and doctors would pay so much per head to those who would exhume freshly buried corpses and deliver them to the laboratory door in the dark of night. In Scotland, this culminated in the notorious case of Burke and Hare, who moved from the robbing of corpses to the creation of them. (See *The Body Snatchers*, below.)

Young Frankenstein faced this same problem. For a man of genius, with the purpose in life that was his, such restriction was intolerable. Was the greatest scientific work of all time to be made impossible because of these ridiculous, outmoded laws? He could not permit it to be so.

And so, the good doctor began to secure human parts wherever and however they could be found. It was a gruesome manner of securing the desperately needed materials. In the dark of night, Frankenstein would enter the village graveyard, shovel in hand, and disinter the fresh bodies of those recently deceased, then load them onto a horse-drawn cart and take them to the laboratory. It was still the custom in those days to leave the bodies of executed criminals hanging from the gallows as a warning to other would-be wrongdoers; these Frankenstein cut down and carted to his workshop. Mary Shelley makes no mention of the possibility that Frankenstein may have fallen into the same crimes and errors of Burke and Hare; the doctor certainly would not have countenanced bringing death to create life. In all probability, murder was not necessary; if it were, perhaps Frankenstein, so intent on his mission, might have been willing to close his eyes.

In his stuffy student quarters in the village of Ingolstadt, Victor dissected and dismembered the bodies, looking always for the very best of what he needed, for it was, from the start, his avowed intention to make this creation of his a creature perfect in every way. Diseased and damaged parts were discarded; only the best were retained and joined to the massive form beginning to take shape on the operating table. His creature, the new race, would be as handsome a thing as he could make him. Poor Dr Frankenstein overlooked the fact that attractive individual elements do not necessarily make for an inviting whole.

Mrs Shelley does not provide us with details as to the actual uniting of the body parts, the interior organs, the vital fluids, etc. Undoubtedly her knowledge of anatomy and medicine did not extend this far. Perhaps it was also her woman's mind that stressed the fact that the body of the creature was to be in every way complete and perfect.

(Let us here digress, for one moment, from Mrs Shelley's writing to speak of the act of creation as it is shown in the Frankenstein films. Mrs Shelley's doctor brought life by chemical means; the later films added the interesting touch of electricity, which permitted spectacular effects.

If Dr Frankenstein was, in a sense, the father of his creation, then lightning was its mother. The secret of the instilling of life into the monster died with Frankenstein, but lightning and electricity were major contributing factors. Frankenstein claimed to have found the seeds of life in certain cosmic rays which had but to be properly harnessed and directed in the correct manner to cause his creation to live and breathe. This was accomplished through the aid of complex electrical equipment.

It was the arrival of this enormous machinery, coming in huge crates by train to Ingolstadt and then carted by horse up the mountainside to the laboratory, that brought the first touch of fear to the villagers. Electricity was still something alien, a force which the average person could not understand. It was new, and it smacked just a bit of black magic. The homes, the public places, the streets of the village were still lit with the feeble, flickering glow of gas lanterns. When the young Frankenstein returned to the village after his education in Geneva, the people did not know what to expect of him. He had been out in the great world, he had assimilated new ideas. It was said he was a scientist, but that meant little to people who had never voyaged beyond their own little village. When the tremendous crates and cases began to arrive and the new laboratory began to take form beside the castle, there was curiosity, but as yet no fear. Then strange things began to happen in that stone monolith. At all hours of the night, the villagers could look up the hillside and see blinding flashes of light; the air was filled with a peculiar humming and crackling sound. Particularly during the violent storms to which that portion of the country was subject, the tower seemed suddenly to be the focus of great and inexplicable activity. The storms seemed, for some unknown reason, to centre about the young doctor's laboratory, the bright forks of lightning striking it again and again, as though God were angry with the work being done there. This was something new, something unknown, considerably beyond the realm of their experience. Whispers began to circulate, and before long the laboratory and the work of Frankenstein began to take on a most ominous meaning.

None of them, of course, would even have dared to guess that what the young scientist was doing was creating life itself.

On a cold, windy night in November, when the air about the tower was rent by terrifying bolts of lightning and the very homes of the village trembled under the powerful peals

of thunder, Frankenstein's greatest dream was realized. His
creature moved, breathed, walked – and lived. He had created
life. He had duplicated the great achievement of the Almighty.
In a sense, Frankenstein had become God.)

The mad scientist has become a familiar figure. Although
this represents a holdover from the dark days when scientists
were feared as madmen and heretics, Frankenstein has become

**Exulting in his freedom, the Monster (Boris Karloff) escapes from
Frankenstein's laboratory to begin his ravaging of the countryside.**
Frankenstein **(Universal Pictures, 1931)**

the prototypes of his species, in itself a particular kind of monster. The mad scientist is one to whom all normal, moral associations have no meaning. His life is devoted, at first, to the greater glory of pure science but, as he progresses in his work, he loses sight of this aim, and directs all his energies, talents and ambitions to the greater glory of himself. He becomes a wild-eyed villain, dressed in the traditional laboratory smock, completely engrossed in his work. He stands before tables lined with test tubes twisted into fantastic shapes, and frightening white and yellow mists curling slowly over the lip of the uncovered beaker and moving like some miniature death fog over the table. He stands by the instrument panel, turning wheels and flicking switches, and the laboratory is filled with ominous cracklings and thrummings, while brilliant, snapping bolts of electricity leap across the spaces from one tube to another. He grows lean and hollow-eyed as he spends twenty-three hours a day muttering strange formulas, mixing vari-coloured fluids which give off choking fumes. His face will suddenly brighten as he cries, 'Eureka! I have it!' He permits no personal emotions to interfere with his work, not even the feelings of those who are dear to him, for none are as dear as his mistress, Science. The beautiful neglected wife stands in the doorway in her flimsy, revealing négligé, waving the promise of sexual delight, pleading with him to end this madness before it is too late, but he angrily brushes her off, driving her into the arms of his best friend. He will stop at nothing to gain his ends; even murder is, to him, permissible in the name of science. Then, suddenly, he will realize that his wife has not been sitting all alone in her room, and he will murder his best friend for doing what he was too busy to do.

Whether Victor Frankenstein falls into this category is open to question. Even today, scientists with new and revolutionary ideas are often considered somewhat mad. That Frankenstein was devoted to his science there is no doubt. In carrying through his purpose he did, in many instances, put himself above the then-existing laws, and the fact that these laws were already outmoded and a hindrance to useful research does not alter this fact. But this does not necessarily mark the young doctor as mad. He worked in fields which were considered holy and beyond the reach of man, but neither is this a mark of insanity. He was branded by the villagers as a dabbler in black magic and unholy rites, a man who had dared the greatest of blasphemies, but neither is this an indication of madness. What may appear as madness in one generation may be enthusiasm of genius in another.

It may well be, however, that Frankenstein did have brief periods of mental derangement. Long, intensive labour on his appointed task undoubtedly brought physical and mental exhaustion, with the resultant inability to see things in quite their proper perspective. It is not surprising that his work became the all of his life, particularly as it neared successful completion. In the great moment of his triumph, when he saw the first signs of life in his creation, certainly a touch of madness was present – the madness of a god who had created life, the madness of mankind's greatest achievement.

But that Victor Frankenstein was not a white-coated lunatic is very clearly evidenced by his reaction to this new life he had created. In the very flush of his great triumph, he was seized by a terrible, chilling fear, a premonition that he had brought evil, not good, into the world. From the very moment that his creature first opened his 'dull yellow eye', Frankenstein's triumph turned to an overwhelming sense of horror and disgust. Perhaps, in that brief moment, he was granted an honest glimpse of the true nature of the monstrosity he was about to release upon the world. When the creature stood before him, extending his yellow hands revealing the raw marks of surgery, Frankenstein saw his creation not as the physically perfect specimen of a wonderful new race of mankind, but as a hideous travesty of humanity, a creature so horrifying that, from the very moment he brought it to life, Dr Frankenstein began to think of its destruction. It was ugly when finished, Frankenstein wrote, but once it had been given life and movement, it became a horror from some unending nightmare.

Victor Frankenstein's reaction to the completion of his work was certainly not that of a madman, but rather of a man who had been living in a long nightmare and had just awakened. Following the terrible night when his creation had first risen from the table a living, feeling and thinking being, Frankenstein became gravely ill with a fever which lingered for months. During this period, he was truly out of his mind, not with the insanity of dedication to the world of science, but with the madness of an unimaginable horror. The monster haunted his feverish dreams, the horror of what he had done weighed on his conscience. Only by forcing from his mind the remembrance of that terrible November night, did Victor Frankenstein regain his sanity and return to the rational world of the living. The Monster had by then disappeared, and no one made mention of the intensive work that had occupied him through the last months. His assistant, too, was gone. No one else had seen the beast. Then, surely, it had been more a creation of his disordered fancy than of his skilled hands? Perhaps the monstrosity had never really existed. Upon his restoration to health, Victor abandoned the former course of his studies and put behind him the horror of what he had done. He refused to believe, even within himself, that he had ever truly succeeded in his work. That nightmare when the creature had risen from the table and walked had been just that – a nightmare, probably engendered by the fever. Thus did he seduce himself, quite ignoring the fact that the nightmare had preceded the fever.

Unfortunately, this new dream world was soon to shatter.

After the terrible incidents of that wild November night had already begun to fade from Victor's mind, he heard of the brutal and mysterious murder of his younger brother, William. Victor immediately rushed to the scene of the crime, arriving at the height of a violent storm. In the brilliant flashes of lightning, he saw before him the monster of his own creation. The beast was gone with the next flash of light, but Victor had seen enough. He knew the truth. The creature, then, did indeed exist, and there was no doubt in Victor's mind that he had slain his brother.

Victor then showed not madness, but a lamentable weakness. A young girl of the village was tried for William's murder, found guilty and hanged, this although Victor knew her innocence. His evil creation had now been the cause of two deaths.

In one of horror's most poignant scenes, the Monster (Boris Karloff) reacts to his first glimpse of sunlight as Dr. Waldman (Edward Van Sloan) strikes from behind.
Frankenstein, (Universal Pictures, 1931)

The revival of this nightmare, which he had been able so completely to put out of his mind, might well have driven Victor to utter madness, but it had quite an opposite effect. Rather, it strengthened his resolve and gave him a new purpose in life – to seek out his evil creation and destroy it.

It was the monster himself who diverted Victor from this course. By way of an impassioned plea for mercy and understanding, the monster managed to convince his maker that he was not completely a creature of evil. He called Victor's attention to the circumstances under which he had been brought to life. He pointed to his gaunt, oversized frame, to the hideous aspect of his face, which caused all who saw him to scream and flee in terror. This was not his own doing, the

monster cried, but the fault of his creator. How could such a
monster as he hope for acceptance in the world of men? Yet
he had been brought to unwilling life and, even to one as himself, life was very dear. He cried out to Victor not to desert
him, to give him the same opportunities that were the right of
all men, be they born of woman or of science. Let him have a
mate, a woman, let Victor create a female as hideous as himself. He swore, in an impassioned plea, that he and this mate
would disappear into the wilds of some uninhabited land and
never again be seen by man.

Were he in truth a 'mad scientist', Victor might have agreed
to the monster's suggestion for the sole purpose of greater
glory. To have created a living being was achievement enough
– to have created two, man and woman, would be greater
glory still. But, once again, Victor was not mad. After considerable thought, he acceded to the monster's request, but not
out of a longing for this greater honour. The truth was, the
monster's words had moved him with a feeling of his own
responsibility, not to the world of man, but to this being he
had created with his own hands. He had brought this monstrosity to unasked life, and could not now tell him he had no
right to existence. Perhaps he chuckled a bit at the thought
that this horrifying caricature was, in a sense, his own son.
What parent can refuse the request of its own child? There is
also no doubt that he implicitly believed the words of the
monster when he promised to take this mate and live apart
from men. Surely the creature had a right to this chance?

Victor commenced his second work of creation on a lonely
island off the coast of Scotland to which, unseen by all but
ever known to Victor, the monster followed him. It was at
this point that Victor truly reveals the sound state of his mind.
The form of the woman, as hideous as the monster himself,
lay before him, cold and lifeless, waiting only for that magnificent moment when life would first flow through her borrowed veins. And it was then that the scientist began to have
second thoughts about what he was doing. Was he not merely
creating a second monster of evil? Even should his two 'children' depart to some wilderness apart from the eyes of men,
what of the future? What of their hideous progeny? Was not

he, Victor Frankenstein, in this little Scottish cottage, about to bring into being a race of demons which would spawn their horror across the face of the earth?

In that moment, if at no other, Victor Frankenstein was wonderfully sane. With cold, deliberate hands and a hard, determined look in his eye, while the monster watched through the window of the cottage, Victor Frankenstein tore to pieces the still-lifeless form of his female creation.

From this point, the life of Victor Frankenstein became an endless nightmare, a horror great enough to drive the strongest mind into screaming madness. From the moment the creature, peering through the window, saw Frankenstein destroy the promised mate, he became, in all respects, a monster in fact as well as name. By this act of destruction of the second body, Victor Frankenstein had become his enemy. All hope was now gone, and any vestiges of human feeling and understanding vanished from the being the young scientist had brought to life. All, all were against him. In his anger, his fury, his soul-destroying hatred, the monster struck out again and again, determined to destroy every possibility of Frankenstein's own future happiness, as Frankenstein had destroyed a future life of peace for the monster.

His next stroke was the murder of Henry Clerval, Victor's closest friend who, concerned about the young scientist, had followed him to Scotland in hopes of inducing him to return home. Victor was finally cleared of the charge that he himself had slain Clerval, but this newest incident of horror brought a relapse of the brain fever which had seized him periodically since the creation of the monster. For months, he lay in delirium, until his father arrived to take him home again.

Back with those he loved, in the familiar surroundings of his own home, Victor once again determined to put behind him forever the horror of what he had done. But always there rang in his ears the words of the monster as the two of them stood over the torn flesh of Victor's broken agreement: 'I shall be with you on your wedding night.'

And the monster kept his promise and brought about the final destruction of the House of Frankenstein. Victor and his beloved Elizabeth were married and on their wedding night

Victor found his new bride lying cold and lifeless on their marriage bed.

This final, ultimate atrocity destroyed forever Victor's hopes of happiness. He was possessed now of only one passion in life – the complete destruction of this horror he had spawned. Through the years, Dr Frankenstein pursued the monster across the face of the earth, hoping always to catch up with him and annihilate this cancer of his own making.

And it was at last, in cold Arctic waters, aboard the ship of a Captain Robert Walton, that monster and maker finally stood face to face again. And here the monster had his final revenge, for when Captain Walton entered Victor Frankenstein's cabin, he found the fiendish beast bent over the lifeless corpse of the man who had created him and brought him to a life of unparalleled horror and degradation. With one last wail of horror, remorse and repentance, the monster then flung himself over the side of the ship and disappeared forever into the frozen Arctic wilderness.

So ended the brilliant, tragic life of Dr Victor Frankenstein, scientist and creator of monsters. Was he mad? If so, it was the madness of genius. Was he insane? If so, it was the insanity of despair. His story is not only his own personal tragedy, but that of the Frankenstein family, for the monster's revenge was complete. Young William Frankenstein had been his first victim, Victor himself was the last. The line had been destroyed, the centuries-old house of Frankenstein had ended at last. Surely the monster's revenge was complete.

The frightening history of Victor Frankenstein might well serve to illustrate the maxim, so popular during the last century, of the intrinsic dangers of a little knowledge. The horrors and tragedies that Frankenstein brought to himself and to the world were a result of his constant quest for truth and light. His intentions were of the best. The creation of life might have been the first step to the extermination of death. The dead might be restored, diseased members might be replaced with healthy ones. A new era might have opened for mankind.

It was not necessarily Victor's fault that his great dream went awry. Perhaps he, like so many other great and brilliant men, merely lived before his time. Perhaps there were ramifications he could not see, which could be foreseen by the science of today.

Thus, to point out Frankenstein as the supreme 'mad scientist' is to do him a great injustice. The mistakes he made were not those of egomania and indifference to the lives of others. If there is true insanity in his tragic tale, it came at that moment of achievement when the monster took his first breath and Frankenstein realized he had succeeded in his great work. From this point, he may have been foolish but, despite periods of long illness, he was never truly insane. We have seen how quickly even that first so understandable elation faded, and the brief 'insanity' with it. His great error lay in not immediately assuming the dreadful responsibility for what he had done. At that very moment of triumph, he realized the enormity of what he had created and realized, too, the potential horror. At that moment, a decisive step would have prevented the tragedy. Rather than try to shut out from his mind the hideous visage of his creation, he should have taken immediate steps for its complete destruction.

Would this have been murder? It is a question difficult to answer. The monster, hideous though he was, nevertheless was a thinking, feeling being in the guise of man. He was possessed – as he indicated in his desire for a mate – of the emotions and longings of man. It is not murder to crush the life of some insect or some highly dangerous animal, but when that animal assumes the form of man, must we not base our decisions on different values?

Perhaps the monster should have been brought to justice by due process of law, to stand trial for the crimes of which he was guilty. Such a possibility, however, immediately presents several obvious difficulties, the greatest of which is the certainty that no one would have believed the wild story about creation of a monster, at least not before it was too late. Even the obvious often finds difficulty of acceptance. If Frankenstein had gone to the magistrate and announced that these crimes were committed by a creature he had assembled and brought to life with his own hands, his sanity would, indeed, have been seriously questioned. At any rate, to go to the magistrate after the monster had committed murder would have been too late.

We must also ask if the monster, being of artificial construction, could have been held accountable for his actions and liable according to the laws and penalties of man. Considering his fantastic strength, would it even have been possible to keep him long in imprisonment?

There is yet another thought with respect to Frankenstein's rights and obligations. As the very creator of this monster, did he not have at least a moral right to take away that life which he himself had bestowed? We may cry 'No', for no less has a mother the right to take the life of her own child. But God had no hand in this strange and monstrous birth. This was a creature brought into being solely by man, a blasphemy, a horror which surely never had a right to live.

The answer to one question of supreme importance may solve the dilemma of Frankenstein's right to destroy the life he himself had created – the question of the soul. Even if man is able to create life, can he also create the soul which can issue only from the handiwork of God? And if not, can we consider his creation truly a man? Is it physical attributes that make a man, or is it that tenuous, unseen force called the soul? Can we label with the term 'murder' the destruction of a violent, monstrous, dangerous, and soulless being?

But Victor lacked the strength of mind and will to destroy his monster, and he permitted it to escape while he recovered from that first horror of what he had done. Here, of course, was his first great error. The next was in standing silently by when an innocent girl was executed for the murder of his young brother. Certainly, by saying nothing at this time, Victor bore on his own conscience the burden of guilt for this girl's death, just as his brother's death was the product of his own hands. Here, perhaps, began that insanity of despair. Had Frankenstein been the stereotyped mad scientist, of course, these deaths would have meant but little to him. Such was not the case.

Victor's agreement to create a mate for the monster was also made from the best of motives. Perhaps he could not bring himself to admit the failure of what he had done; perhaps he was one of those rare, foolish individuals who can not accept the existence of pure evil. Perhaps he was grabbing at straws to delay his acceptance of the inevitable. Whether or not the monster was sincere in his promises to Victor, we cannot say. If we closely examine the words of the monster, before the destruction of his mate brought him to such endless evil, we might possibly find ourselves swayed as Frankenstein himself. Standing, some time later, over the body of his creator, the monster weeps and says to the ship's captain:

While I destroyed his hopes, I did not satisfy my own desires. They were forever ardent and craving. Still I desired love and fellowship, and I was still spurned.

Earlier, he had said:

Once I falsely hoped to meet with beings who, pardoning my outward form, would love me for the excellent qualities which I was capable of unfolding.

Is it so difficult to believe that a being who could speak so eloquently could affect the thinking and beliefs of the man who had created him? Yet perhaps Victor's moment of most rational thought came when he took the still-lifeless body of the woman in his hands and rent it asunder; it was, also, that moment which determined his own ultimate destruction.

What we see then in Victor Frankenstein is not the power-hungry, cold, indifferent mad scientist, but a young man led astray in his quest for knowledge, confused, frightened, even horrified, and completely helpless before the tide of tragedy that swept him and his loved ones to utter and terrible anni-hilation. He was, undoubtedly, a genius, but he was also a very human and a very weak man. His errors were not those of insanity or irrational thinking, but of foolishness, of vacil-lation, of indecision and of his own pitiful weakness. Let us not judge Dr Victor Frankenstein too harshly; his errors might well have been our own.

5

But what of the monster himself? Was this creation of man, pieced together from various organs and members of corpses, given a brain with a criminal element, brought into blazing life by the heavenly fire of lightning, was he, really, Satan incarnate, the greatest evil ever to walk the face of the earth, fit only for destruction, for complete and utter annihilation?

Mary Shelley does not say; she leaves this decision to us. It was in this characterization of the monster that Mrs Shelley reveals her true genius as a writer. She delves with remarkable insight into the mind of the creature, into his thoughts and his emotions, his hopes and fears, his goodness and his evil. He is neither black nor white, neither angel nor devil but, like man in whose image he was made, a combination of these. He was not born with murder in his heart; it was placed there by man himself. To understand more fully the motivations and emotions of the monster, we must understand ourselves, for we have not changed so radically since the people of Dr Frankenstein's day. *Frankenstein* might, indeed, well have been written in our own day, for what Mary Shelley provides is a bitter tale of bigotry, prejudice and intolerance.

It is the very nature of man – today as in the past – to distrust and fear that which is different. Radical change, in any form, is abhorrent to man. Things must always be what they appear to be. Change must be permitted to take its slow and orderly course, to win its gradual acceptance by man, and must not be thrust too quickly upon him. Until this orderly process of change is realized, all must conform; he who does not is shunned, outcast and persecuted.

The monster creation of Dr Frankenstein did not conform to any of the basic requirements necessary to win acceptance by man. He was not born of woman, as man has always been born; his birth was an unnatural one. He came to life in the full strength of his manhood, not as a babe at his mother's breasts. He did not grow from infancy to childhood, from childhood to maturity, from maturity to manhood, as is the natural law of the living. His flesh was the flesh of the dead. His heart came from the grave, his lungs from the corpse of a man hanged for murder. His eyes had once closed in death and been reopened through the machinations of science. Even his brain had once reposed within the skull of another man, a man whose life had been that of an outlaw. He was in all ways an unearthly being, an abomination of nature.

His appearance itself was enough to strike terror in the strongest heart. Dr Frankenstein himself described him as being taller than a man should be tall; his eyes were a dull yellow, his skin had the parchment texture of a long-buried mummy. We can learn to accept ugliness and deformity when they are a natural misfortune of birth, illness or accident, although often our very mode of acceptance is an indication of our powers of cruelty, but few of us can accept ugliness caused by man himself. The monster was hideous in a way that seemed a blasphemy, in a manner that seemed to mock God himself. He was in all ways abominable.

Such a creature as he could never hope to overcome the inherent prejudices and pettiness of man. Wherever he might go, he would be feared and shunned. Hatred would follow him even into a strange land, for the mark of God was not on him. He was born an outcast, and an outcast he would remain.

This is not because he was an unfortunate product of his time. In our own so-called enlightened age, his reception would have been no warmer. What would be the reaction of modern man to the arrival of some nonhuman creature from another world? This is an aspect of our civilization which has frequently been treated by the writers of science fiction. Would such a creature, though his motives in visiting earth might be the most benevolent, be greeted with open arms and words of welcome? More than likely, he would be feared, hunted, destroyed. The world is not yet prepared for such divergence from the plan of creation.

So was it with the monster. Wherever he might show himself, he would be feared and considered an abomination of horror, forever an alien. It is no wonder, then, that he pleaded with Frankenstein to create a woman 'as hideous as myself' with whom he could live always apart from tormenting man.

For the creature was undeniably possessed of finer feelings. He desired love and companionship. He longed to be as other men, he hungered for the warmth of a fireside, of convivial friends and companions, for the handshake of his fellow man, for the smiles of a woman. These, he knew, he could never hope to have.

Through all the blackness and despair of the monster's life, there was but one period when, in a sense, he enjoyed these benefits, and it provides us with the most poignant and moving incidents of the creature's horrifying tale. Searching desperately for the warmth of human companionship, he entered a small village, to be greeted with screams of fear and horror and, finally, to be hounded from the countryside. He took refuge in a mean hovel adjoining the cottage in the forest occupied by an old blind man and his young son and daughter. Unseen, the monster lived for some time in this hovel, his first home, and, peering through an opening in the wall, shared the life of this poor, but affectionate trio. This was clearly the only completely happy period of the beast's existence. During the long evenings, the young couple would seat themselves on small stools before the blind man and he would fill the silent, humble cottage with the bittersweet strains of his violin, and the warmth of their mutual love seeped into the hovel where, like some hunted animal burrowing for safety in his lair, the lonely monster lay and watched and listened. He even, unknown to the three, attempted to assist them in their life of poverty, on more than one occasion leaving cut firewood before the door.

Through the winter and spring, the monster lived thus, completely unsuspected by the three in the cottage, and a new world of warmth and wonder opened up to him.

The gentle manners and beauty of the cottagers endeared them to me. When they were unhappy, I felt depressed. When they rejoiced, I sympathized with their joys.

During this period, there was no trace of evil in the creature. He longed only to live as he was, sharing vicariously the love of the three other living beings. During those long months of listening and observing, he learned to speak; the cottagers' books fell into his hands, and he learned to read.[2]

This incident alone is proof that there was a spark of good within the monster. Had he been accepted, even by just this simple trio of humanity, his life might have run along a gentler, more normal course, and the work of Dr Frankenstein would have been accepted and hailed as man's greatest achievement. Through these happy months, he learned the wonder of human associations, and his only desire was to share them, to feel such warmth directed toward himself.

But, at the same time, he came to a realization about himself which told him, clearly and brutally, that he was not as these friends whose lives he shared:

> I had admired the perfect forms of my cottagers – but how was I terrified when I viewed myself in a transparent pool! At first I started back, unable to believe that it was indeed I who was reflected in the mirror, and when I became fully convinced that I was in reality the Monster that I am, I was filled with the bitterest sensations.

He knew now why all ran in horror when they saw him, why he was feared by all who crossed his path. He knew, too, that these three who had come to mean so much to him would react as others had. Such love as he had viewed during the past months was not, and never could be, for the likes of him. He might enjoy their warmth and affection through the medium of the defect in the wall of his little hovel, but that wall would always remain.

But such distant happiness could not always satisfy the human heart that had been placed in his hideous breast. It may be in the nature of an animal to enjoy such vicarious pleasures, but not in that of man, and before long the monster began to yearn for more direct companionship. One day, when

[2] The monster did speak in the second of the Frankenstein films but, for some reason, apparently lost this ability later.

the young man and girl were away, the monster knocked on the door of the cottage and was admitted by the blind man. For so brief a time, the monster then exulted in his first direct communication. The old violinist had no fear of the stranger; he greeted him with the friendliness of the poor, and the monster was asked into the cottage which he had viewed from the dark and lonely seclusion of his burrow. The blind man could not see the hideous features of his visitor, and thus terror did not follow the monster through the door. He sat with the old man and talked with him; they were the first words he had ever exchanged with any man. Warmth and an unknown sense of peace and comfort entered a heart which had until now known nothing but fear and hatred. Evil seemed a distant thing.

And then the young people returned, and the wondrous dream came to an end in their screams of horror. Sick at heart, the monster fled.

For a time, he seemed to have lost all desire for life. He had known friendship and love; to have shared these emotions and lost them caused a deeper sorrow than never to have known them at all. The full depth of his agony is revealed in his despairing cry, one of the most pitiful in all of literature: 'Cursed, cursed creator! Why did I live?'

But live he did. As a last hope, he determined to make his way to Geneva and throw himself on the mercy of his maker. Even now he had not yet completely become a creature of evil. Seeing a small girl in danger of drowning, he risked his life to save her; the father thanked him with a rifle bullet shot into the monster's arm.[3] This, then, was an example of man's gratitude. Once again, he had no recourse but in flight.

The monster made yet one further attempt to win acceptance from mankind. When near Geneva, he met with an attractive, innocent young boy and conceived the idea of taking this child – too young, surely, to be contaminated by the prejudices of his elders – as his companion, to ease the soul-destroying loneliness which had always been a part of

[3] This incident was included in _Bride of Frankenstein_ in a beautifully touching scene.

his brief life. But the evil of prejudice had entered even the young. Screaming with horror, the young boy threatened repercussions from his father, the powerful Baron von Frankenstein. This was too much for the monster. Filled with fury, he cried, 'I, too, can create desolation!' and his powerful hands closed about the throat of young William Frankenstein.

Thus, with the brutal, cold-blooded murder of his creator's young brother, began the infamous career of blood and horror for which the monster of the Frankensteins was to become notorious. There followed, after the destruction of the monster's proposed mate, the murder of Henry Clerval, the bride Elizabeth and, at last, Dr Victor Frankenstein himself.

One fact, however, stands out clearly when we review the monster's bloody career. These were not isolated, meaningless murders, and it is not accurate to picture the monster as a vicious animal reaching out his bloody hands for all he could grasp. He killed with a terrible purpose, and that purpose was revenge, revenge first upon Victor Frankenstein himself for bringing him to his hated existence, and upon mankind for refusing him the acceptance and understanding for which he craved. His was the horrifying cry of the misanthrope.

There can be no doubt that the monster was, at least at the beginning of his existence, capable of the finer feelings which supposedly distinguish man from the beasts. In his own words, in the most touching and eloquent portions of Mrs Shelley's writing, he pours out his heart to his moved maker, calling again and again for friendship, for understanding, for compassion:

> Let [man] live with me in the interchange of kindness; and, instead of injury, I would bestow every benefit upon him with tears of gratitude at his acceptance.

And this is followed by what is probably the most moving outburst in the novel:

> I am malicious because I am miserable. . . . If any being felt emotions of benevolence towards me, I should return them an hundred and an hundred fold. For that one

creature's sake, I would make peace with the whole kind!

This, surely, is not the cry of an inhuman beast, but the pathetic wail of loneliness and heartbreak of a lost and misunderstood being. Man was not meant to live alone, and the creature was in the form of man. He longed for companionship, but always was repulsed. Even those to whom he intended no harm ran from him in horror. His reaction to this constant rejection is merely another indication of his human nature. He tried first conciliation and only when this failed did he strike out in the only way he could – with the sheer overpowering physical strength of his being. Why must he observe the laws and mores of a race who refused to acknowledge his existence as one of them? He killed, he killed again and yet again, and finally he destroyed the one who was responsible for the existence that had become so odious to him – Frankenstein himself.

Such despair, such hopeless agony, should not be difficult for us to understand. It is in the nature of man to need and want love, but this the monster was never given. The most miserable of us have at some time known the touch of others' compassion, yet the monster was never to know it. Let us not be too quick to condemn.

Yet even as he avenged himself in this terrifying manner, the monster retained those qualities of conscience which place man above the animals. Speaking over Frankenstein's corpse, he says:

> Do you think I was then dead to agony and remorse? A frightful selfishness hurried me on, while my heart was poisoned with remorse. . . . My heart was fashioned to be susceptible of love and sympathy. . . . I pitied Frankenstein. My pity amounted to horror. I abhorred myself. . . . When I run over the frightful catalogue of my sins, I cannot believe that I am the same creature whose thoughts were once filled with sublime and transcendent visions of the beauty and the majesty of goodness. . . . The details [of my crimes] could not sum up the hours

of misery which I endured. . . . The bitter sting of remorse will not cease to rankle in my wounds until death
shall close them forever.

When the monster disappeared into the ice floes of the
Arctic, he was never again seen by man (which may lend
credence to his promise to Frankenstein) and his frightening
story of murder and violence, of loneliness and disaster, came
to an end. He was a murderer, he was an inhuman monster,
he was the victim of bias, of prejudice, of the narrowminded-
ness of the human race. He is remembered as the greatest
evil ever created by man, yet if he had just once been greeted
as a man, welcomed instead of persecuted, understood instead
of vilified, the story of Victor Frankenstein's great creation
might have been the tale of mankind's greatest achievement.

The tragedy and horror of *Frankenstein* lie not in the terror
that was loosed upon the world, not in the innocent lives that
were brought to bloody destruction, not in the downfall of the
great House of Frankenstein, but rather in the tragedy of the
pitifully misunderstood Frankenstein monster. And the tragedy
of this creature is not so much that he was a monster, but that
he was, withal, so much a man.

6

It was in 1931 that Universal Studios decided to transfer the
story of Frankenstein to the screen,[4] thus beginning the long
cycle of monster films which marked moviemaking during
the period of the thirties, culminating shortly before the
Second World War.

For the role of Victor Frankenstein (for some reason, named
Henry in the film), Universal secured a fine young English
actor named Colin Clive, who brought to the role the proper
air of dedication, frustration, bewilderment and, finally,
agony. The character of the warped assistant to the doctor

---

[4] There was a silent *Frankenstein* many years ago, long forgotten.

was given prominence in the film. He was presented as an evil-faced, moronic, diminutive hunchback, in his way as much a monster as Clive's creation. The role was admirably played by Dwight Frye, who also appeared as the madman Renfield in the Lugosi *Dracula*.

The all-important role, of course, upon which the success of the venture depended, was that of the monster himself, and the casting was a long and careful process. There were several important aspects to be considered. The monster must, of course, be horrifying in the extreme – and Universal was a master hand at this – but the studio was not planning a robot-like automaton; the true horror must come, not from the face alone, but from the characterization itself. The monster must, therefore, be played by an actor with the ability to strike both horror and sympathy in the audience. It was also felt advisable to select a performer not yet too well known to the motion-picture public, not yet identified with any particular type of role. The performer chosen was another English actor named Pratt, whose performance secured for him lasting cine-matic fame under the name of Boris Karloff. An air of mystery was added to the film through a press agent's dream – the identity of the actor portraying the monster was not revealed until after the overwhelmingly succesful release of the film.

The Universal make-up department then went to work on the appearance of the monster. The original description pro-vided by Mrs Shelley – gaunt, thin, parchment-yellow – was discarded and an entirely new being was created, soon to become the most famous and familiar of Hollywood creations. The monster was envisioned as enormously tall and ungainly, with many of the physical attributes of a man, but these attributes so exaggerated and extended as to appear abnormal and artificial. The feet were encased in enormous leaden shoes to make walking difficult and unnatural. The long, tapering fingers were extremely white as, indeed, was the entire com-plexion. The wrists were marked with clear and sharply de-signed stitches, indicative of Dr Frankenstein's craft. On either side of the throat was placed a small electrode, through which the life-giving electricity was introduced. The head was large and flat at the top, well-covered with coarse black hair. The face was a nightmare – the cheeks gaunt and drawn, hollowed with black shadow, the lips firm black lines, the eyes deep and sunken, the brow almost Neanderthal. The sum total was the most horrifying creature ever dreamed up by the craft of the make-up artist, and was the imaginative product of Jack Pierce and Karloff himself.

This, then, was the Frankenstein monster as portrayed by the as yet unknown Mr Karloff. Much was made at the time of the eight hours necessary for application of the horrendous and extremely heavy (sixty-two pounds) and uncomfortable make-up. In creating a monster which, despite all its horrors and deformities, still was obviously patterned in the nature of man, the studio showed considerable intelligence. Nothing is quite as horrifying as horrendous man. In the second horror period of the fifties, the various monsters became less and less human in appearance and, as a result, less and less horrifying.

The first *Frankenstein*, produced by Carl Laemmle and directed by James Whale, was a brilliant creative work. Although it leaned heavily on Mrs Shelley's original tale, there were alterations for the purpose of simplicity and pictorial effectiveness. The entire story was laid in the village of Frankenstein, a charming, pleasant town dominated by the massive castle of the Baron von Frankenstein and his family. At one side of this castle, Henry uses a stone tower to serve as his laboratory. It is here he begins his great experiments, having been expelled from the university for unorthodoxy. As his assistant, he takes a mentally defective hunchback who obeys him implicitly. Together, these two open graves and secure bodies of condemned criminals to be used in the great work. The assistant enters the laboratory of the university by night to secure a brain but, in a spasm of fright, drops the vessel holding the brain, which crashes to the floor. In taking a substitute, he unwittingly picks upon one marked abnormal and criminal. In a wild, stormy night, to the accompaniment of flashes of lightning, crackling of electricity and the humming of enormous dynamos, the great creature is brought to life. In a scene which has become a classic of the mad-scientist theme, Dr Frankenstein, seeing a slight movement of the creature's hand, cries, 'He's alive! He's alive, I tell you! He's alive!' The monster is securely chained to the wall in a cell at the base of the tower, where he is constantly tormented by the vicious little hunchback, who delights in thrusting flaming torches into the monster's face. Striking back at this brutality, his first contact with so-called humanity, the monster breaks his chains, hangs his tormentor, and escapes from the tower.

While stumbling along the bank of a brook, he comes upon a small girl sailing blossoms in the stream. With the innocence of childhood, the girl invites him to join in her sport. The monster, not realizing his own terrible strength, accidentally kills the girl. He is thereupon pursued by the terrified villagers, led by Dr Frankenstein himself, who has sadly admitted that his great dream has ended in horror. He and the monster finally come face to face on a bleak mountaintop. The monster, striking out now in fear and terror, overcomes young Frankenstein and carries him to a windmill. The crowd follow him there and, determined to destroy the beast at all costs, set the windmill afire. A fight ensues in the blazing pyre between Dr Frankenstein and his terrible creation, and the monster hurls the scientist from the top of the structure. The doctor's fall is broken by an arm of the mill and he survives, while the creature (supposedly) perishes.

The story is simple, and simply told, while containing considerably more substance than most horror films. For effectiveness and impact, however, it relied chiefly on two all-important factors – atmospheric horror and the performance of Mr Karloff. In both, the makers of *Frankenstein* were extremely fortunate.

We have several times mentioned the advantages and disadvantages of technicolor. *Frankenstein* is one film which benefits greatly from the lack of colour. This is an unrelievedly black and white film. Much of the action occurs in darkest night, with a sky overcast by storm clouds. The final confrontation of Frankenstein and the monster on the mountaintop, against a leaden grey sky, stands out like a painting by an artist of the macabre. Such an effect would have been seriously marred by the use of colour; so it is through much of this brilliant film. Bright colouring has no place in the shadow world of horror. The one possible exception to this is the use of green, aptly termed the very colour of horror. The process of tinting had been frequently used in silent films. Some of the prints of *Frankenstein* were presented, not in black and white, but in a deep, lurid green, and the effect was almost indescribably horrifying. The tint deepened the shadows of the monster's cheeks, made the cold line of his cruel lips seem black. With the advent of technicolor, this process of tinting (green for horror, pink for romance, etc.) was abandoned.[5] It is regrettable that *Frankenstein* is no longer shown with this tint.

In photography and setting, the makers of *Frankenstein* succeeded in building steadily upon the tragic air of gloom that so dominates the film. Only in the village itself is there a touch of cheer and brightness, and this is quickly dispelled by the sudden breath of horror which converts the hamlet into a village shadowed by fear. The gaily decorated streets become cold and forbidding, the people move fearfully and silently. Even Castle Frankenstein is a bleak and oppressively overpowering medieval fortress. The doctor's tower laboratory is a perfect setting for the creation of a monster. Cold, forbidding, it is a stone finger pointing the way to hell. On the ground floor is the heavily barred stone cell in which the monster is first imprisoned. A narrow winding stairway leads up through cold and unadorned walls to the workshop at the summit, filled with the mysterious equipment which has become standard for every mad scientist. Even so apparently innocent a structure as a windmill lends itself to the unrelieved gloom of atmosphere. It stands gaunt and alone on a high, barren hill against a backdrop of scudding clouds.

All the roles were well played, although to the audiences of today it may seem that at times melodramatics rests too heavy a hand on the performers. (Clive, in the ecstasy of his success, is sometimes greeted with titters. This is no reflection

[5] It is still occasionally used. Tinting was beautifully applied in Todd-AO's filming of *South Pacific*, in which particularly sensitive scenes faded out through sold colour – pink for love scenes, lavender for scenes of Bali Ha'i, etc. William Castle, in his horror film *The Tingler*, used a frightening crimson for one of his most impressive scenes, involving blood running from the faucet, etc.

on his ability, but rather an indication of changes in acting style. Silent films were not very far in the past at this time, and the broad techniques of silent films had not yet been completely abandoned.) The casting of Mr Karloff as the monster proved to be a touch of sheer genius, for his performance remains today as one of the great classics of the screen. The role was, in later films, to be played by Bela Lugosi, Lon Chaney, Jr., and Glenn Strange, but none succeeded in reaching the superb heights of Karloff's artistry, and this is strongly attested by the fact that today, thirty-five years later, and although he has since performed finely in many roles not in the realm of horror, Boris Karloff is still the Frankenstein monster, the very epitome of evil. Karloff's monster was a fascinating and terrifying creature of tremendous strength and incalculable fury. His first appearance was a marvel of camera work, as chillingly impressive today as when first shown. Called into the laboratory by Dr Frankenstein, the monster slowly and clumsily walks through the narrow doorway of the dimly lighted room, his back to the camera. Slowly, he turns, and one heavy step takes him abruptly into the area of light. In complete and absolute silence – the constant din of modern sound tracks was, fortunately, not yet in vogue – the camera moves in abruptly for a series of startling close-ups of that hellish face. It remains one of the most frightening moments in screen history, and was doubly terrifying with the original green tint.

And the face itself is another indication of the brilliance of Karloff's portrayal, for his monster was not a walking dead man as he was, unfortunately, interpreted by other actors. The brow was ridged under a white forehead surmounted by the square head with its coarse black hair, the cheeks sunken in shadow. But the true horror of this face lay in its eyes – deepset, glowing eyes that blazed with fury and hatred. One look at those coldly murderous eyes and you knew that here was a creature of incomparable evil. In spite of his great size, the monster was tremendously fast, moving swiftly and violently; there was no escaping him. He was a whirlwind from hell itself, his enormous black body always in motion, the long black arms swinging at his sides, the powerful hands straining and reaching for the throats of his victims. He did not speak in this first film, expressing himself through a series of animalistic growls and cries of fury.

Yet Karloff was not a stereotyped, soul-black monster, for there were moments – as in Mrs Shelley's book – of a peculiar tenderness. To cause even a brief moment's feeling of sympathy for such a horrendous creature was certainly no easy task, yet Karloff carried it off extremely well. One such moment was the monster's first actual contact with sunlight. As he stands in the darkened laboratory, Frankenstein draws back the shutter covering the skylight, and golden sunshine streams down upon the hideous black form which had as yet never been touched by the purity of day. It is an entirely new experience for the creature, totally beyond his comprehension. Slowly, he raises his pasty face to this new wonder, narrowing his eyes in pain at the brilliance of this new element. Muttering low growls of amazement, he lifts his death-like hands and the long, surgery-stitched fingers try vainly to grasp the golden filaments of light.

His contact with the little girl who becomes his second victim is delicately handled. Happy in her play, the girl laughs and the monster responds. The thin black lips part, and the strange, rumbling sound that issues from the cavernous chest is somehow more frightening than his howls of anger and hatred. (The film here ran into censorship trouble. There was originally included a scene in which the monster hurls the little girl into the lake. This was thought too violent, and was cut. The scene as finally shown ended with the monster reaching for more flowers.)

This original Frankenstein film holds up remarkably well today, and is still frequently seen in motion-picture theatres and on television screens. The photography and direction remain classic. In some instances, the performances may seem somewhat outdated (in addition to Clive's creation spasms, Dwight Fry is sometimes guilty of excessive mugging, while the character of Elizabeth, Frankenstein's betrothed, is painfully stereotyped), but Karloff's performance remains a deeply moving experience.

The success of Frankenstein naturally resulted in a sequel.

Some four years later, the same studio released *Bride of Frankenstein* which in some ways surpassed the excellence of the first film.

Perhaps the primary reason for this success was that Mrs Shelley's original story was even more closely followed. The film opened, in fact, with an imaginary reconstruction of the famous gathering during which *Frankenstein* was conceived. Companions ask Mary (Elsa Lanchester) if the fire in the windmill (Mrs Shelley's original Arctic conclusion was abandoned for the flaming climax of the film) was really the end of her story, providing a firm basis on which to lay the sequel.

The monster, of course, did not perish in the fire. Before the flames could destroy him, he crashed through the floor into the water-filled basement. An elderly couple, parents of one of the monster's victims, stand before the flaming mill after the others have gone, determined to see to the complete destruction of the creature. The man falls into the foundation and is slain by the monster. With the aid of the unsuspecting woman (Mary Gordon), who believes the extended hand to be that of her husband, the monster, more horrifying than ever because of his burns, pulls himself from the ruins, throwing the woman after her husband. A servant of the Frankensteins (Una O'Connor) sees the monster and rushes back to the castle with the word that he still lives. When she is disbelieved, she washes her hands of the matter. The monster, meanwhile, pauses to drink and bathe his burned arm in a pool. (There is a touching moment when the monster views his horrible face in the still waters.) A shepherdess, seeing him, falls into the water. The monster rescues her, but he cannot still her cries of terror. Hunters approach and the monster is shot in the arm. The village is alerted and, in a beautifully macabre scene, the monster is pursued through a denuded forest and captured. Trussed like an animal to a pole, he is returned to the village and imprisoned in the jail, placed in a deep dungeon where he is heavily chained to an enormous thronelike chair. This, however, is no hindrance to his great strength, and he escapes, taking refuge in the hut of a blind violinist where, for the first time in his brief, violent existence, he finds warmth, understanding and freedom from fear and persecution. The old man lives alone and, being blind, is unaware of the hideous visage of his visitor. The monster takes up residence with the old man who, believing some unfortunate accident has deprived the monster of speech and left on him the terrible scars he can feel with his sensitive fingers, teaches him to talk. The idyll is shattered when a traveller (John Carradine) enters the cottage. A violent battle follows, and the cottage is set afire.

The monster flees into a deep catacomb in the cemetery, where he comes across Dr Praetorius, an unscrupulous scientist who has managed to create miniature life on his own and has failed to secure Dr Frankenstein's support.[6] It is Praetorius who first puts into the monster's mind the thought of a mate. Frankenstein again finds himself facing his evil creation, who now demands a woman to end his loneliness. Frankenstein at first refuses, but is forced to agree when his bride, Elizabeth, is abducted. A woman is brought to life. When she faces the monster who is to be her mate, she becomes hysterical with fear. The bitter truth bursts upon the monster – that he is an atrocity doomed forever to a life of loneliness. He bids Henry and Elizabeth to leave the laboratory and, his eyes – filled now with sorrow – fixed upon the recoiling form of the newly created woman, he pulls a lever which destroys the laboratory, Dr Praetorius, himself, and the new-made Eve.

In addition to a strong story line, this second film contained all the ingredients which had made the original so successful.[7] There was the fine direction of James Whale, imaginative settings by Charles Hall, the superb camera work of John Mescall. The opening scene in the storm-threatened drawing-room set the air of terror which was sustained throughout the film. The actual story began with several flashback sequences from the original film, which aided the continuity of the story. The basic performers remained the same. The addition of the late

[6] Presentation of Praetorius's miniature figures – a queen on her throne, a lustful Henry VIII, a cardinal, etc. – placed under glass jars was a jarring and rather ridiculous touch.
[7] Michael Egremont wrote a novelization of *The Bride of Frankenstein* that appeared in England in 1936. Never printed in this country, the book has become a rare collector's item.

Una O'Connor, even at this early date the queen of hysteria, as a nerve-torn servant, was a pleasant and not disturbing touch of humour. The evil Dr Praetorius was superbly played by Ernest Thesiger, one of the finest of horror performers.

The name of Boris Karloff now had considerable meaning to moviegoers. The chills of *Bride of Frankenstein* began even before the film itself opened when, to the accompaniment of appropriately sombre music, there flashed on the screen the single word: KARLOFF.

The script of this second film provided Karloff with possibilities of performance of far greater depth and emotional impact than in his first film, and he took full advantage of this. At no other time did the monster seem so human or so nearly sympathetic. The scenes in the fiddler's cottage present a sensitivity never again achieved by a horror film. He learned to speak, in a deep grumble that seemed to come from some labyrinthine depth somewhere in his enormous body. For the first time, he showed sincere affection for a human being – the blind violinist, the only human who ever treated him like a man. This most peculiar relationship, between the huge, clumsy, hideous monster and the frail, gentle, white-bearded old man, provided the highlights of this film. This was probably the only time the expressions of gentleness were to cross the face of the monster. Sitting in the hours of early evening on a small stool at the feet of the kindly old man, smoking a cigar, listening to the fiddler play sad, gentle airs on his violin, the monster even sheds a tear.

During this period of calm and quiet life, the monster clearly revealed the existence of better qualities, and possibility of a useful life if only he had been properly received. This indication was never to appear again.

The climax of the film provided the last sympathetic note ever seen in the long cinematic career of the Frankenstein monster, and it was beautifully played. The monster sits beside the cowering woman, his hands extended, pitifully pleading with her not to be afraid, then realizing at last the hopelessness of the situation. As he stands with his hand on the lever of destruction, gutturally ordering Frankenstein and Elizabeth to 'Go!' the monster seems suddenly a pitiful representation of

The most memorable female in horror films: Elsa Lanchester was the Woman created as the unwilling mate of the Monster.
The Bride of Frankenstein **(Universal Pictures, 1935)**

the failure of man to understand. In this moment, above all, the basic, underlying philosophy of Mrs Shelley's work was realized.

There might be some criticism of the fact that the monster spared the lives of Henry and Elizabeth to provide a happy ending (for all but the monster, of course; monsters may live forever, but not happily!). Certainly the monster had no

reason to feel kindly towards his creator, and possibly Mrs
Shelley's conclusion of their death at the hands of the monster
may be somewhat more logical and dramatically acceptable,
particularly when we consider the violent history of the monster's previous actions. But perhaps something might be said
for the film's conclusion. Did it not at least give a final touch
of nobility to the monster, and place the responsibility for the
failure of the Frankenstein experiment squarely where it
belonged – on man himself?

The female creation of Dr Frankenstein was also perhaps a
bit of a Hollywood touch. Played in an interesting fashion by
Elsa Lanchester (also seen as Mrs Shelley in the prologue) this
very brief appearance was an impressive one. Her movements
were spastic and confused, her understanding of this new life
incomplete. She spoke nothing, for she lived only long enough
to realize the full horror of her proposed mate. She could not
have been termed attractive, but no one could doubt that she
was, nevertheless, a bit too good for her intended companion.
Perhaps Dr Frankenstein had increased in skill, or perhaps
Hollywood simply could not envision a completely horrifying
woman, even if man-made. (Times have changed here, too!)
The long white face bore the livid stitches of surgery, as did
the hands with the incredibly long and tapering fingers. The
hair was a peculiar frizzed pyramid standing out stiffly from
her head, composed of alternate swatches of black and silver;
one might almost think it was standing up from fear. She was
dressed in a long white bridal gown. This may have been quite
appropriate, considering she had been brought to life as a bride
(the sound of wedding bells at this juncture could also have
been omitted), but only Hollywood would have Dr Frankenstein go to such trouble for the creature he feared and despised. (Of course, something had to be done, for in Mrs
Shelley's book the woman makes her brief appearance in the
nude.) The woman's reaction to the monster – she rears back
and hisses almost like a serpent – was superbly done.

After a period of another four years, in 1939, a third film
titled *Son of Frankenstein* made its appearance. There were
several changes of casting in this continuance of the Frankenstein legend. The monster was still finely played by Karloff,

but Dr Frankenstein himself had passed away – supposedly repenting the horrors which had arisen from his unselfish quest for knowledge – and it was now his son, played by Basil Rathbone, who became enmeshed in the tangled skein of the creation story.

While this latest film also had much to recommend it, it did not quite measure up to its predecessors. It was quite evident that the story was beginning to wear thin, and the writers were in trouble.

After many years abroad, the son of Henry Frankenstein returns to his native village with wife and young son, determined to take up residence in the ancestral castle. They are met at the village railroad station – in, of course, a heavy downpour, in the dead of night – by fear and distrust, although he constantly assures the people, and the one-armed prefect of police, that he has no intention of reviving the horror of Frankenstein. However, while rummaging through the ruins of the blasted laboratory, never rebuilt after the monster had destroyed it, the young heir discovers that the monster has not died, after all. Rescued from the ruins by one Igor, he has lain in a secret chamber beneath the laboratory, in a comatose state. Igor is described as a former shepherd who had been condemned to death for the heinous crime of grave-robbing. Although the village succeeded in hanging him, they failed to bring death to Igor. His neck was broken, but he did not die. He lived on, secure in the knowledge that the law would not permit the village to hang him a second time. He has lived through the years in Frankenstein Castle, occasionally sending the monster, during his brief periods of returned strength, into the village to murder, one by one, those who had sentenced Igor to hang. Apparently the monster implicitly obeys him. The son of Frankenstein determines to destroy the monster once and for all, but the fires of creation run as swiftly in his veins as they had in his father and, prompted by the urgings and threats of old Igor, he begins experiments to restore his father's miracle to full strength.

Terror enters the lives of the Frankensteins when it is learned that their young son has been playing in his bedroom with a friendly giant, dressed all in black, who comes to him through the wall. Both Frankenstein and the prefect of police – who, as a child, had an arm torn from its socket by the monster – realize what this means. The Frankenstein monster is walking again. This also explains the mysterious series of deaths in the village. Frankenstein, however, refuses to admit his rejuvenation of the monster, until his child is found in possession of a gold watch given him by the giant and bearing the inscription of Frankenstein's valet, who has disappeared; the body is later found by the prefect in one of the secret passageways in the castle walls. The villagers, convinced that the monster has been returned to life, march on the castle where, in the meantime, using the secret passageways for cover, the monster has taken the sleeping Frankenstein child from his bed and carried him to the laboratory. He is here confronted by the prefect and Frankenstein. The monster drops the child to the floor and a battle follows, during which the monster finally falls to his death into an open pit of boiling sulphur.

This story quite obviously borrowed nothing but the original idea from Mary Shelley. There was no attempt at psychological understanding in this third film, as there had been in the other two. This film was intended as plain horror and, for the most part, succeeded in its aim. Here again, there was fine atmosphere, excellent direction, camera work and performance to lend the needed touches of horror. For the last time, Boris Karloff appeared in the role he had originated, and again he provided a performance of depth and intelligence, although the role demanded less than in the second of the series. Bela Lugosi made the first of several Frankenstein appearances in the role of Igor (he was next to essay the role of the monster himself), giving his usual impressively chilling performance, and the late Lionel Atwill (who became one of the standard mad scientists) lent his authority to the role of the one-armed prefect, with a disconcerting habit of snapping up his wooden arm to hold his monocle.

There were several alterations in detail. The castle of the Frankensteins was not the same structure as shown in earlier films. There was, perhaps, too much of a Hollywood touch in the enormous, cavernous and gloomy structure, with its shadowy, vaulted ceilings, a wooden stairway fit more for a giant than normal men, long, frighteningly dark corridors and catacombic, frigid bedrooms. It provided an effectively morbid and dreadful setting, even if it was not necessarily authentic Transylvania.

The character of Igor, shepherd turned grave-robber, was an addition to the Frankenstein cast of characters. Igor appeared once again in the next film, *Ghost of Frankenstein*, when his warped brain was placed in the skull of the monster to replace that damaged brain which had caused him to lie in a comatose

The Monster (Bela Lugosi) leads Lawrence Talbot (Lon Chaney, Jr.) to Frankenstein's journal. Compare Lugosi's bloated features with Karloff's far more terrifying visage.
Frankenstein Meets the Wolf Man (Universal Pictures, 1943)

state for so many years. (Before his next destruction, the monster spoke briefly with the voice of Igor.) Igor's rather frightening role in this film was, however, of extreme importance, providing a logical explanation for the saving of the monster from the laboratory blast. With his broken neck and his habit of sitting in the tower playing weird and plaintive tunes on a recorder, Igor also added a further element of horror. Perhaps this was another indication that *Frankenstein* was in trouble; it was the first time two monsters had been considered necessary.

With respect to the monster himself, this film offered some highly significant points. As the younger Frankenstein stands with Igor over the comatose creature, he expresses surprise that the monster should have survived the numerous disasters of his life. Igor then points out that the monster cannot die. Thus did the creature achieve immortality, and thus did the studio provide itself with a convenient peg on which to hang the numerous later resurrections of the monster. As a result of the laboratory explosion, however, the monster appeared to have suffered severe damage to the brain cells, which sapped him of a considerable amount of his enormous strength and vitality. Although, for a brief time, the scientific knowledge of Dr Frankenstein restored these qualities to the brute, through a major portion of the film the monster lay in a deathlike sleep. He was destined never fully to recover from the effects of the blast in which his mate had perished and which, apparently, also cost him the power of speech, for he never again uttered more than grunts and growls. He was never again to display the sheer animal strength and fury which had become synonymous with his name, and the chief efforts of all followers of the second Frankenstein were devoted to attempts to restore his strength, efforts which never quite succeeded. As a result, the impact of horror which had become a byword with the name of Frankenstein was largely lost.

In *Son of Frankenstein*, we also see the last attempts to depict the monster as something other than a soulless, heartless and practically mindless beast. In the restored laboratory, after Frankenstein has brought the monster back to consciousness, we have a touching and poignant moment which, briefly, presents a slight reminder of the artistry of earlier films. Frankenstein places the monster before a highly polished mirror in which he can see himself; the monster's reaction to his hideousness is a pathetic one. He draws young Frankenstein to his side and compares himself with the handsome, dashing scientist. An expression of terrible sadness crosses the creature's face. With a low growl of sorrow, he turns the polished surface to the wall.

In his treatment of the small son of the new Frankenstein, a boy of about four years, the monster also revealed – and, for the last time – those swiftly disappearing attributes of warmth and compassion. He made use of the secret passages within the castle walls to gain access to the boy's bedroom, and there sat playing games with him. To the audiences of the thirties, the picture of this hideous creature playing games with a young boy – although never shown – was a particularly frightening one; unfortunately, to present-day audiences it is more likely to stir amusement. The monster even presented the boy with the gold watch of the murdered valet, a gesture of friendship certainly uncommon on the monster's part. At no time did he injure the child, this scion of the hated Frankenstein family, and the small boy, with the inherent trustingness of children, felt no fear of his ugly, ungainly playmate. When the monster finally carried off the youth, through the mysterious passageways to the demolished laboratory, he was careful to see that no harm came to him, and the child seemed to enjoy the excursion, even lifting his hand to aid his strange friend up a ladder. The monster did not take advantage of the opportunity to drop the boy into the sulphur pit, and when he himself was attacked by Dr Frankenstein, the boy was placed out of harm's way. The later monster was not capable of such feeling.

Son of Frankenstein did not end the cycle of films based on the monster of Mary Shelley, but was the last of the series to make any attempt at artistic merit. *Frankenstein* now lost its status as serious entertainment. While there was in later films an occasional gleam of satisfactory horror, largely as the result of atmosphere, the films were lacking in depth, perception

In a publicity still not in the film, the Monster (Bela Lugosi) attends a conference between Talbot (Lon Chaney, Jr.) and the gypsy Maleva, played by the marvelous Maria Ouspenskaya.
Frankenstein Meets the Wolf Man (Universal Pictures, 1943)

and imagination. One became almost a carbon copy of the other.

When Boris Karloff, after the third film, announced his retirement from the series, Lon Chaney, Jr., was thrown into the breach. His *Ghost of Frankenstein* was the weakest of the series to date, marked by one brilliant, unforgettable scene in which the monster stands on open ground and survives – even enjoys – the attack of one bolt of lightning after another. It was apparent, however, that without Karloff, there must be an additional lure. The answer was an additional monster or two.

Frankenstein Meets the Wolf-Man, which we have already

examined, was the first step in this direction. The sole purpose of the film was to bring the two monsters together for the titanic struggle – well staged – and destroy them again. Much of the atmosphere remained – the crumbling castle, the gloomy village, etc., but in other respects the film fell far short of its predecessors. There were none of the deeper undercurrents which had placed the earlier films above the rank and file of horror productions. The truth was, Frankenstein was finished. Never again was the monster alone considered sufficient horror for a film; he had lost his pre-eminence. He had lost Mary Shelley and Boris Karloff.

In *Frankenstein Meets the Wolf-Man*, with Lon Chaney, Jr., as Lawrence Talbot, the monster was played by Bela Lugosi. His hammy performance lacked all the depth, the fury, the sheer animalness of the Karloff characterization. This, of course, may have been the fault of writing and direction, rather than performance. It is strange that so fine a horror artist as Lugosi made such an atrocious monster (and Chaney, as a matter of fact, was not much better). Even the make-up was sadly lacking, and Lugosi's own features were obvious.

The monster became a clumsy automaton, incapable of swift movement, walking slowly and heavily with outstretched arms reaching for his victim. Through most of his later films, he lay in a coma, to be revived only for his destruction at the film's end. He was immensely powerful, but his slowed movements and delayed reactions made escape not too difficult, and thus much of the horror was gone, also diminished by alteration in facial appearance. Where Karloff's monster was a nightmare with its sunken, shadowed cheeks, thin, cruel lips and hate-blazing eyes, the later monster had chubby cheeks and dead eyes and the face of a mindless somnambulist rather than a vibrantly living, evil creature. Karloff's monster was a being of deadly cunning; the beast of Lugosi and Strange seemed to have lost all power of thought as he had of speech.

House of Frankenstein was next in the series. The monster and the wolf-man, after their fierce battle, are frozen into ice. Karloff, travelling with a chamber of horrors featuring the actual skeleton of Dracula, determines to resume the work of Frankenstein. He removes the stake from the heart of

Dracula (John Carradine) and restores him to life until he is destroyed by a ray of sunlight. With the aid of a hunchback whom he has promised a straight body (J. Carroll Naish), Karloff revives both the wolf-man and the monster. Talbot (Chaney, of course) is still seeking a cure from his lycanthropia. The monster (Glenn Strange) goes amok, Talbot is slain by a silver bullet fired from the hand of 'one who loves him enough to understand', the hunchback is thrown from a window of the castle and the monster and Karloff disappear in quicksand.

House of Dracula was written along similar lines. In this one, the evil scientist was played by Onslow Stevens, but the remainder of the cast remained the same, although the hunchback promised a straight body is a girl. Dracula, strangely revived, appears for a cure (all the monsters suddenly wanted one) but is again destroyed, burned in his coffin. Stevens and the werewolf find the monster in the dried quicksand of a seaside cave. Stevens revives him, again promising to help Talbot. But he has been turned into a vampire by Dracula and becomes an evil, mad scientist. He kills the hunchback girl and is in turn killed by the monster, who perishes in a fire, while Talbot, cured at last of his curse, goes on, we hope, to a better and happier life.

While possessing a certain amount of atmosphere and interest through continuance of the legends, these two films were trivia, merely attempting to crowd as many monsters as possible into the first film and to dispose of them for the next.

Although the original monster had finally found his long overdue rest,[8] the ancient family of Frankenstein was not through with monster-making. The efforts of Henry's film descendants were not on a par with his own great achievement. In *Frankenstein 1970*, Karloff appeared as his own future descendant and produced a monster swathed like a mummy, sporting a head covering like an overturned garbage can. A later film, *I Was a Teen-Aged Frankenstein*, presented a young monster with the face of a narcotic addict's nightmare, the

---

[8] We will overlook the film in which the monster and the wolf-man took time off from horror to disport with Abbott and Costello.

The Monster (Glenn Strange) topples the combustible chemicals
that will turn Dr. Edelmann's laboratory into a funeral pyre. This time
there will be no resurrection; it was the last film in the series.
House of Dracula (Universal Pictures, 1945)

flesh a mass of twisted and contorted putty reminiscent of a
child's construction with a lump of clay, with one eyesocket
empty, the other with an eye glaring and half falling from
the face, the nose a flat lump with two nostrils, the mouth a
twisted scar with a few broken teeth, all surmounted by wisps
of straggly black hair. All this was mounted on the beautiful,
powerfully formed body of a young football star. The film
has often earned the distinction of being called one of the
worst horror films ever made.

In the late 1950s, Hammer Studios in England attempted
a revival of the Frankenstein legend, but the two films were
not comparable with the great Karloff films of nearly three

decades before. As with the Hammer Dracula series, these films were in colour, superbly mounted, well photographed, directed and performed, but, unfortunately, lacked in both story content and true atmospheric horror.

These films discarded Mary Shelley's story in favour of a new approach; only the theory of creation was retained. The monster in no respect resembled the creature played by Karloff, and this was a disappointment to the many Frankenstein admirers. Of course, this is not to say that Karloff's monster (which, in turn, in no way resembled the creature described by Mrs Shelley) provides the only correct and accurate portrait, but his characterization has for too long been accepted as the monster *par excellence*. The creature of the English productions – played by Christopher Lee, later such a superb Dracula – was tall and lean, but not physically deformed. There was considerable horror in the white, scarred face, but the imagination of the make-up artist had got a bit out of hand. The original monster was far more manlike than this English version and, consequently, more terrifying. As has frequently been stressed in these pages, it has long been the fault of horror films to rely almost completely on the effects of make-up to create horror, and, with this in mind, the make-up artist has created monsters more and more hideous, but less and less human in appearance. Karloff had, of course, the benefit of superb make-up artistry, but the greatest impact of horror resulted from the actor's characterization and facial expression. He was hideous, he was horrifying, but, distorted though his features may have been, he still had the face of a man. The eyes were in their proper place, the nose and the thin lips were not twisted out of shape. There were no scars, save those of surgery. The monster of these later English productions was different in every respect. With a finely made body came a face that was twisted, the eyes distorted, heavily scarred and only incidentally human. He revealed no emotion, no facial shadings, and there was no attempt at true characterization; the monster was merely a peculiarly unpleasant and powerful machine of destruction.

The setting for these later films was also a mistake. There was here no brooding, cloud-enshrouded castle with dark passages and secret panels, no sharply etched portraits of bare stone and shadow, no storm-clouded skies. Dr Frankenstein lived and worked in a beautiful, sumptuously appointed mansion of plush furnishings, thick carpets and velvet drapes, an atmosphere far more conducive to thoughts of romance than the chill of horror. Technicolor also, as previously mentioned, is not always as successful as stark black and white in creating that air of evil and foreboding which is the very life of horror films.

This is not to say these British productions were without merit. If they had been presented as new horror films, without the direct connection with the famed Frankenstein, they would have been more enthusiastically received. There were several fine moments of horror – one remembers particularly the tremendous fear and suspense of a scene in which the inquisitive servant girl breaks into the doctor's laboratory and explores among the vials and test tubes while the monster creeps up on her – or the appearance of the thickly bandaged, inert and lifeless beast in an enormous tank filled with preservative fluids, awaiting the injection of life – but these were simply not Frankenstein films as the public has thought of them for the past generation and more. The monster finally crashed through the skylight of the Frankenstein laboratory and was, supposedly, dissolved in a vat of acid. There was no attempt to revive him; a new monster was created for the second film.

The superb Frankenstein tales are deserving of new productions with the new, improved techniques of movie-making. That classics of horror can be remade was proven by the Hammer Studios themselves with their superb Dracula films. *Frankenstein*, however, is quite another story. As Dracula, Bela Lugosi gave a fine performance in the role of a particularly evil man, and the very fact that the vampire count appeared as a man, in spite of his supernatural origins, and not a creature created by the arts of make-up, meant the role could be essayed by other capable actors in their own interpretation. Karloff, however, as the monster, presented, in effect, an entirely new species of life. He was its Adam, its first and last representative. A man should be a man, and a

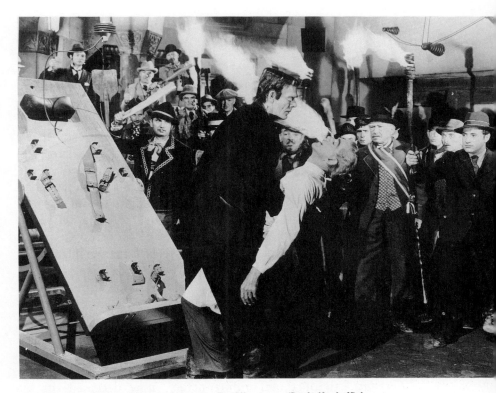

The Monster (Glenn Strange) grasps Dr. Niemann (Boris Karloff) to carry him into the bed of quicksand where they will both disappear. *House of Frankenstein* (Universal Pictures, 1944)

monster should be a monster. Karloff is the monster, and no other form of monster is fully acceptable. It would be interesting to see a remake of the first two – possibly three – of the Frankenstein films, with the monster shown – both physically and emotionally – as he was originally portrayed.

Yet, perhaps even this is not quite the answer. The original Karloff films have suffered but little through the passing of the years. Perhaps it would be best, as in the past, merely to re-release these superb old films again and again and let the audiences delight and shudder to the prime examples of genius in the world of cinematic horror.

7

There have, of course, been other tales of monster-making, both in literature and on the screen, although none of them succeed in acquiring the brilliance of Mary Shelley's novel. Robert Louis Stevenson's famous tale *The Strange Case of Dr Jekyll and Mr Hyde*, which we shall examine in a later section, presents us with a somewhat different method of the creation of a monster, a method considerably simpler than that used by Dr Frankenstein, but also far more dangerous to the creator. Jules Verne's story *The Clockman* is a delightful concoction of witchcraft, superstition and monster-making in which an enormous clock in the figure of a man comes to life and wreaks various kinds of havoc.

Since the introduction of the Frankenstein films, the mad scientist has become somewhat of a staple with motion-picture audiences who like a few chills with their viewing. Generally the scientist has been portrayed by Bela Lugosi (*The Ape Man*), Lionel Atwill (*The Mad Doctor of Market Street*), Ernest Thesiger (*Bride of Frankenstein*), George Zucco (*The Flying Serpent*) – all of them, unfortunately, now deceased – or by Mr Karloff himself. *Island of Lost Souls*, from the story *The Island of Dr Moreau* by H. G. Wells, presented a rotund, polished and frighteningly evil Charles Laughton as the mad scientist on a strange island filled with even stranger characters. The story had a bit of a switch on the creation of monsters, for Mr Laughton – with the aid of science, a religious creed and a powerful bullwhip – took the wild animals of the island and turned them into rather peculiarly monstrous men, one of whom was Bela Lugosi. The film, filled with creeping jungle, black tropical nights, flickering torches and howling animals, with the new creations constantly gathering to proclaim 'Are we not men?' possessed a high level of horror.

The Mad Ghoul presented mad scientist George Zucco with the evil ability of converting the handsome and totally unsuspecting David Bruce into a particularly loathsome monster, a ghoul who requires human hearts in order to live. These

A New Zealand wrestler named Kiwi Kingston (here with Peter Cushing) presented a different Monster; the Karloff features were a Universal copyright.
The Evil of Frankenstein (Hammer Films, 1954)

hearts were generally secured from freshly buried dead, although at times Zucco was not so particular as to the condition of the victims. The film had some highly satisfying moments of horror: the opening, under Zucco's direction, of a freshly dug grave with the ghoul going to work on the corpse with his scalpels, etc. The ghoul was another triumph of make-up. The resemblance to Mr Bruce remained, but the flesh of the face and hands became loathsomely dry and wrinkled, the eyes vacant and expressionless. He became a non-thinking automaton, much like the Frankenstein monster, completely under the evil power of Zucco, and awoke from his periods of horror once again himself, with no knowledge of the terrible crimes he had committed. Zucco, of course, finally becomes a ghoul himself, and Bruce is released from his horror by a bullet well aimed by Turhan Bey.

The mad scientist has become a little madder in recent years, and his creations have not been very satisfying. He seems to be concerning himself these days with not so much the creation of life but experimentation with already existing life forms. Such things are generally accomplished with strange serums, turning women into hornets, men into alligators, creating giants and pygmies and various other unwholesome creatures. The ultimate was achieved in the excellent Vincent Price film, *The Fly*, in which a scientist managed to change heads with the insect of the title, to the ultimate destruction of them both.

The most successful monster of recent years – and one who came closest, in appearance, to the true monster of the Frankensteins – was presented in what must basically be considered a science-fiction tale, Howard Hawks' production of *The Thing*, based on a story by John Campbell, *Who Goes There?* (The title of the film was actually *The Thing From Another World*, shortened for marquee purposes.)

The basic story of *The Thing* is a very simple one. A flying saucer crashes near the North Pole and members of a nearby army base rush out to investigate. Their efforts to preserve the saucer, sunk into deep ice, fail, but they find the form of one of its passengers embedded nearby. The form is cut out of the ice and returned to the base for examination, where it comes to life and wreaks murder and various kinds of havoc. The creature is found to be a vegetable and extremely difficult to kill, since bullets are merely absorbed by the cabbagelike tissue, and destroyed limbs merely regrow. It is finally broiled by electricity.

The film achieved a very high level of horror, the result of tight scripting, brick direction, fine performances and excellent atmospherics. It was not without its flaws – the dialogue was at times too precisely clever, there was the injection of a totally irrelevant and somewhat uncomfortable love story (at the North Pole!), the ever-present wisecracking newspaperman could easily have been omitted – but such minor distractions could be overlooked in the general excellence of the production. The creature, played by James Arness, somewhat resembled the Frankenstein monster; again, the greatest evil comes in human form. He was thin and unusually tall, had long arms, and was completely hairless. Always kept partially

Dr. Neimann (Boris Karloff) and his assistant Daniel (J. Carrol Naish) are about to stumble upon the comotose Monster (Glenn Strange in his first appearance in the role).
House of Frankenstein **(Universal Pictures, 1944)**

in shadow, his face was never clearly shown, yet his tall form dominated the story, a towering and implacable menace.

The tension of the apparently losing battle against the infamous creature builds beautifully, and there were several superb moments of horror from the discovery of the creature to his final destruction as, along a dimly lighted corridor, he moves closer and closer to the beleaguered scientists, only to be struck by cracking electricity and slowly melted into nothing. When brought back to the base in his block of ice, the creature is kept under heavy guard in a refrigerated room. His features are discernible through the ice, his open eyes staring as though fully aware of what goes on about him. Finding this disconcerting, the guard carelessly tosses a blanket over the chunk of ice, not realizing the blanket is electric and in full operation. The ice slowly melts and the Thing is released from his cold imprisonment – the creature's feeding habits are revealed when the bodies of two scientists are found in the greenhouse, hanging head down, drained of their blood. The Thing is trapped in the greenhouse. Heavily armed, the humans gather before the door, while tension mounts. The door is swung suddenly open to reveal the Thing standing directly before them. With a roar of fury, the monster reaches out for them. His hand is caught in the swiftly closed door, and his vegetable fingers snap off. His abrupt appearance before the opened door – the closest look, brief though it is, of his face – is one of the most frightening moments in the film.

8

A cold wind rises from the hills that surround the infamous Castle Frankenstein. A peculiar moaning sound issues from the dark ruins, and we attempt to comfort ourselves with the assurance that the wind has found an opening in the bleak stone. Night, the strange and terrible night of Transylvania, is falling and in the village below us an occasional light appears. A blackness more intense, more frightening than the dark of night, has settled upon us. There is no sound in the village, neither of music nor of laughter. Happiness deserted

this corner of the world many years ago, and has never returned. An errant breeze enters the deserted laboratory where
we stand, and an eddy of dust twists in contorted agony until
it settles once again.

The Frankensteins are gone. The once-honoured family has
crumbled in hatred and disgrace. There are no inquiring scientists of the family to carry on the great and disastrous work
begun by Victor von Frankenstein. The monster, too, is gone
– or so the villagers fervently hope. They have hoped so often
in the passing years, but always that hellish fiend has returned. Will it be so again?

We do not care to enter the castle again, for if there is any
time when ghosts will walk in that blasted pile of crumbled
stone, it is now, when the mysterious night has fallen and the
silver orb of the moon revisits these scenes of unparalleled
horror. Perhaps the wraithlike form of Victor Frankenstein
sits this very moment in the dust-covered library, mourning
the bride he had lost on the very morning of his wedding, his
mind thronging with the countless victims of the monster's
hatred. Perhaps he is not alone – perhaps in that dark corner,
silent, massive, inscrutable, stands the hideous form of the
creature which he, in his knowledge and his ignorance, brought
into being – standing with his eyes blazing with unending
hatred and fury, the thick black lips drawn into a stern line
of cruelty, the sewn hands trembling slightly in remembrance
of the warm throats about which they had once closed.

We walk swiftly down the narrow, neglected path back
into the village, wondering if there is not in us all something
of the Frankenstein monster, something of his loneliness, his
battle against rejection, his heartbreaking cry against the un-
fairness of life. We leave Castle Frankenstein to the ghosts of
the young scientist and the greatest creation in scientific history – the creation he called a man but which the world called
a monster.

THE MUMMY

'And the body was carefully anointed with the proper incantations to the gods and a strip of perfumed linen wound about each joint and the body was placed in the desert tomb to find eternal rest. . . .'

A brilliant white moon, larger and brighter than it is to be seen anywhere else in the world, slowly raises itself over the lip of the desert sands and begins its night-long journey across a sky of deep black velvet sprinkled with diamonds so bright as almost to hurt the eyes. The vast empty desert becomes a blanket of warm silver, and the broad band of the river, by day a muddy, unhealthy brown, becomes the colour of silvered ink.

And then the long beams of the moon strike the sloping sides of the Great Pyramid and turn it into a monument of blue-white pearl.

We are in a very different world now from the wild, fog-choked mountain forests of Transylvania, the home of the vampire, the werewolf, the Frankenstein monster and other unnamable creatures of darkness. But other lands, too, have their horrors and here, in the fiery desert sands of Egypt, marked here and there by some crumbling testament of the glory of a long-vanished age, we will find horror as chilling, as terror-striking, as those with whom we are by now well acquainted, an evil much older than Count Dracula, who had fastened on the living like a blood-hungry leech for a mere five hundred years, an evil, a corruption from the very beginnings of civilization itself.

We enter the dark and silent tomb and the flickering lights of our torches seem to instil with life the brilliant postured paintings on the walls. There is the silence of death all around us. Thousands of years ago, there were others in this tomb, men dressed in long robes, moaning the liturgy of death as the huge stone sarcophagus was slowly borne to its final resting place. They are dust long since, those men, but we would not be too surprised to see them in the long, silent stone corridor that stretches before us. In spite of the hot, fetid air, we shiver a bit, not with the coldness of climate, but with the chill of fear.

For we are here to find the Mummy.

2

As Transylvania is the ancient home of horror, so is Egypt the original home of mystery, and the golden sands of the desert still conceal – in spite of the archaeological explorations of the last century – many of its deepest, darkest secrets. For five thousand years, during a good portion of which most of the world was sunk in the ignorance and poverty of darkness and barbarism, the shores of the Nile were the site of a great and powerful civilization which has seldom been surpassed. The pyramids, the Sphinx, the temples of Abu Simbel, Deir el Bahri, Luxor, Karnak, Thebes, Akhenaten, Cheops, Amenhotep, Nefertiti, Rameses – these names of monuments which still amaze the traveller today, of cities abandoned for millennia, of persons long since fallen to dust, still evoke strange and mysterious pictures to all who hear them. In spite of its recent awakening to the modern world, Egypt today remains one enormous mausoleum – a vast, sunbaked, sand-choked museum of the past.

One of the most mysterious and fascinating aspects of this great civilization was the burial of its dead. In light of the numberless tombs, graves and monuments which pockmark

Another memorable Boris Karloff characterization: Imhotep, revived
3700 years after his burial alive in an Egyptian tomb.
The Mummy (Universal Pictures, 1932)

the Egyptian countryside, it is not surprising that the Egyptian
of dynastic times is often thought of as a somewhat morbid
and morose individual considerably over-preoccupied with
thoughts of death. This, however, is far from the truth. Surviv-
ing documents and artifacts indicate that the ancient Egyptian
was, in fact, a rather carefree, life-loving individual with a
very healthy respect for the pleasures and delights of living,
particularly luxurious living. The wealthy Egyptian surrounded
himself with comfort and beauty just as do the wealthy of
our own time, and it was with the greatest reluctance that he
abandoned the luxury in which he lived. It was, indeed, this
very aspect of love for the good things of life that caused such

intense importance to be placed on the tomb.

The Egyptian firmly believed in a life after death, a life which was a direct counterpart with, of course, certain improvements, of life on earth. This paradise of life in another world was, however, assured only as long as the Egyptian's body and his resting place remained inviolate. With the destruction of his corpse, and the luxuries interred with it, this wonderful Elysium vanished. It was for this reason that the Egyptians erected for themselves mastabas, pyramids, labyrinths and other impressive tombs, all of them constructed in such a way as to be either impregnable or undiscoverable. The more wealth and power a man managed to amass, of course, the more he was assured in the next world, and the more important was his tomb. This was of particular importance to the pharaoh who, after death, joined the ranks of the gods of Egypt – providing his tomb was secure. This vanity on the part of the pharaoh reached its climax early in Egypt's history when Khufu erected the magnificent Great Pyramid. Such burials, of course, were beyond the means of the common people; the wealth and the power of the pharaoh, his family and the various nobles of his court, was indicated by the wealth of the burial. The more common folk often buried themselves close to a pharaoh's grave in hopes of sharing in his deathly glory.

Of equal importance with the inviolability of the tomb was the permanent security of the body itself. The most fabulously appointed tomb, the most carefully concealed grave, would be of no avail if the corpse itself were to fall into decay and dissolution. This preservation of the body was greatly assisted by the dry, desert air of Egypt, but this was not guarantee enough. To be doubly certain that the body would be able to withstand the encroachments of time, the Egyptians resorted to an elaborate and most successful process of mummification. Much of this process – so remarkable that the bodies of pharaohs buried four thousand years ago remain intact and facially identifiable today – is known to us, but there are various important aspects which have become lost through the centuries.

Sir Wallis Budge, formerly of the British Museum, has left us a graphic description of the process of mummification.[1]

First step in the process was the removal of all parts of the body which might be subject to decay and cause general desiccation. The internal organs were removed and placed in large canopic jars, which were later buried in the tomb with the body itself, generally at the foot of the sarcophagus. The process of actual embalming which then followed is believed to have taken anywhere from forty to seventy days, each step accompanied by appropriate religious rites. The mummifier covered the body from head to foot with ten perfumes, giving special care to the head itself. This was done twice. Appropriate prayers followed, and then the entire process was repeated. The backbone was then immersed in a sacred oil and the face turned to the sky. Bandages were laid upon the backbone. Gold, silver and precious stones were placed upon the corpse. The nails of the fingers and toes were gilded with gold, and portions of the fingers enwrapped in sanctified linen. A priest was then called to conduct ritual ceremonies upon the head, which was then partially bandaged. The mouth and face were well oiled and bandaged, together with the ears and the nape of the neck. A sacred bandage was placed in two pieces over the head, and over each ear and nostril and cheek was fastened a strip of linen. Four pieces of linen went over the forehead, two on top of the head, two outside the mouth and two inside, two more over the chin, and four pieces at the nape of the neck. This brought the proper number of twenty-two pieces of linen to each side of the face.

The bandaging of the body itself began with the left hand, which was placed upon a strip of linen. A ring was passed over the fingers, and thirty-six oils and perfumes were applied. The hand was then bandaged with linen prepared in six folds, bearing drawings of the gods. The same was then done with the right hand.

Next step was the rubbing and anointing of the soles of the feet and the thighs. Each toe was wrapped in an individual piece of linen, and linen inscribed with drawings of the gods was placed on each leg. Flowers, oils, perfumes and jewels were placed in the bandages, and the legs and trunk of the

[1] *Egyptian Magic.*

body were then wrapped.

It can thus be seen that the wrapping of a body for mum-mification was not a process of merely winding long linen strips about the body, as is so often believed. Each member was treated separately, preceded and followed by long prayers and invocations to the various gods. Placed at frequent inter-vals within the wrappings were jewels and precious stones.

The well wrapped and perfumed body, now in the traditional form of a mummy, was placed in a wooden coffin carved to represent the human form; this was, in turn, en-closed in another slightly larger coffin. In some such burials, there were as many as three or four of these coffins, each laid within the other like boxes in a Chinese puzzle. In later dynas-ties, such as in the burial of the young Tutankhamen, a gold and jewelled mask was first placed over the head and shoulders of the mummy, and at least one of the coffins was of solid gold. The final sarcophagus was made of stone, carefully and ingeniously sealed so that it was almost impossible to reopen.

The body was now ready for interment in the tomb – the low, many-chambered mastaba of the early dynasties, the impressive pyramid of the time of Khufu, or the rock-cut tomb of the Valley of the Kings during the days of the Amen-hoteps. The tomb was very richly and sumptuously prepared, the walls beautifully painted with incidents of the decedent's life, filled with rich furnishings and treasures to make life in the hereafter more comfortable and familiar to the lost pharaoh.

The pharaoh was placed in the tomb, the tomb was sealed and, it was hoped, forgotten. The deceased ruler had gone to his reward, he had joined the ranks of Osiris and Amon and, so long as his tomb and his body remained inviolate, he would, in even greater measure, enjoy, in the life he had found in the beyond, the luxuries and the pleasures he had known while yet he occupied the powerful throne of Egypt. Nations may rise and fall, Egypt itself may be conquered, liberated, conquered again, but always the Nile would flow along its time-honoured course, bringing life and sustenance to an otherwise parched land, the desert sands would continue through time immemorial to blaze under the burning sun, the

Imhotep's linen wrappings were inherited by Tom Tyler, marking his only appearance as Karis in a new mummy series. George Zucco was the High Priest.
The Mummy's Hand (Universal Pictures, 1940)

pyramids would stand forever in their solitary, stony grandeur, and the pharaohs of this ancient land would sleep, secure and undisturbed, through the passing of the centuries.

But would they? The unfortunate truth is that very few of them really did. It is remarkable that, in all the startling discoveries of Egyptology, the many tombs that have been uncovered, the burial places that have been entered, only the tomb of one such pharaoh – a minor seventeen-year-old king named Tutankhamen – has been found intact. All others have long since been plundered, their riches despoiled, and the after-life of the pharaoh utterly destroyed.

For if they were nothing else, the tombs of these pharaohs were tremendous treasure houses of incalculable wealth. Here, buried with the kings, were gold, jewels, all the riches of the rulers who, while they lived, were the wealthiest and most powerful men on earth. Man was no different three or four thousand years ago than he is today – the lure of gold is ever-enticing, and man during the days of the great pharaohs had just as much respect for the yellow mineral as we do today. Even as Khufu, some five thousand years ago, was busily engaged in erecting his magnificent pyramid, he was given the unhappy news that the richly appointed grave of his mother, recently buried, had already been entered and robbed.

It is sometimes difficult to understand how the ancient Egyptian, living under the harsh influence of his religion and its countless gods, could have had the audacity and the courage to rob the tomb of a buried pharaoh, for such an act placed him under the curse of the gods he dreaded, destroyed his own hopes of a life after death and, of course, if he were caught in the act, meant instant and painful death. Surely the gold he gained by such spoliation was not worth the terrible risk. But it was. Once again, we can only say that man remains man in all times and all lands. The tomb robber of ancient Egypt, like the criminal of today, was always ready to take the chance in view of the profit that was to be gained. The possibilities of untold luxury and riches through the rest of his life completely overshadowed the more distant fear of what happens after death. It might also be pointed out that, even in Egypt, there undoubtedly were non-believers and atheists who would not be deterred by any thoughts of retribution in another life.

The tombs of the pharaohs, unless very cunningly concealed, were almost invariably plundered even before the mortar on the bricks had had a chance to dry. Extremely elaborate precautions were taken to preserve the inviolability of these tombs. There were labyrinths, in which it was hoped any would-be plunderer would become hopelessly lost, to die of thirst or starvation; masses of stone were built in the form of pyramids over the grave itself, with entrances carefully concealed; burials took place in secrecy, at dead of night, in some desolate portion of the Valley of the Kings. But all to no avail. Man's greed soon managed to unearth even the most closely guarded secrets of the dead kings. At various periods in Egypt's history, guards were placed at the tombs in the Valley of the Kings, but the plundering went on, often with the assistance of the guards themselves.

Profitable though it was, this grave robbing could not have been a very pleasant occupation. Let us follow two of these audacious thieves as they set forth in the dark, mysterious night, daring all the gods and spirits of ancient Egypt, their eyes gleaming with lust for gold.

On a dark and moonless night, the grave robbers cross from the right bank of the Nile to the left bank which, from time immemorial, has been the abode of the dead. All is silent, and the movement of the boat across the dark river causes scarcely a ripple in the silent, slow-moving waters. The men are dressed in dark clothing, even muffled to their eyes, to permit them to merge with the night. When their boat reaches the opposite bank, they gather up their tools and silently leap ashore, heading for the hills in which are buried so many of Egypt's dead rulers. There has been a recent burial: another pharaoh has been laid to rest and his tomb, cut deeply into the stone of the mountainside, is choked with gold. It was a secret burial conducted in dead of night, but there are no secrets from evil men with an eye to plunder.

Perhaps as they walk across the deserted, rock countryside, passing the tombs that mark Egypt's greatness, the gods of their ancient land walk beside them, bringing an added chill to the night air. Horus, the hawk god, brushes them with his wings; Osiris glowers at them from the mountain-top, and Toth himself stands ready with his stylus to inscribe their names on the rolls of the dead.

But there, in that little declivity, beneath that shadow cast by the rugged rock, is the tomb they seek. There rests the mighty king, surrounded by gold and semi-precious stones, sleeping through eternity in the midst of wealth beyond the wildest imaginings of those about to seize it.

The grave robbers finally approach the entrance of the tomb. Perhaps they hesitate for the briefest moment when

they see inscribed like an ominous warning on the cold stone
the cartouche of the dead pharaoh, sealing the door of the
cavern in which he lies in hopes of eternal bliss. There is a
curse etched over the doorway, calling the damnation of
Osiris on any who dares defile this final resting place. The
pause is only momentary, however, for the curse of Osiris
will only come after thirty years of the luxurious living to
be gained by entering this tomb. That bridge is to be crossed
in the far distant future.

With a single blow, the cartouche is broken and falls in
pieces on the desert floor. The stone shatters with an explosive
sound as if the pharaoh himself were crying out in protest
against such desecration. The noise rings loud and clear across
the still night air of the mountainous desert, and for a moment
fear touches them again. Somewhat nervously, they laugh at
their own panic. They are alone in the desert, and there is
none to hear them – none, that is, but the dead.

From the moment they enter the tomb, the grave robbers
know they have found riches to allow them ease the rest of
their lives. The room in which they stand is a fairyland of
gold – gold couches, chests, chairs, vases, caskets, the wealth
of a lifetime. Opposite them is yet another door in the wall
which, they know, leads to even greater riches. Eagerly, they
set to work upon this door, smashing, tearing, destroying. Their
lights fall on three couches of wood, encased in gold, a rich
throne of gold, set with semi-precious stones that gleam like
the eyes of evil in the flickering light of the torches. There is
a life-size statue of the late pharaoh, glittering with gold;
there are golden statues of the gods. Everywhere there is gold;
they are in a yellow world, a fantastically wealthy and
precious world. Here are the greatest wonders of the world.[2]

Yet one more chamber, and when they enter this, again
the ever-present gleam of gold. But there is more here. In the
very centre of this inner chamber, dominating the room,
seeming, by the flickering light of their torches, to grow
larger and move closer and closer to them, is the great stone

[2] This and following descriptions are based largely on the find-
ings in the tomb of Tutankhamen.

sarcophagus of the pharaoh himself.

The grave robbers are silent now as they stand beside the sarcophagus. The chamber is lighted by the flickering fire they hold, and the dark shadows are discomforting. Are they shadows, or are they, perhaps, something more? That dark form there in the corner, which seems to loom above them, ever closer, then back again, is it the shadow cast by that statue or is it really the shade of the dead pharaoh, carefully watching this despoiling of his tomb, waiting for the proper moment to strike? With trembling hands, the thieves reach out and touch the cold stone wherein lies the body of the man to whom all this wealth belongs, the man whom they are about to rob not only of gold and jewels, but of eternal life itself. Again, the cold wings of Horus brush against their perspiring faces.

They shrug off these strange fears and set about the difficult task of opening the sarcophagus. The lid, after much cursing and straining on the part of the thieves, is raised at last and, with a heavy crash that echoes and reverberates from wall to wall, falls to the floor, raising a cloud of choking dust. They bend close and see the coffin itself; at its head is painted a portrait of the king. In the firelight the freshly coloured eyes seem to be staring up at them, accusingly, hostilely. Quickly, they remove the coffin lid and fall back in amazement. For beneath this wooden coffin is yet another, of solid gold, glistening in the firelight. Here again is the etched face and the entire form of the great pharaoh, and from head to toe he is clothed in gold set with precious stones. With trembling hands, straining at the enormous weight of gold, the grave robbers remove this last, tremendously wealthy coffin, setting it carefully on the ground. For a moment they gaze at it in wonder, running their eager, trembling hands over the rich yellow surface. Here alone is enough gold to keep them wealthy for the rest of their lives. With the other golden furnishings in this tomb, they will be richer beyond their wildest dreams!

There is one more step. This is not all. Once their greed has been stirred, there will be no stopping them until they have it all. They know that within the linen wrappings of the mummy itself, there will be much wealth – gems, precious stones, more

easily disposed of than the golden statues. They cannot leave
without these.

They turn and look again into the open coffin. More wealth
meets their eyes, for covering the head and shoulders of the
mummy is a glittering, jewel-encrusted golden mask. This, too,
is carefully removed and placed on the floor beside the golden
coffin. Already, there is enough gold here to bring untold
wealth to a hundred men!

Now comes the most difficult and unpleasant operation –
the stripping of the mummy itself. Even the greediest, hardiest
Egyptian must quail before such a task. It is unpleasant enough
to touch the form of the dead, but when that form is the
body of the pharaoh, the great and undisputed master of the
world, a very god, then, surely, there is reason for hearts to
tremble and spirits to fail. Only the thought of the riches
enclosed within those winding bandages is enough to make
them go on.

The mummy lies now uncovered in the last coffin, and the
light casts dark shadows from the sides of the coffin upon the
still white form. The unsteady illumination seems almost to
have restored the power of movement to the dead king, and
he appears to be about to rise in protest at the humiliation
and desecration to be given him at the handling by two of so
lowly a caste. The pharaoh lies on his back, his arms crossed
at the breast, the body tightly wrapped in broad bands of still-
white linen. A strange, musky odour rises from the coffin. It
is the scent of death.

For the last time, the grave robbers hesitate. The tomb,
abode of the dead, is silent save for their troubled breathing.
The gods of ancient Egypt seem to be standing about the
mummy with them, waiting, ready to strike them down if
they profane with their touch the sacred body of the pharaoh.
Outside the tomb, the darkness of night still enfolds the desert
and its mysteries. Perspiration gleams brightly on the fore-
heads of the thieves; fear has added its discomfort to the heat
of the sunbaked tomb.

A trembling brown hand reaches for the white corpse, and
the fingers touch the linen strips, feeling beneath them the
sacred body of the deceased ruler of Egypt. A low moan seems

Lame and half-blind, Karis (Lon Chaney, Jr.) needed only his one strong arm to dispose of his enemies in the endless search for his lost Princess.
The Mummy's Ghost (Universal Pictures, 1944)

to reverberate through the stone cavern, and the thieves desperately try to convince themselves it is caused by a sudden breeze out on the desert, blowing through a slight fissure or opening in the tomb. They move quickly now, for they are frightened, anxious to secure the jewels and leave this place of death with their plunder. Quickly, fumbling, breathing in strained gasps, they unwrap the linen strips from the body of the dead king, pausing every few seconds to lift out some precious jewel concealed by the wrapping, until there is a small pile of priceless, glittering baubles on the ground beside the coffin. The body of the pharaoh himself comes into view, and the hot, stifling air is suddenly flooded with the perfume of the spices used in the embalming.

And now, only the head remains. The naked body of the pharaoh lies completely exposed to their view, profaned, dishonoured. They have not yet been stricken dead for their great crime, and with this comes greater courage. With a slight chuckle of defiance, one of the thieves unwraps the linen about the face. He cries out and falls back. The eyes of the pharaoh are open and staring at him.

And the screams of the two thieves are carried by the wind across the empty, barren waste of desert and lost.

3

There is no horror like that which comes from the grave. We in our time are as much preoccupied as were the Egyptians with thoughts of life after death. People of all lands, regardless of the advance of their civilization, have always been unwilling to believe that death means an end. There must be something more, something beyond, or life itself has no meaning. All religions and peoples have their own defence against so pessimistic an attitude. The body, we are told, may die, but man has an inner something called the soul, which lives on in a state of bliss (depending, of course, on the kind of life one has led) and is, at the final judgment, reunited with the body. The Buddhists believe the soul is born again in another form, again dependent upon the life one has led, while the Egyptians believed the dead join the galaxy of the gods.

Yet we still fear death. Perhaps this is because we cannot escape a certain doubt about this future bliss, or, perhaps, we cannot conceive of a life without the body. Death is too final, too great a change. Physically at least, the dead are dead and so they remain. Any other thoughts are too intense, too profound, for our complete understanding. We find horror in the thought of the dead living again, moving, walking, speaking, even if this walking dead happens to be a loved one. The dead are dead, and that is an end to them. They are placed in the ground, and it is against all the laws of God and man for them to rise again. The dead cannot walk. It is against reason, against logic, against the ordinary course of things.

We scoff at the thought of ghosts. We believe firmly – or so we say – in the existence of that tenuous entity called the soul, which does not perish with the body but lives on eternally, yet we staunchly believe that this soul cannot, under any circumstances, take on either form or substance. This is a ghost, and we all know there are no such things, in spite of the almost overwhelming evidence to the contrary. Once a person is placed to rest in his grave, there he remains, save for that nebulous soul which goes 'somewhere', either heaven or hell, to live on, but always unseen, until it is reunited with the body at the last judgment. But two things are certain – the soul can never return to earth to become a ghost and a dead body can never move again.

And yet, most of us have a dread of cemeteries. Scoff though we may, there are few who would care to spend a quiet evening, particularly about the hour of midnight, in a lonely graveyard. There is nothing that can harm us in a cemetery, since the dead are dead but, well, all the same, we'd rather not, thank you.

Stories of walking dead take various forms. The strolling horrors in the tales of Edgar Allan Poe were generally victims of premature burial. The West Indies have their own gruesome legends of the walking dead in the tales of zombies. Dracula, with his host of vampires, is merely another aspect of the dead who cannot rest in their graves, while the ordinary ghost story seems simply another side of the same coin.

But there is a particular horror about the walking dead of Egypt. In spite of the fact that it may have lain mouldering and fallen into dust in the desert sands for several thousands of years, the Egyptian mummy is a rather frightening figure at best. The dead, after all, should be subject to decay, and there is something not quite Christian about a body which remains intact through so many centuries. The appearance of a mummy, lying white and rigid in its regal posture, arms crossed over its breast, wrapped from head to toe in its white linen bandage, is somehow far more disquieting than the sight of an uncovered modern corpse. The paraphernalia of a mummy's burial – the always mysterious and unknown desert, the tomb cut deep into the rock with the stone passageways but inefficiently lighted by flickering flames of a torch, the mass of the pyramid, concealing secrets forever unfathomable, the gold and the jewels, all these have surrounded the mummy with an air of romance and mystery which a simple Christian burial in a green hillside cemetery could not possibly create.

And then there is the matter of the curse. Every self-respecting mummy is the custodian of an ancient curse, dating back to the time of entombment. Generally this curse takes the form of an invocation to the great god Osiris, god of resurrection, or to the great Amon-Ra, king of the gods of Egypt, to bring violent and sudden death and destruction to all those who dare to enter and defile the tomb of the great pharaoh and thus destroy his chances for immortality. It is difficult to say where the idea of this curse first originated, for it has little foundation in fact. The thought, however, of revenge striking from an ancient grave is a particularly chilling and appealing one and has been used to considerable advantage by writers of mysteries and romance.

From the early excavations of Sir Flinders Petrie, father of modern Egyptology, in the last century, the tombs and treasures of Egypt have held an intense fascination for men. It was not, however, until 1924 that Egypt's ancient past took a firm hold on the imagination of the general public which, aided in the past few years by a series of highly readable books on Egyptological excavation, it has never lost. It was in this year that the expedition of Howard Carter and Lord Carnarvon uncovered the fabulous tomb of King Tutankhamen, known in his earlier years as Tutankhaton and known rather affectionately since 1924 as King Tut.[3]

---

[3] The discovery actually added very little to our knowledge of Egypt's past. Tutankhamen was a minor ruler of the powerful Eighteenth Dynasty, succeeding the heretic Pharaoh Akhenaton (Amenhotep IV), husband of the beautiful Nefertiti. Tutankhamen

The importance of this discovery lay in the fact that this was the first pharaoh's tomb to be found intact and not despoiled. From the moment of the young king's burial some twenty-five hundred years earlier, no one had gazed upon his mummy until the day Howard Carter opened his sarcophagus. The find was immensely, staggeringly wealthy. The public's interest was immediately captured.

There was also considerable talk of a curse. It was said that there was a legend carved in the stone above the sealed entrance, calling down the curse of Amon-Ra upon defilers of the tomb. In following years, whenever a member of the expedition died, lurid tales of the curse of the pharaohs appeared in the more sensation-hungry newspapers. All those who broke into the tomb of Tutankhamen are gone now, since they were rather well on in years when the discovery was made forty years ago, and it is rather likely that they all succumbed from natural causes due to advanced age, and not to the icy hand of a long-forgotten and neglected god of ancient Egypt.

And yet there is one rather curious tale of an ancient Egyptian curse which must be mentioned and which, in the words of Hamlet, 'must give us pause'.

The story is told by the brilliant artist-archaeologist Joseph Lindon Smith[4] as having occurred in January of 1909, and the event involved chiefly Smith, his wife Corinna and Arthur Weigall and his wife, Hortense; Weigall was inspector of antiquities for Upper Egypt.

It all had to do with the curse of Amon-Ra placed on the heretic Pharaoh Akhenaton. When, as Amenhotep IV, this young dreamer became pharaoh, he overthrew the worship of Amon-Ra and other gods in preference for his own god, Aton. He changed his name, deserted the age-old capital of Thebes and constructed his new capital which he named Akhetaton. He then obliterated the name of Amon-Ra from all tombs and

reached the throne probably at the age of thirteen years, dying four years later.

[4] *Tombs, Temples and Ancient Art*, edited by Corinna Lindon Smith.

Hammer Films resurrected Karis in the impressively tall Christopher Lee, who in the following year would assume Bela Lugosi's cape as the new Dracula.
The Mummy (Hammer Films, 1959)

temples, persecuted the priests and brought Egypt close to disaster. When Akhenaton died, probably murdered, Amon-Ra was restored and the heretic pharaoh was placed under the god's curse, his body and soul condemned to wander forever without rest.

Smith decided it was time, after some three millennia, to raise the curse and permit Akhenaton to find rest. The Smiths and Weigalls determined to write and enact a playlet in the Valley of the Kings, in which, through the intercession of Queen Tiyi (the mother of the pharaoh), the curse of Amon-Ra would be removed. Hortense Weigall would portray Akhenaton, Corinna Smith would be Queen Tiyi and Joseph

Smith would appear as Horus, the hawk god; the play was
written by Smith and Weigall. It would be presented at nightfall in the Valley of the Kings, and present would be the leading Egyptologists of the day.

Trouble started early. A single rehearsal, which began well,
was planned three days before the performance. Smith was
quite serious about his little play, and full costumes were provided, even a musician for background effects. The playlet pro-
ceeded smoothly until the moment when Mrs Weigall, as
Akhenaton, made her first appearance. With the first utterance
of Akhenaton's lines, there was suddenly a tremendous burst
of thunder, brilliant flashes of lightning, and a fierce, howling
gale swept down the valley. The rehearsal was stopped and,
in a few moments, the sudden storm passed, after which
Smith and his party resumed their acting. The climax
approached with Mrs Smith, as Tiyi, beginning the beautiful
Hymn to the Aton, believed composed by the pharaoh himself. At the opening lines, a second storm of tremendous fury
swept into the valley, dropping hailstones upon the party,
together with heavy clouds of dust from the desert. Un-
daunted, Mrs Smith continued with the blasphemous hymn;
with her final words, the rain and hail ceased.

That evening, Mrs Smith complained of pain in her eyes,
while Mrs Weigall suffered cramps in her stomach. These ill-
effects were blamed on the sand- and hailstorm.

In the stuffy heat of that night in Luxor, both women were
visited by peculiar dreams. Mrs Smith found herself in the
temple of Rameses II, standing before one of the giant statues
of this pharaoh who had constructed the Ramesseum in honour
of Amon-Ra. The statue seemed to come suddenly alive and
struck Mrs Smith in her eyes with the flail in his right hand.

To the discomfort of the entire party, it was later learned
that Mrs Weigall had experienced an identical dream, save for
the fact that the flail of Rameses had struck her in the
stomach. Both women spoke with extreme discomfort of the
expression of vindictive triumph in the eyes of the 'statue'.

The following morning, both women were severely ill. Mrs
Weigall suffered extreme abdominal pain, and one of Mrs
Smith's eyes was nearly closed. Mrs Smith visited an oculist,

who could not determine the nature of her ailment. The condition worsened until her sight was despaired of and she was rushed to a Cairo hospital. Mrs Weigall, too, was soon hospitalized with a nearly fatal abdominal operation. Arthur Weigall suffered a nervous breakdown and Mr Smith was the victim of an exceptionally severe attack of jaundice. Of the cast of the proposed play, only the musician escaped illness, but his mother, arriving at Luxor, fell and broke her leg. Three other members of the audience, who had arrived early, suffered sudden attacks of illness.

The play was never given; plagued by these sudden attacks of near-fatal illness, Smith and his party abandoned all plans. The Egyptologists who had been invited – including Howard Carter and Sir Flinders Petrie – destroyed their invitations.

What happened to the Smiths and Weigalls may have been merely a series of coincidences. The sudden storms, the peculiar dreams, the illness – perhaps all these have a quite rational explanation. Or perhaps it was something more. Perhaps Amon-Ra, the great god of Egypt, is not dead, but merely sleeps. Perhaps he resented this daring attempt to lift the curse which he had placed upon his desecrator three thousand years ago.

Such is the particular spell of the tombs of Egypt. One of the first and still most readable stories concerned with the horror of the mummy appeared in 1917, some years before the remarkable discovery of Tutankhamen's tomb. This was the long out-of-print novel by Burton Stevenson titled *A King in Babylon*.

It is set in the early days of silent films, shortly before the United States entered the First World War. Movie producer Warren Creel, attempting to stave off financial collapse, comes across an original idea for a film story. He reads a poem by W. F. Henley, *A King in Babylon*, telling in five brief verses of the passionate love of a Babylonian king for his Christian slave, and his attempts to humble her, break her pride, and destroy her. Creel determines to film the story in Egypt, taking with him his wife, cameraman Billy (who narrates the story), an actress named Molly, and one or two technicians. The star of the film is the highly popular and handsome Jimmy Allen;

the female lead will be an unknown French actress named
Marguerite Roland, whom they are to meet in France. Also a
member of the party and an important member of the cast is
a particularly unpleasant papier-mâché mummy. The film is
to be shot at a small oasis outside of Luxor, where for several
years an archaeologist, who will serve as technical adviser,
has been working on some recently discovered ruins.

Trouble begins aboard the ship on its final stage of the long
journey to Cairo, where Jimmy and Marguerite meet for the
first time. Marguerite, for some reason unknown even to her,
becomes petrified with fear at sight of Jimmy, and only Creel's
persuasiveness convinces her to go on. As they leave by camel
train across the desert to their destination, a strange air of
uneasiness falls upon the company. Jimmy secretly complains
that during the night hours, as he lay awake on the desert
sands, something dark and shadowy seemed to pass before his
eyes, bearing with it the unmistakable odour of grave clothes;
he is convinced that something terrible, some unknown doom,
is following him.

At the oasis, a tour of the ruins with the archaelogist, Davis,
has a peculiar effect on Jimmy; he becomes highly agitated
and falls in a faint, blamed on the heat. Creel furnishes a brief
outline of the ambitious story. Jimmy is a modern archaeologist who uncovers the sealed tomb of a pharaoh. Within
the tomb, sealed behind an inner wall, is the body of a beautiful slave, whom the pharaoh had buried alive. Jimmy, the
archaeologist, is actually the reincarnated pharaoh; a series of
flashbacks will carry the story into ancient times and relate
the love story between pharaoh and slave, with its tragic conclusion. This double role necessitates Jimmy's appearing in
both modern garb and the full regal pharaonic robes. His first
costumed appearance as the pharaoh creates consternation in
the ranks of the Egyptian workers; he seems the epitome of
pharaonic splendour. When Marguerite appears in her costume
as the doomed slave, she carries with her the unmistakable
odour of the grave. The two performers fall easily into their
ancient roles, as though they had been born to the parts of
king and slave. Molly, with whom Billy is in love, tells the
cameraman of her growing sense of impending disaster, and

reveals that she has had an experience identical with Jimmy's
– a vague, grey shape hovering over her at night, bearing with
it the musty, desiccated odour of the grave.

Meanwhile, excavation at the ruins has also continued and
Davis finds an intact tomb. Creel utilizes the opening of the
tomb for the film. A small aperture, just large enough for a
man, is made in the door of the tomb and, while the camera
grinds, Jimmy, as archaeologist, enters. When the sequence
ends, Jimmy fails to reappear. When Billy, Creel and Davis
enter the tomb, it appears empty. A closer inspection reveals
a secret doorway, almost invisible. In the inner chamber they
find the large stone sarcophagus of the king; Jimmy kneels
unconscious at its head, his arms about the coffin. In the rear
wall, Davis finds another sealed door, on it a symbol of warning to prevent entry; he announces his intention of opening
this door at the first opportunity. As the four turn to leave
the chamber, a dim grey shape seems to pass before them,
knocking the light from Creel's hand.

Jimmy later tells Billy his overpowering feeling that this
was his own tomb, that someone had taken him by the hand
into the second chamber and ordered him to kneel at the
sarcophagus.

The filming, next day, of the live burial is almost unbearably
realistic. Marguerite fights desperately as the Egyptian extras
try to force her into the tomb, her fingers and teeth inflicting
considerable damage on several of them. She is placed in the
tomb, where she is later found in a coma. While Molly and
Creel tend her, the excited Davis opens the sarcophagus.
When the body of the mummy is seen, it bears a striking
resemblance to Jimmy, who then stuns the company by de-
claring that he is, indeed, the reincarnation of the pharaoh,
and Marguerite that of his murdered love. The mummy is his
own, and behind the sealed door at the rear wall they will
find the remains of the slave he had buried alive. But he insists
she is not dead even now, but has been waiting through the
millennia, waiting to punish him for his terrible crime.

Further horror awaits Billy that night. The coffin of the
dead pharaoh, with the mummy lying within, has been placed
in the tent for safe keeping. Waking during the night, Billy

sees a strangely phosphorescent shape arise from the coffin and glide from the tent, where it is joined by a ghostly shape from the tent of Marguerite. Jimmy is found again sleeping within the inner chamber of the tomb. He directs them to the back wall, insisting that the buried slave is very much alive. They press their ears to the wall and hear signs of movement. It is Tina, Jimmy says, trying to get out at him.

The next day Davis attempts to enter the secret chamber. Jimmy himself is present, carrying a long whip. He is tense, yet strangely exultant and determined. As the door is broken down, Jimmy calls out to his long-lost love, flicking his whip

Lon Chaney, Jr., played Karis in the later films. Like the Monster, he always met a spectacular end, only to be revived for the next production.
The Mummy's Tomb (Universal Pictures, 1942)

at the opening. Davis and Billy peer into the chamber and see
a mummy lying on the floor, dry and withered, dead beyond
a doubt, even though Billy claims to have seen the gleam of
two living eyes. When Creel peers in at the mummy, it has
changed its position. Jimmy bends before the opening and
looks into the dark, narrow tomb. With a slight cry, he moves
quickly back, bleeding from a gash in his cheek.

Later that night, Billy and Molly, seated together on the
fringe of the oasis, see the now-familiar cloudlike shape detach
itself from the ruins and head for the native encampment.
Hearing sharp cries from the native sector, they rush to the
campfire and find the men on their knees in terror, Jimmy
standing in the midst of them, whip in hand, while the dark
shape hovers nearby. The shape, suddenly bearing a striking
resemblance to Marguerite, dashes back towards the ruins,
with whip-cracking Jimmy following. At the very entrance
to the tomb, Jimmy is seen in desperate struggle with the
ghostly form, which apparently is trying to drag the actor
into the tomb. When the others approach, the shape breaks
free and vanishes into the tomb. Creel fires and the already
tottering structure collapses and seals the form inside.

Next morning Jimmy announces his intention of leaving
the company and setting off into the desert. He calls loudly
for Tina, and Marguerite appears. Together, they venture into
the desert and are never seen again.

A King in Babylon is quite typical of the many Egyptian
tomb stories so popular in the early part of the century.
Certainly it is not a classic of literature. It is written in the
rather naïve, goody-goody style of the period, when the
strongest printable epithet was 'Golly!' In its picturization of
Egypt and archaeological workings, it is amateurish and un-
scholarly; it is obvious that the writer had never visited such
sites. The tomb of the pharaoh and his buried love is found
somewhere out in the desert sands, far from any traditional
burying ground. Even the story's ideas are somewhat confusing, for the great days of Babylon had long vanished before
the appearance of Christianity, and the tomb-building pharaohs
of Egypt were dust long before the birth of Christ. Nor did the
Babylonian burial process in any respect resemble that of

Egypt. These inaccuracies meant little to the average reader, for it must be remembered that this book was written some years before the sudden interest in the scholarly aspects of Egyptology. The love story between Molly and Billy is embarrassing and irritating in its naïveté; not even the most innocent teen-ager of today would behave so childishly.

Yet much of the book remains of interest, and it is because it is a fine example of the blending of horror and Egypt, and because many of its elements appear in subsequent tales of its kind, that we have quoted it at such length. The ardent movie fan will be amused by the picture – and in this sense Stevenson is quite accurate – of moviemaking in this very early stage of the industry, when Creel's spectacular production was composed of a leading man and woman, one additional actress, a single cameraman and a few natives. In the aspect of horror, the story remains effective. A disturbing sense of foreboding pervades the work from the first shipboard appearance of Marguerite and her near-catastrophic meeting with Jimmy, and a chill lingers over the portions devoted to the work and incidents in the tomb. The frequent appearance of the mysterious grey shape comes like a cold hand of terror. The gradual preoccupation of Jimmy with thoughts of the past creates an uncomfortable impression. The opening of the tomb, the warning over the sealed door, the first sight of the mummy, the constant tug of war between the pharaoh and his slave which grows stronger through the passing centuries, these are all tried and true elements of mystery-horror.

4

A King in Babylon has never been filmed, but many of its aspects – particularly that of a love that does not die over the course of thousands of years – are present in the various mummy films of later years. First of these, *The Mummy*, of the early thirties, starred Boris Karloff in a simple tale of love and revenge which was also to serve as the basis of the later mummy films which starred Lon Chaney, Jr.

The story tells of an Egyptian of common birth, Imhotep,
who loves Princess Ankhesenamun. When she dies Imhotep
cannot reconcile himself to the loss. He enters the forbidden
temple of Amon-Ra, approaching the statue of the god. In a
small chest in the statue's base is the Scroll of Life. Imhotep
hopes to steal this, to restore Ankhesenamun to the living.
Amon-Ra, however, is not easily robbed. The stone statue
moves, and the flail in the right hand is turned on Imhotep
(strange parallel to the dream of Mrs Smith and Mrs Weigall).
Imhotep is seized in this act of desecration. His punishment is
to be buried in an unhallowed and unmarked grave, with none
of the ancient rites to grant him life in the hereafter.

This original incident of condemnation is shown in flashback. During the film, save for the terrifying re-awakening of
the bound mummy, Karloff appears as a wizened heavily
wrinkled magician, the undead Imhotep, determined to restore
Ankhesenamun to life. Dressed in a one-piece hanging garment,
topped with a fez, with his face a maze of wrinkles, he seems
phenomenally tall and incredibly evil. Those unforgettable
Karloff eyes burn with fury from a face that should have been
dead for some thousands of years. When the body of the
princess is taken to Cairo Museum, Imhotep kneels beside
her sarcophagus in dead of night, with the scroll, but is discovered and again fails in his purpose. In a young girl named
Helen, he sees the reincarnation of his lost love (*A King in
Babylon* again?) and attempts to impress on her knowledge of
her past. The girl calls upon the goddess Isis, who turns
Imhotep to dust, and the girl is saved.

The Mummy, seen too seldom today, is a highly effective
film. The story is carefully and accurately written and, though
much of its performance and direction are now out-dated, it
has the benefit of the reliable Karloff genius for horror.

Karloff made no sequel to this film – one of his first after
his début as the monster – and it was not for some years that
the mummy legend was revived, presenting Lon Chaney, Jr.,
with his most outstanding characterization since that of Lawrence Talbot, the wolf-man.

In the four films of this later cycle, only the original legend
was retained, the other aspects being altered to increase the

In the Cairo Museum, Imhotep (Boris Karloff) stares at the mummy of his beloved Princess. Karloff appeared as the mummy in only one film.
The Mummy (Universal Pictures, 1932)

angle of horror. Primary among the horror build-ups was presenting Karis as a traditional, bandaged mummy. The changes were not an improvement, and much of the effect of the original story was lost. In spite of this, and the fact that the four films were very similar to each other, it seemed for a time that the mummy would become the most popular – and most indestructible – monster since the creation of Dr Frankenstein.

An American archaeological expedition (headed by Dick Foran) finds the long-lost tomb of the Princess Ananka and with it the mummy of a man who had apparently been buried alive. The tomb inscriptions reveal this mummy to be that of Karis, who, through his love for the princess, dared defy the gods and, for punishment, was buried alive in her tomb. (The original legend was shown, as in the original, by flashback, using in at least one instance the original Karloff sequences.) However, it appears that the mummy takes very seriously his guardianship of the tomb and cannot die as long as the body of Ananka is in danger. He kills one of the professors and disappears. The body of Ananka is taken to a museum in the United States and the professor and his family settle down in a small New England town, laughing off the talk of a curse that is slated to befall those who defile the tomb of Ananka.

Meanwhile, in Egypt, the removal of the body of Ananka has caused consternation among the priests of the secret but still very active ancient religion of Amon-Ra. Karis, who has been kept alive through the millennia by the ministrations of this religious sect, has failed in his duty to safeguard the princess. The curse of Amon-Ra must be visited upon those who dared violate her tomb, and the body of the princess must be restored to the sacred hills of Egypt. This now will be the task to which Karis must devote himself.

The ancient high priest of Amon-Ra carefully instructs the neophyte (George Zucco) in what must be done. Here is born the famous matter of the tana leaves. Zucco receives a cask containing a large supply of these ancient leaves. In the full of the moon, with proper ceremony and callings upon the name of Amon-Ra and all the lesser gods of Egypt, and in the ancient vessel made expressly for the purpose, these tana leaves must be dissolved over a low fire and the resultant fluid fed to Karis. The fluid from three such tana leaves will keep Karis alive, while that of nine will give him movement and tremendous strength.

Zucco and his ancient charge journey to America and seclude themselves in the small Connecticut town where Foran and his family live, and where the body of Ananka is now on display to a gaping and non-believing public. Karis succeeds, through his tremendous, overpowering strength, in bringing death, one by one, to the members of the original expedition, but he fails in his attempt to return Ananka to her homeland. He is finally destroyed by fire (a favoured method of disposing of monsters).

But not permanently destroyed, of course. The surprising success of *The Mummy's Hand* made a sequel essential.

Some years later Zucco, now ancient and palsied, turns the destiny of Karis and Ananka into the hands of a vigorous, handsome young priest (Turhan Bey). Karis, badly maimed, still lives and thirsts for revenge and for the return of the princess to Egypt.

The small Connecticut town is now revealed to be the site of a small college. One of its students happens to be a lovely young girl from Egypt, who soon assumes a double importance to the story, for she is actually the reincarnation of Ananka.[5] The young girl already has a handsome young American boyfriend on the campus (Robert Lowery), but the high priest himself soon turns lustful eyes in her direction. (The gods of Egypt should have chosen someone not quite so virile or handsome.) The priest wrestles constantly with his conscience, praying to Amon-Ra to give him the strength to fulfil his great mission and not let nasty personal feelings interfere. The flesh, however, proves considerably stronger than the spirit, and it soon becomes his intention to take the young Egyptian girl for himself and, through the use of the tana leaves and the secret scroll of life, make both her and himself immortal. Karis can shift for himself.

But the whole idea does not at all square with Karis, who, perhaps, has lost some of his dangerous ardour during the passing of several thousand years, and can now devote himself completely to that mission which has been his reason for so extended a life.

Karis abducts the young girl on the priest's orders, but is closely followed by the young college boy who does not quite grasp the significance of what is going on. Learning of the evil plot of the high priest, Karis kills his protector. The girl who is, of course, beautifully gowned in a flimsy and revealing négligé, lies unconscious in Karis' arms as he carries her from his pursuers. In desperation, hoping to shake off the ardent young man and the aroused villagers, Karis heads for the swamps. As they move through the treacherous mud and

[5] Reincarnation is an integral part of all mummy stories. This is rather difficult to understand, for reincarnation is predominantly an Oriental belief which plays very little part in the religions of ancient Egypt.

undergrowth, the years catch up with the young girl and she reveals her true age. As the result of shock following a previous bungled attempt at abduction, the young Egyptian had suddenly acquired a white streak in her raven hair; her entire head becomes the colour of snow. The smooth young flesh of her shapely ankles and slender hands becomes dry and wrinkled and, at last, her face becomes that of a woman who has lived many centuries past her time. (The same sequence was used in the brilliant film version of *Lost Horizon* when Margo, as the young and lovely Lo-Tsen, dares to leave the sanctuary of Shangri-La.) The young lover stands in horror on the bank of the swamp as he sees the mummy Karis disappear into a bed of quicksand, carrying with him an incredibly ancient woman who bears no resemblance to the beauty he had loved.

The next resurrection of Karis became rather confusing. Apparently a good many years have passed. Strange murders are committed in a reclamation project of the bayou, which are blamed on a legendary mummy who had once disappeared in the quicksand. A bulldozer is put to the task of clearing a portion of the swamp and, in doing so, runs its large scoop over the dried mud of what had once been quicksand. The mummy woman, thus released from the burden of earth which has covered her, rises, coated with mud and slime, soon to perish. Karis, meanwhile, has been rescued by yet another high priest from Karnak, still determined, in spite of the apparently insurmountable difficulties involved, to restore the princess to her grave. Karis once again embarks on his career of violence and murder in search of the life-giving fluid of the tana leaves and in hopes of returning his ancient beloved to Egypt. He is, of course, foiled. Badly injured, near the end of his resources, Karis enters the secret crypt where, again, he has imprisoned a lovely woman. Here stands a flaming brazier in which are dissolving the sacred tana leaves so necessary to his survival. He has been pursued, however, by the young girl's lover. (All young girls have lovers in these films; the homely female without such a champion invariably expires.) The young man takes the vessel containing tana juice and casts it to the floor. Desperate, Karis flings himself to the stone floor and tries to lap up the trickling fluid, without which he cannot live. The hardy young lover then raises the brazier of sacrificial fire high and brings it crashing down upon the reclining form of the mummy. Karis disappears in a burst of flame.

(One question, however, is bound to plague the viewer from the very outset – how is it possible for a pair of mummies who disappeared in the quicksand of a swamp in New England to be dug out of the bed of sand in a bayou swamp?)

The various films on the love story of Karis and Ananka might easily have been compressed into one, for all were basically similar and did not reveal a wide range of creative imagination. The story line of Karis' attempts to restore Ananka to her original tomb was the subject of all the stories, and there was little attempt to inject originality into any of them, with the possible exception of the invention of the female mummy. Karis killed his victims by strangulation with his one superpowerful hand, and his course was unswerving in attempting to regain the body of his lost love, crashing through fences, railings and even the sides of barns. The slight variation of presenting a high priest young and handsome enough to develop lust for a young girl actually added little to the story, and was purely a Hollywood touch; it is unlikely that so dedicated and well trained a priest, particularly in so stern a religion as Amon-Ra, could have permitted himself to be so led astray. The story of a deathless mummy, thirsting for revenge and bent on a mission of ancient religion, offers considerable possibilities, but the writers did little to expand on it.

Yet these films were highly successful and, in spite of the flaws and lack of originality, managed to achieve several fine peaks of horror. The mere conception of an Egyptian mummy, supposedly dead for some thousands of years, prowling through the pure Americana of a peaceful New England countryside, is horrifying in itself, and this aspect was heavily stressed – the clean white homes of the Connecticut village, the farms, the sheriff's posse hunting down the monster, the fresh, youthful college students, the very air of clean wholesomeness clouded over by the foul breath from an ancient grave, with a horrible Egyptian mummy blundering in the midst of it all, made an incongruous and frightening picture.

The role of Karis was an unusual one for any actor. He spoke not one word in any of the films, another considerable change from the Karloff mummy, and, enwrapped as he was in the traditional windings of the mummy, his face was never seen (save in flashback sequences). Only his eyes gave life to the white face – eyes ablaze with purpose, fire and hatred. (Eyes are very important in the creation of a monster. The eyes of the Frankenstein creature were the most frightening part of his face, and Dracula's eyes contained considerable hypnotic power. Dead eyes, as in the later Frankenstein films, detract from the atmosphere of horror.) Karis was tall and powerfully built, the white bandages accentuating the strength of his frame. His step was long and slow, determined and inexorable, and there seemed no escape from the long reach of his white arm. (Monsters no longer move swiftly, as once they did. For some reason, a slow, relentless, inescapable pursuit has become more horrifying than a swift attack. The victim, supposedly, is too paralysed with fear to flee.) After his first death in the fire, the aspect of the mummy became even more frightening. His left arm had become paralysed and he carried it in a bent, immovable position across his chest. One eye had been extinguished, leaving an ugly wound, while the remaining eye appeared to blaze even more fiercely than before. Due to injury, the long, loping gait was gone; the left leg had shared some of the paralysis of the arm, and he dragged it behind him. The clean linen of his wrappings was dirty and torn, charred by the touch of the flames. He walked now more slowly, more stumblingly than before, but still with that deadly, unswerving purpose, his powerful right hand extended, the fingers reaching eagerly for the throats of his victims.

Karis provided Lon Chaney, Jr., with his most outstanding horror role since his earlier appearances as the wolf-man, and his performance provided another remarkable character in the galaxy of horror. He made of the mummy a terrifying powerhouse of vengeance and brutality, possibly the most impressive monster since Karloff's portrayals in the early Frankenstein films.

Outstanding among the performances, in addition to Chaney's, was that of the late George Zucco as the evil high priest of

Karnak, later as white and wrinkled himself as an unwrapped mummy, dressed in dark priestly gowns, his hands trembling with age and infirmity. Turkish actor Turhan Bey made an impressively handsome priest of Karnak while Dick Foran, before the unfortunate curse caught up with him, was a cool, efficient archaeologist.

The films contained several outstanding sequences of horror, aside from the standard but effective shots of Karis moving silently and purposefully through the moonlit Connecticut countryside, ploughing unhesitantly through whatever might be in his path, his one good arm ever extended, his foot and a loose twine or two of linen dragging behind him. The scenes of excavation in Egypt were handled in the traditional mys-

Karis (Lon Chaney, Jr.) was given life and movement from the brew of Egyptian tana leaves prepared by the High Priest, in this instance played by Turhan Bey.
The Mummy's Tomb (Universal Pictures, 1942)

terious manner, with insoluble rock-cut inscriptions, flickering torches, half-uttered threats of curses and hints of future evils. There were scalp-prickling scenes of the shadow of the mummy falling across the forms of lovely sleeping women – of the unsuspecting scientist finally solving the riddle of the hieroglyphic inscriptions and burning several tana leaves, just to 'see what would happen', while Karis, answering the ancient call for sustenance, moves ever closer, his murderous hand extended – of the mummy, his single eye ablaze with fury, grasping the throat of his victim in a vice of iron. Probably the peak of horror was attained with the resurrection of the female mummy – the movement of the dried earth after the bulldozer has cleared the ground, the withered hand appearing from the grave, the fingers reaching for the sun, then the dirt-encrusted form of the ancient mummy rising slowly and unsteadily from the ground, staggering and falling, but gaining strength from the sun the Egyptians worshipped.

Such scenes as these cannot fail to please the horror addict, and were largely responsible for the success of this cycle of films dealing with Karis and the lost Princess Ananka.

Hammer Productions of England, following their splendid colour revivals of Dracula and Frankenstein, also released a new technicolor production of *The Mummy*. It is extremely difficult to follow in the steps of successful characterization. Hammer learned this with their Frankenstein films, which were not as successful as might have been expected because of Karloff's permanent association with the role of the monster. This problem was not as great with respect to *The Mummy*, for the original films, while successful, did not have the impact of *Frankenstein*, which had begun the cycle of horror films thirty years before. And excellent though Chaney's interpretation was, it did not make as indelible an imprint in the mind of the moviegoer as had the monster of Karloff.

Nevertheless, *The Mummy* was somewhat of a disappointment. The locale was changed, of course, to England, but the basic story, of undying love, living interment, tomb despoliation and revenge, remained the same. The sexual angle was also retained, with Karis abducting a beautiful young girl.

Apparently, however, it was felt that modern audiences would not accept an unhappy ending, and the young girl was rescued, while Karis sank alone into his grave of quicksand.

Much of the atmosphere of horror, which the earlier films had captured, despite their numerous flaws, was lacking. This may have been due largely to the addition of technicolor (yes, we are again back with the proposition that horror is usually better in black and white) and the use of sets a little too sumptuous and elaborate. The original horror of Karis and Ananka struck simpler people, those of the middle classes, and it was easier for audiences to associate themselves with the inhabitants of a small Connecticut town than with the rich landed English gentry. It was considerably more frightening to see Karis enter the living-room of an average middle-class home than burst into the elegant drawing-room of a lord.

The monster was convincingly and powerfully played by Christopher Lee, and it is amusing to see swords thrust clear through him without putting a halt to his depredations, but horror in the black of night is always more horrifying than in well-lighted, brilliantly coloured surroundings. The scenes of the high priest bowing before the golden altar of Amon-Ra, of the discovery of the ancient tomb of Ananka, of Karis stepping from a beautifully painted sarcophagus, or bursting violently through a pair of French doors, provided moments of horror, but the scenes in the swamp are somewhat artificial and contrived. Karis, in fact, made his home in this film beneath the waters of the swamp and raised himself much in the same manner that Dracula (in *Son of Dracula*) made his appearance at nightfall.

5

The moon has set and the first brightness of dawn lightens the brilliant Egyptian sky. The long night is over and the shades of Egypt's glorious past return to their tombs. The Great Pyramid prepares for the influx of wondering tourists, all with a secret desire to carve their names on stone that has stood through the passage of history. The Sphinx stares coldly

**Karis (Christopher Lee) carries the reincarnated Princess Ananka
(Yvonne Furneaux) to a temporary death in quicksand.**
The Mummy **(Hammer Films, 1959)**

across the desert, mysterious, aloof, ignoring the rabble that
gathers about him as he had ignored the pompousness of a
Roman emperor and a French corporal. The Colossi of Mem-
non sit in silent, voiceless grandeur.

In their as-yet undiscovered tombs, the pharaohs continue
their eternal sleep, guarded by the ghosts of their attendants
and the dread curse of their gods. Perhaps in one of these lost
graves the priests of Osiris still pray to their never-forgotten
god. Through the towering columns of the Hypostyle Hall, the
shades of heavily robed priests still march in silent, solemn
procession. At the Ramesseum, great Rameses still grasps the
flail which can bring death to all who dare to desecrate his
temple.

But the violated tomb of Ananka remains vacant, stripped of its treasures, and Karis no longer guards what no longer needs guarding.

Our visit to the land of mystery is over. There are many horrors here, unseen and unsuspected, which may yet some day burst upon the world. For now, we will leave the desert sands, the graves, the tombs, the pyramids, to slumber on through further uncounted centuries.

And as we step from the dark grave to resume our voyage, there appears over the cliffs on the bank of the glorious Nile the brilliant, scorching rim of the sun, the great god of Egypt, great and glorious Amon-Ra.

THE WALKING DEAD

'A tall figure appears, walking slowly,
looking neither to left nor to right, his
eyes dull and glazed, filled with visions
of the grave. . . .'

There are horrors of the New World as well as the Old. The cold, windswept heights of Transylvania, the fiery desert sands of Egypt, these have their own peculiar horrors, and other portions of the world have theirs. We are still, now, in tropic climes. There is a strange stillness in the night which only the tropics can know. The same silver moon hangs like a pearl orb in the dark night sky but here, somehow, it seems brighter, closer, more intimate. The shadows cast on the ground are the gentle, curtsying forms of the palm tree, and there is a lush undergrowth. Here and there a raucous night-bird casts his challenge to the all-seeing single Eye of Night.

We stand in the dark shadow of a crumbled stone wall, built and destroyed during the violent days of the Conquistadores. We are waiting for our next monster. We may be excused a slight prick of fear, and the perspiration which causes our clothing to cling to us is not strictly the result of humidity. What we are now about to see is not fantasy, legend, superstition. It is truth. This monster exists.

Our eyes are caught by a slight movement at the bend of the deserted dirt road. Slowly, a slender form appears in the cold moonlight, walking silently in our direction. As the form

In the dark Haitian forests, villagers submit to the cult of voodoo. *I Walked with a Zombie*, directed by Val Lewton and starring Frances Dee and Tom Conway, is one of the true horror classics.
I Walked with a Zombie (RKO Radio Pictures, 1943)

comes closer to us, we feel the cold hand of fear begin to close about our hearts.

The creature approaching us is a Negro, tall and as black as the mysterious night. He is completely naked, and the light of the moon casts shadows on his glistening, muscular body. It is a body which proclaims strength, vigour, health. Yet when we raise our eyes and look into the face of this silent figure, we realize that this is the body of a dead man.

The face is a vapid, expressionless mask. The eyes stare lifelessly ahead of him, making no effort to pierce the velvety shadows of night. He walks with an unhurried, yet purposeful gait, his arms hanging limply at his sides, looking neither to left nor to right, seemingly oblivious of all about him. His eyes seem two vacant pools that mirror all the terrors of death.

We are on the mysterious dark island of Haiti, and what we have just seen is a zombie.

2

The horror of the zombie has its origin in a different world, a different time, on nights of terror resulting not from the supernatural but from man's ever-present greed and inhumanity. Two and a half centuries ago, Africa was still the Dark Continent. The vast, mysterious interiors were still untrodden by white men, and there were strange tales of impenetrable forests, mist-enshrouded jungle, tremendous mountains and mysterious plateaus, of strange tribes and horrifying customs. Africa was a frightening, immensely vast area whose riches were as yet untapped. Yet there was one source of wealth which the white man had already discovered, and his interest in the Continent at this time was confined to the merciless exploitation of this new source of riches.

This wealth presented itself in the form of the inhabitants of the areas known as the Gold and Ivory Coasts. There was already a voice raised here and there, declaiming that these peculiar, dark-skinned creatures were actually men, and should be treated as men but none took such talk seriously. The fact remained that these creatures, be they man or animal, subhuman or supermonkey, could be trained to work, and the hotter areas of the Caribbean, where the enervating heat made strenuous work difficult or impossible for the white man, was sorely in need of creatures accustomed to intense heat, who could be trained and put to work on the plantations of sugar cane. The so-called primitive beings of Africa served the purpose admirably.

So began one of the most shameful and horrible stories in the long and violent history of man – the African slave trade.

Once the white man had arrived, night brought a particular kind of horror to the coasts of Western Africa. Here, in the grass-hut villages, the natives lived in constant and deadly fear of the brutal pale-skinned beings from across the sea. In the midst of the quiet African night, he would appear, like some hideous spectral figure, whip in hand, and bring panic, horror and death with him. Grass huts were set afire and as the inhabitants fled from the flames, there were burly arms to reach out for them. Those who were too old or infirm to be of use were slaughtered; babies were torn from the arms of hysterical mothers and tossed back into the flames. The whip, the club, the fist were freely used in gathering together these two-legged animals. The African sky was turned red with the fires of the destroyed villages, and the jungle was torn with screams of fear and terror. Men, women, children, were herded into the Barraccoons, there to await the arrival of the slave traders to whom they would be sold. Families were separated, children taken from their parents, wives torn from their husbands, to await the greed of the hated white man who, after so many centuries, had suddenly discovered the wealth of Black Africa.

When the slave ships appeared off the coast, the captains and the slavers entered into negotiations for the sale and transfer of the slaves. Bewildered, confused, frightened, the natives were forced into the holds of the great ships, the hatches were battened down, and the long journey that was to take them far, far from their native villages, had begun.

Conditions on the slave ships were a nightmare greater than any horror created by the pen or imagination of man. The slaves were chained in pairs, lying side by side below decks. The area was often so small that it was impossible for them to move, or even to sit up. On some ships they were forced to lie in a curved position, the body of one fitting into that of another. There were no facilities for any kind of waste disposal, and the air became foul with the odour of filth and perspiration. The *Brookes* of Liverpool carried some six hundred slaves in this manner in an area a hundred feet long by twenty-six feet wide.[1] The journey generally lasted from six to ten weeks, during which time the slaves were permitted no movement. Once they had taken their places in the holds, the hatches were closed down upon them and kept that way

[1] John H. Spears, *The American Slave Trade.*

throughout the long journey, although occasionally, on a some-what more humane ship, the hatches might be opened for a brief period during the day to permit the flow of fresh air into the prisons; this was not popular with the crew because of the stench that arose.

Loss of life was tremendous, and the captains considered themselves fortunate to reach port with half the cargo still alive. Those who died in the holds were often left there for days, their suppurating bodies increasing the foul stench of these 'living quarters'. If any of the slaves attempted the release of death through self-starvation, the sailors smashed their lips and teeth and, by means of tubes, forced the food down their throats. Dead slaves paid no profit. Captains who experimented by permitting occasional periods on the upper deck to provide the slaves with fresh air and a measure of exercise soon stopped the practice when the miserable primitives indicated a predilection for throwing themselves overboard into the sea.

It is impossible for us to realize the abject misery and horror of these slaves. Uprooted from their homes, torn from their villages, placed like animals in the hold of a ship and embarked on the great ocean which had always been a source of fear and wonder to them, their superstitious minds must have placed them in some sort of limbo which followed death. Many of them became horribly seasick during the voyage, their vomitings adding to the stench and filth of their quarters, which were never cleaned. They knew not what their destina-tion or fate would be, they could not understand why these strange beings with the white skin should do these things to them. Mothers knew they would never again see their children, children cried frantically for parents who had either been slain or sold to some slave dealer. Their previous life had come to an end, and they had been catapulted into a world of which they knew nothing.

Their horror often transferred itself to the seamen of these slave vessels, and many a hardy sailor lived his life with terrible memories he could never lose. Through the long, lonely nights of the voyage, the ship was filled with the cries and lamentations of a people torn from their homes and forced into bondage. The air cried with sudden screams of loneliness, of fear and pain. The stink of the hold befouled the entire ship, and the seamen kept themselves as far as possible from the battened-down hatches. Food, of a kind, was lowered down to the slaves through small openings in the deck, and only the hardiest of the sailors could bear to be so close to this pit. Occasionally one of the hatches was opened and, like a foul miasma, the stench of the hold filled the air. A body was handed up to the men on deck, standing nervously with wet handkerchiefs covering the mouth and nose, and tossed unceremoniously over the side into the sea. Another animal had died, and the profits had been decreased.

The slave trade was not a business for philanthropists, and it is doubtful that many involved in the nefarious traffic ever had serious qualms about what they were doing. We have no record of any captain being softened by the screams of a mother being taken away from her children, and certainly no deckhand was willing to risk his position by displaying a touch of sympathy for the condition of the creatures in the hold. These slaves were not considered human beings, and therefore they were not treated as such. One looks after, to a certain extent, an animal from which a profit can be expected, and this was the extent of the concern of the slave traders. This was not an enlightened era.

Although the slave trade was outlawed in 1817, it did not put a stop to the practise, and many a Yankee New England family based its fortune on this trading in human misery. One of the last slave ships, the *Wanderer*, was a luxurious yacht owned by J. D. Johnson, a wealthy member of the New York Yacht Club, who in turn sold the vessel to Captain W. C. Corrie, another member of the club. No one would have believed that this magnificent schooner, flying the flag of the New York Yacht Club, was actually engaged in the slave trade, yet several cargoes were picked up in the Congo and delivered to Georgia and the Carolinas. The *Wanderer* was eventually seized by the Federal Government and, in 1859, Captain Corrie was erased from the roles of the Yacht Club.[2]

[2] *Ibid.*

Conditions after the banning of the trade became, if possible, even more inhumane. Should a slave-loaded ship be in danger of apprehension, the cargo was simply hurled into the sea, often attached to the anchor chain to prevent the bodies from surfacing.[3]

Once the slaves were landed in the Indies and placed on the market, a new kind of horror began. The agitations for improvement of slave conditions had not yet begun, and the master was accountable to no one for his treatment of his human property. Often they lived in chains, working all through the long day in the fields or the mills, poorly fed, subject always to the whip and scourge, and living in filthy, squalid mud shelters in the open, fully exposed to the elements. No thought was given to his health or his comfort. He was a work animal, and so was he treated. Horses, mules and other animals received better treatment, for they were more expensive and more difficult to replace. A recalcitrant slave, or one who became too old or feeble to work properly, was often merely put to death. F. Van Wyck Mason tells of slaves being buried in sand with only their heads exposed, for the entertainment of visitors to the plantation. The white master and his guests then played at tenpins, rolling heavy balls to the projecting heads, the object being to split them open. While this is but an incident in a novel,[4] there is considerable documentary evidence that such actually was an entertainment provided for visitors. Such treatment was neither unusual nor in any way protested. Slaves were often used for target practice, or set loose on the plantation to provide a particularly thrilling form of hunt.

Such was the condition of the early slaves brought to the West Indies, and so it remained through the better part of more than two centuries. Not even the horrors of the Roman emperors can compare with the treatment of slaves by the supposedly more enlightened people of the seventeenth and eighteenth centuries.

[3] This inhuman action provided a most chilling sequence in the early film *Slave Ship*, which starred Warner Baxter.
[4] *Stars on the Sea.*

The slaves living under such brutality had but one relief, one solace, and that was their religion. This was not the religion of the white man, who professed to believe in a God of love and justice but did not live by His teachings, but a religion of their own, brought with them from the forests and jungles of their distant homes. It was a strange, primitive religion of darkness and evil, smelling strongly of the wild and unknown jungle which white men did not dare penetrate, a terrifying mixture of sacrifice, blood-drinking, beating of drums, wild dancing and sexual orgy, centring about the worship of the Serpent. It promised vengeance and placed in the hands of the slave himself the ability to exact his revenge on these strange white masters who had forcibly removed him from his jungle home and placed him in hopeless, brutal bondage.

It was the religion called voodoo.

Voodoo is a mad world of blackness, of dancing before a blazing fire, accompanied by the wild beating of drums, the screams of the hysterical, the running of blood and the copulation of naked bodies in religious frenzy. It centres about its queen and its king, about the great serpent Dambala, about tiny dolls punctured with long pins and about the walking dead. It is a world completely alien from our own time, a belief repugnant to civilized people, a religion of fetishism and sacrifice, of evil, blasphemous worship of the powers of darkness.

It is a belief which, despite its connection with black magic and superstitions, was very much of a true religion to its believer. Although outlawed in much of the world today, it still has a large number of adherents who gather in secret jungle places, in deserted buildings, in isolated basements and warehouses and observe its rituals. While its followers are mostly Negroes, there have been numerous reports of whites – especially women – partaking in its gruesome ceremonies, which generally culminate in sexual orgy.

The centre of voodooism is worship of the great snake god, the same source of life still adored by many of the more backward African tribes. The serpent god is named Dambala or Vodu, and he is worshipped as the true lord of evil and master of creation, a belief which many peoples have held all through man's history. In voodoo ceremonies, an actual serpent is often the centre of the ritual. Generally a python, the snake is freely handled and caressed by the voodoo queen, who claims to speak the words of the snake god after falling into a trance resulting from the quick caress of the snake's tongue.

The voodoo queen is all-powerful. She rules the beliefs and the lives of her cultists, and is held in greatest dread and awe She is generally a woman wise in the ways of psychology and black magic, sly and cunning, ruthless and completely maddened by her thirst for power. She may be an ancient hag, or she may be incredibly beautiful, as was claimed of the most famous voodoo queen in the history of New Orleans, Marie Laveau, whose name has become a legend. Marie was born some time shortly before 1800, probably in New Orleans, a mixture of Negro, white and Indian blood. She was said to be a strikingly statuesque woman, with fiery black eyes, beautiful features and a dark skin. She began life as a devout Roman Catholic. Marie became the mistress, after the death of her husband, of one Louis De Glapion, and bore him some fifteen children. It was probably through his influence that she first became interested in voodoo.

The voodoo queen at the time was a little-known figure named Sanite Dede, a Negro from Santo Domingo, who was followed by Marie Saloppe, under whom Marie received her training. By 1830 Marie Laveau was the undisputed queen, having, through her arts, driven Marie Saloppe to madness in order to usurp her position.

Marie Laveau remained voodoo queen for some fifty years, until her death at the age of eighty-five. Her career was a fantastic tale of black magic, shrewd intelligence, and ruthlessness, far too detailed to report here.[5] She raised voodoo to one of the most powerful and frightening forces in New Orleans, and was often referred to as 'the boss of New Orleans'.

Not all voodoo queens were as colourful or romantic as Marie Laveau. Many were half-demented creatures, urging

[5] Robert Tallant, *Voodoo in New Orleans*. Mr Tallant also wrote a novel *Voodoo Queen* based on the life of Marie Laveau.

Bela Lugosi (left) carves a Devil Doll in *White Zombie* as he toys with
his latest victim, Robert Fraser, well on his way to becoming a zombie,
in this brooding tale of Haitian voodoo.
White Zombie, (United Artists, 1932)

their followers to gross crimes and indecencies, ever jealous
of their position of power, ruthlessly destroying all rival
queens, ruling with an iron hand that, more often than not,
dripped with blood.

Sacrifice was an indispensable part of the voodoo ritual.
This generally took the form of slitting the throat of a cock or
a lamb. The blood was poured into a large bowl, which was
then passed along the ranks of the celebrants. Each member
of the cult drank of the blood, and the rich warmth of it sent
them into frenzies of religious ecstasy. Often small birds, cats
or other animals were brought to the ceremony. When the
religious dancing reached its height of frenzy, these creatures
were literally torn to pieces and their flesh devoured by the

maddened dancers. In earlier years, small children and babies were sacrificed for their blood.

The devil doll is a small figure, generally not more than five or six inches in height, intended as a double of the enemy it represents; generally, it is made of earth or clay. It is not necessary for the doll to bear physical resemblance to the party represented, but to be effective it must include in its make-up certain parts of the body of the original, generally finger or toenail parings and portions of body hair.

What happens to the doll also happens to the original. Long, sharp needles are used as an exquisite method of torture. When these are thrust into the figurine, the person represented will feel sharp pains in identical parts of his body. If death is desired, a long pin is thrust into the heart of the doll, with the belief that the original will perish of a heart attack. The enemy may be brought to death by strangulation by tying a cord about the throat of the doll and slowly drawing it taut.

The value of the devil doll in disposing of enemies is obvious. In the terms of modern criminology, it can be considered a neat and most secure method of murder, murder in which the killer never actually touches the body of his victim. The practitioners of voodoo have no doubt whatever of the efficacy of the doll. Once it is bruited about that a man, or woman, is being 'devilled', he or she is considered as dead, and nothing can prevent it. It is obvious as well that such a means of disposing of an enemy would have strong appeal for the downtrodden Negro slave. Let the hated white man boss bully and brutalize; his days are numbered. Already death peers through the man's jaundiced eyes, and more and more he complains of the sudden, stabbing pains in his arms and legs. His days and nights become torture, and agony becomes his constant companion. And over the baleful fire of the voodoo queen's chamber of magic, the doll is tortured, pierced, melted, and killed.

For the devil doll, in many incontrovertible cases, really worked and did the job it was intended to do. The terrible voodoo fetish was as feared by the whites as by the blacks. Many deaths in Haiti and other islands of the Indies, during the period of the great power of Voodoo, were attributed to these monstrous caricatures.

The devil doll is no mystery to modern scientific minds. There is no question that the doll really kills, but it does so through the power of suggestion. The intended victim was invariably informed of the fact that a doll had been made in his image and his death is intended. Often more than one doll was made, and these duplicates were placed where the victim would be certain to find them – generally in the bedroom or nailed to the door of the victim's house – with pins sticking from various parts of the body or a cord or wire about the throat as an indication of the pain or death that might be expected. The victim, particularly if he be white, would laugh off the business as savage superstition, but even such a man, raised in a world in which voodoo is a very real power, would often succumb to this manner of auto-suggestion. As time passed and he was advised that nails were being thrust into the arms of the doll, he would begin to suffer twinges in his limbs. When he found, lying on his bed, a doll with a long, murderous needle through the heart, death from fear was often the result.

The devil doll is only one of the horrors of voodoo. There is a greater, one far more widely feared by whites and natives alike, and it provides the New World with its most terrible evil – the zombie.

According to voodoo belief, the zombie is a dead man restored to life as a powerful, emotionless, mindless automaton, an empty shell of a man, complete slave to the will of his master. There is no protection from the relentless pursuit of the zombie for, being already dead, he can not be killed. Bullets will enter his body but cause no damage, and the stab of a knife will cause no blood to flow. He is an invincible foe, an enigma feared and abhorred by the superstitious believers in the cult of the voodoo priest.

The zombie is a result of witchcraft, of spells and incantations on the part of the priest, and is brought to existence in this way: A man dies and is buried by his grieving relatives. The interment is in the native cemetery, a dark and lonely spot beyond the outskirts of the village, unattached to a church or structure of any kind. The funeral services at an end, the attendants depart and the cemetery is deserted. Night falls and, as fate would have it, it is moonless. Silence has fallen upon the land; the natives, living under the crushing heel of superstition, seldom venture forth during hours of darkness. None would dream of approaching the cemetery.

This fear makes the work of the voodoo priest and his followers simpler. Two dark forms detach themselves from the surrounding darkness and approach the freshly dug grave. They bend silently to their ghoulish task, and only the thrust of their shovels into the loosely packed earth disturbs the quiet night. When the shovels touch wood, they are tossed aside and the coffin is raised to the surface. Hoisting it upon their backs, the two men, as silently as before, make their way to the hut of the voodoo priest.

The coffin is set in the centre of the earthen floor of the hut, and the priest begins his work. He injects certain serums into the body of the dead man, bends over the fire and burns the mysterious sacrifice, mutters his obscene incantations. The scene is straight from the dark jungles of Africa, and the two assistants stand quietly and fearfully back in the shadows, their eyes unnaturally white in their black faces, scarcely daring to breathe as they watch the priest go about his work. The room is windowless, and the smoke from the fire seems to cast a screen before their eyes. The stench of the burning sacrifice assails their nostrils as they watch in wild-eyed wonder and superstitious awe.

And then the priest orders the corpse to rise and walk. There is a moment of complete silence, and then a ripple of movement can be seen in the bare arms of the deceased. Slowly, the body begins to rise as the dead man sits up in his coffin. There is not a sound in the firelight as the witch doctor watches in triumph and his assistants tremble with fear. Slowly, the body assumes a seated position. A moment's pause, and those eyes which had so recently closed in death are opened, staring vacantly ahead, devoid of expression or feeling, the eyes of a man who has no right to live. With quiet, effortless grace, the corpse rises from the coffin and stands before the voodoo priest who has raised him from the dead. He is a silent, dark statue of horror, his arms at his sides, his face a mask, his eyes staring sightlessly ahead.

A zombie has been created.

The zombie is now completely under the control of the priest. The creature has no mind of his own, for the doctor may restore the body, but the soul is gone. The zombie will blindly obey all orders given him by his resurrector, even should these orders result in his own destruction. Should he be ordered to walk a certain path, he will walk it, even if it should lead him over the edge of a cliff; he will permit himself to be crushed by a mill-grinding machine if his orders place him in such a position. He walks stiffly, arms always at his side, at a slow but purposeful step, looking neither to left nor to right, his eyes never blinking or revealing the slightest trace of emotion. He will go through obstacles rather than around them, he will brutally and ruthlessly destroy any and all who stand in his way. He requires a minimum of food and no care. He is a perfect mindless, soulless and heartless machine.

No creature of truth, legend, religion or superstition is so terrifying to the superstitious West Indian native as the zombie. He is an unholy being, a man who should be in his grave, restored to the living by the arts of voodoo. This fear is a purely superstitious one, not connected with the usual fear of death-dealing monsters, for in the normal course of events, the zombie poses no great threat to others. He is a monster created by the needs of economy rather than for purposes of evil. The voodoo priest is generally well paid by plantation owners for creation of such creatures, who are used as work horses in the sugar-cane plantations and mills. He is an ideal slave, requiring no attention and little food or sleep. He can be made to work eighteen hours a day at a steady, remorseless pace which never varies from one hour to the next. He need not be paid, he explicitly follows all orders. The voodoo priest implants in the mind of the zombie that he is to give complete obedience to his new owner – the lord or overseer of the plantation – and that obedience neither hesitates nor varies. The zombie is the cheapest source of labour ever discovered.

There are, of course, occasions when the zombie does become a horrifying murderous beast reminiscent of the old-time monsters. His owner may use him as a frightening in-

The popular stage play, *The Cat and the Canary*, was made into a highly successful silent film in which Laura La Plant coped with secret passageways and clawed hands grabbing at her from hidden panels. Martha Mattox, as the sinister housekeeper, stands behind her.
The Cat and the Canary (Universal, 1927)

strument of revenge against his enemies. Short of actual amputation of the hand, the grip of a zombie on a throat cannot be broken. He obeys commands to kill as blindly as commands to pick sugar cane, and he is an implacable, inescapable foe.

It is not difficult to understand the native horror of the

zombie, particularly in the earlier years of slavery. Death was, for them, the only release from a life of brutality and inhumane treatment; they greeted death with open arms. It meant the end of the beatings, of the backbreaking labour, of the heartbreak and misery which were the lot of the slave. Zombieism, on the other hand, was merely another form of slavery which reached beyond death itself. It was the constant fear of the natives that they would be torn from their graves where, at last, they had found rest, to return to a form of slavery even more horrible than that they had known during life. No one was safe from the dangers of such conversion. At times there was a virtual plague of zombies, during which burials were conducted at busy crossroads, it being believed this would foil the priest's plans of exhuming the corpse for his nefarious schemes. The white man, once he became aware of the values of such creatures, became a staunch supporter of the zombie process and closed his eyes to the more questionable activities of the priests. He was interested in a cheap, reliable labour force and, since only these primitives were involved, did not overly concern himself about its source. The plantation owner became rich, the voodoo priest became powerful, and the black slave had but one more misery to be added to the heavy load he carried.

The zombie is not the figment of superstitious imagination or the product of a wild-eyed writer's pen. Zombies did exist and, it is rumoured, still exist.

Just what a zombie is, of course, is quite another matter. Is this really a creature raised from the dead, a corpse dragged from the grave and resurrected by some incredible knowledge of the voodoo priest, a mindless and soulless being from beyond the pall of death?

He is not, of course. The zombie is a living creature – a man or woman – unfortunate enough to fall into the hands of the evil witch doctor and, through the priest's knowledge of various herbs, drugs and, not least, psychology, sent into a life of terrible and perpetual slavery.

The voodoo priest chooses beforehand the man whom he intends to send into the zombie world. Such a candidate is generally someone of considerable strength and health. The witch doctor manages to inject into the body of the future zombie a liquid of his own concoction which has the effect of a slow poison. This poison may be introduced over a period of time, through small doses regularly placed in the food. The victim begins to waste away and it becomes apparent that he has been stricken by some strange and unknown disease. In a matter of a short time, his heart and respiration cease and he lies lifeless, leaving the mourning relatives with no alternative but to see to immediate burial. In such hot and humid climes, this generally takes place within a few hours after death. When the grave has been closed and the relatives departed, the voodoo priest and his assistants disinter the body and take it to the hut of the priest. A counteragent to the death-counterfeiting poison is forced into the 'corpse' which then, in a sense, returns to life. This second fluid, however, has the unfortunate result of completely destroying the brain cells of the victim and he becomes from this point a mindless, unthinking automaton – a zombie. He is, of course, not invulnerable, but the fears and superstitions of the people make him appear so. He is more a slave than ever before in his life, and it certainly would have been better for the poor creature if he had, indeed, died and been placed to rest in the bosom of earth.

3

There are no famous zombie monsters in literature, and he has not made on the screen the tremendous impact of the vampire and werewolf. I recall, during the days of early childhood, reading, in one of the Sunday supplements, an article entitled 'I Walked With a Zombie', written, I believe, by a woman, but the details have long since escaped me. The zombie is met with in books on voodoo or witchcraft, but has not been the object of any major novels of horror.

Probably the most outstanding of zombie films was *White Zombie*, made in 1932 with Bela Lugosi. The film, seldom shown today, featured strikingly macabre sets and the usual domineering Lugosi attitudes. There were also films with titles as *Revolt of the Zombies, King of the Zombies*, etc., which were minor efforts of some years ago and are never seen today; it is, therefore, difficult to pass on their merits or otherwise. There was a striking sequence in the first-mentioned of these films which indicates the effectiveness of this particular field of horror. A number of zombies were utilized as workers by a brutal sugar-cane plantation owner. The task of several of these zombies was to cast baskets of cane into the grinding mill. During the process one of the zombies lost his footing and, together with the basket of sugar cane, tumbled into the press to be ground and, no doubt, become part of the sugar. His accident caused not the slightest delay in the process, or

In *White Zombie*, Madge Bellamy succumbs to the evil Bela Lugosi and is seen here in her coffin, surrounded by an assortment of zombies. But her own zombic state is only temporary, and eventually romance triumphs.
White Zombie (United Artists, 1932)

in the machinelike regularity of the actions of the other zombies. He fell without making a sound and his brother zombies calmly continued their work, casting further bits of sugar cane upon what was now definitely a corpse. It provided a rather striking example of the utter mindlessness of such creatures. This same film featured rather frightening scenes of long lines of tall, dark zombies marching slowly across the darkly clouded skyline of Haiti.

Tom Conway starred some years ago in a chilling little film called *I Walked with a Zombie*,[6] which told of the experience of a nurse called to a West Indian island to tend the mindless wife of a plantation owner. She becomes involved in all the horrors of voodoo and black magic and frequently runs into a particularly unpleasant giant of a zombie. The film was well photographed and had a rich share of chills.

Although, with the possible exception of *White Zombie*, there has been no outstandingly successful film on this aspect of the undead, one striking and frightening zombie does come to mind from, strangely enough, a comedy film.

The Cat and the Canary, a tale of hi-jinks in a haunted house set in the midst of the swamps, was first made as a silent in 1927 with Laura La Plante, Creighton Hale and Tully Marshall, and later remade with Bob Hope and Paulette Goddard. Although it does not specifically fall into the realm of horror, *The Cat and the Canary* was noteworthy for its haunted-swamp atmosphere, its strangely dimming lights, hands issuing from sliding panels and such other tried-and-true methods of providing the audience with a goodly share of goose pimples.

The success of this film naturally brought about another on the same order, with the same stars, titled *The Ghost Breakers*. In this bit of humorous horror, Paulette Goddard inherits an island in the West Indies, reputed to be haunted. Despite numerous warnings, she departs for the island in the company of a radio commentator (Hope), fleeing the threat of gangland justice as the result of a radio exposé; with him is his some-

---

[6] If I am not mistaken, the film was based upon the previously mentioned article.

what hysterical Negro valet, played by the superbly terrified Willie Best. The island contains a wondrously beautiful castle, dripping with cobwebs and mystery, and Miss Goddard's stay is made interesting by a series of ghosts, witches, voodoo dolls, mysterious hands, etc., until it is discovered that the procedure is masterminded by the so-attractive Richard Carlson, Hope's rival for Paulette's hand, for his own interests.

The film was a delightful blending of the sharp Hope humour and satisfying elements of horror. The latter element is introduced at the very opening of the film, with strange figures prowling the corridors of a New York hotel thrown into darkness by a violent electrical storm. The haunted castle, with its cobwebs, its beautiful chandeliers and grand, sweeping staircase, was the perfect setting for a tale of this kind. Most of the action, of course, occurred during the hours of night; there was no electricity in the castle, permitting the use of candles and exquisite candelabra. There was even a burial vault beneath the castle with its huge sarcophagi and massive hand-powered organ.

The high spots of horror were provided by a zombie, an extremely tall Negro, completely bald, with a bold, firm face, clad in native garb. He was kept by the old caretaker in a small hut at the boat landing on the island, from which a wooden stairway led to the castle itself. Here he lay motionless on his back, his vacant eyes staring up at the ceiling, until his services were required. At a word from his keeper he rose and, in true zombie fashion, strolled menacingly through the castle.

The zombie, of course, becomes involved in the comedy antics of Hope and Best, but there was one superb moment of horror with Miss Goddard. Followed relentlessly by the dead-eyed creature, Miss Goddard flees into the castle and up the sweeping staircase. In the dim half-light of the moon, the scene, particularly on the dust-covered staircase beneath the cobwebbed chandelier, provides a more than sufficient number of chills.

4

The world of the zombie is not as well known as the vampire, werewolf and other creatures of this kind. Possibly this is because the zombie's activities are more restricted than those of other monsters. Belief in the vampire and werewolf goes back to classic times; they are part of the folklore of almost all ancient nations. The zombie, on the other hand, is a fairly new arrival to the world of monsters. He has never been a part of European tradition, having originated in the mysterious jungles of Africa and brought to the New World during slave times. He is not surrounded by the wealth of legend which has built itself around the more widely known mon-

In *The Cat and the Canary*, the frightened characters cower around Laura La Plant, facing the villainous Martha Mattox. The film was successfully remade in 1939 as a comedy thriller starring Bob Hope. *The Cat and the Canary* (Universal Pictures, 1927)

sters, but he is, nevertheless, a frightening powerhouse as capable as the vampire of striking fear into the hearts of those who came across him.

It is an interesting fact, by the way, that the horrors of voodoo were responsible for one of the most terrifying and gruesome events in our own history. A minister of Salem, Massachusetts, had in his employ several Negroes from the West Indies. John Indian and his wife Tituba had been brought from Barbados to Massachusetts by Reverend Parris. Tituba was assigned to kitchen tasks, and during this process she often regaled Parris's daughter, Betty, then nine years of age, and her cousin Abigail Williams, with tales of voodoo and black magic. The tales had a strong effect on the two girls, and it was from this simple storytelling practice, grounded in the blackness of voodoo, that there began the terrifying period of witchcraft in Salem.[7]

Voodoo is still a strong, if hidden, force in the Caribbean areas and portions of our own Southland. It lost much of its appeal for the Negro after the days of his emancipation, although much of voodoo lore and ritual was inculcated into Negro Christianity.

But there are still places where the voodoo ritual of death is observed and – who knows – there may still be deserted roadways down which, on bright moonlit nights, a strange figure walks.

[7] Marion Starkey, *The Devil in Massachusetts.*

THE SCHIZOPHRENIC

*'I sought with tears and prayers to smother
down the crowd of hideous images
and sounds with which my memory
swarmed . . . and still, between the
petitions, the ugly face of my iniquity
stared into my soul.'*

London in the middle of the nineteenth century. A sprawling
dark, fog-enshrouded city crouching on the busy banks of the
River Thames. A thick white mist has moved in from the
Channel, blanketing the city in its suffocatingly cold and wet
embrace. The gaslights have abandoned their attempts to force
their rays through the grey-white shield, and have resigned
themselves to remaining dull, circular blots of yellow in a
world of white blindness. The sharp hammer of footsteps
rings loud and clear on the cobbled walks, their sound piercing
the fog. Two nebulous and indistinct grey shapes loom out of
the miasma, talking in strangely hushed whispers, and then
the tap-tap of their walk fades into the distance as they pass
on. A bobby, his tall dark form well covered with a glistening
raincape, ambles unconcernedly along the street, whistling
slightly under his breath. Then he, too, is gone, and the displaced mist closes in once again, holding all in its choking
embrace, covering the city with a thick blanket of silence and
mystery.

And under the cover of this nature-provided shield, evil is
at work. For London, too, has its monsters.

Of all the great cities of western Europe, probably none is so well suited to the existence of monsters as is the ancient city of London. Here they can walk the fog-enshrouded streets of the city, wearing the frequent heavy mist as a mantle to conceal their nefarious activities and to blanket their loathsome appearance. We seldom see them in their homes, and it is never there that their crimes are committed. The inadequate lighting of dim, flickering gaslights spaced so irregularly and infrequently along dark, narrow, cobbled streets, the twisting contours of the alleys and the squares, all plunged into a half-world of indistinct forms and uncertain figures – these combine to make the streets of London of a century ago the habitat of murder and horror.

Our first stop in this new locale, however, will not be the back alleys and deserted squares, but a far more fashionable part of London, a sector of sedate, comfortable mansions which is the time-honoured home of respected members of the medical and legal professions. We will not be forced to wait for the secrecy of misty darkness, for our monster is not a creature strictly of the night hours. As we walk along the calm, quiet lane of neat, orderly homes, we feel that perhaps we have gone astray. There is nothing frightening about this portion of London; surely it cannot be the abode of horror.

But let us walk a bit farther, nearly to the end of the street, until we find ourselves before a peculiar structure, an edifice which does not appear to be in tune with its neighbours. We pause before a small courtyard in which stands a building some two stories high. There is a door in the centre of the ground floor, a scarred, unattractive entry, but the rest of the frontage is blank plaster, with windows only at the sides of the building. There is about the place an air of neglect and desertion.

Let us stand here for a moment, in the shelter of this doorway just across the street from our peculiar courtyard. We are about to witness the startling opening act of a tale of horror set in this quiet and respectable corner of London. Our principal actor is about to arrive on the scene.

Yes, here he comes now. It is a man, small and dark, his face not discernible to us, dressed outlandishly in clothing far

Spencer Tracy provided an excellent portrayal of the role in which John Barrymore had appeared in a silent 1920 film. In the 1932 sound film, Fredric March received a Best Actor Oscar.
Dr. Jekyll and Mr. Hyde **(Metro-Goldwyn-Mayer, 1941)**

too large for a small frame which has about it an indefinable air of deformity. He walks quickly, almost furtively, his head down, apparently in a considerable hurry to reach his destination. In his haste, he is unaware of the playful little girl rushing towards him just around the corner. The child is late for supper, and she knows she will be roundly scolded for her tardiness. The two hurrying figures reach the corner at precisely the same moment, and collide with a heavy thud. With an exclamation of anger and a gesture of intense fury, the little man knocks the child to the walk and purposely and viciously tramples on her as he rushes across the street and enters our mysterious doorway. He takes a key from the folds of his clothing, inserts it and, with a quick, angry glance behind him, enters the building and closes the door.

And in that brief moment, we have seen his face – his ugly, wicked face – dark, hairy, fanged, with deep-set eyes which seem to smoulder and glow with the very fires of hell itself. It is a face that sends through us a terrible chill of foreboding.

For this little, wizened ugly man is our next monster. The courtyard we see before us provides the rear entrance to the laboratory of a prominent and successful physician by the name of Henry Jekyll, and the strange, evil figure who has entered that door is known and both feared and detested by the name of Edward Hyde.

2

The Strange Case of Dr Jekyll and Mr Hyde was one of the last major works to come from the pen of Robert Louis Stevenson. Born in Edinburgh, Scotland, in 1850, Stevenson was dead by his forty-fourth year. In that comparatively brief time, he produced many works which have attained a permanent place in English literature. He was intensely interested in fantasy and the unusual, as is evidenced by several of his works, including the collection of short stories titled *New Arabian Nights* and the later *The Strange Case of Dr Jekyll and Mr Hyde*.

Stevenson was throughout his life an extremely active man, in spite of the fact that he was ill with tuberculosis from an early age. Determined not to permit his illness to blight his life, he took part in many vigorous walking tours of the Continent, which served as the basis for his early writing. It was in 1883 that he produced *Treasure Island*; three years later he revealed his inventiveness and imagination by his account of the tragedy of Dr Henry Jekyll. Seeking for a climate which would prolong his life, Stevenson spent his last years in the tropical paradise of Samoa, where the natives recognized his great talent by conferring on him the name of Tusitala, meaning 'teller of tales'. At the time of his death, he was at work on *Weir of Hermiston*. This unfinished novel is considered by many to be his finest writing.

The Strange Case of Dr Jekyll and Mr Hyde (now more popularly known by its shorter title of *Dr Jekyll and Mr Hyde*) is a brief tale, ranking as one of the most popular and best-known short stories in the English language.

In the best tradition of the Victorian mystery story, *Dr Jekyll and Mr Hyde* opens on a peaceful note, with mystery added to mystery until the shattering climax of the story, when Jekyll's friend, Dr Utterson, bursts into the laboratory and finds the body of the detestable Edward Hyde, but no trace whatever of Dr Jekyll. It is only after this sequence of apparently inexplicable events and after the discovery of Hyde's body that the solution of the mystery is provided in a letter of explanation left behind by the strangely vanished doctor. (This method of storytelling was extremely popular with Victorian writers; even *Frankenstein* and *Dracula* were written largely in the form of letters, documents and diaries.) We of today have, unfortunately, lost one of the prime pleasures of this exciting tale – the element of suspense and surprise – for we are fully aware from the opening pages that Henry Jekyll and Edward Hyde are, in fact, one and the same man.

The story is chiefly related through the experiences of Utterson, in whose hands are later placed the documents of explanation. He has the good fortune of being a close friend of the good Dr Henry Jekyll, as well as his lawyer. Utterson is the very epitome of the Victorian gentleman: staid, respectable, loyal and dependable as the Rock of Gibraltar. (He is always referred to simply as Utterson. This is another aspect of Victorian writing. One was intensely loyal to one's friends, but it was being a bit too publicly affectionate to address these friends by their Christian names.) Utterson has become concerned over the activities of his friend Jekyll, who is sometimes inclined to be somewhat unorthodox in his behaviour and his experiments. A short time before, in his capacity as his friend's attorney, he had been in receipt of a most interesting document from Henry Jekyll, which was nothing less than his will. But a peculiar will it was, leaving all his worldly goods to some unknown gentleman by the name of Edward Hyde.

Nor was this the strangest fact of the will, for these possessions were to go to Hyde not only in the event of Jekyll's death, but also if he should disappear for a period of three months or more. To a friend, such a peculiar document, coupled with Jekyll's recent peculiar, anti-social behaviour, could only be cause for concern.

Utterson's concern is increased following a stroll with his kinsman, Enfield. Their walk takes them to the rear of Jekyll's residence, a little courtyard giving admittance to the laboratory. Here Enfield relates to the attorney a peculiar tale of seeing, on a previous stroll in the same area, a small, wizened and incredibly ugly man knock down a little girl and viciously trample on her body. The child was not seriously injured, but so incensed were the good people of the neighbourhood by the stranger's action that they refused to release him without some retribution to the child. The strange man thereupon entered the door to Jekyll's laboratory, to appear a few moments later with a cheque for one hundred pounds, bearing Jekyll's signature, undoubtedly genuine. Utterson immediately connects this stranger with the mysterious Hyde, the doctor's unknown heir. Close questioning of the doctor's other friends, however, indicates that none of them has actually met Edward Hyde.

Determined to solve this mystery, Utterson conceals himself opposite the laboratory door until the disreputable person again puts in an appearance. He accosts Hyde at the door, introducing himself as one of Jekyll's friends. There is a brief exchange of words before Hyde quickly enters the laboratory, closing the door behind him. In those brief moments, Utterson has examined the stranger and been repelled by him. Hyde is a small man and slight of build, almost a dwarf, and gives an indefinable impression of deformity. The face is a strange, twisted caricature extremely unpleasant to look upon. But above all, Utterson is strongly aware of a sense of most terrible evil about the man. Utterson attempts to see Jekyll, but is informed by Poole, his valet, that he is not in, and Edward Hyde, on the master's instructions, is treated as an ever-welcome guest at the Jekyll home; Poole knows no more about him.

Some time after, London is stirred by the violent murder of

a highly respected, aged citizen, one Sir Danvers Carew. The terrible crime is witnessed by a horrified servant girl who informs the police that she had seen Carew in conversation with Edward Hyde. It appeared that Carew was requesting directions from the little man. In a fit of fury, suddenly and without provocation of any kind, Hyde struck Carew repeatedly with his heavy stick. When the aged man fell to the street, Hyde, in apparent exultation, trampled upon the body until the old man lay still.

Utterson confronts Jekyll with this dreadful crime of his mysterious friend. Horrified, Jekyll swears that he is through with Hyde and will never again admit him to his home. He adds that Hyde will never be apprehended by the police, but will never again be seen in London. He shows Utterson a letter from Hyde, advising Jekyll of his intention to leave London and never return. When Utterson shows the letter to a mutual friend who is a handwriting expert, he is amazed to learn that it is a forgery, written by Jekyll himself.

It is at this time that the fate of another friend becomes of grave concern to the solicitor. Dr Lanyon has always been one of Jekyll's closest friends and, with this in mind, Utterson visits him in hopes of securing his assistance in solving the mystery of Jekyll's actions. He finds Lanyon a figure transformed, ill, wasted, at the point of death. When Utterson mentions the name of their mutual friend, Lanyon orders him from the house. Within a week, Lanyon is dead. He leaves behind an envelope for Utterson to be opened only at his death. When Utterson opens the envelope, he finds within it another sealed envelope to be opened only in the event of the death or disappearance of Henry Jekyll.

The story of Henry Jekyll is coming to a rapid close. One evening, Poole calls on Utterson and pleads for his help, claiming there has been foul play and he believes his master has been murdered. Utterson returns with Poole to Jekyll's home and stands before the locked laboratory. Utterson's presence is not revealed as Poole calls to his master for admittance; a harsh voice orders them to leave. The door of the laboratory, Poole states, has been locked for eight days. A series of notes, left before the door, have sent him to all the neighbouring chemist shops in search of certain drugs which he has been unable to obtain. Only once, when the door had opened to enable the occupant of the laboratory to pick up the breakfast tray, had Poole caught a glimpse of the figure inside. It was Edward Hyde.

Convinced that Hyde has done away with Jekyll, Utterson and Poole break down the door and enter the workshop. They find Hyde stretched dead on the floor, victim of a quick poison, but no trace of Jekyll. Utterson returns to his apartment and opens the envelope left for him by Dr Lanyon.

Lanyon's letter had been written a few days before his death. He had been in receipt of a peculiar letter of instruction from Jekyll, pleading with him to secure from Jekyll's laboratory a certain drawer filled with chemicals and letters. Lanyon was to take this material to his own home, where it would be called for by a man who would identify himself as having been sent by Jekyll. Lanyon follows the instructions and, that same night, is visited by Hyde. Quickly, as though his life depended on it, Hyde mixed a concoction of chemicals and drank it down. Hyde then went into a series of terrible, painful convulsions and, before Lanyon's horrified gaze, became transformed into Henry Jekyll. Lanyon did not long survive this terrible revelation.

The actual story is revealed to Utterson in the second envelope written by Henry Jekyll himself.

Jekyll had always been particularly interested in the constant battle between good and evil in man's soul. He is convinced that man is actually two beings, and he becomes certain that there exists a method by which these two entities can be revealed in a man. He discovers the necessary chemical mixture, prepares it and drinks it. Twisting in agony, he falls to the floor – and rises again as the infamous Edward Hyde. Hyde is younger than his Jekyll counterpart, smaller, but sprier and more agile. This, to Jekyll, is but natural, for there is more good in man than evil, and the villainous *alter ego* would not be so fully developed. A second drinking of the chemical restores Jekyll to proper form.

Jekyll, of course, cannot stop his experiments at this point. Again and again, he drinks the formula that brings Hyde into existence and, in this guise, commits all manner of foul crimes that make his name feared throughout London. There is a certain fascination in this evil self that exists in all men. There is in Jekyll a certain release to be found in the form of Hyde; he is not yet aware of the horrible lengths to which Hyde may carry him.

Disaster strikes soon enough. One morning Jekyll awakens in his bed and finds that, without touching the mixture, he has again become Hyde. This involuntary alteration indicates that Hyde may be getting the upper hand; he abandons the dangerous line of research and, for a time, Hyde disappears. But the call of evil is too strong. Once again, the brew is prepared and Jekyll drinks it down. The result is the murder of Sir Danvers Carew.

The terrible crime, the first murder, causes Jekyll to cry out in horror against himself and yet, at the same time, he realizes his salvation. The brew must never be prepared again, for Hyde faces death if he is found.

But Hyde refuses to remain in concealment. While Jekyll, exulting in his new freedom from the force of evil, sits in Regent's Park, Hyde takes over. The cunning murderer, realizing he is in danger of his life, turns to Lanyon for help, revealing his terrible story and causing that good man's death.

For Henry Jekyll, the horror has just begun. He has lost all control over the transformation into Hyde. His evil self, so much strengthened by the terrible actions of the past months, has now become powerful enough to take the upper hand. The entire nature of Jekyll's physical composition has been so altered through the chemical formula that the transformation now takes place at all hours of day and night. Only through the formula itself is Jekyll now able to return to his proper form.

And then, the last of the mixture is gone, and all attempts to concoct additional brews fail completely. The case is hopeless. Hyde has won.

On this note of complete despair, Jekyll ends his testament, wondering if, when the time comes, Hyde will have the moral courage to destroy himself and thus escape the scaffold.

So does the strange and tragic tale of Dr Henry Jekyll and his evil self, Edward Hyde, comes to a conclusion. Utterson, no

Many film historians still consider the 1920 *Dr. Jekyll and Mr. Hyde*, starring John Barrymore (center), the best of the several films based on Robert Louis Stevenson's novella. Unlike later actors in the role, Barrymore depended more on facial contortions than elaborate makeup.
Dr. Jekyll and Mr. Hyde (Paramount Pictures, 1920)

doubt, received a certain amount of consolation from the fact that Hyde did, indeed, manage to take his own life before discovery, and therefore his friend, Henry Jekyll, was spared the ignominy of death on the gallows.

This is a gem of a story, brief, superbly told. Stevenson's method of writing was clear and lucid, Victorian in style, but not slowed and cluttered by the long paragraphs of description so common in Victorian literature. The writing is leisurely, building up slowly and inexorably to the tragic climax, every word essential to the story. It carries with it the comfortable, solid air of Victorian London, of studies lined with leather-bound volumes, of blazing fires in the hearth and soothing glasses of ruby-red wine. Dr Jekyll rushes to his destruction, but the story moves with a steady pace, slowly and pitilessly to its conclusion. In spite of the scientific undertones, we feel it would not be as effective if placed in, say, a modern American scientific laboratory. For Henry Jekyll is a man completely out of his time, and in that fact lies much of the horror of the tale.

Dr Jekyll and Mr Hyde is from its opening lines a superb tale of horror, and yet it is difficult to point out any particular scenes as the chillers. Stevenson makes little or no attempt to construct the usual atmosphere of horror, of dark shadows, of creeping monsters. His atmosphere is of an alien belief introduced into the staid London of Queen Victoria; in that, there is horror enough. He does not concentrate on surroundings, on descriptions of an evil at large in the evening mists, or even on the transformation of Jekyll into Hyde, which is briefly passed over. There is no attempt to describe Hyde's evil deeds, save for the murder of Sir Danvers Carew; these are left to the reader's imagination.

Yet the horror is there, nevertheless, rich and unnerving. We read the brief mention of Henry's agonies after drinking the formula of transformation, and we somehow see the doctor twisting, gasping, moaning on the floor of his laboratory, we view the terrible physical changes, we see him at last rising to his feet and standing before the mirror to face the hideous countenance of his own evil self. We are not provided with a description of Hyde's wicked mode of life (such, of course, would not have been permitted in Victorian writing), but somehow it is a simple matter for us to envision him prowling through the dark, misty streets, the clothes of Jekyll too large for his smaller frame, the collar of the dark cape carefully raised to conceal his hideous features. We catch an unnerving glimpse of his fanged teeth and evil eyes as he passes a gas lamp, we see the upraised cane, the joyful glint in the evil eyes, and we hear the chuckle of pleasure when another crime has been successfully committed.

Stevenson makes little actual mention of horror, but no reader can escape the cold hand of horror that pervades every page of this strange tale.

Dr Jekyll and Mr Hyde, critics point out, is a story of schizophrenia. Stevenson, through the use of this fictional form, has
given us a sort of Aesop's fable, in which there is so much
more than meets the eye – a parable of the endless war between good and evil which constantly rages within a man's
heart, soul and mind. What was accepted in 1886 as a simple,
rather exciting little story, was really very much more, was
really a lesson in life, but the people of the time were not yet
at the educational level to comprehend it. The terrible realities
of schizophrenia are much clearer today than they were in the
days when Stevenson wrote, and to us the story is easier to
comprehend. We all have an Edward Hyde lurking somewhere
within us, waiting only for the brief moments when he is able
to take the upper hand – these are the times when we lose our
temper, when we bring pain and unhappiness to others and, in
the more violent cases, when we commit acts of violence. In
our own troubled time, we have seen the tragic results of un-
controllable schizophrenia – the suppposed good and moral
young woman who suddenly gives every indication of being
a prostitute, the brilliant young student who suddenly commits a heinous crime, the teen-age youngster who takes an axe
to his mother. It is of people like these that Stevenson was
writing in his brief, unforgettable story.

Undoubtedly, there is much to be said for this viewpoint.
No one can deny the schizophrenic aspects of this tale, but
the result of all this dissection has been to distort the original
point of Stevenson's writing and has done him something of
a disservice.

The fact is, Robert Louis Stevenson was not writing a
morality play or a medical treatise. He was writing a story,
and a very interesting and well-concocted one at that. It is
unlikely that he had any other purpose in mind. Undoubtedly,
he was aware of the perils of schizophrenia and its attendant
horrors, and it is certainly more than possible that he had this
in mind when he wrote his story.

But let us not attempt to distort his reasons for writing.
Stevenson was not a prophet, nor a sage. In medical knowledge, particularly psychiatry, he was not what is often
referred to as 'a man ahead of his time'. His interest in such

things was merely the more or less cursory interest of a writer. He penned *Dr Jekyll and Mr Hyde* as a bit of entertaining fiction, and that was all. There was no hidden meaning behind his writing. If we are able to get some kind of morality lesson from his story, so much the better. However, we should not approach this fine tale as a history of a medical case. The change from Jekyll to Hyde was not, as some would have it, merely a psychic transformation, but an actual physical alteration. Once Jekyll swallowed the concoction of which he alone knew the ingredients, Dr Jekyll no longer existed, either in physical or mental form. Edward Hyde picked himself up from the floor, different in every way from Henry Jekyll, even to the point of stature. Stevenson makes this very clear. To pretend the transformation was anything but complete is to strip the tale of its delightful horror and destroy much of its pleasure.

3

The filming of *Dr Jekyll and Mr Hyde* has presented several problems. This is strictly what is generally referred to as a 'star film', one of those stories in which the protagonist is of special importance, and the success or failure of the film depends on the actor in the title role. Stevenson's character requires an actor of considerable stature; this is particularly true since the performer portrays two completely different roles. Another great difficulty in filming this story of the schizophrenic doctor is the story content itself, for Stevenson's work is not a full, rich novel, but a compact, tightly woven short story. There are few characters and a scarcity of incident. Most of the tale is provided by various letters and documents; there is a minimum of dialogue. As it stands, the story seems rather poorly suited for film. It has always been the task of the screenwriter to build upon the characters and the incidents provided, and others to fit easily within the framework of the story, and yet maintain the original tautness of the tale. This has permitted an enlargement on the nefarious activities of the villainous Hyde, a stressing of the trials and agonies of poor Dr Jekyll, and the insertion of the apparently vital love story which does not necessarily contribute to the effect of the film, but aids the box office.

Despite these problems, there have been no less than five major films based on Stevenson's great story. These all deserve comment, and at least two of them have been impressive. The earlier films, unfortunately, are seldom seen today and it is, therefore, difficult to pass detailed judgment.

Dr Jekyll and Mr Hyde was one of the earliest masterpieces of literature to be attempted by the silent screen. It was in 1913 that Universal Studios presented the first version of Stevenson's story. (Literary classics were extremely popular film fare in the early days of silent films.) Starred in this long-forgotten museum piece were King Baggott and Jane Gail.

The second production, only seven years later, was in every way more memorable. The star was the great John Barrymore, who had already made twelve silent films, none of which had been particularly successful. Filmed by Paramount in their Long Island studio in 1920, *Dr Jekyll and Mr Hyde* established Barrymore as one of the great performers of the silent screen. He made an impressively handsome Jekyll and, complete with fangs and talons, a terrifying Edward Hyde. Starred with him was the lovely Martha Mansfield and the popular actor Louis Wolheim, but the discovery of the film, portraying a rather lurid dancer in one of Hyde's London dives, was a lovely girl named Nita Naldi.

The dual role was a natural for an actor of Barrymore's talents, permitting him to please his feminine admirers with his suave and charming portrayal as the unfortunate doctor, and giving him an opportunity for some splendid scene chewing as Hyde. It is an actor's dream role, and Barrymore enjoyed every moment of it.

The success of this film was immediate, and it remains today an impressive production. The writers overcame the obstacle of limited story by combining Stevenson's original tale with various portions of Wilde's *Picture of Dorian Gray*, but apparently no one quarrelled with such writer's license. Barrymore was to make use of his Hyde make-up several years later

The 1920 silent version of _Dr. Jekyll and Mr. Hyde_ was a curious combination of Stevenson's tale and Oscar Wilde's _The Picture of Dorian Gray_. It was a triumph for John Barrymore (left). _Dr. Jekyll and Mr. Hyde_, (Paramount Pictures, 1920)

in _The Sea Beast_, based on Melville's _Moby Dick_, as Captain Ahab.[1]

The dual role of the London doctor was to prove highly helpful to the career of another young actor when, in 1932, _Dr Jekyll and Mr Hyde_ was produced for the talking screen, with the starring role played by a young performer who was still a comparative newcomer to the screen. Fredric March had been appearing on the stage since 1920, but did not appear in pictures until nearly a decade later. His performance in 1930 in *Manslaughter* gained him the important role of the Roman centurion in De Mille's epic *The Sign of the Cross*, and it was in the following year that he firmly established himself with his performances in the title roles of Jekyll and Hyde.

Horror films, thanks to the work of the late Lon Chaney and the more recent Boris Karloff (*Frankenstein* had appeared the previous year), had already begun that era of popularity at the box office which is now referred to as the great horror cycle, and the more terrifying aspects of *Dr Jekyll and Mr Hyde* were strongly stressed, providing a frightening atmosphere, an excellent story, and a fine cast. March's make-up was of the utmost importance (in the early thirties, the make-up man was king) and he was presented as a horrifying picture of vice, with a face that might well be considered the epitome of evil with its tousled black hair, its fanged teeth, deep-set eyes and withered flesh. The film was both a critical and box office success and March became the first – and, alas, only – actor to receive an Academy Award for a performance as a monster.

The next *Dr Jekyll and Mr Hyde*, which appeared somewhat more than twenty years ago, was probably the weakest of the Hollywood efforts. Spencer Tracy appeared in the title role, and was ably supported by two of the then reigning Hollywood beauties, Ingrid Bergman and Lana Turner. In spite of this excellent cast, and the fact that the film was sumptuously and artistically produced, well directed and finely played, it failed to receive the critical acclaim expected. Chief fault undoubtedly lay with the writing which, in an effort to be artistic, was cumbersome and dull, burdened with heavy-handed fantasy and meaningless dream sequences. Emphasis was placed on Jekyll's romantic involvements, which slowed the story almost to a crawl.

[1] Silent screen expert Joe Franklin mentions there was a second minor *Jekyll and Hyde* this same year by Louis B. Mayer. Not very successful, this one placed the location of the story in New York and presented the entire tale as a dream. Mr Franklin also points out there was yet another such film starring Conrad Veidt.

Tracy's performance was, nevertheless, an extremely interesting one. Barrymore and March, despite their great ability as performers, had relied heavily on make-up to create the effect required as Mr Hyde, but Tracy kept the make-up to a minimum, preferring to fall upon his own facial expressions and characterizations to create the sense of inner evil. He was most successful, for his Hyde was a twisted, wild-eyed monster in its own way every bit as terrifying as the fanged and clawed predecessors.

It was inevitable that the Hammer Studios would get around to Stevenson's tale, and this they did in 1961. Although it received the same care as all Hammer productions, the same excellent colour and fine performances, it was the least successful of all the Hammer horror classics, and the most disappointing of all Jekyll-Hyde films.

The fault again lay in the writing. This version presented an embarrassing mishmash of infidelity and rape with few of the finer qualities of the original story. Dr Jekyll is a brilliant but dull scientist married to a beautiful, youthful wife who is having an affair with a money-grubbing scoundrel. The gentle Dr Jekyll – who permits neighbourhood children to play in his garden – concocts the serum which changes him into Hyde, and begins his life of decadence. At a local dance hall, he takes as mistress the featured near-nude snake dancer. Here he also sees his wife with her lover, and realizes the truth about his marriage. In the form of Hyde, he attempts to seduce his own wife, but fails. Pretending friendship, Hyde then offers to act as go-between for Jekyll's wife in her hopes of obtaining a divorce and marrying her lover. He arranges a dinner for himself, the wife and the lover, in the rooms of his mistress above the dance hall. He then locks the lover into a room with the dancer's boa constrictor, while he rapes his own wife. Dazed, the woman finds her horribly slain lover. She falls to her death through the dance-hall skylight, crashing in a shower of glass into the midst of the dancers. Hyde, meanwhile, strangles his mistress. To throw suspicion off himself, he murders an old man of the neighbourhood and places the body in his laboratory, which he sets afire. The body is assumed to be that of Jekyll, whose death is declared accidental, and Hyde, now content to live as himself, is declared Jekyll's heir. But while leaving the courtroom after this decision, Hyde suddenly reverts to Jekyll, and the jig is up.

The film, so completely involved in sexuality, had little to recommend it. There are no outstanding scenes of horror, and much of it is more embarrassing than interesting. The rape scene is crude and vulgar; the film seems composed of one bedroom scene after another. It also contains the lewdest and most tasteless exhibition of can-can dancing ever filmed.

The role of Jekyll-Hyde was played by Paul Massie, and here was the greatest divergence from Stevenson's original idea. Jekyll was a sombre, brown-bearded, intent, devoted scientist – reliable and dull. Hyde, on the other hand, was young, tall, dashing and handsome. The transformation merely required Massie to remove his beard, stand a bit straighter, and get a woman-loving glitter into his eyes. This is certainly the first instance in which the evil Hyde was made to appear rather appealing. Although it is nothing new, of course, to show evil in rather attractive packages, this was an interesting application and a rather novel theory for the Stevenson story. Unfortunately, it destroyed the aspects of horror in the film.

Not the wildest imaginings of a script writer could restore to life a Jekyll-Hyde who died as the result of a virulent poison. It is quite another matter to permit Frankenstein's monster to survive fire, flood, quicksand and various other means of certain death, for the monster is not a human being and, therefore, not subject to the laws of life and death that govern human beings. The same might be said of such enduring monsters as the wolf-man, Dracula and Karis. Hyde, however, despite his evil and supernatural transformation, was a man, and when death comes to one such as he, it is final. The only solution would appear to be constant remakes of the story; this grows monotonous after a time. The Hammer production was titled *House of Fright*, a rather innocuous and meaningless title, but in none of the advertising was it mentioned that this was the old Jekyll-Hyde story; apparently it was feared that another version of the tale would have little drawing power.

Hollywood, of course, conceived a different escape from this monotony. Let Dr Jekyll remain in his self-appointed grave, but let his story continue in his progeny. We might wonder at the legitimacy of such progeny, for Stevenson makes Jekyll a bachelor; of course, it is quite possible that Jekyll indulged in other forms of hanky-panky besides what went on in his laboratory.

Dr Jekyll was first given a son in the form of dashingly handsome Louis Hayward (who deserved better than what Hollywood gave him) in a film aptly titled *Son of Dr Jekyll*. The son apparently had a sister, who presented herself to the world in a minor little effort called, aptly, *Daughter of Dr Jekyll*. The taint of Hydeism affected not her, but her guardian, Jekyll's best friend, played by Arthur Shields. The writers became terribly confused here, for the taint suffered by Jekyll appeared to have been lycanthropy, while the means of death is strictly vampirical.

Stevenson's work, as that of Mary Shelley and Bram Stoker, will manage to survive any number of poor, weak versions.[2] It remains the greatest fictional tale of schizophrenia and will provide future generations of readers with the same delightful thrills of horror and suspense that it has offered for nearly three-quarters of a century.

4

The house and laboratory of Dr Henry Jekyll still stand, long vacant and forgotten. No light gleams from the windows of that tragic home, and in the laboratory the dust of many years covers the test tubes and equipment which Henry Jekyll put to such terrible and tragic use. Like Victor von Frankenstein a century earlier, Henry Jekyll had dared to probe with his ever-inquisitive mind into matters which, perhaps, it is better for man not to know, and, like Frankenstein, he paid

[2] Even Boris Karloff once played Hyde, in a comedy with Abbott and Costello. The film did not add to the credit of Stevenson or of Karloff, but perhaps the man who brought the Frankenstein monster to such terrifying life was entitled, after so many years, to a little romp of nonsense.

a terrible price for the quenching of his thirst for knowledge.

The fog is beginning to lift now, and before long the first faint, barely discernible glow of dawn will begin to brighten the sky. There is little time left us here in London, for a strange and terrible figure awaits us in the dark, dank sewers of Paris. We must travel quickly if we are to meet the other schizophrenic monsters of this ancient city.

We find ourselves in a quiet, sumptuously furnished drawing-room of a period shortly before the turn of the century. Here, too, as in all our visits, we find the dust of neglect, for this room and this house have long been empty. Again, we wonder what horror this pleasant, if stuffy, chamber could have held.

And then we see it, hanging there upon the wall. It is a portrait, a beautifully painted picture of a strikingly handsome young man, a man vibrant with youth, his skin smooth and unblemished, his hair rich and golden. We wonder who this man might be, this very personification of all that is beautiful in the young. We look closer, to the bottom of the frame, and we have found our monster.

The painter of this remarkable portrait was one Basil Hallward, and it is a portrait of his friend, Dorian Gray.

Seeing this portrait of himself had a very strong and terrible effect on young Dorian Gray. When Hallward presented the work for his criticism, young Dorian stood silently before it, admiring the beauty of the execution, admiring the youth and elegance of his own form. And before his eyes, that form faded, withered, grew lined and old, just as he would some day lose his youthful beauty, become absent-minded, doddering, old, old, old.

It was then that Dorian Gray uttered those fateful words, expressing the wish that the portrait would assume the burden of his years, the harshness of living, the decay and dissolution of frustration and despair, while he remained forever young, handsome, unblemished.

And the fates heard Dorian's words, and they laughed and granted his wish, plunging Dorian into a life of corruption, licentiousness and decadence.

Dorian Gray lived for pleasure. He found this pleasure wherever he sought it, and cared nothing for the thoughts and feelings of others. He descended into vileness and obscenity, crime and evil, yet always he remained young, and no trace of the blackness of his soul appeared on the smoothly handsome, ever-youthful face.

But it was different with the portrait. For the picture became the mirror of his soul, and each vice, each crime, each bit of evil added another line of loathsomeness to the ageing face in the painting. When his callousness caused the suicide of the girl who loved him, a smear of crimson appeared on the talon-like hands in the painting. The scandals, the blackmail, the suicide of a close friend – all these left Dorian Gray untouched, while his portrait deteriorated to a loathsome monstrosity of decay.

But his evil life finally catches up with him. Worn out by his own degeneracy, he murders his friend Hallward and, in a fury of madness, stabs the cursed portrait with the same knife. But he has slain his own soul. When the room is entered, a body is found lying on the floor under the superbly beautiful portrait of Dorian as a young man:

He was withered, wrinkled and loathsome of visage. It was not till they had examined the rings that they recognized who it was.

The Picture of Dorian Gray[3] is a superb work of insidious horror, written by Oscar Wilde in 1891, nine years before his terrible and untimely death. The tale stirred a storm of controversy as 'indecent' and 'decadent'. The fact that this superbly written story is an allegory presenting the career of a youth who makes his choice between good and evil, does not detract from the constant sense of horror. The cold hand of fear clamps the reader every time Dorian enters the chamber in which hangs the portrait, and sees etched on the hideous face the mark of his latest crime. The longing for evil

[3] The book is often erroneously referred to as *The Portrait of Dorian Gray*.

that drives Dorian from crime to crime, to blackmail and murder, and finally to self-destruction, presents us with an engrossing, terrifying study of man. Dorian, too, is a schizophrenic, presenting to the world a face of beauty and youth while the portrait reveals the horror of his soul.

The Picture of Dorian Gray provided the theme for several minor silent film productions, but was given full treatment in the early 1940s, with Hurd Hatfield as Dorian and George Sanders as Hallward. The film was a critical and artistic success. Superbly mounted, it featured strikingly loathsome portraits of Dorian, shown in colour.

5

Had we time, we could visit other frightening creatures of nineteenth-century England. London could tell us of the mysterious murderer known as Jack the Ripper, who prowled the streets of the city in 1888 and was never apprehended. There have been many theories of the Ripper's identity, including the belief that he was a prominent citizen suffering from schizophrenia. Among the many novels on this theme, the most successful was *The Lodger*, written by Marie Belloc Lowndes in 1913.

The film *The Lodger*, though departing considerably from Mrs Lowndes' novel, presented a high in horror. The murderer was a mysterious madman who had a penchant for slaying actresses, a result of his brother's suicide following an unhappy love affair with an actress. The mysterious lodger of the title roamed the foggy streets of London with a black bag, and burned mysterious substances at night. He fails, however, in his attempts to slay a dance-hall queen (Merle Oberon) and, cornered, leaps to his death in the Thames.

The success of the film was largely due to the brilliance of a young actor named Laird Cregar. An impressive, large man, Cregar, still in his twenties, was hailed by no less an authority than John Barrymore as one of the great actors of our time. His agonized facial expressions lifted this film to superb heights. Soft-spoken, seemingly completely gentle, somewhat mystic and dreamy-eyed, Mr Cregar gave a performance which showed promise of starting a new series of psychological horror films.

This promise was strengthened by Cregar's next film, *Hangover Square*, based on a novel by Patrick Hamilton, also the tale of a schizophrenic in Victorian London. Cregar appeared as a brilliant pianist-composer sent into spells of amnesia by any slight jarring sound, during which time he committed various brutal murders. The film was brilliantly presented, with all the best atmospheres of nineteenth-century London – the fog, the gaslights, the dance halls. Its peak of horror was the celebration of Guy Fawkes' Day. A huge bonfire was prepared, and on it Cregar placed the body of his latest victim. His guilt, however, is suspected by the Scotland Yard inspector (George Sanders), who arrives to take him into custody as Cregar is presenting his latest piano concerto at an elegant drawing-room recital. The building catches fire and all occupants flee. Cregar, realizing the truth of his dual nature, remains at the piano and, as the flaming structure collapses about him, thunders the final powerful chords of his concerto.

In this impressive Wagnerian setting, Cregar's career also came to an end, for this brilliant performer died before the release of the film, in 1944, at the age of twenty-seven.

Robert Louis Stevenson provided Hollywood with another superb tale of Victorian horror in *The Body Snatchers*. This tale of Scotland during the days when doctors had to contend with laws which forbade the dissection of the human body is a classic of horror. The notorious Burke and Hare had already been put to a justified death for the horrors of grave robbing, and the hands of doctors interested in research to gain a knowledge of the workings of the human body were tied. Some there were who engaged in activities which, were they revealed, would mete them the same fate as Burke and Hare. One such doctor was that played by Henry Daniel. A brilliant teacher and surgeon, particularly interested in the healing of paralysis, he must have subjects for his work. Through the aid of an unscrupulous hack driver named Gray, played by

Boris Karloff, he manages to secure these subjects. Gray delivers the freshly exhumed corpses to the rear door, is paid his fee, and departs. Karloff, of course, soon creates his own subjects. In one striking sequence, a young blind girl stands singing on a dark and foggy corner in Edinburgh. The evil Karloff pulls up with his hearselike hack, and the song is abruptly cut short. Daniel, because of a carelessness in his earlier years in which Gray had played a part, is unable to break loose from the influence of the evil driver, and finally is compelled to murder him.

The film was a combination of all that is best in a motion picture of this type. The photography of fog-enshrouded Edinburgh was striking, the scenes presented in low-keyed lighting, with heavy use of shadows and dark close-ups. In the role of the doctor was one of the most accomplished, most incisive performers of our time, and Henry Daniel's characterization of a dedicated and brilliant scientist converted into a haunted, terrified murderer was one of the finest performances in a brilliant career. Karloff, of course, was a superb villain. Shabbily dressed with a long, wollen muffler about his neck, his hair long and dirty-white, generally unshaven, he lived alone in a squalid little room behind the stable where he kept his hack and his horse.[4] He was unctuously obsequious when it suited his purpose, harshly and brutally vicious when the need arose. Bela Lugosi appeared as the doctor's somewhat moronic handyman. When he finds the body of one of Karloff's self-made subjects in one of the laboratory vats, his simple, muddled mind conceives a method of making easy money through blackmail. He visits Karloff's stable quarters and threatens exposure if he is not paid for his silence. In a dramatically photographed scene with light coming only from a flickering fire, Karloff easily lulls Lugosi into a sense of false security by pretending to give him what he wants. Lugosi is, of course, then promptly strangled.

The climax of the film is one of the most superb touches of the macabre in film history. Daniel, having finally murdered

---

[4] Karloff was always superb in films of old England, as witness his fine performances in *Bedlam* and *The Haunted Strangler*.

his tormentor, finds himself in urgent need of another body. He and his young assistant exhume the freshly buried corpse of a stately old woman and load it into his carriage. The doctor and the student sit together in the single seat with the body, in a large sack, propped up behind them; the doctor is driving. The road is a rough and rocky one, and the carriage is tossed violently from side to side as it starts back to Edinburgh; despite the student's efforts to keep the corpse in position, it frequently falls against the driving doctor. The horror of the grave robbing, the wildness of the night with the black, cloud-covered sky torn by jagged streaks of lightning, combine to create an atmosphere of overwhelming horror in Daniel's tortured mind. As he drives faster and faster down the mountain road, he seems to hear, in a harsh and terrible whisper, the evil voice of Gray, promising to be ever near him, even in death. The doctor's eyes grow wild with fear. There is a slight delay as one of the wheels of the carriage sinks into a rut in the road. The student leaps down to free it and, as he does so, the corpse once again falls against the doctor. He touches the face and is convinced that the features have changed. When the light of the lantern is drawn closer, Daniel finds himself facing the still, white corpse of Gray. He then utters one word which, filled with despair and anguish, is one of the most superb utterances in films: 'Gray!'

The doctor whips the horses into a fury and the carriage leaps ahead. The body of Gray becomes now fully exposed, the terrible white form of the grave, and the heavy rains fall upon it as it is illuminated by the flashes of lightning. The doctor cannot keep the corpse from him, and it almost seems that he and the dead man are locked in a furious, macabre struggle. Daniel loses control of the carriage and it crashes down a slope and overturns. When the young assistant reaches the scene, he finds that the doctor is dead and the corpse is, indeed, that of the recently exhumed elderly woman.

6

But the sun is close to rising, and we must bring to an end our visit to the city on the Thames. Another monster awaits us, in the dark, dank and gloomy world of the sewers of Paris, and we must not make him impatient.

THE PHANTOM

'Imagine ... Red Death's mask suddenly come to life ... to express, with the four black holes of its eyes, its nose, and its mouth, the extreme anger, the might fury, of a demon; and not a ray of light from the sockets!'

We stand in the dim light by the quiet shores of a lake of blackness in a world so thickly enshrouded in night that the beams of our lantern cannot penetrate to the other side of the inklike body of water. At our feet is a small white boat, capable of holding no more than two or three people, seeming like a vivid white scar on the dark surface of this world, bobbing gently in the slight soundless movement of the tideless water. Above us, behind us, around and before us, there is nothing – nothing but a black world, a world seen, even suspected, by few people, a world containing its own peculiar evil and horror. There is a small rockfall to our right as a huge grey rat, its eyes burning like twin fiery beacons in the feeble light of our lantern, scampers from these invaders of his silent world. The slight sound echoes and rebounds like an avalanche through the stone cavern. For this lake is not a body of water under the clear, cold sky of heaven; its still surface has never reflected the twinkle of the stars or the romantic light of the moon. We have descended through five levels of dark mystery, have traversed corridors long forgotten save by the army of rats which are everywhere underfoot, have come

The Phantom (Herbert Lom) faces the soprano (Heather Sears) whose career he has secretly guided at the Paris Opera.
The Phantom of the Opera (Hammer Films, 1962)

into contact with walls of cold, unrelieved stone which have never seen the light of day and down which, at various points, trickles the cold, dirty waters of the sewers. We have gone deeper and deeper into the earth, leaving the world of light and sanity far above us, into a world of utter silence in which is a complete absence of colour, save for the unrelieved

monotony of the world of night. And we have come at last to
the silent, forgotten shores of this underground lake, deep in
the bowels of the earth, hidden, forgotten, unknown, directly
beneath one of the great metropolises of the world.

And as we stand in this silent, mysterious world of everlasting night, there drifts down to us, from far above our
heads, dimly and but faintly heard, the sound of glorious
music.

We step unsteadily into the little white boat and start
slowly across the lake which seems composed of some particularly black and vile-smelling ink. The sound of our oars, dipping in and out of the smooth surface of the water, is shat-
teringly loud as we move slowly towards the opposite shore,
so close by, yet lost to our sight in this world of darkness.
Our hearts seem to hesitate in our breasts as we approach the
dangerous centre of the lake where, in former times, those
who dared to venture upon the surface were beguiled by the
alluring song of the siren, rising from beneath the water itself.
There were those who were unable to resist the strange, age-
old call of the witch of the lake and, heedless of their danger,
bent over the side of the boat, striving desperately to see the
beautiful creature from whom the glorious tones issued. Closer
and closer they bent toward the surface of the water until,
suddenly, there was movement beneath the smooth, dark
mirror and two strong, powerful arms reached up for them
and dragged them, silent and unresisting, down into a watery
grave.

With a slight, almost imperceptible jolt, the little white
boat makes contact with the opposite shore. As we step from
our ancient vessel, the rim of our iron lantern strikes against
the gunwale, and there is a sound as of thunder in the vast
empty chamber, pealing through the long, mysterious corridors, seeking out the forgotten nooks and crannies of this lost
world. We pause, frightened, although we know there is no
longer anything to fear in this dead world, and then walk on
down the corridor before us until we come at last to a wall
which seems effectively to bar any further progress. But a
light pressure of the hand in the upper right corner and the
wall swings slowly, silently aside. It closes behind us and we

are once again alone in a dark and silent world. There is a
flare of light and suddenly we find that we are standing in a
luxurious, elegantly furnished drawing-room of the period of
Louis Philippe.

Well may we stand in amazement at what we see, for it is
apparent that someone of exquisite taste and sensitivities had
once made his home here, five dark stories below the level of
the ground. The room is furnished with the greatest opulence.
There are comfortable chairs, exquisitely carved tables, a rich
divan, brilliant paintings upon the walls. Beautiful silk and
satin draperies hang before windows that look out upon nothing. There is a large, superbly carved mantelpiece. Above it
hangs a mirror in a gold frame, and upon the mantel itself are
two curious ebony boxes. We open these, thinking to find
jewels and some fabulous treasure, but instead we see two
strangely carved figurines – one the model of a scorpion, so
lifelike that we shy away in fear from the poisonous barb in
its tail, the other a grasshopper that seems about to leave its
place of temporary rest and bound across the room. To the
right of the mantel is a small flight of folding steps against the
wall, leading up to a window, placed high, near the ceiling,
which seems, to us, to look out upon nothing but blackness,
as do all the windows in this most peculiar abode.

At the far side of the room is an enormous pipe organ,
covered now with a thick coating of dust. Upon the music
rack are several sheets of musical manuscript paper, thickly
blanketed with a frightening mass of tiny black notes with
wiggling tails. Across the top of the first sheet scrawled in
huge black letters, is the title DON JUAN TRIUMPHANT.

And on the bench before the organ, greying with the dust
of passing years, is an old violin, and a full-length, smooth,
featureless mask.

Just past the organ there is another small room, and as we
cross its threshold, we are struck with a terrifying presenti-
ment of death. For the room is black and scarlet – black walls
and scarlet satin hangings. It is bare of all furniture save one
curious and frightening object in its very centre, surrounded
by draperies the colour of newly spilled blood. It is an open
coffin.

We stand silent and more than a little frightened, in the midst of this abandoned luxury, marred by this graphic reminder of the grave, and voices raised in a chorus of song drift faintly down to us from the levels above.

We have come to a strange place indeed in our quest for horror, to a shrine of music, a temple devoted to the beauty of soul-thrilling sound. We are standing now in the fifth cellar of the Paris Opera House, far, far below the level of the stage.

But even here, so far removed from the wilderness of Transylvania and the burning sands of Egypt, here in one of the most beautiful and civilized cities in the history of the world, here in the very heart of modern living, even here, we will find horror.

For we are standing in the secret home of Erik, and here before us is the coffin in which slept the dread and powerful Phantom of the Opera.

2

The exquisite city sprawled along the banks of the gentle Seine has known many monsters in its two thousand years of existence, and in Paris nothing ever really dies. In the darkest hours of night on the Ile de la Cité, you can stand in the Paris Notre-Dame and, gazing up to the magnificent squat square towers of the cathedral, see the twisted, deformed figure of unfortunate Quasimodo, his arms embracing the aloof cold garcoyle of Le Penseur, asking why he, too, could not have been made of stone. The spacious beauty of the fountained Place de la Concorde still seems to ring with the horrible chuckle of Madame la Guillotine. The Place de la Bastille still rings with the agonizing screams of the mysterious Man in the Iron Mask.

The Paris Opera is one of the architectural wonders of modern Europe. Site of the structure was chosen in 1861, during the glittering days of the Empire, but the various nineteenth-century upheavals of the course of French history postponed its completion for more than fifteen years. By the time it opened its doors, the Empire was a glorious memory of the past and France was in the period of its Third Republic. The opulent design, the fantastically luxurious furnishings, all were reminders of the Empire glory and found instant acceptance in the hearts of luxury-loving Parisians. In at least the architectural sense, the Paris Opera House is the most famous in all of Europe.

The structure is composed of some seventeen floors, including five deep and vast cellars and subcellars beneath the building. These lower levels, although occasionally used for storage purposes, have been, for the most part, vast and empty, seldom visited or explored, serving chiefly as support for a weight of approximately twenty-two million pounds. The size of the opera house is almost inconceivable. According to an article in *Scribner's Magazine* in 1879, just shortly after the structure was first opened to the public, the building contains 2,531 doors with 7,593 keys. There are nine vast reservoirs, with two tanks holding a total of 22,222 gallons of water. Fourteen furnaces (at the time) were used to provide heat, with nearly five hundred grates to distribute warmth to cold corridors and chambers. There was a stable with a dozen or more horses, used in the more ambitious productions, dressing-rooms for five hundred people, together with one hundred closets for the instruments of the orchestra. The building is a vast maze of enormous stairways and massive corridors, marble columns, gold design, paintings, frescoes, statues. There have always been unconfirmed rumours of a vast lake in the subcellars – a river, according to some – but there is no documentary evidence of this. Such a lake is, however, a possibility, since so much of Paris stands upon water. These underground areas are today cut through by several railway tunnels.[1]

It is this enormous, fantastic and beautiful edifice that Gaston Leroux used for the scene of his novel *The Phantom of the Opera*. Leroux, born in 1868, started his career as a journalist and later became a popular writer of detective and mystery stories. Although he is little read today, he secured a form of immortality through his most famous work about the opera phantom, still a favourite with readers of old-time mys-

[1] Details are provided in the Prologue to *Phantom of the Opera*.

Landlady Kate Lawson demands her rent from the gentle composer
Claudin (Claude Rains) soon enough to become the fearsome acid-
scarred Opera Phantom.
The Phantom of the Opera (Universal Pictures, 1943)

tery and horror. The book first appeared in 1911, sixteen
years before the death of the author. Although it is no longer
easily available today, the character of the protagonist is, by
way of various film versions, as well known today as when he
first made his appearance on the literary scene.

3

The story of *The Phantom of the Opera* is placed almost entirely in the huge, rambling Paris Opera, beginning on the
night that the two managers of the opera, Debienne and
Poligny, are entering into retirement and handing over control to two other gentlemen, Moncharmin and Richard. The

principal characters of this somewhat involved tale are the lovely singer, Christine Daaé, her lover Raoul de Chagny and his brother Philippe, who is the Comte de Chagny, the two new managers, and the mysterious phantom, Erik, generally referred to as the opera ghost.

At the time of the opening of the story, the Paris Opera has for some months been plagued by the ghost, a wraith, an unknown and rarely seen figure who has brought constant terror to the members of the organization. This unwanted guest made his presence known in various uncomfortable ways. His ghostly voice was apt to be heard at any time and in any part of the structure, issuing from the walls, from the ceiling, from the very air itself, but without providing a single clue as to the actual whereabouts of the speaker. It was apparent that he resided – if a ghost can be said to reside – somewhere in the opera house, although no one was able to guess where. Unlike most ghosts, he is also in need of material sustenance, for the managers of the opera are required to pay him twenty thousand francs a month to ward off the various catastrophes which seem to befall the members of the troupe if this stipend is not promptly paid at the beginning of each month. Payment of this strange salary is made in one of the loge boxes. Box number five is on the ghost's orders reserved at all times for his private use, and woe betide any other occupant! At the beginning of each month, an envelope containing the francs is placed on a ledge in this box. How the ghost secures the money is another of the many mysteries that surround him. The box is very closely watched at all times, no one is seen to enter or leave it. Yet, invariably, by the end of the performance, the envelope, which has never left its position on the ledge, is found to contain only worthless bits of paper. There is also further evidence that the unseen ghost has been in the box – a box of sweets or a five-franc tip is left on the shelf for the cleaning woman, Mme Giry, who insists she has actually heard the ghost in the box, conversing with an unseen female companion. The constant strain of dealing with this phantom figure has contributed heavily to the decision of Debienne and Poligny to go into retirement.

The ghost has actually been seen on at least one occasion; at any rate, Joseph Buquet, chief scene-shifter, claimed to have seen him one day in one of the upper cellars. The distraught man described the phantom as being extraordinarily thin, wearing evening clothes over a skeleton frame. His head was that of a dead man's skull, with no nose, and eyes so deep set that they could not be seen.

For months, every untoward event that occurred at the Opera was attributed to the opera ghost, and the mere mention of him was enough to send the members of the chorus and ballet into paroxysms of fear. A falling bit of scenery, a cold suffered by one of the prima donnas, even poor box office receipts, these were all blamed upon the activities of the opera ghost. He was everywhere. He completely dominated life within the walls of the great Paris home of operatic music.

And even on this night, just before the speeches in honour of the outgoing managers, the ghost has struck again – Joseph Buquet – he who had once seen the phantom – is found dead, hanging from a beam in the third cellar, in the very spot where he had reported his encounter with the ghost. It is even reported that the phantom himself, dressed in the long scarlet robes of the Red Death, with no mask to cover his death's head, has been seen at the various little parties held in several parts of the house on this night.

The opera has on this evening been the scene of a great new triumph – the first stellar appearance of Christine Daaé, a lovely young girl who had previously sung only minor roles. On this particular evening, Carlotta, the prima donna, had been taken ill – the ghost's work again, no doubt – and Christine had been rushed in to sing Marguerite in the production of *Faust*. She had created a major sensation, and there were many surprised comments by those who had heard the young girl sing many times before, but never in so exquisite a manner.

Among these is the young Raoul de Chagny, who has known Christine as a child. He is the brother of Philippe, the Comte de Chagny, who is some twenty years his senior. Overcome with sudden love for the young singer, Raoul rushes back to her dressing-room after the performance, to find the small chamber crowded with admirers. He finds himself rather shabbily welcomed by the young singer and is asked to leave with the others when she expresses a desire to be alone. With the conceit of young lovers, Raoul convinces himself that Christine's true intention is to be alone with him. He conceals himself in the corridor until the others have gone and then, excited and happy, he returns to her door. To his dismay, just as he is about to burst into the room, he hears a man's voice, demanding that his beloved must love only him. Christine's response assures the unknown man that on this night she has sung only for him, that she has given him her soul. Shattered, Raoul moves away from the door and conceals himself again, waiting for them to leave, anxious for a glimpse of his rival. But when Christine appears, she is alone. Raoul rushes into the dressing-room to find it empty.

The troubles begin for the new managers on the very next morning, with a note from the ghost himself, reminding them that box five is to remain his exclusive property, threatening disaster if the box is sold. The letter also contains a demand that Christine be permitted to sing that evening. The managers are inclined to laugh off the story of the ghost as a practical joke, probably perpetrated by their predecessors.

Raoul, meanwhile, has managed an interview with Christine, who explains to him the sudden improvement in her voice. Her father, a violinist, had been her original coach and promised that, upon his death, he would send to her the angel of music to continue her training. Shortly after her father's passing, the angel had appeared, and it is he who has been coaching her for the past few months. The instructions are received in her dressing-room, delivered by a mysterious voice belonging to someone she has never seen. It was this voice Raoul had heard while standing outside her door. Raoul, with the jealousy of a man who suspects a rival, disbelieves her story, and Christine leaves him in anger.

The managers, meantime, have decided to defy the ghost. The star of this evening's *Faust* will be Carlotta, and the managers themselves will view the performance from the controversial box number five. As further protest to the ghost's demands, Mme Giry is fired as an accomplice, her place to be taken by M. Richard's concierge, who is to be in the audience this night.

The phantom reacts quickly to this bit of defiance. The managers receive a second threatening letter, again demanding that Christine sing in the place of Carlotta, that box five be returned to its rightful occupant, and that Mme Giry be reinstated in her post as keeper. The managers ignore this new demand. At the same time, Carlotta also receives a threat, ordering her to relinquish the role to Christine, hinting at dire misfortune should she dare to sing. Carlotta, feeling this is a plot engineered by Christine herself, also ignores the warning.

When the curtain rises on *Faust*, the managers are in box number five, Carlotta appears in the stellar role, Christine is once again in a minor supporting role. It is during the second act that disaster strikes. While moving confidently through one of the major arias, Carlotta's voice fails her. The managers become aware of an uncomfortable, alien presence in the box. A ghostly voice whispers to them that Carlotta is singing to bring the chandelier down. With a tremendous roar, the massive chandelier above the auditorium crashes to the floor. Among those killed is M. Richard's concierge, slated to replace Mme Giry.

Several days after the tragedy, Raoul receives a note from Christine, who has unaccountably disappeared from the opera house. The note suggests that they meet at the opera masquerade. Christine there tells him that they will never meet again, that she will never again appear at the Opera. It is obvious she is both unhappy and frightened. Determined to find and destroy this so-called angel of music, Raoul enters Christine's dressing-room, hoping to solve the mystery of the voice that comes from nowhere, but he finds nothing. Christine, unaware of Raoul's presence in the dressing-room, enters, weeping, calling mournfully for someone she refers to as 'poor Erik'. Suddenly Raoul hears singing – a man's exquisite voice, issuing from behind the walls. Christine rises and calls to Erik as the voice moves closer. She crosses to the full-length mirrors from which the voice swells ever stronger, and then, in a sudden blaze of light, is gone. Raoul's efforts to solve this strange disappearance prove futile.

But Raoul has not seen the last of his beloved, for Christine returns to him some two weeks later. She takes him to the roof of the opera house, far above the rest of Paris, for only here, she says, are they safe, for all the underground belongs to Erik. She has now learned the truth – her vocal coach is

Claude Rains was a soft-voiced menacing Phantom in the splendid Technicolor remake that also starred Nelson Eddy and Susanna Foster. *The Phantom of the Opera* (Universal Pictures, 1943)

not the angel of music, but a mortal man with a more-than-mortal voice. She does not love him, but is compelled to return to him again and again, lest some dreadful disaster befall the Opera and its members. His name is Erik, and he loves her with a terrible, all-consuming love. Sitting huddled in the safety of the roof, Christine tells Raoul the entire terrible story.

This mysterious voice spoke with her, instructed her, sang for her in thrilling and magnificent tones, but remained always a voice without form or body. There were daily instructions, and he was harsh in his tutelage, but under his hands Christine blossomed into a superb and brilliant artist, firmly believing he was the angel of music sent by her father. But when Raoul entered her life, the voice became suddenly still, returning only after Christine promised to see the young man no more. The night of the falling chandelier Christine learned the secret of the mysterious mirror in her dressing-room. The full-length panel opened at a slight touch in one of the upper corners, to reveal a dark and unknown passageway behind the walls of her room. In the darkness, a hand reached out for her – a hand cold and hard as bone itself. She screamed and struggled when a man in a large cloak, wearing a mask, took hold of her and forcibly led her down the passage into the depths of the secret regions beneath the Opera. After a nightmarish walk through a maze of dark, twisting stone corridors, they reached the silent shore of an underground lake; this they crossed in a small white boat. Suddenly Christine found herself in a sumptuous, well-lighted drawing-room. When the mysterious man in black told her not to fear, that she was in no danger from him, Christine realized she was at last in the presence of the voice, her angel of music.

In anger, Christine attempted to snatch the mask from the face, but was held back with the warning that she was safe only as long as she did not touch the mask or attempt to see what was beneath it. The figure, identifying himself only as Erik, then dropped to his knees and, weeping, poured out his love, imploring her to remain with him in his underground home and sing only for him. He revealed the elegance of his strange palace, but frightened her by the appearance of his own bedroom, where he slept in an open coffin as a reminder to himself of the intransigence of life. All he had he offered her, if she would but love him and never try to see his face. Finally he seated himself at the large organ and, playing with strong, thunderous tones, called Christine to sing to him. Her voice trembling with fear, Christine began to sing, moving ever closer to the strange figure so engrossed in his music. With one quick and sudden gesture, she tore the mask from his face. With indescribable horror, she saw a death's head with black holes for eyes, nose and mouth, with no ray of light from the dark sockets of the eyes. Erik forced the poor girl, nearly out of her mind with fear, to look upon his horrible face, telling her he was a corpse from head to foot, a creature too horrible to be seen by mortal eyes.

With the passing of the shattering sense of horror, a deep feeling of pity came over Christine as she saw the hideous creature crawling at her feet, begging for love and forgiveness. At last she agreed to stay with him for two weeks, during which time she managed to some extent to overcome her horror. Only when she promised to return to him did Erik permit her to leave.

But as she sits with Raoul on the roof, Christine reveals her fear of the phantom, and agrees to flee from Paris with Raoul following the next evening's performance.

And as they talk, the phantom, concealed behind a nearby buttress, listens to their every word.

The ghost makes his next move the following evening. Christine, starred in the night's performance, achieves a great triumph. But suddenly, during the climax of one of the final scenes, the stage and theatre are plunged into darkness. The blackout lasts only for a moment, but when the lights come up again, Christine has vanished.

Raoul has no doubts as to where Christine has gone. His only question is how to find a way into the dark bowels of the opera house. Here he is aided by a mysterious figure known simply as the Persian, a tall, bearded man often seen about the Opera, although his reason for being there is unknown and no one has dared question him about it. He now reveals to Raoul that he was once chief of police to the Shah of Persia, and a long-time foe of the ghost. The two men solve the mystery of the mirrors in Christine's dressing-room and make their way into Erik's world.

Raoul and the Persian prowl for some time in the dark corridors of the huge edifice, aided only by the light of a lantern. They come across some of the strange inhabitants of this dark world – the furnacemen, dark, gnomelike figures who stoke the massive furnaces of the opera house and are seldom seen in the light of day; the door-closers, old former employees of the Opera who have had jobs created for them in order to keep them alive, and spend their older years seeing that the many doors of the opera house are kept closed. They have an encounter with a horde of rats and the frightening figure of the man who is employed as rat-catcher. Raoul assumes they are headed for the lake, but the Persian, aware of Erik's bag of tricks, informs him they would never cross the water alive. Through his magnificent art of ventriloquism, at which Erik is the supreme master of all time, the phantom causes all crossers of the lake to hear the voice of a siren, and when the boatmen lean closer to the water in hopes of seeing this legendary underwater dweller, Erik, concealed (through one of his many magical arts) beneath the surface of the water, reaches up with his long white arms and drags them to a watery grave. There is one other entrance to Erik's underground lair, at the spot where Joseph Buquet had been found dead. They seek out this secret entrance and drop into what the Persian immediately recognizes as the torture room.

This frightening six-cornered chamber is composed entirely of mirrors, with no apparent possibility of escape. There is an iron tree and a hangman's rope. The Persian shudders; he has seen such a room before.

But their primary concern is Christine, and through the wall, they hear the singer and Erik in conversation. Erik has given her a terrible choice – marriage with him or death for her, for himself, and for others. When Erik leaves the room, Raoul and the Persian make their presence known to Christine, who has been tightly bound and cannot move to indicate to them the whereabouts of the secret door. The phantom returns and Christine's fears tell him that there is someone in the torture chamber. The Persian's pleadings are to no avail; the chamber is suddenly flooded with brilliant light. The torture has begun. The heat in the room increases to an almost unbearable point. The Persian realizes they have one of two alternatives – roast to death or use the rope as a means of escape by hanging.

The torture of the heat is increased by a series of frightening illusions, aided by Erik's ventriloquist's powers. The Persian searches for the hidden spring which he knows will open the secret door, but the hours pass, the heat increases, and the secret eludes him. They are close to death when the Persian presses a nail beneath the iron tree and a portion of flooring gives away, plunging them into a dark cellar lined with long rows of small kegs, filled with gunpowder. They realize it is the phantom's plan to blow up the opera house during the evening performance.

Raoul and the Persian return to the torture chamber, calling to Erik to abandon his mad scheme; the phantom ignores their cries. It is time for Christine to choose. On the mantel are two small figures, a grasshopper and a scorpion. If Christine will wed the phantom, she need only turn the scorpion and the gunpowder cellars will flood with water; if she prefers death, the turning of the grasshopper will ignite the powder and destroy the Opera and all in it. After a moment of agonizing indecision, the singer turns the scorpion. The waters flood into the cellar and torture chamber, almost drowning its two occupants.

When the Persian regains consciousness, he finds himself in his own home; one of the conditions of Christine's agreement was that no harm should come to Raoul or the Persian. Raoul has disappeared, and Christine is not heard from again, nor is Erik. For a time, Paris papers are filled with the mystery of the sudden disappearance of the young man and the brilliant singer. The mystery deepens when the Comte de Chagny, Raoul's brother, is found dead by drowning on the shore of the lake beneath the Opera, a victim of 'the siren', while searching for his brother.

Some weeks later, the Persian has an unexpected visitor – the phantom himself. Erik tells him he is dying of love for

Christine. The young singer's plight had touched his cold heart. She had given every indication of remaining true to her promise and becoming his wife, but her unhappiness was painfully apparent. Whenever he bent to kiss her, she did not draw away, but horror shone in her eyes. When she herself placed her warm lips on his hideous forehead, Erik knew for the first time the true meaning of compassion. He wept, and Christine wept with him; she pitied him and held his cold, skeletal hand in her own, filled with warm and youthful life. Against this proof of the singer's gentle heart and goodness, the evil of the phantom could not prevail. He tells the Persian that he has released her from her promise and permitted her to go off with Raoul, asking only that she return to bury him herself in the depths of the Opera cellars when he dies, as he knows he soon must, without her.

Three weeks later, the Persian receives the brief notification that Erik, the phantom of the Opera, is dead.

With this, the tale of the phantom of the Opera comes to an end. It leaves, of course, a great deal unanswered, which M. Leroux clears up in a brief epilogue, presented in the form of a talk with the Persian shortly before the latter's death. (Leroux explains that he had become acquainted with the Persian during his attempts to learn the truth of the phantom legend, resulting in his writing of the book. Such methods, intended to present a work of fiction as fact, were common in those days.)

The Persian explains that Erik was born of so hideous an aspect that even his mother forced him to wear a mask at all times. He fled from home to become a freak in a travelling circus, and then attracted the attention of the Shah of Persia, who called upon him to perform at the palace. Erik became part of the Shah's court, securing considerable power, which he freely used to gain his own ends. It was here, as a diversion for the Shah, that he first devised his fiendish torture room. Finally his power became somewhat of a menace to the Shah himself, who ordered Erik's execution, the task being assigned to the chief of police, none other than the Persian. Erik, followed by the Persian (who took this opportunity to flee a coming purge), fled to Paris and became a contractor. Determined to lead a normal life despite his aspect, Erik plunged into the social swim of Paris, but found himself dreaded and avoided. He was then employed in the construction of the Opera, which enabled him to build his own secret home deep in the bowels of the earth, abandoning for all time the society which had no place for him.

Erik achieved most of his successes through trickery. He was the world's greatest ventriloquist, and made use of this ability to create the siren of the lake, the ghostly voices of the Opera, the croaking of prima donna Carlotta on stage. His intimate knowledge of the secret passageways and doors of the Opera permitted him to come and go as he chose, and his feats of legerdemain explained many otherwise inexplicable happenings. The monthly stipend he had actually picked from the manager's pocket even before it was placed in box number five, deftly replacing it with the envelope of paper. Among his many talents, he was an expert at strangulation, permitting him to dispose of many of his enemies.

Leroux concludes his strange story with the discovery of the phantom's skeleton during construction work at the Opera. As for Christine and Raoul, they were never seen again.

4

The Phantom of the Opera suffers from many of the flaws we noted in *A King in Babylon*, which was written some six years later. The writing is often stilted, generally naïve, the characters are caricatures of life. Christine is impossibly pure and wholesome, a typical example of the long-lost breed of helpless, defenceless women; Raoul is irritatingly patient and understanding. The Age of Chivalry still shines through this work. Raoul, in spite of his consuming passion, would never think of taking advantage of Christine, even in the most advantageous circumstances. The phantom is incomparably evil, yet even he, while he has Christine imprisoned in his underground palace, respects the purity of womanhood and spends most of his time on his knees pouring out his love and pleading for understanding and compassion. It is difficult to conceive of any present-day villain behaving with such regard for feminine chastity; perhaps modern emancipated woman does not rouse such chivalrous feelings. It might also appear that Christine was more highly conscious of her honour than women are today; she could have saved the situation in the underground lair by merely pretending agreement to marriage, but it seems this never occurred to her. Though under duress, she had given her word to marry the phantom, and she was a woman of her word.

These flaws, again, are not necessarily of the writing itself, but of the time in which the writing was executed. Europe was in a state of ferment and indecision, but the First World War had not yet erupted when Leroux penned his story. It was still a world of gentility and propriety, a world in which good always prevailed and evil was inevitably overcome. Four letter words were not permitted in polite society, either in spoken or in printed form. The more intimate possibilities between the sexes were not mentioned by writers; if some daring author should be so careless and improper, 'the right kind' of people certainly would not read him – at least, not openly. Vulgarity in speech or action had no place in literature; love was a spiritual longing, never to be confused with animal lust.

Leroux's story is often confusing and sometimes difficult to follow. Despite later explanations, it is not always completely clear just how the phantom manages his little artifices. His monumental passion for Christine is also somewhat difficult to understand, for she seems in every way quite an ordinary, rather dull, young lady.

But in his picture of life in the Paris Opera, particularly in the dark nether regions known only to the initiate, Leroux has composed a fine brooding work of horror. The Opera House becomes a world of secret panels and passageways, of long, dark stone corridors, peopled by unknown wraiths and monster rats, of underground lakes and waters, of an existence lived in complete darkness, made all the more mysterious by the fantastic world of glitter and colour upon the stage directly above these mysterious depths. The phantom,

with his ghost appearances and half-appearances, his horrifying death's head, becomes a chilling figure of unknown
evil.

In many monsters, we find something to pity. We can feel
with deep sympathy the longing of the Frankenstein monster
for friendship and understanding, the agony of Lawrence
Talbot during his transformation into a wolf. Perhaps we can
even, just a little, pity Dracula for his endless battle against
the forces which would destroy him, and Karis for his
attempts to prove undying love and devotion. There are
times, also, when we can feel a surge of pity for the Phantom
of the Opera – the little boy who was so hideous that his own
mother forced him to wear a mask. The home he erected for
himself beneath the Opera House of Paris was merely another
mask, another attempt to conceal his own hideousness from
the eyes of the world that rejected him, as it does monsters
of all kinds. There is in the phantom, in his loneliness, his
alienness, much of the Frankenstein monster. When one such
as he falls in love, we can find time for sympathy. His constant
weeping and crawling at the feet of his goddess may be repugnant to us, but we cannot help but be moved by the depth of
such a love. And in his final scenes with the Persian, in which
Leroux's writing reaches its finest emotional peak, when Erik
speaks of the wonder of being looked upon without fear by a
beautiful woman, of actually feeling the warmth of a woman's
kiss on his horrible face, surely then we cannot feel too much
fear and hatred for this monster who had the misfortune to be
born with a great heart and a terrible ugliness.

It is difficult to avoid comparison between the phantom's
hopeless love for Christine and the great passion of Quasimodo
for the gypsy girl, Esmeralda. Leroux, in fact, was obviously
strongly influenced by Victor Hugo's classic *The Hunchback of
Notre Dame*. Hugo had his cathedral, his monster, his air of
love and loneliness, his beautiful girl; all these elements are
present in Leroux's less important work. Even the conclusion
is the same – as the phantom's body was found in the depths
of the Opera long after the end of the tale, so was Quasimodo's
skeleton later discovered in the vault of Montfaucon.

In his final release of Christine, the phantom, perhaps, does not behave entirely true to form. After what we have seen of the intensity of his longing and passion, his soul-searing loneliness, it may seem somewhat unlikely that Erik would so relax his hold on Christine after she has finally succumbed to his importunings and given her word to be his forever. But we have, fortunately, never been in quite the same position in which Erik found himself; possibly we can not quite realize the effect of a woman's kiss on the face of a man who had never before known the meaning of tenderness and compassion. Then, too, at the time Leroux wrote his tale, novels were the pastime of women, and they would not have expected any other ending – or accepted it – but one in which Christine and Raoul lived happily ever after.

5

We have gone into considerable detail in retelling the sad and frightening story of The Phantom of the Opera, since the book by Leroux is no longer generally available. The phantom is, nevertheless, one of the best known creatures of horror, and it is the screen that is responsible. Gaston Leroux's novel – which has often been called 'a spanking good story' – cannot stand the tests of a classic and in all probability would have been long forgotten or, at best, relegated to the class of the ancient mystery tale, had not Universal Studios taken hold of it, greatly enlarged on the angle of horror and turned it into one of the classics of the field.

Universal's famous silent production of The Phantom of the Opera was released in 1925. I was not yet born at the time and, unfortunately, have never had the opportunity of seeing this greatest of Lon Chaney, Sr's classic films. Certainly its reputation has not diminished with the passing of the years. In the realm of make-up, Chaney was supreme in his time. As the phantom, he appeared as Erik is presented in the original story – with the head and face of a skull. The terrifying scene in which Chaney is unmasked at the organ is one of the greatest classic scenes of horror. It has been shown many times in silent-screen memory films, and is as chilling

A two colour Technicolor process heightened the effect of several
scenes, including Lon Chaney dressed as Poe's Red Death at the
masked ball.
The Phantom of the Opera (Universal Pictures, 1925)

today as when first presented; the scene was excellently re-
staged in the James Cagney film on the life of Chaney, titled
Man of a Thousand Faces. This first *Phantom of the Opera*
closely followed Leroux's story, with such touches as the
torture chamber, the hand dragging victims into the underground lake, etc. The young lovers were played by Norman
Kerry and Mary Philbin. There were elaborate sets of the
catacombs and the opera stage, with various scenes presented
in the startling innovation of colour, and the scene of the

falling chandelier was one of the great spectacular scenes of the day.

Joe Franklin insists[2] the Chaney film was far more thrilling and exciting than the 1944 remake of Universal, a sumptuous technicolor production with beautiful music, brilliant sets and exquisite costuming. This may be true, yet the later production had much to commend it, particularly in a superb performance by Claude Rains as Erique Claudin, the phantom. The advent of sound, of course, was a blessing for a film of this type, and there was considerable operatic production, presenting Susanna Foster and Nelson Eddy as the romantic interest.

Considerable liberties were taken with the story in this new version of Leroux's book, and the tale was considerably tightened and simplified. Erique Claudin is a violinist in the orchestra at the Paris Opera. His life's ambition is to be recognized as a composer, and to this end most of his effort is directed. The lovely Christine is a member of the opera chorus; not even the singer is aware that he has been paying for her voice lessons for many a year. The violinist has always worshipped the soprano from afar, and he is convinced that she will some day be recognized as a great singer. To Christine, he is merely a member of the orchestra.

The years soon catch up with Claudin, and his hands become crippled with arthritis. As a result of his inability to perform adequately, he is released from his post at the Opera, the director feeling that the violinist has, through all his years with the organization, put aside more than sufficient funds to meet his needs. This, of course, is not the case, for Claudin has spent all his savings on the secret voice lessons for Christine. The publisher, Pleyel, to whom Claudin has submitted his great concerto, is now his only hope, both to secure funds on which to live and to continue Christine's lessons. Pleyel, however, refuses to see him. Claudin calls again and again at the office, but is unable to make his way past the legions of secretaries. On his last visit, he is told his manuscript has probably

[2] *Classics of the Silent Screen.*

been thrown into the trash basket, and is lost. Claudin becomes violent, for he has submitted the only copy of his great work, and it cannot be duplicated. While he argues with the employees of the publishing firm, the great maestro, Liszt, visiting Pleyel, comes across the manuscript and begins to play, first slowly, then enthusiastically, recognizing the touch of genius. Hearing his music from behind the closed doors, Claudin is convinced that he has been robbed. He bursts into the inner office and attacks Pleyel, accusing him of piracy. Pleyel's female assistant, terrified by this seemingly unwarranted attack of a madman, hurls a dish of acid into Claudin's face. Screaming in unbearable pain, the violinist dashes from the publishing house and seeks shelter and comfort in the dark, wet sewers of the city.

This is the beginning of Claudin's life of darkness. He takes residence in the catacombic cellars of the Opera House and becomes known and feared as the Phantom of the Opera. His hand is soon felt throughout the establishment, always strangely in support of Christine.

Determined to give the soprano the deserved opportunity of shining before the music-loving populace of Paris, Claudin slips a potent drug into a drink given to the prima donna, Madame Biancarolli. Unable to sing, she is replaced by Christine, who scores a tremendous success. Claudin, wearing a long cloak and hood and the full-face mask which is never removed from his face, stands alone in the darkness of the opera cellars and hears the exquisite voice come gently down to him.

But Madame Biancarolli is not so easily tampered with. She insists she had been drugged in a plot in favour of Christine and demands that the young singer be dropped from the Opera roster. The management bows to her will. In his insane fury, Claudin, gaining access to the prima donna's dressing-room through the secret passage behind its walls, strangles her.

He does not, however, fully achieve the desired result; Christine, while returned to the Opera, is kept in the chorus. The young singer, meanwhile, has not been unaware that the mysterious phantom works in her behalf. His voice comes to her through the walls of her dressing-room, promising that she will be the toast of Paris. Christine, confused and frightened, leans for help and support on her two rival suitors, the star baritone and the inspector of police, both determined to save her and win her for his own.

Claudin again communicates with the managers of the Opera, demanding that Christine be starred in the next production, hinting at great tragedy that will befall the house if they refuse. The managers do just that, and another singer is signed to take Biancarolli's place.

There is a full house that evening, a glittering display of the best of Paris society. Having been alerted to the possibility of some new move on the part of the phantom, the police are out in full force, placed inconspicuously in strategic parts of the

The senior Lan Chaney stunned audiences with his makeup in the 1925 silent version of *Phantom of the Opera*, which was somewhat more faithful to the original novel than later productions. *The Phantom of the Opera* (Universal Pictures, 1925)

audience. The Russian opera calls for a large chorus of men wearing robes and masks, and this permits the placing of officers backstage and in the chorus. It also, however, gives Claudin freedom of movement, posing as one of the cast.

While the opera progresses, Claudin climbs above the stage and out over the audience, to a point where a massive crystal chandelier hangs over the auditorium. He begins to saw away at the heavy chain from which the chandelier depends, knowing that the sound of the music will drown out his own noises. With a mighty crash, the chandelier falls upon the audience.

In the chaos and confusion that follow the falling of the chandelier, Claudin rushes backstage and takes Christine by the hand, indicating that he is a police officer sent to lead her to safety. The frightened young singer follows him, not suspecting the identity of the cloaked figure until he opens a gate that leads to the cellars. Her screams are cut off by the phantom's hand and the two disappear into the depths of the underground.

Claudin, attempting to soothe Christine with his assurances that she is in no danger, leads the young girl through dark and mysterious corridors, lower and lower, ever deeper into the very bowels of the building. When they reach the dark, silent underground lake, they move quickly along its shore until they reach the secret doorway that opens into Claudin's underground lair. He assures Christine that she will not be harmed, but pleads with her to live with him in this secret world of darkness, where she will sing for him alone.

Meanwhile, in the Opera House above, the baritone and inspector plan to set out in search of Christine. The astute baritone has, by now, managed to guess at the identity of the phantom, and has conceived a plan to bring him out into the open. Liszt is brought onto the stage of the now-deserted theatre and told to play Claudin's concerto. The great pianist seats himself at the piano and his powerful fingers strike the keys as the baritone and the inspector enter the cellars.

In the phantom's lair, Claudin has been startled by the sound of his concerto. Incensed at what he considers thievery, he sits at the organ and plays in concert with Liszt, the sound guiding the two would-be rescuers to Christine's place of

A turn of the scorpion means life for Christine (Mary Philbin); a turn of the grasshopper means death. The Phantom (Lon Chaney, Sr.) watches.
The Phantom of the Opera (Universal Pictures, 1925)

imprisonment. They find their way frequently blocked by rockfalls and realize that the entire underground structure is crumbling.

Meanwhile, both on the stage and in the dark chamber, the brilliant tempo of the music increases, and with it grows the fury of Claudin's playing. He becomes uplifted by his own music, forgetting all but the tremendous torrent of sound from the organ. He calls upon Christine to sing as he plays. Christine, wondering how this frightening figure could have used as the basis of his concerto a simple little folk tune from her childhood days, begins to sing, edging ever closer to the musician who, engrossed in his music, is unaware of her approach. With a quick, sudden movement, Christine rips the mask from his face. He stops playing and rises in fury, turning the full horror of his face, terribly burned and seared by acid, to the young singer. She screams as the baritone and inspector rush into the chamber. The inspector fires at the hideous figure and the reverberation of the shot causes the crumbling stones to collapse. The three flee in terror and make their way rapidly through the dark corridors, while the weight of the Opera House falls upon the phantom and destroys him.

The Phantom of the Opera was, of course, far more than just a horror film. It boasted exquisite production, beautiful colour and fine direction. In the cast were top-notch performers and fine singers. The operatic sequences – featuring primarily music of Chopin and Tchaikovsky – were superbly mounted and beautifully sung. There may possibly be some argument for the belief of horror aficionados – and of silent film devotees like Mr Franklin – that there was too much opera and too little actual horror, but to those who enjoy both music and horror – and there were, undoubtedly, many of these in the audiences – this new version of *The Phantom of the Opera* was a sheer delight.

Young Susanna Foster (she was not quite twenty at the time) scored a considerable success in the role of Christine. Added to her fresh, red-haired beauty was a remarkably fine and true operatic voice, for an unfortunately brief time the most popular classic voice on the screen.[3] This was one of the last of Nelson Eddy's screen appearances, following his many

[3] Miss Foster followed the success of this film in the following year with another beautifully presented technicolor horror titled *The Climax*, in which Boris Karloff furthered her career at the Paris Opera through hypnotism. (Apparently no one thought she could make it on her own.) As the malevolent Dr Hohner, Karloff had in his home the coffin-vault of a woman he had killed, the embalmed body mounted in true Hollywood fashion on an impressive catafalque with silken hangings. Karloff eventually perished in the fire that destroyed this room. *The Climax* was the inevitable Hollywood attempt to cash in on a new, successful idea, begun by *The Phantom of the Opera*, but, although impressively produced with strikingly beautiful operatic sequences, it did not equal the success of the earlier production. Miss Foster, after a few more surprisingly minor and ineffectual films, married singer Wilbur Evans and retired from the screen.

successful films with the late Jeannette MacDonald, and his somewhat wooden performance was more than compensated for by his vocal contribution.

Claude Rains was no newcomer to horror films, although *Phantom* was his first in this genre in many years. He had, in the early thirties, scored a tremendous success as the original Invisible Man in H. G. Wells' superb tale, and was also the father of Lawrence Talbot in the first of the wolf-man films. As Erique Claudin, he gave what was easily one of his most memorable performances. His justly famed silver voice was a sharp and startling contrast to the evil of the role and the chaos he caused. He was quietly and effectively sinister.

The appearance of the Rains phontom differed considerably from that of Chaney, which so closely followed Leroux's description. There was here no death's head with empty sockets for the nose and eyes. Certainly, however, Rains' features were every bit as frightening, and the abrupt removal of the mask caused as many terrified screams as those which greeted the exposure of the Chaney skull. The entire side of Rains' face was a mass of burned and seared flesh, the eye destroyed, the mouth twisted, the burned face a horror of blue and red scars. Even the light blue, featureless mask, covering all but the mouth, which Rains wore through most of the film, presented a peculiar horror of its own.

The script writers revealed a sound sense of effect in their alterations of the original story. The screen play was considerably easier to follow than Leroux's original, with its many extraneous sections on the ghost's private box and the monthly stipend. The Persian appeared but briefly in the film, with strong emphasis on the police inspector. This omitted the interesting but not really necessary incident in the phantom's torture chamber and the rather curious and not wholly acceptable explanation of the phantom's past at the court of the Shah. By making Erique Claudin a member of the opera orchestra, long and involved explanations were avoided. The omission of the phantom's grand passion for Christine was a major change in the story, but a beneficial one. The addition of love would have added nothing but further complications to the story; the phantom's love for Christine in the original is often unsatisfying, confusing and embarrassing.

The falling chandelier was, of course, the highlight of the film, as it was also in the Chaney production. The chandelier was a massive structure of crystal diadems and gas jets, hanging far over the heads of a glittering audience garbed in the height of the day's fashion, the sparkle of their jewellery almost outshining the chandelier itself. On stage at the moment was a very colourful scene of Russian barbarism, a camp of Tartars toying with a captive princess; the superb music was based on a theme from Tchaikovsky's Fourth Symphony. While the audience listened to the crashing music and watched the cast and horses on stage, Claudin, wearing a fur-lined cape and hood and the blue mask that covered all but his twisted mouth, sawed industriously at the thick chain holding the chandelier. The Russian princess took centre stage and began her aria. Her full, rich voice soared to its peak of emotion when, suddenly, her eyes became wide with horror, and the note was replaced by a scream of terror as she saw the massive chandelier sway, then crash down upon the audience. The scene was superbly executed.

There were many other telling scenes in this fine film. The throwing of the acid into Claudin's face in the publisher's office caused many a shudder in the audience; Claudin's screams of pain as he sought the dark world of the underground were chilling; the ghostly voice issuing mysteriously from behind apparently solid walls; the shadow of the phantom gliding so silently about the corridors of the Opera House; the hand dropping something into Biancarolli's goblet; the superb removal of his mask – all assisted in building up the tense horror of the film.

This is one example of horror in which technicolor was decidedly an asset.[4] The opera mountings were exquisite, the scenes of Paris beautiful. The incidents within the cellars were dimly illuminated and well photographed, lending an eerie air of unreality to this most important locale of the film.

The Phantom of the Opera was one of the horror revivals made by Hammer Studios and – strangely, in a studio which has turned out such superb work – the least successful, in no way comparable to the Rains film, although the phantom

Hammer Films presented the Phantom in a film that, despite a fine performance by Herbert Lom, was not as successful as the production with Claude Rains.
The Phantom of the Opera (Hammer Films, 1962)

[4] Again, I must emphasize that I have not seen Chaney's silent film, and therefore cannot make an honest comparison. It is often an advantage not to have seen the original version of a classic which has been well remade, for it is then possible to judge a film on its own merits, without comparisons. I have no doubt of the genius of Chaney's portrayal, but films of the old days often take on a gloss that over-emphasizes their qualities. The same may be said of *The Hunchback of Notre Dame*, which I have often seen. For its time (1923) Chaney's version of this superb story was startlingly powerful, and remains so today. Chaney's performance was possibly the greatest of his career, and forty years later is still a masterpiece of acting. Nevertheless, the RKO remake of 1939 remains, for sheer sweeping grandeur and dramatic impact, one of the great films of its kind, and the performance by the late Charles Laughton, complete with hump, bandy legs and horrible, distorted face, is one of the classics of the macabre.

was well played by Herbert Lom. Hammer failed badly
on production values in this film, and the Opera House
appeared like little more than a country summer theatre. The
lair of the phantom was a ludicrous pile of theatrical furniture
on the very bank of a swift-running sewer. The eagerly awaited
falling-chandelier scene was reserved for the conclusion of
the film, when a small and unimpressive ceiling lamp fell on
the phantom and killed him. The film was marred by inadequate music, overemphasis on sex, and a generally poor
script.

6

We need search no longer in the vast, empty, echoing chambers of the Paris Opera House, for there is no phantom there
today; these are events more than a half-century in the past.
The long, mysterious corridors beneath the great structure are
vacant and unused. It may be that a dark shape now and then
glides silently through the gilt and marble hallways of the
Opera, down the broad marble grand stairway, haunting the
dressing-rooms, but this is only a shade, and a shade can do
no harm.

In the tumbled rubble of the nether world of the Opera
House, a silent violin and a blue, featureless mask continue
to gather dust. Erik or Erique Claudin, the opera ghost, the
Phantom of the Opera, lies at rest somewhere in the catacombic depths of the structure he had helped to build, and
perhaps the glorious sounds from the stage above drift down
to him through the lonely darkness and bring him peace.

THE HUNCHBACK

Never till now was I aware
of how hideous I am.
When I compare myself with you,
I cannot help pitying myself,
poor, unhappy monster that I am . . .
I am something frightful,
neither man nor brute,
something harder, more shapeless
and more trampled upon, than a flint.

———QUASIMODO

We are not yet ready to leave the City of Light. This sprawling, ancient metropolis stretching along the banks of the River Seine, which has witnessed the passing of history over some two thousand years, can teach us much about horror, fear, disaster. The good and evil of two millenia have cast their shadows over this beautiful city, and its ancient buildings can tell many a story to hold us spellbound. The Paris Opera has already revealed to us the story of the strange and mysterious Phantom who once lived within its deep, dark cellars. We must now cross into the Cité to another great architectural treasure, where we will meet one of the most famous monsters of all time.

But we must go back in time now, for the Paris of our monster is quite a different city from that of our time, or even of the time of Eric of the Opera. We must travel back through the rush of history, glancing only briefly at the various aspects of the City . . . Paris under the heel of the Nazi conquerors, back further beyond the days of World War I, which was the war to end all war, even beyond the days of Louis Philippe, which are still too recent for us. We visit briefly the dazzling Paris of the Emperor Napoleon, built upon the confusion of the First Republic, which, in turn, arose from the indescribable horrors of the bloody Revolution. We glimpse a lovely, courageous but foolish queen being driven in a tumbrel to her appointment with the guillotine, and still we must go back. We pass over the frivolous Louis XV in his gambols with the Pompadour and du Barry, view with horror a Henri IV slain in his carriage on the rue de la Ferronnerie, only twenty-five years after the murder of his father, the third Henri. Back, back we go, to the tragic tournament in which Henri II was slain in fulfilment of the prophesy of the mysterious Nostradamus, back to the beginning of the sixteenth century to the young Charles VIII struck down by an accidental blow on the head.

At last our backward pace slows as we reach the last quarter of the fifteenth century, for here we have reached our destination in time.

The Spider King sits upon the throne of a France torn by turmoil and dissension. Cruel, harsh, brilliant, progressive, the eleventh Louis has ruled medieval France some twenty years, and perhaps even he suspects that he is approaching the end of his vigorous life. He has overcome the traitorous Burgundians and brought prosperity to his sprawling, violent nation.

It is the year 1482.

Paris is already a vast metropolis. It has expanded far beyond the cradle-shaped island called the Cité on which it was founded by the legions of Julius Caesar before the beginning of the Christian era. In 1482 there are three distinct sections of the city: the Cité, the Université on the left bank of the Seine, and the Ville on the right bank of the great river. The Cité holds the churches, the

Université the great seats of learning, and the Ville the palaces.

In the Cité, already nearly two centuries old, stands the great cathedral of Notre-Dame.

This is a sprawling city, a violent and colourful one, typical of the medieval period, where side by side exist the fantastic luxuries and frivolities of the royals and nobles, with the incredible poverty and hardship of the lower classes. The streets are narrow, filthy alleys, the several stories of the buildings almost touching at their upper floors, trapping the sunlight. The unwary travel-ler, skirting his way about pools of foul-smelling filth, is apt to receive a deluge of slops upon his head from a suddenly opened window. Life has little value in this world, and mugger and murderer freely go about their business. Richly caparisoned dandies, their horses better clad than the average Parisian, ride recklessly through the streets, holding themselves grandly aloof from the rabble, not overly concerned if their horses happen to ride down a child or two. Thieves and beggars number in the thousands, living in their own fantastic world called the Court of Miracles. Here only the initiated are admitted. Others enter at the risk of their lives, but at the end of the day the lame can walk and the blind can see.

Gypsies are prevented from entering the city by heavy guards at the city gates, for Paris is still a walled town. An iron chain prevents free entry or exit from Paris, and this barrier is never lowered for a member of the thiev-ing gypsy tribes. The Church is everywhere supreme, and the bloody Inquisition freely lays its murderous hands on all accused unbelievers. Heretics are tortured and burned at the stake; the penalty for thievery is the gallows, and the pillory is the shame for lesser crimes and misdemeanours.

The magnificent cathedral of Notre-Dame de Paris is the center of the religious life of the city. The starving, ragged poor stand in awe before this glorious Gothic structure with its great squat bell towers, its slender central spire, its magnificently carved portals, its gargoyles and demons that seem to glare down at them with a promise of hell fire. With the impressive pageantry and beauty of the ceremonies of the Church, the poor are lulled into a feeling of good will and security in the next world and perhaps, for a short time, they manage to forget the gnawing pain of empty, shrivelled stomachs and the annoying bites of the lice that cover their bodies. Here and there might be a person who feels the fortune expended on construction of this monument to God might have better been applied to feeding the poor; but this is not an enlightened age, and the poor themselves take great pride in Notre-Dame. What matter if they are hungry, so long as God is exalted.

The great bells of Notre-Dame ring daily over the crowded, bustling city of Paris, their full, rich, resonant tones reminding the people of the God who watches over them all, rich and poor alike, merely asking them to worship and adore.

The ringer of those bells is our next Monster.

Our tour of the bustling city takes us to the Palace of Justice, and here we will pause, for a great, noisy crowd has gathered. One glance tells us that we have arrived at a moment of festivity, for there is much singing and dancing, much drinking and laughter, and the crowd is in a holiday mood. Thieves move quiet and unnoticed through the throng, snipping here and there at a purse string, while the beggars extend their dirt-encrusted hands or exhibit their mutilations, true or false, in hopes of melting the hearts of the happy Parisians.

We have arrived during the Feast of Fools, that riotous celebration with which Paris and all Europe observe the Feast of Epiphany. The Parisians have gone wild with rejoicing. All cares and worries are forgotten; even poverty is pushed into the background. This is a day when only Joy rules. There is to be a fine display of fireworks in the Place de Greve, and a May tree. The poet, Pierre Gringoire has been trying, with little success, to draw some attention to his great Mystery now being performed, but the people have already become interested in something of more importance . . . the selection of a Pope of Fools to reign over the festivities.

A small, windowlike opening has been provided, and through this are thrust all the hideous, ridiculous, laughable, revolting faces in the city. The ugliest will be Pope of Fools.

One after another, the most unattractive faces in Paris are presented to the gaze of the viewers, to be greeted with laughs, cheers, hoots of derision, exposed backsides. It is no shame on this day to be homely, for this is the one day in the year when ugliness has its own reward. Each face seems more ludicrous than the last, and the uproar increases with each ridiculous or revolting visage.

And then, suddenly, there appears at the opening a face so hideous, so repulsive in its ugliness, so frightening in its malformation, that the shouts of laughter turn to screams of terror and women turn their eyes away from a countenance that makes them think of Satan himself.

The large, misshapen head is covered with stiff, red bristles. In the approximate center of the face is a large, twisted nose, covering a small mouth filled with jagged and irregular, discolored teeth, surmounting a pointed, forked chin. A single tooth, like a yellow fang, protrudes over the horny lower lip. The right eye is completely concealed by an enormous wart and the left is ringed by the same red bristles that cover the head. Closer examination reveals the rest of the creature to be as twisted and deformed as the head. Encompassing the entire back is an enormous, mountainous ridged hump, and there is a similar deformation at the chest; the legs are bowed, the hands as immense and monstrous as the feet.

For a moment the audience is dazed with horror, and then the cries of acclamation begin. Here is a creature as ugly as the Devil himself, a hideous aberration, an obscene caricature of the creature made in the image of

The magnificent 1939 version of *The Hunchback of Notre Dame*
wonderfully recreated medieval Paris, particularly the Cathedral of
Notre-Dame, and boasted a superb cast. Here Quasimodo (Charles
Laughton) faces the terrified gypsy girl, Esmeralda (Maureen O'Hara).
The Hunchback of Notre Dame (RKO Radio Pictures, 1939)

God. Here, indeed, is a being so supremely ugly that his
very ugliness becomes a thing of beauty.

The Parisians have found their Pope of Fools and we
have found our next monster. This is Quasimodo, the
hunchback of Notre-Dame.

2

It may seem somewhat of a literary blasphemy to include in a book of horror one of the greatest pieces of
literature produced by the Western world. This is no

lurid tale of grave robbing, of mad scientists and long-reaching, blood-lusting creatures of darkness; rather it is the towering production of a brilliant mind, one of the greatest fruits from the pen of one of the most gifted writers we have ever known.

The Hunchback of Notre-Dame is, nevertheless, among these other things, a work of horror. For its principal figure, Quasimodo, the hideous, deformed, and terrifying bell-ringer—while he may not be as blood-hungry and murderous a beast as others we are now familiar with—is, at least in appearance, as much of a monster as the creation of the good Dr. Frankenstein. For more than a century he has brought chills of fears and fascination to readers all over the world. He is not a supernatural being, an artificial creation, but a man, like Eric the Phantom. To the people of his time he was a monster, and so is he considered today. He is another horrifying creature of the great writers of the last century.

It was in 1831 that Victor Hugo, who was not yet thirty years of age, produced the novel he titled *Notre-Dame de Paris*, first of a series of novels that over the next half-century were to make him immortal in the world of literature. Although Hugo began work on his novel in 1829 and completed it in January of 1831, the actual writing of this lengthy book occupied him for only six months of this time. A tremendous amount of research was necessary before the actual writing of the story, and for well over a year Hugo immersed himself in studies of Paris during the time of Louis XI. He came intimately familiar with every nook and cranny, every inscription within the cathedral of Notre-Dame, for it was his determination to be historically accurate in every detail of his work, and to be completely familiar with the structure he intended to use as the home of his protagonist. The result was the institution of an entire new literary concept: the writing of fiction based upon actual fact, in which the central figures may be real or not, but which are accurate in historical detail.

Although it made a great name for the author, *Notre-*

Dame de Paris was not at first well-received. In its portraits the greatest monsters are members of the priesthood
and the greatest evils are perpetrated by the Church
itself. The book thus came as a considerable shock to
Catholic France. With its central theme of a priest's lust
for a pagan gypsy girl, *The Hunchback of Notre-Dame*
was most certainly not a Christian book.

It is not the province of this writing to give an analysis or a detailed commentary on the various literary
values and qualities of *The Hunchback of Notre-Dame*,
as the novel came to be known. Here, we are only interested in the aspects of horror contained in this tale—and
in these the story abounds. Hugo brought tremendous
realism to Esmeralda the gypsy girl, Frollo the evil priest,
Pierre Gringoire the Poet, Clopin the King of the beggars, Captain Phoebus the rogue and rake, Gudulo the
mad recluse and, above all, Quasimodo himself, the
deaf, hunchbacked bell-ringer of Notre-Dame. Much of
the power and force of this work is due to the clarity
with which these figures are drawn. As with Mary Shelley's great book, the horror would be lost if the Monster
were not a sharply defined, believable creation.

And above all these characters—the good and the bad,
the pure and the evil, the beautiful and the hideous,
dominating every portion of the story—is the true hero-
ine of the tale: the magnificent cathedral of Notre-Dame.

3

The story is too well known to require detailed retelling
here; a brief summation will serve, in order for us to
point up the moments of horror.

The moving force of the tale is the lovely Esmeralda,
an orphaned gypsy girl who has never known her parents. Despite the Paris ban on gypsies, Esmeralda manages to enter the city during the riotous celebration of
the Feast of Fools. She dances in the squares and per-
forms tricks with her intelligent goat, then passing

through the audience with extended tambourine for con-
tributions. Her dancing is viewed by the priest, Claude
Frollo, who immediately becomes possessed with lust for
the young girl.

The ward of Frollo is Quasimodo, who is employed as
the bell-ringer of Notre-Dame. Quasimodo was a monster at birth . . . ugly and deformed, hunchbacked, mentally deficient. As an infant, he had been left before one
of the altars at the church. Here he was seen by Frollo
who, in a rare burst of sympathy, took the unwanted
child under his care. Since the assumption of his duties
as bell-ringer, Quasimodo has also become deaf. He is
never heard to speak and it is assumed, mistakenly, that
he is mute as well.

Frollo turns to Quasimodo, who obeys him implicitly
in all things, in his lust for the gypsy girl. At his urgings
Quasimodo attempts to abduct the girl, but his plan is
foiled by the arrival of the guard, led by Captain Phoebus,
who rescues Esmeralda and imprisons the hunchback.
When brought to trial, Quasimodo is given a double
sentence for his crime: he is to be publicly whipped and
then exposed to the Paris mob for an hour on the revolving pillory set up before Notre-Dame. The whipping star-
tles him, for the poor fool has not realized the turn of
events, but he bears it stoically. On his knees, his hands
bound behind him, he is mocked, reviled, and stoned by
the same people who only the previous day had hailed
him as their Pope of Fools. When he pleads for water, he
is loudly hooted until Esmeralda herself climbs the pillory and eases his thirst. Quasimodo spends the remainder of his time on the pillory in awed silence.

The gypsy girl has meanwhile become a married
woman. The poet, Pierre Gringoire, has made the mistake of wandering into the beggers' Court of Miracles.
He, too, has been tried . . . by Clopin, the King of
Beggars. Found wanting in proficiency as a thief, Pierre
was sentenced to death, unless one of the feminine inhabitants of the Court will take him as a husband.
When no offers are forthcoming, Esmeralda saves his

life. It is a marriage in name only, meaning little to those involved. Esmeralda has found another love: Captain Phoebus, her rescuer from the hands of the hunchback. The handsome, dashing, and unprincipled captain has readily entered into a passionate affair with the dancer. When Frollo hears of this, he hides himself in the room where the lovers meet. While the gypsy girl and the captain are locked in an embrace, the priest leaps from his place of concealment, stabs the captain, and flees. Esmeralda is arrested for murder.

Under torture, Esmeralda confesses to the slaying of her lover. The priest Frollo, convinced that only a witch could make him so forget his churchly vows, is on the ecclesiastic panel that condemns her to be hanged before Notre-Dame.

Near the place of execution there lives a crazed recluse named Gudule, whose infant girl had been taken from her sixteen years before and slain by a band of gypsies, leaving Gudule with only a shoe as a reminder of her child. Since that time, Gudule has immured herself in a small cell, which she never leaves. She is a strange and terrifying figure of insanity, constantly pouring oaths and imprecations upon the gypsy race. She screams her triumph as Esmeralda, on her way to the gallows, is led past her cell. Phoebus also watches the procession from the balcony of his latest love. Seriously injured by Frollo's attack, he has recovered, but cares little about the fate of a gypsy girl.

And from his perch high on the battlements of Notre-Dame, Quasimodo watches the preparations for the execution. In her plain white shift, Esmeralda kneels on the steps of the cathedral and does penance. Quasimodo, who has developed a worshipful love for the gypsy girl since the incident on the pillory, grasps a long rope left hanging down the face of the building by laborers, swoops down onto the steps, seizes the girl, and swings high into the tower with her, claiming the time-honored Church right of sanctuary.

While both friends and foes of Esmeralda plan to res-

cue her from Notre-Dame, the gypsy girl is tenderly
cared for by the hunchback, who makes it clear to her
that she is safe as long as she does not step from the
church. He provides her with food and other necessities,
concealing himself behind masonry to spare her the horror of seeing his face and form.

The vagabonds from the Court of Miracles hear that
the right of sanctuary is to be abolished and the gypsy
removed from the cathedral. Determined to rescue her,
they march on Notre-Dame under the leadership of the
indomitable Clopin, and attempt to wrest her from the
hands of Quasimodo. The hunchback, fearing they have
come to hang the girl, fights them off by dropping heavy
stones and timbers from the towers, left behind by laborers repairing portions of the church. This merely slows
the advance of the vagabonds and it soon becomes apparent they will succeed in breaking into the cathedral.
Almost insane with fear and panic, Quasimodo desperately searches for a means of battling the invasion; his
eyes fall upon the enormous vats of lead ready for use in
the construction work. He manages to light huge fires
under the vats and pours the molten lead upon the
vagabonds in the square, inflicting tremendous loss of
life and turning the square into a smoking scene of
massacre.

While Quasimodo is engaged in fighting the attackers,
a darkly clad figure bursts in upon Esmeralda, claiming
he has come to take her to safety. The frightened girl
goes with him, across the Seine and to the Place de
Greve, the site of executions. Here the dark figure reveals himself as Frollo. He offers Esmeralda an ultima-
tum: either she must be his, or she will be hanged. In a
torrent of words, Esmeralda pours out her hatred and
loathing for this man who was her nemesis, assuring
him she would rather die than be his. Frollo drags her to
Gudule's cell. The recluse, overjoyed at being able to
assist in the death of a hated gypsy, reaches through the
bars of her hermitage and holds tightly to Esmeralda's
arm while Frollo summons the guard.

But just before the arrival of the troops, Gudule spies an infant shoe that Esmeralda wears on a string about her neck. The gypsy girl informs Gudule that the shoe is her own, the sole memento of her long-lost mother. Gudule realizes the girl is her own child.

The discovery has come too late. Desperate, Gudule pulls the girl into her cell and attempts to conceal her from the soldiers, but without success. Gudule fights the guard furiously, pleading for the life of the child she has found after sixteen years of mourning, but to no avail. Esmeralda is dragged to the gallows, while the hysterical mother clings to her legs and is carried along. Gudule's embrace is forcibly broken and she falls, dead, to the ground. As her lifeless body is carried away, the rope is placed about Esmeralda's head and she is hanged.

After the violent death of the gypsy girl, Quasimodo disappears and is never seen again in the vicinity of Notre-Dame. Some two years later, his skeleton is discovered in the vault of Montfaucon, where hanged prisoners are interred. The skeleton lies in embrace with that of Esmeralda. When attempts are made to disengage the remains, they both crumble into dust.

4

This, in substance, is the story of *The Hunchback of Notre-Dame*. No brief summary, of course, can do justice to the tremendous, panoramic sweep of the tale, to the wealth of its colorful characters and to the brilliance of its writing. It is one of the greatest works in French literature.

The success of horror depends primarily on two elements—atmosphere and characterization—outside of story content itself, and we should pause here for an examination of these facets.

There are locales that lend themselves readily to atmospheric horror. Primary among these, of course, is the graveyard, closely followed by the haunted house or castle and the mad doctor's laboratory. Any enormous, ancient, dimly lighted structure, honeycombed with passages and narrow stairways, possibly with a secret stair here and there, can be extremely effective. Certainly these elements are present in the vast and ancient edifice of the cathedral of Notre-Dame. The reaches of the cathedral, lighted but dimly by candles that cast flickering shadows on its stone walls, the narrow, winding stone stairways illumined only occasionally by an unsteady torch in a wall bracket, the intricate maze of the bell tower with its huge cradles for the bells, its hanging ropes, its wooden ladders, combined with the dark mystery of a violent medieval city with its narrow, unlighted streets . . . here, certainly, we have a locale that can easily build an atmosphere of horror.

In his characterizations, Hugo was equally successful. They are all firmly drawn, neither completely black nor completely white. Esmeralda is a simple, uneducated teenaged girl raised in a world of prejudice and violence, an innocent tool of Fate, rushing to destruction because of the foolishness of her own heart. In may ways, she is not much different from the young girls of today. She arrives alone in Paris, fresh from life in a gypsy caravan, and is dazzled by the sweep and excitement of the great city. The poverty, filth, and violence mean nothing to her; this is a tremendous new world. She meets Captain Phoebus, handsome, wealthy man-of-the-world, a soldier who, like Prince Charming, arrives on a white horse to rescue her from the clutches of evil. She could do nothing but fall in love. Blind to his many faults, she surrenders herself to this great passion, the first of her young life. Claude Frollo, a man considerably older than she, severe and unhandsome, garbed in the somber frock of the Church, can arouse only fear in her heart. She looks at Quasimodo as a creature of horror. She cannot understand his motives, nor can she conceive of such a creature being possessed of human feelings and emotions. He is a hideous caricature who has no place in a girl's dreams.

Quasimodo is one of the most memorable characters in all literature. He is hideous, terrifying, a misanthrope, one of the most dreaded creatures in Paris. He is generally believed to have made various pacts with Satan, and it is held that a mere glance at his distorted features will cause a pregnant woman to miscarry or give birth to a monster as deformed as himself. Parisians swear they have seen him flying above their rooftops in the dark of night, and he is held accountable for sudden deaths due to heart attacks or apoplexy. Only the protection of the even more feared Frollo saves him from violence at the hands of the mob. In all his twenty years, there is but one occasion when Quasimodo finds even a token sort of acceptance from the people, and that is when his hideousness raises him to the post of Pope of Fools. He exalts in the position, laughing, his horrible face twisted by grimaces of pleasure, carried on the shoulders of his courtiers until the sternly disapproving Frollo appears and orders him back to his post at Notre-Dame. The bell-ringer's popularity is short lived, for the next day, when he is exposed on the pillory, the populace pelt him with insults and refuge. There is no doubt of the horror that Quasimodo inspires in the hearts of the people of Paris. He is a monster.

Yet here again, as with all truly "great" monsters, we see a glimmer of something else, a slight trace of humanity under that terrifying edifice. He moves us to pity, and while we are horrified by the appearance and actions of Quasimodo, we cannot help but feel sorry for him. Abandoned at birth by a horrified mother, he has lived ever alone, apart from companions, having no contact with anyone but his protector, Frollo, to whom he gives complete and somewhat touching loyalty. The cathedral of Notre Dame is his home and his world; he has never known any other. His only friends are the great bells that are in his charge, and on these he lavishes the love and affection of which none think him capable. He gives them names, and through the long quiet nights, when he is more alone than ever, he sits and talks with them. He knows he is hated and feared within Paris, and so he keeps away from the city, walking the streets, when necessary, only under cover of the night. He realizes he is a monstrosity, twisted in mind and body, in no way like the tall, handsome, straight-limbed men who sometimes come into the cathedral. Only behind the sheltering walls of Notre Dame, which he knows more intimately than any of the priests or acolytes, can he find a measure of peace and security.

But within the twisted frame there is a heart, and Esmeralda unwittingly finds her way into it by a simple act of kindness, the giving of a drop of water. When Frollo commands the hunchback to kidnap the gypsy girl and bring her to him, Quasimodo obeys blindly, for it would never occur to him to question his master. He gives no thought to Esmeralda. He has, perhaps, seen her dance in the square, but she is part of the world from which he is barred. His slow mind does not even wonder at the purpose behind Frollo's command. He is merely obeying the precepts of his guardian. His subsequent arrest, trial, and punishment come to him as a considerable surprise. He has done no wrong, for the commands of Frollo cannot be wrong. Why, then, is he being punished? His greatest cause for concern is fear of Frollo's wrath, since he has failed in his mission. The first measure of surprise enters his dull mind when his shirt is stripped from his body and he feels the first touch of the lash on his massive hunched shoulders. His simple, twisted mind is unable to cope with what is happening to him; he cannot understand the forces that move men to acts he cannot comprehend. He does not understand the bite of pain of the lash on his shoulders, the undisguised joy of the crowd who laugh with pleasure each time the great iron-tipped thong comes down on his body.

But kindness is one thing that even the poor hunchback can understand. When he calls for water, the crowd heaps abuse on him. But then the crowd makes way for Esmeralda who gives him water to drink. Kindness is a virtue that Quasimodo has seldom encountered, and he is amazed by it. When Esmeralda raises the gourd and pours water into the gaping mouth, he looks up at her in awe and reverence, and is silent. The gathered mob, whom he has never harmed, has mocked and ridiculed him, while this lovely young girl, who has every reason to fear and detest him, has had pity upon him. Perhaps, as the wheel of the pillory turns, Quasimodo is silent while revolving this paradox in his poor, confused mind.

These, then, are the chief actors in this powerful story . . . a gypsy girl, a mad priest, a lustful captain, a poet, and a hunchback. Placed together, they add up to one of the most fascinating groups of people in all of literature.

But is this truly a work of horror? This may seem somewhat of a sacrilegious notion to those who are accustomed to think of horror as rather lurid, not very serious fiction, of interest mostly to readers of limited mentality, concerning itself with impossible situations and even more impossible characters. To many, horror is not a subject to be taken seriously, belonging somewhere in the realm of fairy tales, superstitions, and creatures from outer space.

Yet, we need only cite *Frankenstein*, which is a great classic as well as one of the primary works of horror. Certainly if the presence of a monster is an indication of horror, this novel belongs in that category, for Quasimodo is as fine a monster as can be found. But the introduction of such a creature is not enough; he must be surrounded with the proper atmosphere, his monstrosity must be reflected in the attitudes of those about him, otherwise he is more to be pitied than feared. In this, Hugo succeeds remarkably well, for there are many fine scenes of horror here.

A dark, brooding fear hovers over the poet's entry into the Court of Miracles, the attack of Frollo on Phoebus is carried out silently and swiftly, the flickering flames of a baleful fire lights the torture chamber where Esmeralda is taken for her Ordeal. Beautiful Notre-Dame itself becomes a veritable stage of horror as fine and chilling, in its way, as the laboratory of Victor Frankenstein or the castle of Count Dracula; for this is the home of that frightening troglodyte, Quasimodo. Through the dark passageways and twisting stone stairways, lighted but fitfully by flickering torches, the deformed bell-ringer moves silently and swiftly unseen but ever suspected, the soft padding of his feet casting daggers of fear into all who hear his steps. While Victor Hugo titled his

In his greatest film role, Quasimodo in *The Hunchback of Notre Dame*, Lon Chaney solidified his position as the "man of a thousand faces." Two years later, he further consolidated his claim by his performance in *The Phantom of the Opera*.
The Hunchback of Notre Dame (Universal, 1923)

work *Notre-Dame de Paris*, the fact that this great novel is known today as *The Hunchback of Notre*-Dame is a clear indication of how this central character has forced his hideous image on the minds of the readers.

4

There have been several film versions of Hugo's classic and, like productions of *Phantom of the Opera*, these films capitalized and expanded upon the aspects of horror in the tale. A very early silent version titled *The Dancer of Paris* has long since been effectively forgotten; Esmeralda was played by Theda Bara.

Two years before his appearance as the Phantom of the Opera, Lon Chaney scored a tremendous triumph in *The Hunchback of Notre*-Dame, one of the most ambitious of Hollywood's silent film productions. The film was released in 1923, and the numerous still photographs clearly indicate the power of Chaney's characterization. His Quasimodo was a small, wizened creature with gaunt features and a thin, twisted frame. Chaney's performance greatly increased his stature as an actor and not merely as a man with a tremendously versatile hand at makeup. Chaney wore a breast-plate attached to his shoulder pads to which, in turn, was connected the seventy-pound rubber hump. A leather harness connected these various articles, which made it impossible for Chaney to stand erect. A rubber, skin-tight suit, covered with animal hair, was worn over this unwieldy contraption. Behind the fanglike set of teeth in Chaney's mouth was inserted a contraption to keep the mouth forcibly open. This horrendous makeup was conceived and applied by Chaney himself.

The film was made at a cost of $1.5 million, a tremendous sum at that time. Patsy Ruth Miller appeared as Esmeralda, Tully Marshall as Louis XI, Raymond Hatton as Pierre Gringoire, and Ernest Torrence as Clopin. Norman Kerry appeared as Phoebus, and Brandon Hurst was

Frollo. The film was a tremendous success and still ranks as one of the masterworks of silent film. In *Man of a Thousand Faces* James Cagney effectively recreated Chaney's version of the pillory scene.

Comparison between silent and talking versions of the same film are odious, for there are too many differences in production values. For this writer, the RKO-Radio version of *The Hunchback of Notre Dame* in 1939 ranks as one of film's greatest achievements.

An exceptionally fine cast was gathered for this new production. Sir Cedric Hardwicke, already well-known for the incisiveness of his characterizations, was a brilliant Frollo, an iron-minded man with a face of finely chiseled marble and a cold, severe eye, tormented by strange lusts and desires that had no place in the heart and mind of a man of the cloth. In his film debut, Edmond O'Brien was an ingratiatingly frivolous and amusing Gringoire. Allan Marshall was correctly handsome and aloof, if rather bland, as Captain Pheobus. The role of Clopin, King of Beggars in the Court of Miracles, considerably enlarged from the book, provided Thomas Mitchell with one of his most impressive roles. His Clopin was an incredibly dirty, ragged, roguish, unscrupulous, and thoroughly delightful scoundrel, courageously leading his men on until his death at the very portals of Notre-Dame. The Spider King, Louis XI, one of France's most interesting and colorful monarchs, is a natural for the screen. Although his importance in Hugo's original work is limited to the latter portions of the story, he appears frequently in the film. The wily king, just approaching his sixtieth year and near death, is riddled with disease, himself physically deformed, feeble and aged before his time. The art of printing has been introduced to France, and the brilliant Louis is keenly aware of its tremendous importance for the future of the world. The aged monarch is ever approachable by his people, Esmeralda herself appeals to him at Notre-Dame, and as a result of his intervention, she is put to Trial by Ordeal, which unfortunately condemns her. The performance by

Harry Davenport, complete with ermine robes, bathtub and the famous medal-lined hat, remains the classic characterization of this ruler, who was interested in justice but severe and uncompromising in its practice.

The role of Esmeralda was played by an eighteen-year-old Irish beauty who was also to make a considerable name for herself in Hollywood. Although this was Maureen O'Hara's fourth film, she had not aroused much notice until another film made earlier that same year, *Jamaica Inn*. Her performance as Esmeralda established her as a star.

Quasimodo was played by Charles Laughton, contributing one of the classic portrayals of the screen. Laughton already had numerous brilliant performances to his credit. Seven years earlier, for his unforgettable performance as King Henry VIII, he had received the Academy Award. He had come close to a second Oscar in 1935, for his unforgettable Captain Bligh in *Mutiny on the Bounty*. The opportunity of playing Quasimodo was too great a temptation to resist, and he returned to Hollywood from England, where he had been living and working in recent years.

The Laughton Quasimodo was physically very close to the kind of monster Victor Hugo had created. The left side of the face was covered with a sheet of sponge rubber, which completely concealed his left eye; a false, dead eye was placed somewhat lower down on his cheek, giving the face a lopsided appearance. The mouth was small and twisted, scraggly with broken teeth, the hair scanty, unmanageable. Laughton was of course a rather stout hunchback—he could not see the advantage of going on a rigid diet just to play a monster—with an enormous ridged hump and extremely bowed legs. In spite of his size and ungainliness, Laughton moved with grace and agility. The overall impression was one of the most satisfying monsters of makeup since the miracle of Karloff's Frankenstein monster. Laughton's own opinion was that he had never seen anything quite so hideous; from all accounts, he never even saw the completed film.

Transferring so large and involved a novel as *The Hunchback of Notre-Dame* to the screen is a seemingly insurmountable problem, and considerable abreviation is necessary, while retaining all the basic elements of the story. (This is just the opposite problem to that encountered in filming *Dr. Jekyll and Mr. Hyde,* which is only a novella.) This task is perhaps particularly difficult when working with a story as well known as Hugo's. In this instance, the writers did a laudable job. Slightly more emphasis was given to the characters of Pierre Gringoire, Clopin, and Louis XI, while various minor roles were completely omitted, among them Gudule, the recluse. While this unfortunately cancelled the extremely melodramatic incident of Gudule's pleas for her daughter, the character is not essential to the story. The affair between Esmeralda and Phoebus became a fairly innocent flirtation rather than a full-scale sexual affair (after all, the censors were still around) and Pheobus was stabbed and slain in an open garden during a festival, rather than in the intimacy of a trysting place. In line with the trends of the day, which claimed tragedy was not box office, the film was given a happy ending, with Esmeralda granted final amnesty and Quasimodo standing in the belfry of Notre-Dame, watching her and Gringoire riding out of his life. This conclusion was the greatest liberty taken with Hugo's story, and the only serious objection to the script. (The later version with Anthony Quinn returned to the tragic conclusion, but neither this nor Technicolor could make this a really interesting production.)

The film was expensively mounted and brilliantly directed and produced, setting a new and high standard for realism and accuracy in historical films. It provided a stirring picturization of life in medieval Paris and its mob scenes; the celebration of the Feast of Fools and the storming of Notre-Dame by three thousand vagabonds was handled with the touch of a Cecil De Mille. The film was lensed in black and white, but the lack of colour is not missed. (This, of course, was the year of

Gone With the Wind (which included another fine performance by both Thomas Mitchell and Harry Davenport); after that a spectacle in black and white became
unthinkable.

The most spectacular aspect of the film was the splendid reconstruction of Notre-Dame on the back lot; the
same lot that had been used in Chaney's film. The massive set seems authentic in every way, both in its interior and exterior, down to the last gargoyle. I was much
younger the first time I climbed the stairway of the bell
tower of the real Notre-Dame, but it was a haunting
experience. The dark, narrow, winding stone steps, their
centers rutted by centuries of climbers, but dimly lighted
by occasional slits in the wall, take one eerily back into
the past, and are just as shown in the film. I would not
have been surprised to see Quasimodo leaping down
above me.

Certainly the greatest single asset of the film, and the
chief force of its horror, sprang from the bravura performance of Charles Laughton. He spoke but little throughout the film, the bulk of his performance being in
pantomime, at which Laughton was a master. He was
often accused of being a "ham," and his facial grimaces
as Quasimodo probably added weight to this accusation.
Someone has truthfully said, however, that his was the
very best quality of ham.

Laughton's Quasimodo was a fascinating mixture of
horror and pathos, of good and evil, of cruelty and
kindness. He moved quickly, expertly, from one mood to
another, totally dominating the film, giving one of his
finest performances in a brilliant career.

The film also provided interesting illustrations of the
effect of mingling horror with the more mundane. The
tone of horror is introduced early in the film in the first
quick view of the hunchback . . . his single expressive
eye watching the dancing Esmeralda while he is concealed in a dark alley. When Esmeralda, sensing his
stare, becomes frightened, he withdraws, and we have a
teasing glance of his twisted form in flight.

The touch of horror is then eased by the riotous celebration of the Feast of Fools, but returns with a vengeance with the next abrupt appearance of the deformed bell-ringer. When during the choice of the King of Fools (for obvious reasons, the film could not dub him Pope of Fools) the horrifying visage of the hunchback for the first time bursts upon the screen as he thrusts his head through the opening, we have one of the most satisfying moments of horror in screen history. The effect is greatly heightened by the sudden, abrupt, and complete silence that freezes the merrymakers with fear.

As with Karloff's creature, no photographs were released of Quasimodo's face before the film opened, or for some time after. For publicity, still photos from the film only showed Quasimodo in semidarkness or shadow, as a huge, misshapen but faceless form. This quite naturally increased the ultimate impact.

Immediately following Quasimodo's first full-faced appearance on the screen, through a clever twist of mood, we encounter the first touch of pathos in the tale of the hunchback. It is obvious that Quasimodo enjoys his new exalted position as King of Fools. Wearing the traditional court-jester's belled crown, the troglodyte is carried on a litter through the streets of Paris. Like some hideous toad, he squats on the litter, his deep-throated roar of laughter rising above the shouts of the crowd. Then Frollo appears, watching with stern disapproval. When he orders Quasimodo down from his perch, the hunchback's face becomes serious and frightened. He lowers himself from the litter and, the fool's crown dangling from one hand, follows his master back to the cathedral. Several members of the crowd, objecting to this removal of their newly crowned king, attempt to indicate their disapproval but are quickly cowed by the menacing visage of the hunchback. The effect is that of a child's holiday spoiled by a scolding parent and, for a moment, Quasimodo does not seem quite so terrifying.

But horror returns almost at once with the attempted seduction of Esmeralda. Facing arrest as a gypsy, the

Charles Laughton was the ultimate Quasimodo. In one of his greatest performances, Laughton brought to the title role of *The Hunchback of Notre Dame* the very essence of horror, despair, and pathos.
The Hunchback of Notre Dame **(RKO Radio Pictures, 1939)**

dancer flees into Notre-Dame, where she appeals personally to the King. Louis places her in Frollo's care until her case is examined. The lustful priest guides her up the darkly winding stone stairway to the bell-tower.

Suddenly the horrible figure of Quasimodo appears before her. Screaming with terror, she flees, and Quasimodo, on Frollo's orders, follows her into the streets of the city. Darkness has fallen upon the narrow, dirty, and unlighted alleys of Paris. The fear of darkness encountered in the danger-filled, unprotected streets of medieval cities is a fear that has never left the human subconscious. The closely packed buildings block the brightness of the moon and stars; windows are tightly curtained and little light escapes into the streets, gleaming dully on stone walls and puddles of stagnant rainwater and slops. Esmeralda, sensing that she is being followed, walks slowly and fearfully down the dark alley, keeping close to the shelter of the stone wall, pausing occasionally to peer behind her. But she fails to look above her where, moving swiftly but quietly on top of the wall, Quasimodo follows, the infrequent light of the moon etching his hideous face. And then, suddenly, he drops from the wall in front of her. Esmeralda stops, frozen with horror, as the terrible creature approaches her, grinning and beckoning with his fingers.

Later in the film we once again have an offsetting of horror by the pathos of Quasimodo's trial and punishment. He stands before the tribunal, his hands tied before him, uncomprehending, bewildered and docile. In his deafness, he fails to hear the questions put to him regarding his name, age, and occupation. He stands, breathing heavily, bored and confused, looking indifferently about the court. Realizing at last that he has been spoken to, he pours out a torrent of responses to the questions that had been put to him some minutes before, leading the magistrate to believe he is mocking the court; the result is the addition of one hour on the pillory to his sentence of whipping.

What follows is one of the classic scenes of film-making. The pillory is a large wooden platform set up before Notre-Dame, somewhat above eye level. In its center is a circular second platform, which rotates at the application of a lever. Here criminals are whipped and then

presented to public view, with the gathered mob free to
vent their displeasure in whatever manner it sees fit,
provided no one actually sets foot upon the platform
itself. Here Quasimodo is taken after his trial. Stripped
to the waist, the horrifying noduled mass of his deformed back is revealed to the excited crowd. He is
placed on his knees on the rotating circle, his hands tied
behind him. Until the first stroke of the lash falls on his
naked back, he is silent and submissive at which point
he turns his head in surprise. Again and again the thick
leather thongs, tipped with bits of metal, fall upon the
humped ridge, until tiny rivulets of blood trace their
crimson course down his body. He twists and squirms,
cries out with the heavy voice of a bull, then is silent.
The leather of the whip has become softened by blood
and perspiration, and is replaced with a fresher instrument.

The scourging completed, a length of sackcloth is tossed
over Quasimodo's bleeding shoulders and he is left to the
mercies of the people. He kneels silent and unmoving,
his bullet-shaped head thrust forward, his single eye
glowing with hatred and humiliation, while the crowd
taunts and mocks him. After a time he breaks the silence by calling hoarsely for water. The crowd jeers; a
man mops a rag in the muddy water under the pillory
and tosses it into Quasimodo's face; he knocks it free
with convulsive movements of his shoulders. Then
Esmeralda slowly and silently mounts the pillory. Laughton here indulges in one of the most poignant bits of
pantomime ever recorded on screen. He looks up at the
gypsy girl with awe and a touch of reverence, moving
his heavy, bound body in an effort to avoid besmirching
this angel, trying to conceal his hideous face. Slowly,
then, he tilts his head back and opens his mouth while
the dancer raises her gourd and permits a stream of
water to fall over the parched lips. Quasimodo drops his
head abruptly, the lips brushing the back of her hand in
a silent gesture of gratitude, and he endures the remainder of his punishment in stoical silence.

A touch of non-Quasimodian horror follows when Esmeralda, on trial for the murder of Captain Phoebus, is put to torture in hopes of a confession being forced from her. A trapdoor is opened in the floor of the court- room and through it comes the baleful flicker of the torturer's fire; it seems a door opening into hell. The frightened gypsy girl is taken down the small flight of steps and finds herself in a chamber of horrors, lined with instruments of torture at whose purpose she can not even guess. A low fire burns in a stone brazier beside which stands a tall, muscular man whose head is com- pletely concealed by a large black hood; only his cool, indifferent eyes are revealed by two narrow slits in the fabric. Esmeralda is seated and an iron boot is placed on her small white foot. Slowly, remorselessly, the screws on the boot are tightened, biting agonizingly into the tender flesh. She screams. . . .

The film attains its greatest heights of both pathos and horror in its scenes in Notre-Dame itself, after Esmeralda has been rescued by Quasimodo and lives there in uneasy sanctuary. She is given the small cham- ber that has been Quasimodo's home since he attained the position of bell-ringer. The hunchback, like a faith- ful guardian dog, sleeps on the floor across the doorway, thus effectively barring passage to those who would harm his ward. He gives her a high-sounding whistle with which to summon him when she is in need; this high pitch he can hear. Each day her food is placed on the floor at the entrance of her chamber; Quasimodo then conceals himself so the sight of his face will not mar her appetite. He explains to her that he is deaf, plaintively asking, "You wouldn't think there could be anything else wrong with me, would you?"

He rings the bells for her, introducing them by names he has given them, leaping onto the massive swinging forms, laughing and hooting in the excitement of com- panionship, carried away by the ecstasy of thunderous sound, one of the few sounds he can still hear. Esmeralda looks on in horrified fascination as the enormous humped form leaps from one bell to the other, until finally the overpowering noise of the great bells and the horror of Quasimodo's exultation drive her from the bell tower and back to her chamber.

These scenes are among the moist poignant ever filmed, beautifully directed and superbly performed by both parties. At no other time in films does a monster of horror appear in so sympathetic a light. It is impossible, at this point, to be horrified by Quasimodo. The feeling he creates is one of great pity. It is a lasting tribute to Laughton's great talent that the hideous appearance of this deformed creature is, for a time, almost forgotten.

The vagabonds march on Notre-Dame for the climax of the film. In the dark of night, carrying blazing torches and weapons of all descriptions, three thousand ragged men and women converge upon the square before the cathedral, determined to storm the structure and carry Esmeralda to safety. Quasimodo, equally determined to preserve the adored Esmeralda, is seized with panic. In the strange half-light, the twisted, gnomelike figure moves quickly about the platform and gallery between the bell towers, tossing the workmen's beams down upon the crowd of vagabonds. He lights the fires under the vats of molten lead and the hideous monstrosity prances about in the light of the flames like something out of a nightmare. He stands precariously on the very rim of the gallery, holding onto the slender columns, laughing horribly as he watches the slaughter below, his twisted mouth gaping, the single eye glowing with triumph.

And then, the shrill scream of Esmeralda's whistle reaches his ears. She is in danger, and all else is forgotten. Quasimodo rushes to her sanctuary to find her in flight from Frollo. All his loyalty to the priestly figure vanishes as a horrific pursuit follows between the casings of the giant bells, Frollo in his black habit relentlessly followed by the wizened figure of the monster, his one eye now ablaze with fury and the lust for blood. They meet and Quasimodo raises Frollo high in his hands and hurls him to death from the gallery of the cathedral.

These scenes are rich with horror and excitement. One does not need Technicolor, for brilliant splashes of colour might have been a distraction in these darkly shadowed sequences.

The film then ends on a quiet, pathetic note. Before his death, Frollo had confessed his guilt to his brother, the Archbishop of Paris who, in turn, had gone to the king and revealed the truth. Freed by the monarch himself, Esmeralda leaves Notre-Dame in triumph, as Quasimodo watches from his gallery high in the cathedral. His world has now ended. He has slain his guardian, Frollo, and now has lost the only being he has ever dared to love. He leans against one of the hideous gargoyles with which the gallery is studded . . . no more hideous than himself . . . and sighs. His hand runs over the stone of the deformed creature, and he whispers, "Why was I not made of stone like thee?" The camera moves for a distant shot of Notre-Dame, with Quasimodo appearing simply as another of the cold stone figures.

The Hunchback of Notre-Dame opened at the Radio City Music Hall in 1939 and was highly acclaimed (although some critics still insisted they preferred the Chaney version). It seems to have increased in status over the years. It has been reissued several times, but I caution those who wish to experience the full impact of this film not to watch it during its occasional television presentations in which a film of just under two hours length is presented in a commercial-lanced version of just 90 minutes.

6

A later film version of *The Hunchback of Notre-Dame*, released in 1956, presented Anthony Quinn as Quasimodo and Gina Lollobrigida as Esmeralda. The film was spectacularly produced in Technicolor, and well performed and directed but it did not achieve the success of

The first colour version of *The Hunchback of Notre Dame* was filmed
in France in 1957 and starred Anthony Quinn. Gina Lollobrigida
played Esmeralda. Its major advantage was that it restored Victor
Hugo's tragic ending, which had been considered unsuitable for the
1939 version.
The Hunchback of Notre Dame (1957)

its predecessor. As previously mentioned, this version of
Hugo's great classic did not adopt the happy ending of
Laughton's film (happy, that is, for Esmeralda), nor did
it return to the original Hugo conclusion of Esmeralda's

hanging; Miss Lollobrigida was killed by an arrow shot into her back during the battle before Notre-Dame. The final scene, however, was a satisfying copy of Hugo's own epilogue: the discovery of the two intertwined skeletons in the place of public burial.

Quinn's Quasimodo relied on somewhat less makeup than did Laughton's. Behind the twisted left side of his face, with it partially covered eye, Quinn's own features were clearly discernible, and his hunchback sported a full head of black hair. Quinn's performance, however, was in the best tradition of the impersonators of the bell-ringer of Notre-Dame. The failure of such a spectacular film is difficult to understand.

Anthony Hopkins fared no better in a 1982 TV version of the film. Perhaps there is such a thing as too many remakes. The Quinn film was the third version in some thirty-five years. There was nothing strikingly different about this film (aside from colour) to set it apart from its predecessors. Remakes of such horror classics as the Dracula and Frankenstein films are continually successful because of the element of surprise. The stories are never identical to the previous filmed versions. The best example of this is the Frank Langella *Dracula*, which varied widely from the original. With the film about Quasimodo, the element of surprise is largely gone. It is one thing to take liberties with a comparatively little-known "classic" as *Phantom of the Opera*, but quite another to tamper with a story as thoroughly well-known as Hugo's tale.

The popularity and the commercial expectations of these two films might also be indicated by the houses in which they played. Although the Quinn version opened at a first-run house in New York, it could not boast the prestige of a Music Hall opening. When the Laughton film was reissued in New York many years ago, it appeared as the sole attraction at the Palace for a successful run. Quinn's film appeared as a reissue on a double-feature program in a third-rate grind-house on West Forty-Second Street.

We might also return to our original premise for the relatively lukewarm reception of the Hammer Frankenstein remakes. Boris Karloff had made the role of the Monster so completely his own, it was difficult, if not quite impossible, for any other performer, no matter what his capabilities, to attempt the part with much success. Even Glenn Strange, who succeeded Karloff, was never more than adequate; but then, the same could be said for the scripts.

The same might be said of Quasimodo. Through rerelease and the (highly abridged) television showings, the younger generations have been permitted to view Laughton's magnificent portrayal. It is one of those roles that become the exclusive property of a particular performer, at least until sufficient time has elapsed to permit the earlier performance to be forgotten. Laughton is the definitive Quasimodo (and remember, not many have even seen the Chaney version.) This holds true of at least two other great Laughton characterizations. He is still the perfect idea of Henry VIII, despite later performances by Richard Burton and others, and he is also the perfect image of Captain Bligh in *Mutiny on the Bounty* (1935), in spite of Trevor Howard's strong performance in the 1962 remake. While comparisons can be odious, they will always be made.

7

It is unlikely there will be another Quasimodo, at least for a good many years to come. The taste for historical epics has faded, and they are too expensive in these days of soaring costs. *The Hunchback of Notre-Dame* cannot be made on a shoestring. As with so many of the great films of the past . . . and this is particularly true of the magic year of 1939, in which Laughton's film was released . . . it would be much wiser merely to rerelease the flawless originals of such films, which are as moving and exciting today as they were a half-century ago. The remake of a classic is seldom as memorable as the original.

But Quasimodo will never suffer the oblivion that has befallen many movie monsters who have run their course and finally lost acceptance by the public, for he will live on imperishably in the pages of one of the greatest literary works of the Western world.

A visit to the awesome cathedral of Notre-Dame de Paris takes one back into the dark mysteries of the medieval age. It is impossible to gaze upon the magnificent edifice, to walk between its great stone walls, in its higher galleries and platforms, above the hideous stone gargoyles frozen in their expressions of horror, without feeling the shadow of the ugly, deformed, feared and lonely Quasimodo, the hunchbacked bell-ringer of Notre-Dame.

THE CREATORS OF HORROR
I

The Alcoholic:
'I became insane . . . with intervals of
horrible sanity.'

The man before us now has often been called one of the two or three true literary geniuses produced by this country. He is small of build, slender, well formed. He fits his clothing well. There is about him an air of elegance, of poise, of self-assurance. He is much at home in these genteel, comfortable surroundings. One can see he is a gentleman, with all that word implies. He is an extremely handsome man, in a wild, almost gypsy manner. He holds his proud handsome head erect, black locks of his thick hair fall appealingly about his broad, pale forehead, and his large, unusually dark eyes flash with intelligence. Women, who have always been strongly attracted to him, often call him 'beautiful', although there is nothing unmanly in his attitude or appearance. They say he is a kind, gentle, devoted and considerate, charming and gracious man. He might be a matinée idol. He smiles winningly, his white teeth flashing, and his voice is soft and well modulated. He does credit to any drawing-room graced with his presence.

But let us see this same man later in the course of the evening. The surroundings are quite different. We are in a tavern, dark, filthy, filled with hawking, coughing, spitting, swearing men and laughing, loose women. Our matinée idol sits alone at a table against the wall, a glass in his hand and a bottle on the table before him. There is no gracious air about him now. Those dark eyes are bleary and bloodshot from drinking and there is in them the memory of things perhaps never before seen by man. He moves with abrupt, nervous gestures and the corners of his mouth tremble slightly. His dress is stained with drink, the collar of his shirt open, his trousers begrimed with dirt. There surrounds him an air of impending disaster. He is young, just in his thirties, yet he looks now far older, and already death has tapped him on the shoulder.

We are in the presence of the master, the greatest writer in the field of the macabre and the horrible. He is an alcoholic, an inveterate gambler and, if whispers are true, a narcotics addict.

His name is Edgar Allan Poe.

He was born in Boston in 1809, son of an unsuccessful actor and an English actress. Poverty brought death to both parents before he had reached his third year. He was then adopted (although not legally) by a well-to-do Virginia merchant named John Allan. Although Allan was, in later years, to complain that Poe never indicated the smallest gratitude for what was done for him, the merchant saw to it that the boy was well educated, first in England and later at the University of Virginia. Poe, although never much interested in schooling, was an alert boy who did well. When he had enough of this 'nonsense', he ran off to join the army, and was stationed for a time on Sullivan's Island in South Carolina, which was later to become the scene of his famous tale *The Gold Bug*.

His cleverness soon earned him a commission to West Point where he did quite well. But during this period, John Allan remarried and Poe's situation took on quite a different cast. He came to the decision that this second marriage of his guardian might well result in children who would supplant him as Allan's heir, and he saw his hoped-for inheritance slip away. The prospect of army life became less appealing, and he determined to leave the Point. Much has been made of this part of Poe's life, with claims that he was discharged from the

Academy because of his propensity for gambling; it is unlikely that he was the first or last of the young cadets to indulge in this rather harmless vice. Poe was discharged from West Point because he wished to be discharged; he deliberately neglected his studies and absented himself from his classes. The West Point incident is generally considerably overplayed by hostile biographers who wish to paint him in the blackest possible tones; in a character as full of flaws as Poe's, there is no need to rely upon invention.

At the age of twenty-four, Poe's first story, *Ms. Found In a Bottle*, achieved considerable success and earned for him an editorial post on the *Southern Literary Messenger*. But already the most fatal of all his vices had appeared, and before the year was out Poe had lost his position because of excessive drinking.

In 1836, he married his cousin, Virginia Clemm, and another chapter of his peculiar tragedy was begun. Poe was 27; his bride was 13. Poe's touching devotion for little Virginia is possibly the only aspect one can find in his life that is decisively in his favour. He loved her dearly, and most of his finest love poetry was written in her honour. For a time, he seriously attempted reform to give Virginia the kind of husband he felt she deserved.

But the marriage was a difficult one. The Poes lived ever on the borderline of poverty and, to make matters worse, Virginia suffered all through her brief life from tuberculosis. Poe himself fell ill with the same disease. Friends and literary circles attempted to aid the young couple, but the proud Poe did not graciously accept their assistance.

And then, in 1847, at the age of twenty-four, Virginia Poe died, 'retaining her fragile and childish beauty to the last'.

Only the most romantic writer could claim that Virginia's death was a blow from which Poe never recovered, that it was this loss that drove him to the dissipation which ended with his own death. The seeds of decay had always been in the young writer, and they now merely reappeared. Virginia's death had, if nothing else, removed the sole sobering influence in his life.

Nevertheless, Poe did keenly feel his loss, for his love for

Virginia had been true and sincere. A strange morbidity
settled upon his mind and he turned more and more to the
oblivions of alcohol. He suffered a lesion of the brain and
spent many hours in the delirium of fever, finding it difficult
to separate the periods of sanity and madness. He became
obsessed with sex. Always attractive to women, he now
became involved in a series of sordid scandals with prominent
and wealthy women. He ran out of funds and once again
knew the pangs of hunger. He had now no friends to assist
him, for he had alienated them with his libertine way of life.
He did little writing in these days, for he had also earned the
enmity of the magazine editors who previously had so eagerly
sought his stories. He became involved in unpleasant and
embarrassing controversies with various writers of the time,
and his furious exchanges with Henry Wadsworth Longfellow
became the literary scandal of the day. He was scheduled to
marry into a prominent and wealthy New England family,
then appeared drunken and disorderly at the home of his
intended, and was shown the door. He seemed to fall deeper
and deeper into degeneracy.

For one brief period toward the end of his life, however,
Poe seemed to regain his senses. After a protracted bout of
drinking with some cronies in Philadelphia, he determined on
reform. He went to Virginia, taking up residence in his old
home town of Richmond, and joined a temperance society.
He began a series of lecture tours which proved successful,
resumed contact with his old friends and, for a time, it seemed
that he had indeed found himself. This hope became stronger
when it was learned that he was again to marry, a widow of
long acquaintance who had, for some reason, never quite lost
her faith in him.

This marriage, too, was fated never to materialize. En route
to New York to make arrangements for the wedding, Poe
stopped at Baltimore and once again fell in with the evil
influences of his wilder days. These friends urged him to put
aside his good resolutions and celebrate his coming marriage
in proper spirit. Once begun, Poe needed little urging, and one
drink followed another. Some hours later, in a state of total
drunkenness, he staggered out of the tavern. It was a cold

and rainy night in October. Throughout the night, Poe wandered the streets of the city, in delirium, babbling in half insanity, until finally he collapsed into the gutter. He was taken to a hospital and there, on October 7, 1849, he died. He was buried beside his beloved Virginia.

The great genius of American letters had lived only forty years.

Few writers have been as little understood and as grossly misunderstood as Edgar Allan Poe. We have seen two sides of him, and it is difficult to understand which side was the true one. Was he the coarse, obscene, self-centred, arrogant drunk as pictured by so many of his time, or was he the kindly, generous, affectionate and devoted gentleman pictured by his many female admirers? A safe judgment is to say that the truth lies somewhere between the two. That he was an alcoholic, of course, there can be no question. His chief biographer, Rufus Griswold, delighted in recalling as many derogatory incidents as possible and, unfortunately, many of these have been accepted without question. Griswold writes of him walking the streets in fits of insanity, muttering curses, his eyes wild, braving all kinds of violent weather.

Certainly he was not an admirable man, yet people are too often prone to condemn others for succumbing to vices of which they know nothing. It is rather trite to say that Poe was more to be pitied than scorned, yet surely this was the case. Weak-willed, mentally unsound, Poe's brief life was one of torment, frustration, dissipation and tragedy. He might have been a character in one of his own stories.

Of his genius as a writer, there can be no question. It is interesting to note that he was at first more widely acknowledged in Europe than in his own country, and this is still somewhat the case. He was viciously and bitterly condemned by Longfellow, an otherwise kind and gentle New Englander who could not be expected to understand the torments of such a mind as Poe's. Henry James, who certainly should have appreciated Poe's writings of the macabre, claimed that only a primitive mind could see anything worthwhile in this alcoholic's crazed writings. His editor Griswold, whom Poe later appointed as his executor, detested the writer, and his biography presents a viciously distorted and hateful account of Poe's life and character.

Yet Baudelaire called Poe a 'wizard of letters'. The American was the most respected writer in Europe since Nathaniel Hawthorne. Alfred Lord Tennyson (undoubtedly thinking primarily of Poe's poetry) freely pronounced his opinion that Poe was the greatest genius of American letters.

It is, fortunately, this opinion of genius that remains today. Poe was remarkable in various literary fields. He ranks with the greatest of poets with verses that often contain haunting elements of tragedy. There is no poem in our language more beautiful than *Annabel Lee*, of which his dead wife was the subject. *Lenore* is another tale of tragic love, while such poems as *The Bells* and *The Raven* firmly established him in this field. His poetry has a sweeping, other-worldly grandeur that few other poets have been able to capture.

But it is in his short tales – which he termed 'tales of the grotesque and the arabesque' – that Poe achieved immortality. The effect on literature of his tales of terror was tremendous. In *The Murders in the Rue Morgue*, he produced what has been called the world's first detective story, while *The Gold Bug* elevated deduction to an art. Auguste Dupin in *The Purloined Letter*, predated the great Sherlock Holmes.

Poe's literary world was one of insanity, peopled with strange phantoms, tortured minds and souls, hideous crimes, undying revenge and hatred and emotions such as few people, fortunately, have ever experienced. His characters are not pleasant people: the men are strikingly handsome, generally extremely wealthy, but morbid, melancholy and thoroughly unpleasant company, while the women are beautiful, ethereal and, more often than not, mad. His settings are Gothic; ancient, crumbling castles with cobwebbed stone stairways, secret passageways and damp, dripping dungeons, bleak and blasted countrysides blanketed with fog and noxious vapours.

In these tales, Poe revealed the state of his brooding, strangely melancholy mind and the wild fantasies of alcoholism. There is no brightness in any of these tales; they are as dark, sombre and hopeless as the mind and life of their creator.

Poe was obsessed with the theme of premature burial, which

As the two greatest horror figures of the time, Boris Karloff (second
man from left) and Bela Lugosi (right) often appeared together. In this
one, Karloff proved to be the good guy.
The Raven (Universal Pictures, 1935)

occurs again and again in his stories. Love, to him, was a
terrible, all-consuming passion which did not end with death,
but went beyond the grave itself. He stressed the dangers of
inbreeding, and many of his characters are insane due to
generations of intermarriage in old families. He relished
macabre methods of revenge and then generally added a peculiarly terrifying twist in which the avenger became the victim
of his own diabolical inventions. Poe's characters were beings
of overpowering emotions, and death was no barrier to them.
Love, hatred, revenge, all extended beyond the grave to bring
insanity to the living.

It was not a pleasant world in which Poe lived in his mind.

A lifetime of brooding, of alcoholism and other dissipations, was bound to extract its mental toll. No man of sound mind could have conceived such horrors. The stories are typical of the man.

The stories of Edgar Allan Poe are too well known to require detailed retelling here; we will content ourselves with a superficial examination of some of the outstanding ones.

Probably the most famous is *The Fall of the House of Usher*. Appearing in 1840, a product of that bleak and hopeless period following the death of Virginia, this is probably the most superbly atmospheric tale in American literature. From the first description of Usher's mansion – the dreary countryside, the bleak, fog-filled swamp, the massive, crumbling structure of the manor house – a pall of tomblike gloom falls upon the reader. The deathlike atmosphere of the surrounding area is complemented by the dreariness, the air of death and horror which pervades the house. Here lives Roderick Usher, last bearer of an ancient name, crushed under the terrible fear – nay, the certainty – that his sister, Madeline, has been placed while still living in her tomb. Usher hears her cries, her desperate attempts to escape the sarcophagus, and is driven to madness by his fear. When Madeline actually appears before him, bloody and insane from living interment, Roderick dies of horror. The tale ends on the same frightening note on which it began as the blasted manor collapses and

the deep and dank tarn . . . closed sullenly and silently over the fragments of the House of Usher.

This is a simple enough tale, but Poe's artistry of characterization and atmosphere make it a classic. There is not a single word of cheer or pleasantness to brighten this overpoweringly sombre and gruesome story. The House of Usher is an ancient, decaying mansion occupied by the last of an ancient, decaying family. It breeds horror; the massive chambers, the dungeons, the walls themselves exude an air of ageless terror.

The ingredients of this story – insanity and premature burial – appear frequently in Poe's tales. In *The Premature Burial*, he examines with delicious horror the incomparable terror of

waking living in a tomb. The central figure in this tale is a
man subject to fits of catalepsy in which he assumes all the
appearances of death. It is his constant fear that he will one
day be buried alive. This terror grows steadily until he is too
frightened to leave the comparative safety of his own home,
where his servants are aware of his dreadful disease. He
secures oaths from the servants that under no circumstances

**Vincent Price (here with Mark Damon) became the star of Roger
Corman's beautiful series of films based on tales by Edgar Allan Poe.**
House of Usher **(American-International, 1961)**

will he be buried until actual decomposition of his body has begun. The family vault is remodelled so as to permit opening from within, with arrangements for light, food, air and water. The coffin is provided with a special lid which can be opened from inside, and from the roof of the tomb is suspended a large bell, with which he can call attention to his plight. The young man finally, after a horrifying experience in which he mistakenly believes himself to have been buried alive, cures himself of both his fears and his catalepsy. It is an unusually happy ending for Poe, and it exhibits, perhaps, an unusual knowledge of psychology on the writer's part.

This fear of premature burial was not strictly a figment of Poe's tortured imagination, for such incidents occurred with a frightening frequency. Montague Summers[1] gives many terrible instances of this particularly horrible fate, pointing out that catalepsy, with its counterfeit of death, has often resulted in burial before life has actually left the body. In many such cases, the so-called deceased, buried in a shallow grave, managed to dig his way to freedom. Permanent insanity was generally the result of this horrifying experience. Exhumation of bodies frequently provided graphic and terrible evidence of the supposed decedent's attempts to escape the tomb.

Summers relates a particularly horrible account of a young woman who had slipped into a state of catalepsy and was pronounced dead. Completely paralysed, unable to speak or to move, the young woman was yet wholly aware of all that went on about her. She was conscious of the arrangements for her funeral, aware of every movement as she was placed into her coffin and friends and relatives passed by to pay their final respects. The agony of the woman was beyond comprehension as she strove desperately to give some sign that life remained. Only the accident of the body being pierced by a pin worn by one of the mourners saved her from the terrible fate of premature burial. When a drop of blood appeared on her body, it was realized that she still lived. Summers also mentions a man of Harrisburg who apparently died after a long illness. His wife, terrified at the prospect of his being

[1] *The Vampire, His Kith and Kin.*

given premature burial, would not permit interment until actual decomposition had begun. At the third day, she noticed that her husband's eyes had opened, and it was discovered that he still lived.

Summers did not mince words in his writing, and his various descriptions of horror are for strong stomachs only. He graphically describes autopsies being performed on a corpse in a cataleptic state which suddenly exhibits signs of life. When such an autopsy was performed on the body of Cardinal de Espinosa, Grand Inquisitor of Spain during the reign of Philip II, it was discovered that the heart was still beating.

We of today, of course, have little reason to fear the accident of premature burial, but in Poe's day the danger was still very real. Anyone of Poe's melancholic turn of mind could easily imagine the horrors of awakening to complete darkness, feeling the confinement of the coffin, the sudden, horrible realization that you lie living in the grave, the cries of anguish and insane fear, the scratching of the fingernails on the lid of the casket, the desperate, animalistic attempts to dig through the smothering earth to freedom.

In another of his finest stories, *The Cask of Amontillado*, Poe combines the theme of living burial with that of implacable hatred and revenge. Fortunato is lured into his enemy's cellar by promises of a taste of exquisite amontillado, and he is there buried alive in the wall of the cellar. This device has often been used by other writers as well.

Poe's characters commit terrible, brutal crimes, but are often found out by the voice of conscience, for this sick-minded writer understood the twistings and workings of the human mind. Such is the case in his chilling tale *The Tell-Tale Heart*. An electric air of suspense is constructed by the description of the terrible, hated eye of the victim – a pale blue, vulture-like eye with a film over it – and by the diabolical plans for the old man's murder, with the murderer entering the bedroom carefully, night after night, during the course of the week. Finally the old man awakens and the light of the lantern falls on the terrible eye, inciting the murderer to his terrible deed. While the victim's heart beats loudly with fear, the deed is brutally done and the body buried beneath the floorboards.

Vincent Price is walled up alive in his tomb, in a sequence based on Poe's story "The Cask of Amontillado."
Tales of Terror **(American-International, 1962)**

The murderer brings the police into the very room and, in his bravado and self-confidence, places his chair over the very spot beneath which the body lies. But his own conscience betrays him as he believes he hears the terrible, frightened beating of the dead heart, louder and louder, although the police seem to hear nothing. In a fit of insane fear, the murderer confesses his crime and reveals the body.

There is similar just retribution in *The Black Cat*. This tale begins with an act of typical Poe brutality – a man, imagining his cat avoids him, cuts out the creature's eye with a penknife. The mutilated cat then follows its master everywhere until, in distraction, he hangs the creature. When, shortly after, his home burns, the image of a hanged cat is etched in smoke on one of the burned walls. A stray cat follows him home one night and, in the morning, is found lacking an eye. In a fit of fury, he raises an axe to slay this second beast. When his wife objects, he turns the instrument on her and kills her, walling up her body in the cellar. The crime is detected when the sound of a cat is heard issuing from behind the wall of this makeshift crypt; he has walled up the living animal with his wife's body.

One of Poe's most harrowing tales is *The Pit and the Pendulum*. A victim of political intrigue is imprisoned in a cell of particular horror. He is strapped upon a narrow bed, surrounded on all sides by a tremendous pit, teeming with large and vicious rats. Above him swings an enormous pendulum with a razor-sharp edge. Each swing of this macabre instrument brings the knifelike edge closer to his body. It is an ingenious, typically Poe, mode of torture and a gruesome manner of death. The prisoner is eventually, after the pendulum had already begun to cut through his flesh, freed from the prison by a change of political forces in the government. Only a mind such as Poe's could have conceived so diabolical a device.

And so on and on through all of Poe's tales, one horror follows another in a world of insanity such as has never been conceived by any other writer. It is little wonder that a gentleman like Henry Wadsworth Longfellow could find nothing appealing in this wild-eyed, melancholy young man with his dark and hopeless stories, his tales of distorted minds and twisted lives. The worlds of Poe and Longfellow did not seem part of the same universe. Longfellow's world was filled with gentle love, heroism, warmth and beauty; Poe's bitter world was the prison of his own imagination.

The brief macabre tales of Edgar Allan Poe were little used by Hollywood in the great horror period of the thirties. Bela

Lugosi appeared in a dreary, unimpressive version of *Murders in the Rue Morgue*, which made use of an extremely unrealistic gorilla. Karloff's films *The Raven* and *The Black Cat* owed little to Poe.

In recent years, however, there has been a tremendous revival of interest in Poe's tales by American-International Studios. This studio has been responsible for some of the most childish and inept excursions into horror ever inflicted upon the public, filling movie houses with an assortment of teen-aged monsters and an impossible galaxy of half-human, half-animal creatures. The financial gain resulting from these juvenile bits of horror, however, enabled American-International to apply themselves seriously to the translation to the screen of tales by Edgar Allan Poe, resulting in some of the most brilliant examples of horror yet filmed.

The first of these productions was *The House of Usher*, with Vincent Price as Roderick Usher. This film was a superb combination of atmospheric horror, fine writing and ingenious use of colour. Poe himself would have been delighted by the bleakness of the surrounding marsh, the decayed mansion, the general air of ancient horror which hovered over all. Various dream sequences were cleverly shown in tinted, hazy photography. Artistically and sumptuously produced, *The House of Usher* compared, in quality of production, with the best of the Mike Hammer efforts. The concluding scene, in which the Usher mansion slowly slips into the black and yellow swamp, was an exquisite painting of the macabre.

One of the finest horror films in years was American-International's production of *The Pit and the Pendulum*, a superb example of the best elements in this field, deserving of more than passing notice.

Richard Matheson, himself a superb writer of the macabre, expanded Poe's original brief tale into a terrifying eighty-five minutes, replete with scenes of sumptuous horror and brilliantly directed by Roger Corman. The tale is set in an ancient Spanish castle, home of Nicholas Medina, descendant of a brutal grand inquisitor. Elizabeth, his wife, has died under mysterious circumstances, and her brother, Francis, not content with the vague report of her death, visits the castle to determine the truth. He learns from Dr Leon that Elizabeth had died of fright. Nicholas escorts Francis to the dungeons and the medieval torture chamber where his father had plied his infamous trade. The chamber is filled with evil devices. It was here, in the Iron Maiden, that Elizabeth had been found dead. Nicholas finds in the torture chamber a compelling fascination. As a young boy, he had concealed himself here and watched his father torture and murder his mother and uncle, whom he suspected of adultery. Nicholas, however, is now obsessed by the fear that he has buried Elizabeth still living; strange sounds heard in the night lend credence to this. It is finally determined to open the crypt and satisfy Nicholas that his fears are groundless. When the crypt is opened and the lid of the coffin removed, they find a horribly contorted body which had obviously clawed desperately for release. During that night, Nicholas hears his wife calling to him. He descends into the crypt and sees Elizabeth issuing from her tomb. He flees into the torture dungeons as Elizabeth comes closer and closer. He falls to the floor in what appears to be death. His good friend, Dr Leon, enters and the conspiracy between him and Elizabeth is revealed. Elizabeth had not died, but joined with Dr Leon, her lover, to drive Nicholas mad. But Nicholas is not yet dead. He hears their confession and a battle follows in which Leon is slain and Elizabeth, her mouth gagged, is thrust into the Iron Maiden. Nicholas is now wholly insane; his mind having reverted back to the past, he believes himself to be his father, faced with the facts of his wife's adultery. When Francis enters the torture chamber, Nicholas takes him for the villainous uncle. He seizes Francis and takes him to the chamber of the pit and the pendulum; he straps the youth to the slab and the pendulum begins to swing. Francis is rescued by other members of the household, and Nicholas falls to his death in the pit.

The film is brilliantly made. The settings of the castle and, in particular, the torture chambers and dungeons are like a surrealist's nightmare. Poe's constant air of brooding horror hovers over every scene. The story content, though considerably different from Poe's original tale, is in every respect true to the Poe spirit, and Matheson reveals considerable knowledge of the workings of Poe's mind by including in his story the Poe themes of premature burial, insanity and revenge.

In no other film of horror has technicolor been put to such excellent advantage. This presents new techniques introduced by American-International which – if continued on the same superb scale – may go a long way towards recognition of the horror film as a particular form of cinema art. The standard use of colour in a film of this type, as previously mentioned, generally adds little to the atmosphere of horror. Rambling mansions, ancient castles, period costumes always look very well in colour, but a gloomy laboratory or tower retreat is more often more impressive in black and white. Universal, in its earlier years as a horror studio, never used technicolor. American-International, however, has applied colour to the horror itself, and the results are extremely gratifying. Nicholas' insanity is shown in a veritable madhouse of colour. The screen becomes a glaring blotch of crimson, with Nicholas' contorted features etched in the colour of blood, the walls of the dungeon a deep, dripping scarlet. A most interesting combination of solid colour and hazy photography is applied to dream sequences (as it was in *The House of Usher*), in which the screen fades almost imperceptibly from a solid blue to green to red and the characters take on a fuzziness typical of the indistinctness of dreams. The camera, too, comes in for a considerable share of credit by strange, uncomfortable angles and lightning swift movement. The final result was a film quite different from any other presentation of horror. It is, in effect, a novel and exciting experiment in what may very well prove to be a new classic form of presentation.

The film contained several impressive scenes of shock horror, outstanding among which was the discovery of Elizabeth's body in the opened coffin. Briefly, in a sudden abrupt and close shot, the camera reveals the hideously distorted form, the hands like claws reaching for the lid of the casket, the mouth twisted in a soundless scream of horror. The pit and pendulum scene is set in a tremendous stone chamber, its walls painted with nightmarish figures of black-cowled monks. Far below is the pit, with its jagged rocks onto which Nicholas falls to his death, and above is the massive steel pendulum, swinging slowly, steadily lowering to the helpless victim strapped to the slab beneath it.

The conclusion of this film is a brilliant twist of which Poe would heartily have approved. With the discovery of the conspiracy between Elizabeth and Leon there is, for a moment, a feeling of disappointment. Is the entire tale to end in the conventional triangle? Such, of course, is not the case, for Nicholas revives and the horror is just to begin. Nicholas falls to his death and the audience begins to gather its things to leave the theatre, expecting THE END to flash on the screen. But the most superb moment of horror is yet to come. Francis and Catherine, the late Nicholas' sister, mount the stone stairway leading from the dungeon. Francis, bloody and battered, leans heavily on the new heiress. Catherine pauses at the doorway, glances back into the dungeon with its instruments of

Vincent Price cowers in fear at strange sounds in the family crypt, where he believes he has buried his sister alive. John Kerr is at far left. *The Pit and the Pendulum* (American-International, 1961)

horror, and calmly announces that this chamber will be sealed and never entered again. It seems the conclusion of the film. But with these words, the camera swings abruptly to the Iron Maiden and we see the face of the gagged Elizabeth, her eyes wide with horror as she hears the words that seal her living in the tomb. Coming on the heels of the quiet let-down assumed to conclude the film, the effect is shattering.

The cast assembled for this production was a good one. Vincent Price appeared as Nicholas Medina. Price by this time seemed fair to assume the mantle of horror king worn in previous decades by Chaney, Karloff and Lugosi. After a long and successful career as the suave and gentlemanly killer, as in his first great success *Angel Street*, Price had, a short time before, starred in a highly successful horror film titled *The Fly* and in a number of William Castle stunt horror films such as *The Tingler*, *The House on Haunted Hill*, etc. Price's method of horror is not that of the classic monsters. It is a horror dependent, not on make-up, but on mental aberration. Suave, polished, noted for his fine speaking voice, Price frequently has a rather lamentable tendency to overplay, particularly in facial expressions, but he has become the number one horror star of the day.

Appearing as the evil Elizabeth was Barbara Steele, a raven-haired beauty who had previously scored heavily in *Black Sunday*, and Francis was ably portrayed by John Kerr.

The production of *The Premature Burial*, starring Ray Milland, boasted the same exquisite production values of previous films, centred about a brooding manor and a delightfully frightening mausoleum. Here, again, dream sequences were of considerable importance and, fascinatingly coloured, added much to the horror of the film, particularly the sequence in which Milland believed himself buried alive. The film presented a rather disturbing element, however, which had also marred the later Hammer productions – a rather uncomfortable emphasis on promiscuity.

In the thirties, Universal attempted to inject additional horror into their films by the inclusion of several monsters instead of one. American-International decided to include several well-known horror names in *Tales of Terror*, which starred Vincent Price, Peter Lorre and Basil Rathbone.

This interesting film presented three of Poe's tales, all of them featuring Price. *The Black Cat* combined this tale with *The Cask of Amontillado* in an interesting script which had the superbly evil Peter Lorre take revenge on his wife by walling her and the supposed lover, Price, into the wall of the cellar – together with the cat which gives the entire scheme away. *The Facts in the Case of M. Valdemar*, a tale of mesmerism, permitted Price to don particularly horrifying make-up as a dripping and decaying corpse who strangles Basil Rathbone. The third story of the tale was the lesser-known *Morella*, a frightening tale of possession of the dead. Although *Tales of Terror* was not quite as successful as the previous Poe films, it was an interesting, well-done experiment with the short horror stories.

It is difficult to connect the stories of Edgar Allan Poe with comedy, yet American-International dared this in their version of *The Raven*, loosely (very lossely) based on Poe's great poem. The film was a rather rollicking comedy of witchcraft in some bygone age, filled with magic and humour and, now and then, a touch of horror. Boris Karloff and Peter Lorre were pitched in a delightful test of magic with Vincent Price, in which the late Mr Lorre wound up as a rather large, black raven.

The stories of Edgar Allan Poe provide a rich field for the makers of horror, and they are just now being tapped. If American-International can steer clear of the pitfalls which the Hammer Studios appear to have fallen into, the stories appear to be in highly capable cinematic hands.

THE CREATORS OF HORROR II

The Rhode island Recluse:
'The world was at one time inhabited by
another race . . . who yet live on outside,
ever ready to take possession of this
earth again.'

A thick mist has crept in from Narragansett Bay, cloaking the old city of Providence in a mantle of soft blue-white. The enormous clock in the old church tower has long since struck the hour of midnight. The streets of the city are generally deserted, and only here and there does a golden sliver of light pierce the greyness. It has rained earlier in the day, and the silence is broken by the monotonous drip-drip of rainwater from the eaves of dilapidated buildings which have been standing for centuries. A cold wind has blown in from the bay, bringing with it the first bitter touch of winter.

Suddenly a dark shape seems to loom out of the mist, walking towards us. We step aside and allow him to pass. He is a peculiar figure of a man, tall and extremely thin, heavily wrapped in a greatcoat, hat and muffler. Above the cloth of his scarf, wrapped about his chin and lower face, we see cheeks and a forehead that are almost spectrally white, and a pair of alert, blazing eyes that seem to be peering into a strange, seldom-seen universe. He walks silently, looking neither to left nor right, and in a moment, he is gone and the mist closes in again as though he had never been.

We have seen the one man who can truthfully be called the successor to Edgar Allan Poe. Known as the Rhode Island recluse, his name is Howard Phillips Lovecraft.

Providence, Rhode Island, situated on an arm of Narragansett Bay, is one of New England's oldest and most traditional cities. Its history stretches back over more than three centuries, to the time in 1636 when Roger Williams, banished from Salem for his religious opinions, founded a settlement in remembrance of God's providence to him in his distress. The city is today the thriving, populous capital of the state, but even now, along the wharves, in the older portions of the town, can be seen mementoes of its past: the great days of the sailing vessels and clipper ships, the austere Puritanism which once governed its people and, perhaps, memories of a darker, more sinister day.

Winter in Providence can be bleak and bitter, the sky leaden with dark, scudding storm clouds, the icy grey waters of the Narragansett whipped into white-capped anger. Fog rolls often in from the bay, shrouding the silent city in a white funereal wrapping. The sun sets early, and Providence becomes a strange world of blacks and greys, of wispy, ghostlike alleys peopled by the strange imaginations of writers like Poe, who spent some years of his twisted, unhappy life here.

And here, too, lived Howard Phillips Lovecraft, one of the strangest and most interesting figures ever to appear on the American literary scene. With the possible single exception of Poe himself, Lovecraft was the supreme master of the tale of horror and the supernatural.

Lovecraft was born in Providence in 1890, and it was there that he spent most of his comparatively brief life. Always sickly, spending most of his childhood in invalidism, he was never able to participate in the usual outdoor games and sports of boyhood, and was inclined from the first to studiousness; he remained a scholar throughout his life. His interest in the supernatural and the unknown began at an early age, and he delighted in exploring the ancient folklore and legends of New

England. For a time, he wrote an astronomy column for a Providence newspaper, indicating an interest in the stars which occasionally appears in his stories.

H. Phillips Lovecraft, as he styled himself, might well have served as a model for some of his own characters. His semi-invalidism had given a permanent pallor to his face which, combined with his extreme leanness, created an almost cadaverous impression. He could not bear cold and, during the harsh winter New England months, was seldom out of doors. He spent the long evenings at work in the excessive warmth of an overheated study, conjuring from New England's past a galaxy of ghouls such as seldom has been introduced into the pages of literature. In spite of his discomfort, it never occurred to Lovecraft to leave New England for some warmer region of the country. He visited Charleston and New Orleans, purely as an antiquarian interested in the legends of the South, but he never remained long from his Providence home.

He slept badly and but little; weather permitting, he took long walks through the city in the darkest hours of night, and during these nightly strolls, the brilliance and garishness of modern Providence disappeared and he felt himself walking through the dark streets of an ancient town, peopled with experts in black magic and witchcraft, with strange beings never really seen by man. For Lovecraft did not enjoy the cold, mechanistic age of the time in which he lived. The twentieth century was an era without romance, without legend, and he preferred more distant times; the eighteenth century was his favourite. Much of his writing reveals this obsession with the past.

Lovecraft was a great admirer of the writing of Edgar Allan Poe and the English supernaturalist Arthur Machen, and this admiration is apparent in his own writing. His stories combine the highly literary quality of Poe with the mystic airs and backgrounds of Machen. But there the similarity ends, for Lovecraft was, above all, a writer of complete and almost unimaginable originality.

In a letter to a friend, Lovecraft explained the basis of these stories. (Boris Karloff mentions that Lovecraft's letters often ran to a length of fifty thousand words!):[2]

> All my stories, unconnected as they may be, are based on
> the fundamental lore or legend that this world was in-
> habited at one time by another race who, in practising
> Black Magic, lost their foothold and were expelled, yet
> live on outside, ever ready to take possession of this earth
> again.[3]

This quotation fully sums up the terrifying tales of H. P.
Lovecraft. He created an entire new lore of the supernatural
which influenced writers of horror in his own time and after.
As Machen wrote about the mysterious folklore of Wales,
Lovecraft centred his work about the ancient and lost legends
of the deceptively peaceful-appearing New England countryside, which he peopled with strange monstrosities and unknown horrors. Although an occasional story is placed in
England or some other part of America, the bulk of Lovecraft's
work has its setting in the deep, mysterious forests of Maine
and Vermont, or in Providence itself. He spoke of ancient
tales, of Indian superstitions, of the dark legacies left behind by
the Salem witchcraft days. The centre of the black arts used
in his stories is the fictitious town of Arkham, seat of Miskatonic University in Massachusetts, an institute of doubtful
higher learning, specializing in studies of witchcraft and
associated sciences. He enjoyed writing of lost languages, and
in their delirium his characters often spout completely unintelligible phrases, such as *'Ph'nglui mglw' nafh Cthulhu
R'lyeh wgah'nagl Fhtaga'*. This mysterious jargon is the long-
lost language of the Outsiders, taught by Cthulhu and his
breed to those they visit in dreams. Lovecraft also writes frequently of the supposed blasphemous works of black magic,
to which his more villainous personages constantly refer, such
as the 'Necronomicon' of the 'mad Arab Abdul Alhazred'.
   Lovecraft's tales are superbly written. Probably no other

[2] *And the Darkness Falls*, edited by Boris Karloff.

[3] *Great Tales of Terror and the Supernatural*, edited by Herbert
   Wise and Phyllis Fraser.

writer of horror – including the master Poe himself – was so successful in creating the very atmosphere of horror, fear and terror. His stories are a fantastic series of 'charnel-house, slathers of primordial evil, cosmic ghouls and demons, terrifying entities that have no name, and lands that exist neither in time nor in space'.[4] A highly literate man, Lovecraft used the English language in its most perfect and elegant form. There is no cheapness or vulgarity in his writing. The tales contain little dialogue, and abound in description, particularly of the horrible and the monstrous. Perhaps here, too, he was voicing his discontent with the time in which he lived, for his writing seems almost Victorian – the leisurely, incomparably rich and elegant style of a Dickens or a Stevenson. It has been demonstrated again and again that this style of writing is by far the most effective for stories of horror. Lovecraft's are, indeed, among the best-written short stories produced in this country, and only their content – for too often, even now, the writing of horror is not considered as serious literature – prevents them from being considered models of form and style.

Certain elements appear and reappear in Lovecraft's stories. One of these refers to colour. The generally restful shade of green was, for this master of the macabre, the very colour of horror. (Remember the tint of the original *Frankenstein?*) Lovecraft's descriptions were often painted in most livid colours, and it was always green that predominated. In *The Strange Case of Charles Dexter Ward*, a rather lengthy tale which appeared after the death of the author, spirits of the dead are called up by the use of a mysterious powder which gives off noxious green fumes. The invisible monster of *The Dunwich Horror* leaves enormous tracks that are filled with green slime. Many of Lovecraft's characters dissolve into pools of foul-smelling green slime, as in *The Thing on the Doorstep* and *The Shunned House*.

Lovecraft conveyed horror through other senses, as well. In both *The Dunwich Horror* and the excellent *The Haunter of the Dark*, an atmosphere of terror and tension is con-

[4] *And the Darkness Falls*, edited by Boris Karloff.

structed by strange sounds 'like the lapping of the sea'.

The monsters in Lovecraft's tales were seldom fully described. It is a clever writer who leaves something to the
imagination of his readers, for such imagination can often
create greater monsters than the pen of the most gifted writer.
In *The Whisperer in Darkness*, creatures from another world
are described as resembling large pink lobsters, but that is as
far as Lovecraft will go. In only one instance does he give a
detailed description of a monstrosity. This is in *The Dunwich
Horror*, in which the monster, at the time perishing in the
inevitable pool of green slime, is described as having the face
and hands of a human being, but a body which contains no
human elements. The chest resembles a crocodile, the back is
yellow and black like the skin of a snake. Below the waist, he
is covered with thick black hair; from the abdomen depend a
number of green tentacles terminating in open mouths. On
each hip is an enormous eye, and in place of a tail is a long
feeler terminating in another mouth. One wonders why, in
this particular instance, Lovecraft decided to go to so much
trouble to provide an exact description which, in truth, is not
very satisfying. A rather vaguely defined horror is often more
terrifying than the one which is clearly outlined for us. Lovecraft, in most of his writings, reveals clear understanding of
this. The greater monster of this same tale is invisible to all.
Seen or unseen, however, Lovecraft's monsters all have a good
deal in common. They move with slurps and gurgles, and
usually dissolve into pools of noisome green slime.

The creation of structures of horror – haunted houses, laboratories, castles, etc – is a favourite pastime of all writers in this
field, and here, again, Lovecraft was a master. In an early story,
The Picture in the House, he goes into considerable detail to
describe the hidden horrors to be found in a ramshackle,
tumbledown farmhouse such as can often be seen along deserted country lanes in the less-populated backwoods of New
England. Innocent-appearing farmhouses they may be, but
to a writer of Lovecraft's fertile imagination, even these
become the haunts of strange monsters of the past. In this
particular tale, one such tumbledown shack is the home of
an old man who sustains his life by feasting on the flesh of

passers-by. Another superbly atmospheric tale is *The Haunter of the Dark*. Here the structure of horror is a massive, dreary, deserted church made of black stone, located in an Italian section of Providence. Lovecraft's pen brings the church very sharply to the view of the reader – the dust-enshrouded pews, the crumbling stone columns clung with glistening cobwebs, the odour of mould and decay, the occasional gleam of sunlight pouring timidly through a shattered window. In the belfry lurks an ancient, unknown and unseen horror which, when innocently released, is deterred from its depredations by the circle of electric lights which surrounds the church. *The Shunned House*, a tale of vampirism, presents a more traditional haunted house, about which lingers an unhealthy air, and near which nothing grows but a strangely luminous grey fungus.

There are some aspects of horror which must be treated with the greatest care, in order to avoid accusation of bad taste. Lovecraft treats frequently of cannibalism. One of his earliest tales was *The Rats in the Walls*, which tells of a harrowing cult of cannibalism in the secret dungeons of a ruined English abbey. The same subject is broached in the abovementioned *The Picture in the House*. Under Lovecraft's hands, the subject becomes harrowing and gruesome, but never actually offensive.

In 1928, Lovecraft produced a story titled *The Call of Cthulhu*, in which he established the legend of a former race of giants which had once ruled earth and lost its power through the use of black magic and other evils. These creatures came from some planet beyond our own galaxy, long before the appearance of man on this world. They ruled through countless centuries and then lost their hold. They did not leave, nor did they perish. They went into deep sleep, a sort of suspended animation, in their great cities, and there they sleep still, waiting for the day when 'the stars will be in their proper position in the heavens' and they will rule earth again. The great chief of these Outsiders, as they are called, is Cthulhu himself, sleeping in his monstrous green-slimed city of R'yleh, somewhere beneath the waters of the southern Pacific. He is described as a horrifying creature 'miles high', with the head and tentacles of an octopus, the scaly body of a dragon, with a pair of small, rudimentary wings. He visits humans in their sleep and, in this manner, keeps alive the worship of himself and his people.

This is the tale told in *The Call of Cthulhu*. The horror of the Old Ones is first revealed during a period of violent global earthquakes centred in the South Pacific. Various persons describe strange, frightening dreams in which they find themselves in a sunken city filled with vague, terrifying forms, covered with greenish slime. Some dreamers carve hideous statues or speak and write in unknown tongues. In the swamps of Louisiana, the police break up an obscene cult which worships a monstrous statue named Cthulhu. In the Pacific centre of the quake, a group of seamen come face to face with Cthulhu. They beach on an island risen as a result of the quake and manage to open an enormous, curiously carved green door. Cthulhu rises from the opening – a massive, green, gelatinous mass of horror. The seamen flee, but Cthulhu follows, not deterred by the sea itself. He swims after the ship and is stopped only when the vessel sails directly into the mass, cutting it into several fragments. As the ship turns again to flee, the severed bits of the monster are reuniting. Cthulhu then returns to his city, the island again sinks beneath the waves, and great Cthulhu sleeps – and waits.

This story first appeared in *Weird Tales* in 1928, and its success was tremendous. The idea of an ancient cult of Old Ones caught on quickly and, with Lovecraft's blessing, other writers built their own stories upon the legend. *The Call of Cthulhu* is by no means Lovecraft's best work, but probably his most lasting contribution to literature was his creation of the great Cthulhu myth.

Lovecraft himself returned to Cthulhu in several other tales. The green slime, the terms Yog-Sothoth, Cthulhu, Yuggoth, reference to the Old Ones, these were all to become staples of his work.

These elements were probably never put to better use than in his superbly terrifying *The Whisperer in Darkness*. In this story, Lovecraft builds what is probably his strongest atmospheric groundwork for the horrors to come. He begins with a description of the unprecedented floods that struck the mountain regions of Vermont in 1927. It was reported that people saw strange things floating down the swollen streams, peculiar crablike bodies, pink in colour, as much as five feet in length, such as no one had ever seen before. They bring to mind ancient Vermont Indian legends of creatures flying between earth and their own planet with a cargo of stone not available on their own world. Albert Wilmarth, of Miskatonic University, enters into correspondence with one Henry Ackeley, a scholarly resident of the area who claims to have seen the creatures. Ackeley sends Wilmarth a recording he has made of a conversation between a man and some creature who speaks in a disturbing, insectlike buzzing sound obviously not human. There are strange references to Cthulhu and Yuggoth. Continued correspondence from Ackeley reveals his certainty that the creatures are aware of his knowledge and that he is in danger. It becomes obvious that their correspondence is being tampered with. Matters grow worse, and Wilmarth receives a hysterical letter telling of a siege at Ackeley's farm by the pinkish creatures and the humans who aid them. The telephone wires have been cut and Ackeley cannot leave the farm. Yet on the following day, a second typed letter arrives in quite a different tone. Ackeley has been contacted by the Old Ones who have revealed their plans for the good of mankind. He has agreed to help them and, in return, will be taken to their far-distant home. He urges Wilmarth to join him. When Wilmarth arrives, he finds Ackeley suffering from a severe attack of asthma which has incapacitated him. Entering the room where Ackeley awaits him, Wilmarth finds that, in his illness, his friend cannot bear direct light, cannot leave his chair, and speaks in a curious, hoarse whisper as he tells of the wonders the Outsiders have revealed to him. The strange creatures are large, pink, crablike beings with huge leathery wings which permit them to fly through space. Their base is Yuggoth, the unknown planet beyond Neptune, but their home is the far-distant world of Cthulhu. Humans who aid them in their work will be transported to Yuggoth, not in

human form but by a mental process in which their minds
will be removed from their bodies and kept forever alive in
an electric metal capsule. Wilmarth, horrified, determines to
flee, taking his friend with him. During the night, he sneaks
downstairs to Ackeley's room, but he is not there. In the
chair are his clothing and a mass of green slime, with the lifeless hands and face of Ackeley. On this air of terror and mystery, this frightening tale comes to an end.

This rather lengthy tale is superb in its suspense. What
better way to open such a story than with mysterious reference to monstrous pink 'things' floating down a swollen river?
Here again is the green slime. Lovecraft's characters often
speak in a whisper to disguise differences in voice quality
which might betray their identity and origin.

The copyright of this tale is 1931, just one year after the
discovery of the planet Pluto, 'the mysterious world beyond
Neptune'. For the first time, we are provided with a definite
explanation of one of the terms of Cthulhu-mology. Yuggoth,
referred to as 'the gateway to the Old Ones', is Pluto, the
dark, distant planet. The existence of Pluto was suspected
for some years before its actual discovery, and Lovecraft who,
it should be remembered, was something of an astronomer,
may have early decided on this cold world as the home of his
creatures. Even this far-distant world, however, is not quite
far enough distant for Lovecraft's purposes, and he makes it
quite clear that Yuggoth is merely an advance base for the
beings, whose home is in a far more distant part of the sky.
Today's science-fiction writer would probably mention Alpha
Centauri.

For the story is, of course, as much science fiction as it is
horror, and it holds an important place in that particular field
of literature. The theme of alien creatures conquering earth
by taking over the minds of its inhabitants is one of the most
popular themes in science fiction today, used to particular
advantage in Heinlein's *The Puppet Masters* and Jack Finney's
superbly terrifying *The Body Snatchers*.

Yet *The Whisperer in Darkness*, which makes such excellent horror, is not very satisfying as science fiction. Lovecraft
was wiser in the science-fiction aspects of his other tales,

where he leaves details vague and ill-defined, for he was no scientist. Possibly the excitement caused by the discovery of Pluto had an exhilarating effect on Lovecraft and he felt the urge to apply this discovery to his writing. There can be no quarrel with the appointment of Pluto as Yuggoth, but the method of interplanetary travel of the crablike creatures is juvenile. They bridge the approximate distance of three and a half billion miles on huge leathery wings. Even the youngsters of today could not accept such an explanation. Certainly in Lovecraft's time, enough was known of the problems of space travel to rule out such a method, although we must not, of course, expect Lovecraft to write with the scientific accuracy of present-day writers. Yet it is unfair to seize upon this absurdity and point it up as a flaw in the story. In the world of horror (and this was, remember, basically horror, not pseudo-science) anything is possible. Jules Verne sent his characters to the moon by the aid of a monster cannon, and this bit of palpable nonsense does not detract from the spell of his writing.

On the other hand, Lovecraft's frightening earlier tale *The Colour Out of Space* (1927) is sheer science fiction in the very finest tradition of this field of writing.

The Colour Out of Space refers to the effects of the landing of a strange meteor in a scarcely populated wood west of Arkham. The meteor exudes a strange colourless and odourless gas and then gradually dissolves. But the area in which the meteor landed becomes the centre of a peculiar blight in which all vegetation turns a peculiar grey. Trees, plants, animals and insects grow to abnormal size, but become so brittle that they fall apart at the touch. A strange madness seizes the members of the family of Nahum Gardner, on whose farm the meteor came to rest. Gardner's wife and sons are locked, in their madness, in separate attic rooms, where they are later found to have deteriorated into grey indescribable monstrosities which give off a foul stench. The grey blight finally gathers itself together and, in a tremendous blast of light which completely destroys the Gardner farm, shoots up in the sky.

This is both horror and science fiction at its best. The story

appeared in a 1927 issue of *Amazing Stories* and if written today would undoubtedly appear in one of the numerous
science-fiction magazines as an example of the best writing in
the field. Once again, the monster is and remains invisible, but
the effects of its arrival on earth and the horror of its depredations are all too clear. It is a horror that grows and spreads,
from foliage to animals to humans. It is referred to, in the title
itself, merely as a 'colour' from out of space. There is no
attempt at scientific explanation, and the monster leaves as
suddenly as it had arrived. Yet Lovecraft ends this tale on a
quiet note of horror, for he says there remains a faint lumin-
osity about the shattered Gardner farm, and the villagers
swear that the blasted greyness of the sector grows broader
year after year.

Lovecraft was the author of one of the most superb short
stories in the English language. *The Outsider*, appearing in
1926, is written in the first person, and the writer is not
named. All his life has been spent in a ruined castle filled with
dust, bones and decay; he has never seen sun or sky. One part
of the castle, a tall tower, seems to extend above the treetops
which serve as a barrier to the rest of the world. One day,
weary of his lifelong imprisonment, he climbs this tower and
finds a trapdoor in the ceiling. When he lifts this, he is in a
dark room lined with shelves of marble and peculiar oblong
boxes. A doorway leads him into a long corridor, at the end
of which he sees the glow of moonlight. Reaching the end of
this corridor, he is disturbed to find that his long climb has
not brought him to a dizzy height; he is at ground level. He
makes his way through the dark countryside and approaches
a castle from which there are lights and the sound of music.
Peering in through an open window, he sees a large chamber
filled with dancing people. This is his first contact with others,
and he moves eagerly to join them. Just as he enters through
the window, a sudden fear seizes the dancers and with screams
of terror, they flee the castle, leaving him alone. He glances
about him, searching for the cause of this sudden fear, and
sees a hideous, unearthly creature too horrible to describe – a

mouldy, disintegrated travesty of humanity. He stretches out his hand to seize the obscene monster and touches 'a cold and unyielding surface of polished glass'.

This little gem of a story is one of the greatest classics of horror and Lovecraft's masterpiece. It has been said that, had Lovecraft signed this tale with the name of Poe, it would without question have been accepted as the work of the master, both in content and style. In his taut, terrifying descriptions, Lovecraft reaches heights which few others have attained. A character study of a monster, the story has a strong and unusual element of pity, for the creature, having faced the horror of the mirror, returns to the graveyard, through the vault and back to his underground lair, realizing that he is forever an outcast and an abomination. He is probably the most sympathetic monster in all of literature, and Lovecraft's mastery makes him one of the most fascinating.

This, then, is the strange and ghoulish world of H. P. Lovecraft. There are many other stories, for despite his relatively brief life, Lovecraft wrote prolifically. *Pickman's Models* relates the terrifying tale of a painter of the macabre who used, as his models, indescribable creatures from the very bowels of the earth; *Cool Air* brings the horror of a living dead man to a Manhattan brownstone; *In the Vault*, in a more traditional tone of horror, tells of the terrible vengeance of a slighted corpse when the curate is trapped in a vault. One of Lovecraft's most frequently anthologized tales, *The Thing on the Doorstep*, is a frightening story of demonic possession, in which a dying woman seizes both the mind and the body of her weakling husband; the previously mentioned *The Dunwich Horror* is another tale of the Old Ones, living in human form while planning to re-enter the world of the living.

Most of these stories had their first appearance in pulp magazines, particularly *Amazing Stories* and *Weird Tales*, which were responsible for the emergence of many a fine horror writer. Lovecraft's stories are as yet strangely untouched by the film industry. Many of his tales would not seem to lend themselves readily to films (neither, for that matter, do Poe's), but a capable script writer might make an engrossing film from *The Colour Out of Space* or *The Whisperer in Darkness* or *The Dunwich Horror*; many films have borrowed heavily from Lovecraft's ideas.[5]

It is often the sad fate of writers to fall into a decline of popularity soon after their passing and this, unfortunately, has happened to Lovecraft. In the mid-forties there was a surge of interest in the horror tale, and Lovecraft was widely read. His most ardent disciples, August Derleth and Donald Wandrei, formed a publishing-house in Wisconsin, named Arkham House after Lovecraft's mythical town, which did much to bring Lovecraft's work to public attention. Probably the finest collections of his tales were the Arkham House books *The Outsider and Others* and *Beyond the Wall of Sleep*; unfortunately, both have long been out of print. Derleth, a personal friend of Lovecraft's, was responsible for the first appearance of many of his tales in book form in his excellent Rinehart anthologies *Sleep No More, Who Knocks?, The Night Side* and *Night's Yawning Peal*. Random House's monumental publication of 1944 *Great Tales of Terror and the Supernatural*, included *The Rats in the Walls* and *The Dunwich Horror*, while *The Thing on the Doorstep* appeared in the excellent Boris Karloff anthology, *And the Darkness Falls*. In 1945, Tower Books released *The Best Supernatural Stories of H. P. Lovecraft*; this fine edition, which sold for less than a dollar and included some fourteen of Lovecraft's best tales, has also been long unavailable. Joseph Payne Brennan, another fine writer of horror who owes much to Lovecraft, wrote *H. P. Lovecraft: A Bibliography* in 1952 and, three years later, *H. P. Lovecraft: An Evaluation*.

In his chosen field, Lovecraft has no peers, with the possible exception of Poe, whom he himself called 'the master', yet within a few years after his death Lovecraft was little read and almost forgotten. While Poe is ranked with the great

[5] It has recently been announced that an English studio plans to film *The Strange Case of Charles Dexter Ward*. One of Lovecraft's longest stories, this is an engrossing tale of witchcraft, black magic and vengeance from beyond the grave.

writers of American literature, Lovecraft's name is not even mentioned in most encyclopedias and literary collections.

Howard Phillips Lovecraft died in 1937, aged forty-seven years, leaving behind him a tremendously rich legacy of ghouls, monsters and assorted horrors. The years have not been kind to his memory, but perhaps the pendulum is now beginning to swing in the other direction. We are in a period of revival of the literature of horror, and it would be impossible to overlook this titan. In the past year or two, many fine anthologies have appeared, and H. P. Lovecraft is represented prominently in all of them; the possibility of films based on his stories may do much to revive interest in his tales, and we may yet see the day when Howard Phillips Lovecraft, the Rhode Island recluse, will take his proper place in American literature at the side of the revered Edgar Allan Poe.

The Creators of Horror III

The Mystic of Wales:
'Is there no serenity to be had anywhere
in this world?'

He might have stepped from the pages of any book by Dickens. A mystic, a student of the occult, he was yet a man who found tremendous enjoyment in being alive. He was a big man with a pink complexion, light blue eyes and sparse white hair. He was a courtly man, always the gentleman, but at times his voice would sound with the roar of a bull. He generally affected a battered felt hat in order to conceal his bald pate, but his white hair was worn long, fitting companion to the old-fashioned black cape which was generally slung across his shoulders. He was a gentleman of the old school. He was one of the great writers of his time, but his works brought him little financial reward. He seemed to move in a dream world of his own creation – a world of elves, fairies, the Little People, of Arthurian romance, of gallant knights whose sole purpose in life was the quest for the Holy Grail. He was a figure of the days of chivalry, rudely transported into a world of modern confusions, noises, odours and wars. He is remembered for a series of remarkably other-world stories, one of which became so widely accepted as truth that his authorship of it has been forgotten. His name was Arthur Machen.

This distinguished man was born at Caerleon-on-Usk in

Wales, and there are few stronger examples of the influence of birth on a man of letters. The Roman legions had known his town as Isca and here, more than a century after the collapse of Rome, Arthur Pendragon held court. Machen was never to escape his Celtic background, nor to forget the tales of fairies, elves and romance which were an integral part of his child-hood. Although he spent much of his later life in London, Arthur Machen was always a spiritual descendant of the days of King Arthur.

He was born in 1863, and lived a long and vigorous life, dying some eighty-four years later in December of 1947. The bulk of his best work was done fairly early in life, before and during the First World War. His writing interests began while he was yet in his teens, when he published at his own expense a poem entitled *Eleusinia*, of which no copies now exist. In London he worked as clerk, teacher, and actor with a Shake-spearean group; he married one of the ladies of the company.

Machen lived a lonely, retired life. He was a shy man who lacked the ability of insinuating himself into the company of others. His long nights were spent in the solitude of his rooms, studying, meditating, writing, dreaming of the fantastic worlds that surrounded him. His first book appeared in 1884, titled *The Anatomy of Tobacco*, a curious work which bore no re-semblance to his later writings, and which achieved little success. He eked out a rather precarious living in subsequent years by providing English translations of French literature; he was responsible for the monumental six-volume translation of *The Memoirs of Casanova* that is still standard today. The monetary reward for such labour was small.

In 1894 appeared the first of the tales that were to bring him fame – a thick volume containing *The Inmost Light* and the unforgettable tale *The Great God Pan*.

Machen was very much concerned with the effect on other-wise normal people of too much preoccupation with matters of the occult and supernatural, and this is revealed in his first two prominent tales. *The Inmost Light* tells the story of Dr Black and his beautiful wife, a most devoted and popular couple in the then small village of Harlesden. Suddenly Mrs Black is seen no longer, and is rumoured to be dead. Dyson, who narrates much of the story, passes the Black house one day and sees peering from the window a terrible face resembling Mrs Black but possessing an expression which could not be described as human. Shortly after, Mrs Black's death is officially reported. Dyson, questioning the surgeon who performed the autopsy, is told that examination of the brain revealed it to be something inhuman. Not long after, Black himself dies, screaming of the theft of something of great value from his sordid rooms. The theft proves to be that of a jewel of incomprehensible value. With the jewel, discovered later, is an explanation written by Black. His marriage had put a temporary stop to his occult studies, but in time the lure again became irresistible. He had found a way to create tremendous wealth in the form of an enormous opal, by destroying the life and soul of his wife. The light of his wife's soul was stored in the jewel, and she herself had perished.

This is an interesting little story, though not one of Machen's best. Mystery is heightened by the search for Black's tremendous wealth, but the solution is somewhat of a letdown. It is never made quite clear just what is the connection between his wife's 'inmost light' and the jewel which, in some way, manages to destroy her.

In this same volume appeared *The Great God Pan*, undoubtedly the most famous of all Machen's stories, a terrifying tale of the madness which follows an encounter with the ancient satyr god Pan. The story concerns primarily a woman named variously Helen Vaughan, Mrs Herbert, and Mrs Beaumont, one of the most evil women in all literature. There is a chilling little preamble to this rather lengthy story when one Clark is witness at a little experiment conducted by a Dr Raymond, who believes that a slight operation on a portion of the brain will permit one to see a very real world beyond our own. The experiment is conducted on a girl named Mary, whom Raymond had literally picked out of the gutter. It is a complete success, and the poor girl comes face to face with the Great God Pan. The result for her, unfortunately, is complete idiocy.

The rest of the tale follows the evil life of the daughter who results from this brief union between Mary and Pan. She is an exquisitely beautiful woman without a soul, who spreads death and horror wherever she goes. When she is seen dancing in the woods with a naked man of horrible visage, she drives the viewer, a young village boy, into insanity. She marries a man named Herbert and by initiating him into various and sundry horrors, drives him to insanity. As Mrs Beaumont, she becomes the social toast of London; various prominent men who become involved with her are driven to suicide by the horrors to which she introduces them.

Fate, of course, finally catches up with her and she is, herself, driven to suicide. She lies on her bed, her blackened body changing form, twisting and writhing, from that of a woman to a man, from a man to a beast and, at last, to a horrible, crawling mass of corruption.

The story rambles somewhat and is even, at times, a bit difficult to follow, but the overall impression is one of tremendous, unmentionable horror, of loathsomeness, of an ancient evil abroad in the streets of modern London. Machen gives free reign to his vivid imagination. *The Great God Pan* remains his most widely-read tale, and has achieved for itself the status of a classic of English literature.

The first group of Machen's stories was followed by *The Three Impostors*, in which Machen imitated the style and pattern of Robert Louis Stevenson's *New Arabian Nights*. Included in this collection were two chilling examples of Machen at his best. *The Novel of the Black Seal* is concerned with a small black stone, inscribed with strange and indecipherable characters, found by Professor Gregg. The stone is undoubtedly ancient, and bears a peculiar resemblance to the Sixtystone, a sacred object of some wild, mysterious savages of the inner areas of Libya. The professor's interest is whetted when he hears of similar characters having been inscribed on sandstone in a western portion of England, inscriptions that could not be more than fifteen years old. The professor takes a house in the area and begins his studies of the stone. He learns that a woman named Craddock had given birth to a weak-minded son, named Jervase, after having been found in a state of hysteria on this strangely inscribed sandstone. Gregg is convinced that the stone, the strange characters, the widow and her son are in some way connected with the mysterious and evil Little People, whom Gregg believes still exist, possessed of considerable power. He takes the boy Jervase into his house and very closely watches as the lad falls into sudden fits, spouting unintelligible languages. When Gregg manages to decipher the stone, he utters the strange words to the boy during his fit and sees a horrible change come over Jervase as he slips from humanity into a strange, loathsome beast. The words on the seal are those which can reduce man to the ancient reptile from which he has sprung. Holding the key to these mysteries, Gregg sets off to confront the Little People and is never seen again.

Machen did not view the Little People – elves, fairies and leprechauns – in the same light as children do, as rather quaint and harmless creatures who live in strange caverns under the forest and can easily be tricked into use of their magical powers, or made to reveal their hoards of gold. To Machen, these Little People were extremely foul and evil creatures of the same race as the devils who partook in the horrible and blasphemous feast known as the Witches' Sabbath. At one time, his imagination told him, there was but the one race of man, but a certain small group, imprisoned by superstition, somehow fell behind the advances of the rest of the race. Retaining some of their ancient and evil powers, this group went underground, while the remainder of mankind progressed to the status it enjoys today. But these Little Creatures still survive in obscure places and they occasionally make use of their still terrible powers. Machen's tales are filled with persons, generally children or young people, who start across a field or a meadow and are never seen again; they have been taken by these Little People to be sacrificed in one of their terrible rites held in secret places, during the frightening blasphemy of the Witches' Sabbath. The lightly populated areas of Wales are happy hunting grounds for the Little People, which explains many of the superstitions of the ancient Celts. Forests are particularly dangerous, and sunken areas or small valleys dipping suddenly between two hills, for these are the favoured homes of the Little Folk who wage an endless war with mankind, in hopes of securing once again their former power. (This sounds almost like Lovecraft's cult of Cthulhu.)

Machen made strong use of this myth in *The Shining Pyramid*, one of the tales written after the period of the First World War. Two friends, Dyson and Vaughan, meet in London; the latter tells of most peculiar happenings at his country home. On an ancient pathway behind his house, he has seen what appear to be a series of signals: old arrowhead patterns on the path in the form of marching men, an inverted bowl, a pyramid and a half-moon. Dyson goes to the country with Vaughan in an attempt to solve this mystery. It soon becomes evident that the signals are formed in the dead of night, by beings able to see in the dark. Further signs are made on stone walls at a height of just over three feet, which leads Dyson to believe that these 'persons', able to see in the dark, are of extremely small stature, yet obviously not children. The mystery deepens with the disappearance of a girl from the village. Tracing the route of the disappearance, Dyson comes upon a depression of the earth which he is certain is the bowl in the signals. He is now of the opinion that the signals point to a gathering of the Little People in this inverted bowl for the ceremony of seeing the Pyramid. He and Vaughan conceal themselves on the rim of the bowl and witness a horrifying sabbath of the Little People, in which the lost girl is immersed in the pyramid flame of sacrifice.

As in many of Machen's tales – and this holds true of many of the writings of horror – this story is more terrifying for what it does not say than for what it does.

To return for the moment to *The Three Impostors*, this collection also included *The Novel of the White Powder*, which again presents the subject of man's reptilian origin, a favourite Machen theme. A young man, Francis Leicester, causes his sister considerable anxiety by his complete immersion in his studies. The sister prevails upon their doctor to give the young man what we would call today a vitamin pill, in the form of a white powder prepared by a local chemist. The change in the man is almost immediate. He loses interest in his studies, and becomes involved in various unsavoury frivolities, until his health begins to suffer. His sister now has quite a different cause for concern. The young man's wildness continues until he becomes a shadow of his former self. Finally he locks himself in his room and is seen no more, his meals being left outside his door. Glancing up at his window one afternoon, the sister sees a horrible, inhuman face (this is another of Machen's pet methods of creating horror). When the maid finds a peculiar sticky substance dripping from the floor of Francis' room, the sister again turns to the doctor for help. They burst into her brother's room to find a blasphemy on the floor, a dark, putrid mass melting and bubbling, with the eyes of Francis. The doctor destroys the monstrosity. Analysis of the white powder reveals impurities which converted the harmless substance into the powder called the Wine of the Sabbath, used in the Witches' Sabbath to reveal the worm of putrescence in man. This powder had transformed Francis into an obscene horror.

These two stories – *The Black Seal* and *The White Powder* – have outlived the volume in which they first appeared. Both are written in first person, both narrated by women – the first by a governess, the second by the sister. They are both typical of Machen's leisurely Victorian style, but in both instances the horror begins with a gentle atmospheric touch and builds to a frightening crescendo. They also reveal Machen's intense interest in what he terms 'the original form of man', for many of his characters dissolve into a putrid mass. In *The White Powder* we can clearly see Machen's influence on Lovecraft; this tale brings to mind certain aspects of *The Colour Out of Space*. Lovecraft freely admitted his debt to the Welsh writer, of whom he said:

Of living creators of cosmic fear raised to its most artistic pitch, few if any can hope to equal the versatile Arthur Machen, author of some dozen tales . . . in which the elements of hidden horror and brooding fright attain an almost incomparable substance. . . .

After his marriage, Machen abandoned the writing of supernatural tales for journalism, and did not return to fiction until the period of the First World War.

Machen became obsessed with the thought that the hatred and evil unleashed by the war could find its counterpart in the revival of other, more ancient evils. This is the theme of a striking, brief tale titled *Out of the Earth*. This narrates the sudden vicious savagery of the children in a particular portion of Wales, previously known for its gentle, kindly people. Investigation reveals that these monsters are not actually children at all, but the Little People, who have risen from beneath the earth to rejoice in the turbulent times, when they see people following their own violent ways. The story was the first of several on this theme.

It was towards the end of the war that Machen wrote *The Terror*, one of his finest stories, based on this theme of evil begetting evil. The insect and animal world, infected by the atmosphere of hatred which blankets the world, rise against their human masters. Throughout Wales and England, there are strange deaths, some of which appear accidental, some suicides, others obvious murder. The mystery is solved by the finding of a manuscript in a farmhouse where the master lies dead in the yard, pierced through the side to the heart, and others of the family dead of thirst indoors. The manuscript relates a harrowing tale of the sudden attack of the livestock, one of which gores the master; the animals then prevented the family from going for water. When some occupant of the house opened the windows to gather rainwater, a monstrous cloud of moths attacked him. With the aid of these facts, the other deaths are solved – men and women pushed over cliffs by docile sheep, or trampled to death by horses, armies of monstrous rats converging upon factories to attack the workers, vast clouds of moths setting upon people, suffocating them by force of numbers. The uprising is put down, but Machen points out the danger of a recurrence, when hate covers the world and the beasts believe that man has abandoned his throne of superiority.

This probably remains Machen's most readable story. It is plain horror, without the mystic elements that sometimes becloud his other tales. It is, unfortunately, rather heavily laced with Machen's wartime hatred of the Germans who, in their 'villainy' and 'barbarity' are at first considered quite capable of turning insects and animals against men through some devilish kind of ray. This is later ruled out, but Machen's anti-German sentiments somewhat mar the pleasure of this tale; politics, after all, has no place in the fantasy world of horror.

(This theme of the revolt of the animal world has been used by other writers since Machen's time. Birds are generally the villains, as in Daphne du Maurier's tale, recently filmed by Alfred Hitchcock.)

It was in 1914, shortly after the battle of Mons, that there appeared in the London *Evening News* Machen's *The Bowmen*. This was a short, fanciful tale in which the spirits of the bowmen of Agincourt come to the rescue of the hard-pressed English soldiers at Mons and, with their phantom bows, rout the Germans. A war-frightened world, seeing such an item in a newspaper, immediately latched onto the tale as a literally true indication that God was on the Allied side. Even today, this strange tale of the archers of Agincourt is often included in books recounting 'unexplained phenomena'. Machen's authorship has been almost forgotten. He himself never forgave his readers for this, and in several subsequent tales, Machen makes rather bitter reference to this forgotten story, so widely accepted as a factual account.[6]

When Machen reached his sixtieth year, he turned to other forms of writing, producing a three-volume autobiography and an account of the Elizabeth Canning case. He ceased writing completely when he entered his seventieth year, and from then until his death in 1947, he lived with his wife and two sons in quiet retirement in the south of England, a retirement greatly assisted by a Civil List pension that had been granted him.

Machen never earned what could be called a comfortable living from his writing, but this never seemed to trouble him. He enjoyed life, was a clever and witty commentator on our times, and believed money was for spending rather than hoarding. He possessed very strong opinions on every imagin-

[6] In his book *Forgotten Mysteries*, R. DeWitt Miller takes exception to Machen's claim of authorship. Miller claims reports of the incident were circulated in August, whereas Machen's story did not appear before the end of September.

able subject, and could not be swayed from them. He did not care for the modern world (once again we are reminded of Lovecraft) much preferring the ancient days of Britain before and during Roman times. *The Hill of Dreams*, which he wrote in 1907, is a curious and beautiful book about a Welsh boy who escapes from the unpleasantness of modern living into a dream life in ancient Roman Britain. Although it took Machen no less than ten years to find a publisher for this novel, it is today considered his greatest work. The folk of legend and faerie were often more real to him than the flesh-and-blood creatures who were part of his everyday life. Although he never quite escaped the poverty of his early days, he faced life with a mixture of humour, wonder and excitement. He was a kindly man, generous and benevolent to all. He had, unlike so many of his contemporaries, a profound respect and admiration for America and Americans.

Philip Van Doren Stern has truthfully said that one must acquire a taste for the writing of Arthur Machen.[7] The same, of course, may be said for many of the classic writers of horror. Machen was strongly influenced by Shakespeare, Scott, Stevenson, and Poe. The writing is Victorian, slow, leisurely. There is much subtle thought, much inference, much background. His tales reflect the loneliness of his life and his knowledge of local folklore and custom. He was a romantic writer who painted on broad, gloomy landscapes of his native country, delving into horrors more ancient than ghosts and vampires, which once held sway in a world very different from the world of today, but are no less living and powerful in our own time. In some of his tales as, for instance, *The Bright Boy*, the reader grows a little impatient and wonders if he will ever come to the point of his tale; *The White People* begins with a seemingly endless discourse on what is and what is not sin. Yet one is always well rewarded for wading through what may appear to be extraneous pages. This is not the style of the modern horror tale, with its swift movement, its crisp, abrupt prose. This is writing of a far more leisurely time and

[7] Arthur Machen, *Tales of Horror and the Supernatural*, edited by Philip Van Doren Stern.

a more leisurely people. The change of pace of modern living is largely responsible for the fact that such works do not today receive the attention they merit.

It is unfortunate that Machen, too, has joined the ranks of authors who are not as widely read as they should be, although the period of his neglect seems to be passing. As far as I have been able to determine, none of his tales has been filmed, although several of his stories would adapt themselves interestingly to such a purpose. On the occasion of the recent publication of a new edition of *Tales of Horror and the Supernatural* in London Cyril Connolly seized the opportunity to praise his work, and avow his own personal addiction to it, at some length in *The Sunday Times*. In England *The Hill of Dreams* and *The Three Impostors* have been republished, and paperback editions of some of his stories have also been published. He appears in most anthologies of horror and had his day in America when Carl Van Vechten and Vincent Starrett first introduced Machen's work to the American reader in the twenties. If his writing is considered too leisurely, too mystical, too polished and elegant for readers he cannot be said totally to lack supporters in the staid and classic world of horror.

We have visited only three of the outstanding craftsmen in the literature of the weird, the uncanny and the terrifying. There are many others whose presence would be of interest to us, for the field of horror is an extremely broad one, and the number of writers who have either specialized in, or delved into, this particular aspect of literature is almost endless.

We might visit Prussia in the earliest years of the last century and see a strange, dramatic-looking man with a mass of wild hair, tight, narrow but sensual lips, large and deep eyes ringed with shadows. This is E. T. A. Hoffmann (Ernest Theodor Wilhelm; Amadeus was later substituted for Wilhelm in tribute to Mozart), one of the early great writers of fantasy and horror, of whom Christopher Lazare has written:

In European literature, Hoffmann's unmistakable mark can be seen in the work of . . . Hans Christian Andersen . . . in Hugo, Alexandre Dumas . . . Hoffmann's is the theme of dual identity . . . which inspired Robert Louis Stevenson in 'Dr Jekyll and Mr Hyde' and 'Markheim'; his signature is the Gothic melancholy and Teutonic Romanticism which charged the work of the Brontës . . . In America, Hawthorne's preoccupation with the ancestral curse can be traced to Hoffmann's 'The Legacy'. Longfellow literally borrowed whole pages of fantastic description from the same source for his prose romance 'Hyperion', and the inestimable indebtedness of Poe's horror stories to Hoffmann's 'Tales' has motivated the admirable detective work . . . of a dozen monographs. . . .[8]

Until he died in 1822, aged forty-six, a bitter, disillusioned, pain-racked man, so shrunken in body that his nurse was able to carry him in her arms, Hoffmann wrote a galaxy of strangely fantastic tales which have gained the name of Gothic romances. These works – Don Juan, The Double, The Vow, Berthold the Madman among others – have never been widely available to the American public, and he is chiefly remembered today for his influence on other writers and the fact that his tales are the basis of Offenbach's great opera The Tales of Hoffmann.

Or we might visit Ambrose Bierce, born of a poverty-stricken Connecticut family, an uneducated man who came out of the Civil War a full major, and who wrote some of the most literate and chilling tales of horror in the English language. Bierce was in his seventies when, in 1914, he went to Mexico to take part in the incredible adventures of Pancho Villa, and was never heard of again.

We might visit for a time with the elegant Henry James, who was an American writer who spent most of his life in Europe and finally abandoned his American citizenship for British. He was responsible for some of the most frightening

[8] Tales of Hoffmann, edited by Christopher Lazare.

ghost stories in the English language, including the immortal
The Turn of the Screw.

Or we might visit some other great and famous writers of
the last century – Sheridan Le Fanu, or Wilkie Collins, whose
books *The Moonstone* and *The Woman in White* were among
the first modern mystery novels, or there is the Italian-born
American F. Marion Crawford, whom we have previously
mentioned as the author of a brilliant tale of vampirism. Later
in the century, there was Montague Rhodes James, often described as the Lovecraft of the ghost story, or H. G. Wells,
who excelled in horror as he did in science fiction, and that
curious individual H. H. Munro, who wrote such delightfully
malicious tales under the simple name of Saki.

We might also pay brief visits to the modern craftsmen of
horror – August Derleth, who rescued Lovecraft and many
another writer of horror from oblivion with his fine anthologies, and who has written many a fine tale of horror himself,
or Ray Bradbury, whose tales both of horror and of science
fiction bear an unmistakable stamp of wild, unearthly beauty
that has become his trademark; or such other fine horror
writers as Fritz Leiber, H. F. Heard, Theodore Sturgeon,
Richard Matheson.

Indeed, few writers have been able to resist the lure of the
supernatural, the brisk chill of fear, the terrifying touch of
horror. The world of literature is the world of imagination,
and there is little that stirs imagination so much as the unknown, unsuspected world of darkness and the creatures that
inhabit the darkness, those fears inherited from our most re-
mote ancestors, and never quite forgotten by any of us, even
in this most modern and unsuperstitious of worlds.

EPILOGUE: 1966

As the sky to the East brightens with the golden touch of dawn, the creatures of darkness lose their powers and return to that terrifying limbo from which they have come. The lid of the vampire's coffin creaks as, sated with his night's feeding, he returns to his damned sleep. The werewolf pauses, trembles and slowly resumes the form of agonized man. The mummy returns to the painted sarcophagus in which he has so fitfully slept through the millennia. The laboratory of the mad scientist falls silent as, worn and weary from his insane endeavours, he removes his white coat and falls exhausted onto the narrow cot for a few nightmare-haunted hours of repose. As man awakens to the rich promise of another day, the evil beings of the night enter their uneasy, damned sleep until they are once again restored to movement by the gentle kiss of the moon.

We have seen many horrors in this long night; we have met many of the monsters who have haunted the imagination of man through all the long, tortuous centuries of his existence. We have seen the vampire indulging in his horrid feast, the mummy pursuing his ageless need for vengeance, the unbelievable agony of him cursed with the sign of the pentagram. The soulless and mindless zombie. The cry for love of a man forced to conceal his hideous face beneath a mask. The tragedy of the accursed Frankensteins and the soul-searing loneliness of their great creation. The battle of the good and the evil natures in man. We have visited the bleak, hostile mountain regions of Transylvania and the mysterious, burning

Massive cobwebs and crumbling stone stairs were an essential in these early films. Irving Pichel (left) here faces his own nemesis (Otto Kruger) beyond a cobwebbed barrier.
Dracula's Daughter **(Universal Pictures, 1936)**

sands of Egypt. The fog-enshrouded streets of old London and the brilliant glories of Paris. The unknown, drum-throbbing depths of the African jungle and the languid, menacing tropical paradise of the islands of the Indies. We have watched the creation of our greatest masterpieces of horror, have seen the alcoholic genius of Poe, the loneliness of Lovecraft and the mysticism of Machen.

There is much more we could see, there are many more we might visit, were the night longer. We might enter the staid and stolid manor houses of England and feel the chill touch of the supernatural as a spectral form materializes before our eyes, or stand in the ruins of a castle on the Rhine to meet the ghostly shade of a Teutonic knight. New Orleans and Charleston have their own frightening legends of ghostly visitors and there are those who maintain that insubstantial wraiths still prowl the streets of old New England on dark and silent nights. The glorious, crumbling temples of ancient Greece could tell us much of this world of horror.

There are the terrors of witchcraft and black magic, which we have but briefly noted. Salem is still haunted by the holocaust created by the tales of a Negro servant and the hysteria of two imaginative children. We might have visited the blasphemy of the Witches' Sabbath or the Black Mass and seen the indescribable horrors attendant on the worship of Satan. The smoke of burning faggots has not yet completely cleared from the air, and if we listen closely perhaps we can still hear the screams of the witches and the warlocks fastened to the stake in the village square. Here, indeed, is a black world of horror that will forever haunt the soul and the conscience of man.

Giantism creates a world of horror all its own. We might have gone to Skull Island, that wildly mysterious home of the all-but-invincible King Kong. Sir Arthur Conan Doyle, Jules Verne, H. G. Wells, among others, wrote of lost worlds and continents which still tremble under the heavy gait of the dinosaur. In our own time, the effects of radiation on insect and animal life have resulted in wildly imaginative tales of gigantic ants, spiders, etc., attacking man, and underwater atomic testing has released long-sleeping reptilian monsters of the past.

Nor should we forget the horrors of the future, unknown and, because of this, even more terrible to contemplate. The creations of the great science-fiction writers of our time may well become the legends of horror for future generations, the strange and terrible life forms from other worlds and the, perhaps, inevitable struggle against terrors more dangerous than that of the vampire and the werewolf.

But our concern has been primarily with the great monsters of the past, and our journey is now done. A sudden hush has fallen upon the earth, a hush of expectance and of hope. A new day is about to begin, with all its promise and beauty. For one last moment, the moon seems to linger above the crest of the hill, as though hoping to hear a familiar voice, calling her back. But the cry is not made and, almost with a sigh, the rim of silver quietly fades and is gone.

Earth is silent. In the East, a new, stronger glow has spread upon the sky, touching the delicate clouds with a tinge of gold. The monsters will walk again, but for now, they sleep, and earth belongs to man.

EPILOGUE: 1989

The great Monster of Dr. Frankenstein walking back-ward into the cold stone laboratory of his creator and then turning to present to the world for the first time that hideous visage in a series of terrifying closeups; the white, sinuous, wormlike fingers of Count Dracula emerging from the coffin in which he sleeps, to raise the creaking lid so he can rise for his bloody nightly repast; the agonized features of the Werewolf as he stares up to the full moon and begins his dreadful transformation; the gleam of light in the desiccated face of the Mummy as he slowly opens one eye to see again the world he had left thousands of years before; the horribly deformed bell-ringer lurking in the shadows of Notre-Dame—these are the classic creatures of horror.

It is unlikely that our dear old tried-and-true monster friends will ever walk again. They have had their day, and it has been both a long and satisfying one, presenting us with many memorable moments of true horror. There is no danger they will ever be really forgotten, for in one way or another, they are all part of our heritage. The agonies of the werewolf, the blood lust of the vampire, arise from misted legends many centuries old, part of the dark folklore of many nations. Such ancient tales are always remembered even though actual belief in them may be gone.

And the awesome splendours of ancient Egypt will always be shadowed by the ever-mysterious form of the

Mummy. Who can enter the Egyptian room of a great
museum and stand at the mummy case, staring like
Imhotep at the tightly linen-wrapped form of what thousands of years before had been a living human being,
and not think of the chilling tales of the walking dead?
The schizophrenic has become a figure of medical fact
and will always bear the dread name of Jekyll-and-
Hyde, who, admittedly, carried the ailment to extremes.
There are still those in the dark mountain jungles of
Haiti who believe in the existence of the mindless zombie stalking with menacing slowness along the lonely
country roads; and two of the architectural jewels of
Paris still seem haunted by the masked Phantom and the
troglodyte Hunchback. Frankenstein is no longer just a
name from a novel; the word itself has become part of
our language.

The greatest figures of the world of darkness were first
presented to us in literary works that have stood the test
of time. *Frankenstein* and *Dracula* are as engrossing and
chilling to readers today as when they first made their
appearance so many years ago; surely there are few who
are not familiar at least with the names of these two
most terrifying creatures. *The Hunchback of Notre-Dame*
remains one of the masterworks of literature, and perhaps the Broadway appearance of *Phantom of the Opera*
will again arouse interest in this minor classic (as has
been the case with *Les Miserables*). The brevity of the
fanciful nightmare tales of Poe, Lovecraft, and Machen,
the terse novella of *Dr. Jekyll and Mr. Hyde* make them
easy reading for those today who are too often impatient
with books of greater length. Perhaps the motion picture
industry, to which we must be grateful for giving these
creatures a tremendous popularity beyond the printed
page, may even have directed some to seek them out in
their original literary form.

They have perhaps become too familiar to us, and
such familiarity can blunt even the reactions of fear. It
is impossible to describe the incredible impact of the
face of Karloff's Monster when it first burst upon the

screen in 1931. Today it is surely one of the most familiar and most easily identified faces in the world, and
that initial first-time shock impact is lost forever. We
see those hideous green features glaring at us from shop
windows on every Hallowe'en, and even the little kids
are no longer so much afraid of it.

The Frankenstein Monster was the first to lose that
sense of instant horror, but at least partially responsible
was the unfortunate lack of care taken with his later
appearance. Once Boris Karloff abandoned the role, the
makeup artists seemed to lose their interest in that magnificently horrible visage; a mask would have done as
well, or perhaps even better. The face became stoic,
rigid, the expressionless eyes drained of all emotion; the
creature again became mute and, at least for a time,
blind, and Boris's frighteningly powerful creature of destruction deteriorated into a clumsy, stumbling automaton, a zombie, awakened from his constant state of
comatose sleep only long enough to provide a crashing
or blazing finale for the films in which he appeared. The
first signs of this great Monster's decay could already be
seen in the square, bloated features when Lon Chaney, Jr.,
assumed the role; unfortunately, television presentations
of his *Ghost of Frankenstein* do not even include the
most powerful scene in the film, with the Monster standing on open ground during an electrical storm and exulting under the constant bolts of lightning. The Monster's
position as the most terrifying creature of all time was
effectively destroyed by the pathetically inept imperson-
ation by Bela Lugosi (for which indifferent scripting and
incompetent editing must also share the blame). Not
even Glenn Strange could fully restore him.

The story of Victor Frankenstein and his blasphemous
work is simply a novel, not a legend, quite complete
within itself. The rather vague conclusion of the story,
however, with the Monster vanishing forever into the
frozen wastes of the North, makes one wonder if perhaps
Mary Shelley herself was not quite finished with him.
Did authors write sequels in those days? (This makes the

clever preface to *Bride of Frankenstein* seem quite plausible.) We cannot draw upon legends to continue the Monster's story, save for those gradually built into the film scripts. Igor's statement to Wolf Frankenstein that the Monster could not die seemed an inspiration at the

The genius of Boris Karloff's performance lay in the power and vibrancy he brought to the character, unequaled by later performers. *Frankenstein* (Universal Pictures, 1931)

time, offering endless opportunities for future films but script writers failed to live up to its potential. The story line soon began to wear thin. That became all too painfully apparent in the later films, in which the Monster was little more than a last-act supporting player to Count Dracula and Lawrence Talbott. Karloff knew what he was doing when he left the series after the third outing.

The vampire has had a longer, more active life, for there always seemed other aspects of the old legends upon which to build a new story. *Dracula, Prince of Darkness* revived that part of the legend stating that a vampire cannot cross running water. (Of course, other aspects of the "legend" were sheer writer's imagination.) The vampire count did not share the Monster's immortality, but he was a wilier opponent and very difficult to destroy. Also, there was only one Frankenstein Monster, whereas anyone could become a vampire. But before long, these stories became redundant as Hammer doggedly refused to permit the evil vampire to rest in peace; the films were saved only by their still impressive production values. A bite on the neck is still just a bite on the neck, no matter how it is done.

The Mummy's popularity soon faded when audiences became a bit tired of Karis's eternal search for the woman he had loved three thousand years before and constantly sought in reincarnated form. How often can you tell that tale? The sight of a lame, twisted, one-eyed mummy trailing his loose dirty linen wrappings through a wholesome all-American town in New England was a novelty, but even that began to pale. There have been other mummies beside Imhotep and Karis, but these were found in generally lurid low-budget films with little value.

The infamous Jekyll-Hyde, the mad Phantom and the pathetic Quasimodo were basically one-story characters who could best be presented in remakes that, with the noted exception of *Phantom of the Opera*, were seldom comparable to their originals.

The tales of Lovecraft and Poe still provide inspiration for horror films, but somehow they never seem as good as they should be, and what appears on the screen generally bears very little resemblance to the original story. Lovecraft's work is perhaps even wilder and more terrifying than that of the master Poe himself, and they should make outstanding films in this genre. Unfortunately, Lovecraft never found a film-maker like Roger Corman with his lovingly lavish interpretations of Poe, nor a Vincent Price who found in them his own niche of the terrible.

We live in a graphically violent time; you'd think civilized man would have by now gone beyond such things. Newspaper pages devoted to film ads are filled with blazing guns of all sizes and descriptions. Violence is a necessary element of horror, but it has never been so graphically illustrated as in today's films. The violence in earlier productions seems somewhat more subdued and subtle, sometimes shown merely in shadow, without the revolting blood-letting and dismemberment that today turns the screen into a huge blob of crimson every few moments. The famous scene in *Frankenstein* in which the Monster hurls the little girl into the lake was excised from the print as too gruesome. That would certainly not happen today; the audience would explode with delight at the scene. The fact that this sequence has been restored in video cassettes (as have some of the more brutal excised scenes from the original *King Kong*) is a clear indication of the current penchant for violence.

As a result of this preponderance of violence and massacre in such films today, the all-important elements of good writing and characterization have been largely lost. No one is particularly interested in these creatures any longer, aside from their fascination as killing machines. Today's audiences are not concerned with motivation, introspection, inner feelings, right versus wrong. They become restless with too much talk. They simply want to see the axe fall again, the blood to flow in delightful rivers of crimson and gore. They have neither the patience nor the time for pity.

Well, at least these grand old films have not rotted

away in some musty Hollywood vault of a film graveyard, as has been the fate of too many great productions
of the past. The final resurrection of Count Dracula was
on the cassette of a VCR, and Karloff's moving and
terrible Monster can now find a home in your own
living room.

I was somewhat hesitant when it was suggested that I
add a new final chapter to this edition of *Horrors!* What
more could I have to say? I had dealt with the terrible
creatures of the past, the strange beings that are no
longer in vogue. The classic creatures, to repeat once
again a term you have often encountered in these pages.
I do not in any sense consider myself an "expert" in the
entire broad field of horror and pseudo-horror and its
many allied branches, but simply in the certain aspects
of the genre that particularly interested me. That period
was almost twenty years in the past when this book was
first written, and has now become a closed chapter. To
carry this further, to include less impressive and far less
worthy creatures who did not belong would be to tar-
nish the specialized nature of the work I had tried to
provide; and to turn *Horrors!* into just another blood-
and-gore recital, defeating its purpose and intended value.

Perhaps writers have become too strongly influenced
by the possibilities of motion picture and television sales.
I always have the impression that many writers today
construct their scenes according to how they would look
on film; they write with a film director staring over
their shoulders, rather than the muse of literature. This
seems particularly the case in works of horror and in
those sizzling sex novels at which women writers are so
remarkably and disturbingly adept. There is no question
that the style of contemporary horror writers is perfectly
suited to the modern age. The classic works of horror
were written in the brooding, more leisurely Gothic style
that is so conducive to atmosphere: crenelated castles
rising starkly against a dark sky, isolated decaying mansions, misted graveyards. I experimented with this style
in my own Frankenstein novel titled *Creature*, a modern

sequel combining the elements of the original story and films, while still maintaining the atmosphere of an older time. I wanted as much as possible to adapt to the style Mary Shelley herself might have used. I was gratified to find that many of my readers understood what I was trying to do, although one publisher rejected the work with the comment that I am "probably the last true Gothic." That perhaps makes me something of an anachronism, but I was pleased.

A highly successful Broadway production of *Dracula* in 1977 resulted in a new filming of the Stoker story with the play's star, Frank Langella, as the vampire Count. (*Frankenstein* also made a Broadway appearance in 1980 but unfortunately lasted only one performance.) Langella provided quite a different breed of Dracula from the classical restrained Lugosi and the athletic Lee. His Dracula was younger, more handsome, highly sensuous. He moved with a wonderful grace, spinning that famous cape as though it were part of his body, and he spoke in smooth, richly mellifluous tones. One could easily understand that women would surrender to his hypnotic charm and dashing appearance.

The character of Professor Van Helsin, Dracula's most implacable foe, provided Laurence Olivier with another of those old-man-with-heavy-accent roles which he has frequently presented in recent years. His Van Helsing was older, more intense and more obviously Dutch than the more quietly restrained portrayal of Edward Van Sloan in the original film.

Although the new production diverged considerably from the original story, the basic elements remain, and there was some fine atmosphere, thanks to excellent photography and use of color, mostly darkly shaded, and an eerie, powerful score by John Williams.

There were also some fine shock elements, such as Dracula crawling headfirst down an outer stone wall and staring with unblinking eyes, still upside-down, through the bedroom window of his next victim. Particularly effective was the finely photographed sequence in which Van Helsing confronts his hideously transformed vampire-daughter in the dark, dripping, rat-infested caves beneath Carfax Abbey. The concluding scene was a sharp departure from the traditional dispatch of the feared vampire. Trapped aboard a ship in which he hopes to make his escape, Dracula is hauled by block and tackle up to the mainmast to disintegrate in the blazing light of the sun.

I'm afraid I can't be very complimentary about more recent horror films. They are best termed "shock films," for that seems their sole purpose. No more staid and beautiful women, scientific serious-minded men; we now have primarily rambunctuous, brainless, sex-starved teen-aged stereotypes.

What could be more juvenile than the apparently endless series of films based on the dire events that await the unwary on every Friday the 13th? A group of lively, nubile, and obviously sex-starved teenagers are terrorized by a particularly vicious and murderous luna-tic in their mountain cabins. The films are incredibly bloody, the numerous murders interspersed with hotly panting kids concerned with the undoubted joys of sex. Yet it seems we are to have one of these films for every possible Friday the 13th, for despite the ominous reputa-tions of those cabins, the stupid kids return again and again, with the same results. I forced myself to sit through the first two of these numerous Friday blood-and-sex affairs, but nothing could convince me to go on with the apparently endless tale of the goalie-masked Jason.

I don't deny there are some effective fright scenes in such films, but such scenes should not be the sole inter-est of a film. What it amounts to is simply having someone jump out at you and say "Boo!" every few moments. When they're not being slaughtered, the young girls seem always to be undressing, hotly rolling in the grass, or jumping into bed with someone; the only pas-time that interests the young boys is the quest for female flesh, in warm and living form.

I suppose *Halloween* (1978) started it all, but this was

a somewhat superior film of its kind, largely due to the
always impressive presence of the soft-spoken Donald
Pleasance. We of course have had more than one Halloween massacre, with diminishing result. Holidays seem
popular times for massacres; they have even tried it
with Christmas and a murderous Santa Claus! Not my
genre.

As for the so-called creatures of these films, how can
you feel pity or sympathy for them? They wear hockey
masks. They lurk, breathing heavily, behind bushes and
move the branches aside (just enough so the audience
can see a vague "something" there) to look at a pretty
girl. They conceal themselves in dark corners, they whisper names, they appear as dark shadows or black hulk-
ing forms when a door is suddenly opened. They seldom
speak, we have no facial closeups to indicate emotion.
They wield their axes, knives, whatever primitive tools
that best spill blood and dismember bodies.

The films are much too long. Those in particular that
deal with the "average" teenager in a small town en-
countering mass murderers have far too many lengthy
segments of what is supposed to be a depiction of the
teener's lifestyle. The attention, whatever there is of it,
lapses and quickly needs another shock scene to bring it
back again. That's part of the titillation, of course: keep
them wondering when the blood will flow again. Perhaps the teenagers don't mind so much. It makes them
think the girl walking down the comfortable middle-
class street from her school to her home, carrying books
in her arms (she is never seen to open one of them) and
flirting with the handsome football hero senior while a
dark menace follows in the shrubbery, might be themselves. *The Mummy* and *Dracula* ran only 75 minutes,
with none of it wasted fill-in time. Well, perhaps you
can't blame the audiences of today. Who would plunk
down five to seven dollars to see a film that runs just
over an hour?

Horror films of the early years often boasted a cast of
stellar players who would lend distinction to any pro-

duction, with supporting roles played by such outstanding actors as Hull, Ohland, Bellamy, Rains, Griffies, Ouspenskaya, Byington, and many others. With few exceptions, the "stars" of the current films are quickly forgotten; there is nothing in performance or characterization to make them memorable. They don't have to be actors; they simply have to be cute.

There are too many remakes, and in these pages we have often seen the errors of such a mistaken device. I have never seen a remake as good as the original (again, with the exceptions of *Phantom of the Opera* and *The Hunchback of Notre-Dame*), and that is not merely due to fond recollections, although I suppose these remakes might seem acceptable if one hasn't seen the original. Look what they did to poor *King Kong*! They not only made him a man in a gorilla suit, but had to hype the scene by starring him in a gaudy, raucous carnival rather than in the more sedate and thus more frightening theater, and they took him from the Empire State Building which surely more closely resembled the tall trees of his primitive world, to the characterless World Trade Center. The original production of *The Cat People* was a superb black-and-white chilling minor masterpiece filled with atmosphere and the frightening sense of the unknown; the remake, in blazing colour, was a revolting mishmash primarily concerned with sex.

To step slightly out of my own era for a moment, I might make mention of a few more in the remake syndrome. *The Thing* was a taut, terrifying thriller; its remake destroyed its own possible merit by being too long, and the tight sense of ever growing fear was lost. *The Fly* was a ridiculous idea to begin with; but it was certainly well done. So was the remake, but too much of the regurgitation turned my stomach at last. The new *Invasion of the Body Snatchers* wasn't really bad, but it could not in any respect measure up to the frightening little black-and-white original. It was a mistake to transfer the action to Los Angeles; most of us found it easier to relate with the people of a small town like Santa

Mira. Anyway, it was nice to see Kevin McCarthy reprise his memorable hysterical pleas for help. *The Island of Dr. Moreau* would be acceptable if you have never seen *Island of Lost Souls;* how could Burt Lancaster equal the splendid, unctuous evil of Charles Laughton? Perhaps fond memories do get in the way.

It's not that there have been no interesting films bearing at least superficial resemblance to my genre, but they are few. I've always been strangely haunted by a 1972 film that Ivan Butler described as an interesting oddity. *Horror Express* is certainly that. It appears rather difficult to classify. Some call it a black comedy, others a parody, still others merely an adventure film. It is all of these, but it is also rather engrossing horror.

The entire action, save for its opening in a railroad station, takes place on the Trans-Siberian Express, which made for some splendid colour snowbound Siberian photography. (Oh, I know it was not actually filmed in Siberia, and the train-in-the-snow shots were miniatures, but it was all very effective anyway.) It stars the two Hammer stalwarts Peter Cushing and Christopher Lee, with—believe it or not—Telly Savalas as a bald Russian official.

The story concerns itself with the shipment across Siberia by an archaeological society of a curious humanoid corpse found in the icy wastes. It is soon apparent that this ancient relic (the missing link? An alien from outer space who has lost his way?) is not quite what it seems. There are strange emanations from the crate in which the creature lies, passengers on the train have peculiar visions of prehistoric worlds and creatures, eyes are seen to glow from the crate and a hand reaches out . . . you get the idea. It's great fun and well-made; there are already signs of its becoming something of a cult film. There is also a terrific score by John Cacavas.

I can perhaps place this film on the fringe of my genre, since there is something of a Frankenstein theme here, although the similarity to *The Thing* is even stronger. *Alien* also falls into this same fringe category,

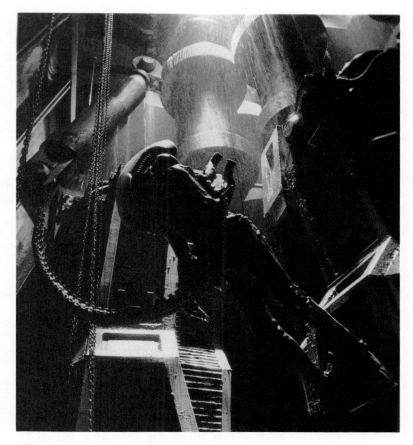

Alien, an updated variation of the Frankenstein myth, was a modern classic of science fiction horror. During the course of the film, the terrifying Creature slaughters a space crew.
Alien (20th-Century Fox, 1979)

but this tremendously frightening film, is, of course, sheer science fiction.

Using the word "horror" in a film title is a natural come-on, but more often it is little more than an attention-getting ripoff. We have already had horror hospitals, circuses and, naturally, high schools. *Horror Express* was justified in its use. I am also reminded of *Horror Hotel*, although this is a tale of modern New

England witchcraft rather than actual horror. Another strangely forgotten little jewel, it features Christopher Lee, but the true star of the film is the Lovecraft-like town of Whitewood, always surrounded by creeping mist and filled with witches who have a tendency to burst into flames at the sight of a cross. It has a clever story with some truly terrifying scenes, doubly effective (in the brooding style of *Black Sunday*) in its deeply shadowed black-and-white photography.

I have previously mentioned my displeasure over *Abbott and Costello Meet Frankenstein*. I did not like to see my favorite characters turned into the butt of a comedy team. I can view it a little differently today. It may have been a parody, but in spite of some terribly silly sequences (such as Costello sitting unknowingly on the lap of the Monster, whom he calls "Junior"), there was authentic atmosphere and Lugosi, Chaney, and Strange seemed for the most part to take themselves quite seriously. Abbott and Costello films do not hold up nearly as well today as the films of their greater predecessors Laurel and Hardy, but this one now seems the funniest and most original.

It is peculiar that it took nearly a quarter of a century before the next Frankenstein parody, and this the best of them all. The tremendous success of Mel Brooks's *Young Frankenstein* (1974) is not likely to be surpassed in its kind, and even I must admit there were moments when I laughed aloud (somewhat guiltily). In spite of those lapses in taste that are to be expected in any Brooks film, *Young Frankenstein* is often hilarious, with at least two glowing performances.

Gene Wilder is fine as young Dr. Frankenstein, who is very much embarrassed by his heritage and insists on being called "Fronkensteen"; his scene with the moving bookcase concealing a secret passage is a true comedy classic. The late Marty Feldman, of those startlingly protruding eyes, gives one of the funniest performances in any "horror" film. He, too, insists on proper pronounciation ("Eye-gor" not "Ee-gor") and the hunch on his back has a curious habit of shifting shoulders. Using a ridiculously short cane, he even makes the old "walk this way" joke seem hilarious. A delicious performance. My major complaint with this film is that in its final segments, with the Monster appearing in public as a song-and-dance man, the horror is displaced by sheer slapstick, and I cringe at the singing of "Ah, Sweet Mystery of Life" in scenes of sexual ecstasy with the Monster.

Brooks was wise to make this film in black-and-white; in spite of the comedy element, it faithfully captures the

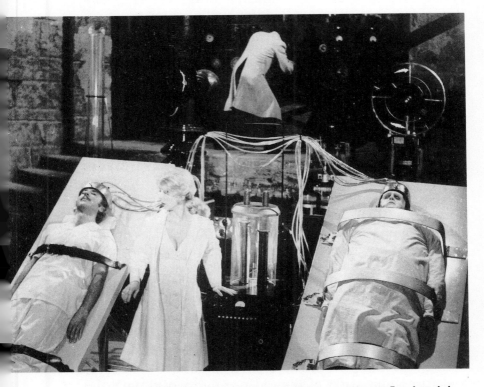

A strange transference is taking place between Young Frankenstein, Gene Wilder (left), and the Monster (Peter Boyle). Terri Garr is the confused blond, and Marty Feldman is at the controls. The Mel Brooks film was a hilarious spoof, despite what many would consider serious lapses in taste.
Young Frankenstein (20th-Century Fox, 1974)

eerie atmosphere of the earlier classics. I'm rather surprised that film historian Leslie Halliwell prefers *House of Dracula* as the best of the horror parodies, although it was not intended as such and thus is a parody in a much gentler vein.

The George Hamilton film *Love At First Bite* did not quite do for the vampire what Brooks had done for Frankenstein, although it, too, is heavily laced with one-liners, many of them very funny. It seems often strangely heavyhanded for a comedy. The opening scenes, in Dracula's castle, are the best, but then I do always prefer the classic background; Dracula in New York does not impress me. (London at least has more fog.)

The undoubted best performance in this film, the Feldman of the production, is that by Arte Johnson, with his lunatic giggle, constantly scampering about in search of roaches and other unsavory items to add to his curious diet. Placing a reading light in Dracula's coffin was a wonderful idea; his reading of girlie magazines while he rests is something of a Brooks touch. But for me the film has too much ethnic humor, although having Richard Benjamin try to scare Dracula off with a Star of David was good for a laugh.

Also, Hamilton's performance seems strangely bland and uninspired. His accent is too patently phony, a not-very-good imitation of Bela Lugosi. Perhaps he was having too much fun; it would have been better had he taken himself more seriously. Anyway, I did like the great chase scene toward the end of the film, and the two vampires in bat-form flying off together.

Salem's Lot is the best of the newer vampire films. It has its flaws, perhaps primarily the fact that it is too long. It succeeds because of a solid story (Stephen King, of course), fine performances, an authentic air of terror, and its combination of the old vampire world with the new.

Writer David Soul arrives in the New England village of Salem's Lot (wonderful name) to write about the mansion known as Marsten House, where terrible things had happened in the past, and in which an aunt of his had worked at a previous time. The strange events are not yet at an end. There has arrived in the town a suave, mysterious, very gentlemanly dealer in antiques (James Mason), who is preparing to open a shop in the village not for himself, but on behalf of another party, whose arrival is always stressed as being "imminent." This other party, in fact, is a vampire who is switching operations to this new locale and whose immediate goal is to convert the entire village into a nest of vampires; his ultimate goal goes much beyond that. One by one, the villagers die strange and terrible deaths, to be resurrected as vampires who increase the blood-drinking population. The writer eventually realizes what is going on and devotes himself to the dangerous task of defeating the vampire's plans.

There are some quite remarkable scenes here. There is a touch of the old Dracula when a young boy, converted into a vampire, "mists" himself into his brother's bedroom and urges him to join the exclusive new club. A female corpse lies under a sheet in the doctor's office while the writer, knowing what will happen, frantically constructs a makeshift cross. The cloth moves, the woman rises as a snarling vampire, and is dispatched when the cross is seeringly pressed to her forehead. (She simply disappears.)

The most interesting aspect of the film is that the great vampire responsible for all this carnage, whose way is being prepared by Mason, is not a polished, immaculately dressed Transylvanian nobleman like Dracula, but actually the terrifying Nosferatu, most horrifying vampire of them all, first brought to the screen in the 1921 silent German film *Nosferatu* with Max Schreck. (A fitting name: the German for "terrible" is "schrecklich.") Here indeed is a true monster: the bald head, green skin, burning eyes, and crimson lips, the incredibly long fingernails.

Nosferatu's first startling appearance is very brief as he attacks a prisoner in the local jail, but when we next see him the effect is powerful. A priest is sitting at a kitchen table with a mother, father, and their young son, who has been "beckoned" by the two vampire brothers who had been his playmates. The room begins to rattle and tremble; crockery falls from the walls as from the antics of a poltergeist, and then a massive black form rises from the floor and reveals itself as the snarling, hissing Nosferatu. He kills the priest and the boy's parents, which is important to the plot, for the boy becomes a rather unlikely partner in the writer's campaign to stamp out the plague of the undead.

The entry of the writer and the young boy into Marsten House takes us back to the good old days. There is a decided resemblance (on a less grand scale) to Dracula's castle in the massive, dark, and empty house; there are even curtains of cobwebs. They find the coffin of Nosferatu and open it to the sunlight. In true good old vampire-destroying style, the writer pounds a stake into the vampire's heart—really *pounds*, while Nosferatu moans, hisses, reaches out his long fingernails to grab at his slayer's throat. A good, classic ending to the story.

But unfortunately not to the film, although it would have been wiser to end it there. The writer and boy now determine to root out vampirism wherever it is to be found, knowing they are hotly pursued. This takes them to Guatemala, which serves primarily as an opportunity to dispatch the writer's girlfriend, who has also become a vampire.

Among the films flaws are the number of scenes simultaneously followed, requiring abrupt cuts from one scene, to another, back to the original, back to the other, and so on. This becomes confusing. For some unknown reason the evil Marsten House seems always to be flood-lit. Some liberties are taken with the vampire legend that were not really necessary. The eyes of the vampires glow weirdly as though a golden light bulb had been placed behind them. A startling effect, but a vampire's eyes, if they glowed at all, would be red in colour, not gold. The entry of the two young brother vampires into a bedroom is also peculiar. They float in on the mist, like a leaf in a breeze; I don't remember vampires ever doing that. It was interesting to have such young vampires, though. Despite the flaws it remains an excellent film; there is a delightful touch in the very last moment of the film: the full moon very briefly bears the imprint of a human skull.

Of all our old monsters, the werewolf has done best in most recent films, thanks primarily to new techniques in filming, and the marvelous tricks that can now be done through special effects. *The Howling* (1981) is as fine a werewolf film as has been made.

A dauntless television reporter suffers a long period of traumatic nightmares after she is attacked in a porno film booth in Los Angeles while on a special assignment. A psychiatrist suggests she seek help at his establishment called The Colony, where he attempts to help the mentally troubled. But The Colony is inhabited by werewolves and the reporter's attacker is among them, brought together by the good doctor (also one of them). His foolish hope is to find some way that werewolves, feeding on their own herd of cattle rather than humans, may become assimilated into society. (At least a novel idea!) But all hell breaks loose, the doctor is killed, the werewolves revolt, and those who do not meet the classic fate of a silver bullet are locked in the barn and burned. Most of them, anyway.

This is a very frightening film. There is enough atmosphere here to satisfy anyone, even me: the forests along the beach are constantly swirling with curly blue-white fog, the moonlit nights are filled with the howling of wolves, and The Colony's "patients," who seem like reasonable, normal people (if John Carradine constantly howling for death to "end it all" could be considered normal) soon reveal their nature.

There is fear in almost every scene. In one sequence the reporter is trapped in one of the cabins, and the fury of a werewolf is terrifying as he practically tears the fragile building apart to get at her. The reporter's husband is attacked by a nympho-werewolf and infected. He meets her in the woods, and following a partial transformation with the hair sprouting from his face, saliva dripping from his fanged mouth as he raises his head to bay at the moon, he rolls and couples with her in the grass in grand animalistic lust. The burning of the werewolves is spectacular. Locked in the blazing barn they transform into animal shape and howl, scream, and battle to escape their pyre. Hairy, clawed hands and arms burst through the crumbling flaming walls and the air is filed with screams and wolf howls.

Not all the werewolves perish in the fire or succumb to the silver bullets, for as the reporter and a friend drive away, their car is surrounded by enormous upright wolves who attack, slashing through the metal fabric of the car to get at them. One manages to break into the car and is killed by a silver bullet; it is the reporter's husband. There is a superb ending. Back at the TV station, the reporter, trying to stress the perils of lycanthropy, turns into a snarling, howling wolf onscreen.

The great transformation occurs when a female friend of the reporter's sneaks into the office of The Colony to search the files for information as to just what the hell is going on. She is confronted by the peep-show were-wolf, and the transformation begins.

It is absolutely awesome, a masterpiece of makeup and special effects. First there is the pulsation of the cheeks, the throat, and forehead. The fingers slowly extend, become hairy, and turn into claws. The entire body trembles; the trousers split. Ears suddenly raise themselves through the hair of the head as the face becomes more hirsute. Saliva drips from the mouth. In an incredible sequence, the jaw extends further and further until it has become an animal's fanged muzzle. The effect is electrifying.

Excellently photographed and tautly directed, the film starred Patrick McNee as the werewolf doctor who utters an expression of gratitude when a silver bullet finally sets him free, and Dee Wallace is effectively terrified as the victim reporter. *The Howling* is a classic among films concerned with lycanthropy. (There have since been Parts II and III, unfortunately; neither compares with the original.)

An American Werewolf in London (1981) is not far behind in excellence; this one includes touches of humor that *The Howling* lacks. (This is not a criticism of either film.) The story begins on the always fascinating moors. David and Jack are two young Americans on a walking tour of Europe, perhaps a bit bored by the dreariness of the moors, which promise little in the way of female companionship. They are likable fellows, and the banter between them is light and humourous. Their very first appearance seems a touch of comedy: a truck pulls to a stop on the moor road and our young Americans are found among a mass of sheep, perhaps going to slaughter. Symbolism, of course. In the gloomy village of East Proctor, they stop at a tavern called The Slaughtered Lamb, whose name board depicts an extremely bloody wolf. Despite the warnings of the dour inhabitants of the tavern, the two again venture onto the moors, where they are attacked by a werewolf; Jack is killed and David is bitten, ending up in a London hospital where no one will believe his story.

David is taken into the home of a protective nurse (the love interest). The undead Jack appears and advises David he will become a wolf at the full moon. In this form, David kills half a dozen people and awakens naked in the wolf cage at the London zoo. He buys a fist full of balloons from a young boy and uses them as strategic cover until somewhere he finds a woman's bright red coat. He raises eyebrows when he stands on line for a bus, wearing the coat and showing a pair of very hair legs. (Yes, I wondered, too: If he awoke naked in the wolf-cage, where did he get the money to buy the balloons and to pay his bus fare?) David knows now that he is a werewolf and fears for his nurse lover. When he fails to have himself arrested by making a scene in Trafalgar Square, he places a phone call to his Long Island home, and in the most touching scene of the film, asks his younger sister to tell their parents that he loves them. He finally changes again in a Piccadilly cinema when he finds himself sitting beside Jack (whose makeup in this scene is ludicrously bad). David creates chaos in Piccadilly and is killed by a silver bullet.

David's transformation is as frightening as those of *The Howling*, perhaps a bit more subtly presented. Throughout a long, uncomfortable day, he senses what is coming. He is restless, cannot remain still, has no appetite, cannot interest himself in television, wanders aimlessly about the apartment, stands on the stoop where a cat raises its back and hisses at him. He feels an itching throughout his body. And then the transformation. The difference between David and the werewolves of *The Howling* is that David does not want to be a wolf, whereas those at the clinic enjoyed the sense of freedom and power the wolf form gave them. David screams in pain and writhes agonizingly on the floor as he feels the terrible changes in his body; it is a scene very well played by David Naughton.

These two films make very valid points about the legend of lycanthropy that were not possible in earlier productions. The werewolf here is not just a man who develops certain animal attributes. The legend clearly states that a man so afflicted actually turns into a wolf. Lawrence Talbott remained something of a man. He walked on his hind legs, with a slight crouch, and in form remained a man save for superficial changes in his nose, limbs, and hairline. In these two later films, the werewolf becomes a true wolf, a total animal with silver fur and red eyes (the legend states these are the signs of a werewolf), with no resemblance to a man except, perhaps, for the fact that the lycanthrope is able to stand erect on his hind legs.

There was always a particular difficulty about the early werewolf in the matter of his clothing. Talbott turned into a wolf, but still wore man's clothing. This is directly counter to the legend. The wolf form could not possibly be contained in the strictures of clothing; in both the above films, the clothing is torn from their bodies by their expanding forms. This provided a very serious problem with the censorship laws of the time. Today those laws no longer apply, and we can see the demise of the lycanthrope strictly according to legend: when Davis is finally shown dead in the area of Piccadilly Circus, he is totally naked.

The werewolf is thus the only one of my classic creatures to have moved successfully into the modern world. Compared to our present-day lycanthrope, the Lawrence Talbott portrayed by Lon Chaney, Jr., is simply a particularly hairy man with strange habits. Yet perhaps the semihuman form permitted us to feel greater sympathy for him.

Terror does not belong to the bright golden hours of sunlight; night is its world, the full moon its symbol. Even more civilized man can feel a touch of uneasiness during the night hours. Strange shadows and unexpected sounds startle us. We wonder what the shadows may conceal. For too many ages, we have been afraid of the dark. Vampires. Werewolves. Assorted Monsters. They will always be there, lurking at the back of our minds, misted images from the past. We remember and preserve them in our literature, our legends, and in the new visual world of films.

But we no longer fear them.
Do we?

FURTHER READING

Anobile, Richard J., editor, *Frankenstein*. New York; Universe Books, 1974 (a frame-by-frame presentation of the film)

——*Dr. Jekyll and Mr. Hyde*. New York: Universe Books, 1975 (a frame-by-frame presentation of the film)

Bojarski, Richard, and Beals, Kenneth, *The Films of Boris Karloff*. Secaucus, N.J.: Citadel Press, 1974

Borsnan, John, *Movie Magic*. New York: St. Martin's Press, 1974

Budge, Sir Wallis, *Egyptian Magic*. Secaucus, N.J.: University Books, 1958

Butler, Ivan, *Horror in the Cinema* San Diego: A. S. Barnes, 1979

Florescu, Radu, and McNally, Raymond T., *Dracula*. New York: Hawthorne Books, 1973 (A biography of Vlad the Impaler)

Florescu, Radu, *In Search of Frankenstein*. Boston: New York Graphic Society Books, 1975

Frank, Alan G., *The Movie Treasure of Horror Movies*. London: Octopus Books.

Franklin, Joe. *Classics of the Silent Screen*. Secaucus, N.J., Citadel Press, 1947

Halliwell, Leslie, *The Filmgoer's Companion* (4th edition). New York: Avon, 1974

——*Halliwell's Hundred*. New York: Scribners, 1982

Higham, Charles, *Charles Laughton: An Intimate Biography*. Garden City, N.Y.: Doubleday, 1976

Huysmans, Joris Karl, *La Bas*. Secaucus, N.J.: University Books, 1958

Keel, John. *Jadoo*. New York: Julian Messner, 1957

Lanchester, Elsa, *Elsa Lanchester Herself*. New York: St. Martin's Press, 1983

Leland, Charles Godfrey, *Gypsy Sorcery and Fortune Telling*, Secaucus, N.J.: University Books, 1962

Lenning, Arthur, *The Count*. New York; Putnam 1974 (a biography of Bela Lugosi)

Leroux, Gaston, *The Phantom of the Opera*. Indianapolis: Bobbs-Merrill, 1911

Lindsay, Cynthia, *Dear Boris*. New York: Knopf, 1975

Loederer, Richard A., *Voodoo Fire in Haiti*. Garden City, N.Y.: Literary Guild, 1935

Lovecraft, H. P., *Best Supernatural Stories*, August Derleth, editor. New York: World, 1945

Ludlam, E., *A Biography of Dracula*. Slough, Buckinghamshire, England: W. Foulsham & Co., 1962 (a biography of Bram Stoker)

McNally, Raymond T., and Florescu, Radu, *In Search of Dracula*. New York: Galahad Books, 1972

——*The Essential Dracula*, New York: Mayflower Books, 1979

Machen, Arthur, *Tales of Horror and the Supernatural*, Philip Van Doren Stern, editor. New York: A. Knopf, 1948

Mank, Gregory William, *It's Alive!*. San Diego: A. S. Barnes, 1981 (a detailed fiftieth anniversary history of the Frankenstein films)

Menville, Douglas and Reginald, R., *Things to Come*. New York: Time Books, 1977

Miller, R. De Witt, *Forgotten Mysteries*. Secaucus, N.J.: Citadel Press, 1947

Noblecourt, C. Desroches, *Tutankhamen*. Graphic Society Books, 1963

Pitts, Michael R., *Horror Film Stars*. Jefferson, N.C.: McFarland, 1981

Poe, Edgar Allen, *Tales*. Garden City, N.Y.: Fine Editions Press, 1952

Rovin, Jeff, *The Fabulous Fantasy Films*. San Diego: A. S. Barnes, 1977

Seabrook, William *Witchcraft: Its Power in the World Today*. San Diego: Harcourt Brace, 1940

Shelley, Mary, *Frankenstein*. New York: Pyramid, 1957

Smith, James Lindon, *Tombs, Temples & Ancient Arts*. Corinna Lindon Smith, editor. Norman: University of Oklahoma Press, 1956

Starkey, Marion, *The Devil in Massachusetts*. New York: Knopf, 1950

Stevenson, Burton, *A King in Babylon*. New York: Dodd, Mead, 1931

Stevenson, Robert Louis, *The Strange Case of Dr. Jekyll and Mr. Hyde*, New York: Arco Press, 1964

Stoker, Bram, *Dracula*. New York: Heritage Press. 1965

Summers, Montague, *The Vampire, His Kith and Kin*. Secaucus, N.J.: University Books, 1960

——*The Vampire in Europe*, Secaucus, N.J.: University Books, 1961

——*The Werewolf*. Secaucus, N.J.: University Books, 1966

Tallant, Robert, *Voodoo in New Orleans*. New York: Macmillan, 1946

Tropp, Martin, *Mary Shelley's Monster*. Boston: Houghton Mifflin, 1976 (a remarkably detailed study of the nature of the Monster)

Underwood, Peter, *Boris*. New York: Drake Publishers, 1972

Usini, James, and Silver, Alain, *The Vampire Film*. San Diego: A. S. Barnes, 1975

Venables, Hubert, *The Frankenstein Diaries*, New York: Viking, 1980

Walpole, Horace, *The Castle of Otranto*. London, England: Folio Society, 1976

Wilde, Oscar, *The Picture of Dorian Gray*. Cleveland: Cleveland Fine Editions Press, 1947

Wolf, Leonard, *The Annotated Dracula*. New York: Clarkson N. Potter, 1975

——*The Annotated Frankenstein*. New York: Clarkson N. Potter, 1977

FILM LIST

The following is a partial list of horror films which may be of interest to the reader. The list is necessarily incomplete. Others, in fact, will be found mentioned throughout the text. This list is intended as a cross section of films rather than a list indicative of quality or importance. For the most part, foreign-language productions (such as the brilliant Mexican films on the vampire, *Nostradamus*) are not included. VCR indicates that the film is available on video cassette. The reader should bear in mind, however, that additional video cassettes are constantly being released.

Alien. 1979. Tom Skerritt, Sigourney Weaver, VCR.
An American Werewolf in London. 1981. David Naughton. VCR.
Ape Man, The. 1943. Bela Lugosi.
Before I Hang. 1940. Boris Karloff, Edward Van Sloan.

Black Cat, The. 1934. Boris Karloff, Bela Lugosi.
Black Friday. 1940. Boris Karloff, Bela Lugosi.
Black Sleep, The. 1956. Basil Rathbone, John Carradine, Bela Lugosi, Lon Chaney, Jr.
Black Sunday. 1961. Barbara Steele, Arturo Dominici.
Blood of Dracula. 1957. Sandra Harrison.
Blood of the Vampire. 1958. Sir Donald Wolfit, Barbara Shelley.
Body Snatchers, The. 1945. Boris Karloff, Bela Lugosi, Henry Daniell. VCR.

Bride of Frankenstein. 1935. Boris Karloff, Elsa Lanchester, Ernest Thesiger, Colin Clive. VCR.
Brides of Dracula. 1960. David Peel.

Cabinet of Dr. Caligari, The. 1919. Conrad Veidt. VCR.
Cabinet of Dr. Caligari, The. 1962. Dan O'Herlihy, Glynis Johns.
Cat People, The. 1942. Simone Simone, Kent Smith, Tom Conway. VCR.
Climax, The. 1944. Boris Karloff, Susanna Foster, Turhan Bey.
Cry of the Werewolf. 1944. Nina Foch, Steven Crane.
Curse of Frankenstein. 1957. Christopher Lee, Peter Cushing.
Curse of the Werewolf. 1961. Oliver Reed, Richard Wadsworth, Justin Walter.

Dead Men Walk. 1943. George Zucco, Dwight Frye.
Dead Of Night. 1945. Michael Redgrave, Georgie Withers. VCR.
Dr. Blood's Coffin. 1961. Kieron Moore.
Dr. Jekyll and Mr. Hyde. 1920. John Barrymore, Nita Naldi.
Dr. Jekyll and Mr. Hyde. 1932. Fredric March. VCR.
Dracula. 1931. Bela Lugosi, Dwight Fry, Edward Van Sloan. VCR.
Dracula's Daughter. 1936. Gloria Holden, Marguerite Chapman, Irving Pichel, Edward Van Sloan.

Fly, The. 1956. Vincent Price. VCR.
Frankenstein. 1931. Boris Karloff, Colin Clive, Dwight Fry, Edward Van Sloan. VCR.
Frankenstein Meets the Wolf-Man. 1943. Bela Lugosi, Lon Chaney, Jr., Maria Ouspenskaya, Ilona Massey. VCR.
Frankenstein 1970. 1958. Boris Karloff.
From Beyond the Grave. Peter Cushing, Donald Pleasance. VCR.

Ghost of Frankenstein. 1942. Lon Chaney, Jr.
Ghoul, The. 933. Boris Karloff, Ernest Thesiger.
Golem, The. 1920. Paul Wegener.

Halloween. 1978. Donald Pleasance, Janice Lee Curtis. VCR.
Hangover Square. 1945. Laird Cregar, Linda Darnell, George Sanders.

Horror of Dracula. 1958 Christopher Lee. VCR.

House of Dracula. Onslow Stevens, John Carradine, Lon Chaney, Jr.

House of Frankenstein. 1944. Boris Karloff, John Carradine, Lon Chaney, Jr., J. Carroll Naish.

House of Fright. 1961. Paul Massie.

The Howling. 1981. Patrick McNee, Dee Wallace. VCR.

I Walked with a Zombie. 1943. Tom Conway, Frances Dee. VCR.

Hunchback of Notre Dame, The. 1925. Lon Chaney, Patsy Ruth Miller.

Hunchback of Notre Dame, The. 1939. Charles Laughton, Maureen O'Hara, Sir Cedric Hardwicke. VCR.

The Invasion of the Body Snatchers. 1956. Kevin McCarthy, Dana Wynter. VCR.

Invisible Man, The. 1933. Claude Rains, Una O'Connor. VCR.

Invisible Ray, The. 1936. Boris Karloff.

Island of Lost Souls. 1932. Charles Laughton, Bela Lugosi.

I Was a Teen-Aged Frankenstein. 1957. Gary Conway.

King Kong. 1933. Robert Armstrong, Fay Wray. VCR.

London After Midnight. 1927. Lon Chaney.

Mad Love. 1935. Peter Lorre.

Man Who Laughs, The. 1928. Conrad Veidt.

Mark of the Vampire. 1935. Bela Lugosi, Carol Borland. VCR.

Mask of the Red Death, The. 1962. Vincent Price.

Monster, The. 1925. Lon Chaney.

Mummy, The. 1932. Boris Karloff. VCR.

Mummy, The. 1959. Christopher Lee, Peter Cushing, Raymond Huntley.

Mummy's Curse, The. 1944. Lon Chaney, Jr., Peter Coe.

Mummy's Ghost, The. 944. Lon Chaney, Jr., John Carradine, George Zucco.

Mummy's Hand, The. 1940. Tom Tyler, George Zucco.

Mummy's Tomb, The. 1942. Lon Chaney, Jr., Turhan Bey.

Murders in the Rue Morgue. 1932. Bela Lugosi.

Mystery of the Wax Museum, The. 1933. Lionel Atwill.

Nosferatu. 1921. Max Schreck. VCR.

Old Dark House, The. 1932. Ernest Thesiger, Boris Karloff, Charles Laughton, Raymond Massey.

Phantom of the Opera, The. 1925. Lon Chaney, Sr., Norman Kerry, Mary Philbin.
Phantom of the Opera, The. 1943. Claude Rains, Nelson Eddy, Susanna Foster. VCR.
Pit and the Pendulum, The. 1962. Vincent Price, John Kerr, Barbara Steele.

Return of Dracula, The. 1958. Francis Lederer.
Revenge of Frankenstein, 1958. Peter Cushing.
Revenge of the Zombies. 1943. John Carradine, Veda Ann Borg.
Revolt of the Zombies. 1936. Dean Jagger.

Son of Frankenstein. 1939. Boris Karloff, Bela Lugosi, Basil Rathbone.
Spider Woman, The. 1941. Gale Sondergaard.

Thing, The. 1951. James Arness, Kenneth Tobey, Dewey Martin. VCR.
Tales of Terror. 1962. Vincent Price, Peter Lorre, Basil Rathbone.

Unknown, The. 1927. Lon Chaney, Sr.

Walking Dead, The. 1936. Boris Karloff.
Werewolf of London, The. 1935. Henry Hull, Warner Oland, Spring Byington, Ethel Griffies.
White Zombie. 1932. Bela Lugosi. VCR.
Wolf-Man, The. Lon Chaney, Jr., Claude Rains, Bela Lugosi, Maria Ouspenskaya, Ralph Bellamy. VCR.

Young Frankenstein. 1974. Gene Wilder, Marty Feldman, Peter Boyle. VCR.